Using SPSS for Windows

Using SPSS for Windows
Analyzing and Understanding Data

SECOND EDITION

Samuel B. Green
University of Kansas

Neil J. Salkind
University of Kansas

Theresa M. Akey

Prentice Hall, Upper Saddle River, New Jersey 07458

Library of Congress Cataloging-in-Publication Data

GREEN, SAMUEL B.
    Using SPSS for Windows: analyzing and understanding data/Samuel B. Green,
Neil J. Salkind, Theresa M. Akey.—2nd ed.
        p.   cm.
    For Version 9.X of SPSS.
    Accompanied by a computer disk with all files needed to work through the lessons.
    Includes bibliographical references and index.
    ISBN 0-13-020840-X
    1. Social sciences—Statistical methods—Computer programs.
    I. Salkind, Neil J.   II. Akey, Theresa M.   III. Title.
HA32.G737   1999 <MRC>
300'.285'5369—dc21

99-41419
CIP

Editorial director: Charlyce Jones Owen
Editor in chief: Nancy Roberts
Acquisitions editor: Jennifer Gilliland
Associate editor: Anita Castro
Editorial assistant: Tamsen Adams
AVP/Director of production and manufacturing: Barbara Kittle
Managing editor: Mary Rottino
Production editor: Kari Callaghan Mazzola
Project liaison: Randy Pettit
Manufacturing manager: Nick Sklitsis
Prepress and manufacturing buyer: Tricia Kenny
Marketing manager: Sharon Cosgrove
Electronic page makeup: Kari Callaghan Mazzola and John P. Mazzola
Interior design: John P. Mazzola
Cover design director: Jayne Conte
Cover design: Karen Salzbach

This book was set in 10/12 Times by Big Sky Composition
and was printed and bound by Banta Company.
The cover was printed by Phoenix Color Corp.

Printed in the United States of America
10 9 8 7 6 5 4 3 2 1

ISBN 0-13-020840-X

PRENTICE-HALL INTERNATIONAL (UK) LIMITED, *London*
PRENTICE-HALL OF AUSTRALIA PTY. LIMITED, *Sydney*
PRENTICE-HALL CANADA INC., *Toronto*
PRENTICE-HALL HISPANOAMERICANA, S.A., *Mexico*
PRENTICE-HALL OF INDIA PRIVATE LIMITED, *New Delhi*
PRENTICE-HALL OF JAPAN, INC., *Tokyo*
PEARSON EDUCATION ASIA PTE. LTD., *Singapore*
EDITORA PRENTICE-HALL DO BRASIL, LTDA., *Rio de Janeiro*

This book is dedicated to our parents and to our children.

Contents

Preface

The development of easy-to-use statistical software like SPSS for Windows has changed the way statistics is being taught and learned. No longer do students have to learn a system of elaborate code to conduct simple or complex analyses. Instead, students simply enter their data into an easy-to-use data editor. Then they can select items from a pull-down menu to make appropriate transformations to variables, click on options from another menu to create graphs of distributions of variables, select among various statistical analyses by clicking on appropriate options, and more. With a minimal amount of time and effort, the output is displayed, showing the results.

Researchers also have benefited from programs like SPSS for Windows. They do not have to spend time reacquainting themselves with the ins and outs of a statistical software package or learning new programs for conducting analyses that take hours to master. They also don't have to teach assistants how to write code to produce analyses, or examine and reexamine code that has produced error messages that do not really indicate what is wrong. Everyone can just point and click.

In general, programs like SPSS for Windows have improved the quality of life for students who are learning statistics, for teachers who are teaching statistics, and for researchers who are applying statistics. Nevertheless, many users of these programs find "doing statistics" an arduous, pleasure-free task. They still are faced with many potential obstacles and feel overwhelmed and stressed rather than challenged and excited about the potential for mastering these important skills.

What are some of the obstacles that students, in particular, face when they are trying to conduct statistical analyses with SPSS for Windows?

- Obstacle 1: Although SPSS for Windows is extremely easy to use, many students and first-time users find it very complex. They have to learn how to input data into the Data Editor, to save and retrieve data, to make transformations to data, to conduct analyses, to manipulate output, to create graphs, to edit graphs, and so on.
- Obstacle 2: Students can feel helpless. Although they can point and click, they are frequently confronted with new dialogue boxes with many decisions to make. Their instructor does not have the time to talk about each of the options, so students feel as if they are making uninformed decisions.
- Obstacle 3: The amount of output and numbers produced by any statistical procedure is enough to cower most researchers if they are forced to explain their meaning. How can students who are taking statistics for the first time feel confident about interpreting output from an SPSS procedure? In trying to understand output, they are likely to face language problems. For example, "What is a Sig. F? Is it the same as the *p*-value that the instructor is talking about? No, it couldn't be, or she or he would have told us."

Researchers, graduate students, and more advanced undergraduate students are going to face additional obstacles.

- Obstacle 4: Users can think of a number of different ways to analyze their data, but they are unsure about which way would yield the most understanding of their results and not violate the assumptions underlying the analyses.
- Obstacle 5: Even if users make all good decisions about statistical approaches and understand the output, they still must write a results section that conforms to American Psychological Association format.

Using SPSS for Windows: Analyzing and Understanding Data was written to try to help readers overcome these five obstacles.

Part I, "Introducing SPSS," was written to address Obstacle 1, while Part II was designed to attack the other four obstacles.

Part I consists of seventeen lessons divided into four units. It guides students through the most basic of SPSS techniques and uses a step-by-step description.

Unit 1, "Getting Started with SPSS," shows the student how to get started using SPSS, including a survey of the main menus, how to use SPSS help, and a brief tour of what SPSS can do.

Unit 2, "Creating and Working with Data Files," goes through the steps of defining variables, showing how data are entered and edited, printing SPSS data files, and importing and exporting information to and from SPSS.

Unit 3, "Working with Data," describes how to find and replace data, recode and compute values, sort data, and merge and split files.

Unit 4, the final unit in Part I, titled "Working with SPSS Charts and Output," teaches the student how to create and enhance SPSS charts as well as how to work with the SPSS output and SPSS tables.

Part II, "Working with SPSS Procedures," consists of twenty-seven lessons, divided into six units. Each unit presents a set of statistical techniques and a step-by-step description of how to conduct the statistical analyses. This is not, however, a cookbook format. We include extensive substantive information about each statistical technique, including a brief discussion of the statistical technique under consideration, examples of how the statistic is applied, the assumptions underlying the statistic, a description of the effect size for the statistic, a sample data set that can be analyzed with the statistic, the research question associated with the data set, step-by-step instructions as to how to complete the analysis using the sample data set, a discussion of the results of the analysis, a visual display of the results using SPSS graphic options, a results section describing the results in APA format, alternative analytical techniques (when available), and practice exercises.

Unit 5, "Creating Variables," shows how to create new variables from existing ones and shows the basic procedures for describing qualitative and quantitative variables.

Unit 6, "T Test Procedures," focuses on comparing means and shows how to use a variety of techniques, including independent and dependent *t* tests and the one-sample *t* test.

Unit 7, "Univariate and Multivariate Analysis-of-Variance Techniques," focuses on the family of analysis-of-variance techniques, including one-way and two-way analyses of variance, analysis of covariance, and multivariate analysis of variance.

Unit 8, "Correlation, Regression, and Discriminant Analysis Procedures," includes simple techniques such as bivariate correlational analysis and bivariate regression analysis, as well as more complex analyses such as partial correlational analysis, multiple linear regression, and discriminant analysis.

Unit 9, "Scaling Procedures," focuses on factor analysis, reliability estimation, and item analysis.

Unit 10, "Nonparametric Procedures," discusses a variety of nonparametric techniques, including such tests as the binomial, one-sample chi-square, Kruskal-Wallis, McNemar, Friedman, and Cochran tests.

New to This Edition

Version 9.0 of SPSS introduces a wealth of additional features, including the features listed below.

For Charts

- Drag and drop new variables, and update charts on the fly
- Split a single chart into multiple panels for side-by-side comparisons
- Paste "live" charts into applications that support ActiveX objects

For Statistics

- New ANOVA procedure with custom models and post hoc tests
- Robust Levene test to compare variance between groups
- Harmonic and geometric means now available in the Means procedure
- Interclass correlation in the Reliability procedure

For Data Management

- Display descriptive variable labels instead of variable names in dialog boxes
- Variable labels (not variable names) can be up to 256 characters long
- Include a date and time stamp in journal files for archiving

Output

- Use Layered Reports procedure that provides summary reports with each subgroup in a separate layers
- Pick the output format you want
- Control default column width in pivot tables and save column width settings in the Data Editor
- Online Help
- Results Coach provides an annotated sample output that helps you understand how to interpret your results
- "Ask Me" help is a natural language interface that helps you find the answers you need without needing to know any complicated jargon

The Student Disk

Using SPSS for Windows: Analyzing and Understanding Data comes with a student disk that includes all the files you will need to work through each lesson. Part I uses several data files, among them one named Crab Scale Results and another named Teacher Scale Results. These will be introduced as you work through the first seventeen lessons. They can also be seen in Appendix A.

Part II contains two types of data files. The first you can use as a sample data file when learning a particular SPSS procedure, such as paired-samples *t* test or factor analysis. These files can be easily identified since they are named, for example, Lesson 22 Data File 1 or Lesson 35 Data File 2. Also used in the second half of the book are sets of data files for completing lesson exercises. These are named, for example, Lesson 22 Exercise File 1 or Lesson 35 Exercise File 2. Since Windows 95 and Windows 98 allow for long file names, these file names can be detailed descriptions.

Other Features of the Book

Typing Conventions

There are two basic typing conventions that are used throughout the book:

- Bold characters indicate actions that should be taken when using SPSS. New terms also appear in bold.
- In Part I, a sequence of actions is indicated by an arrow like this →
  For example, if a certain procedure requires clicking on the File menu and then clicking the New option, it would be represented as follows.

1. Click **File** → **New.**

Examples

Each lesson includes step-by-step procedures, with copious illustrations of screen shots, for successfully completing a technique with sample data. Exercises at the end of each lesson allow you to practice what you have learned.

Tips

Lessons contain tips that will help you learn SPSS as well as teach you short cuts that make SPSS easier to use.

Acknowledgments

No book is ever the work of only the authors. *Using SPSS for Windows: Analyzing and Understanding Data* was first contracted with Chris Cardone, whom we would like to thank for giving us the opportunity to undertake the project. Chris remains a good colleague and a better friend. We would like to thank Burton L. Alperson of California State University at Los Angeles and Bernard S. Gorman of Nassau Community College for reviewing the manuscript. We would also like to thank Prentice Hall editor Jennifer Gilliland and, especially, Prentice Hall editor Anita Castro, who helped keep all the pieces of this project together. Finally, we would like to thank Kari Callaghan Mazzola for doing a wonderful job of producing this book.

Thank you for using this book. We hope it makes your SPSS for Windows activities easy to learn, fun to use, and helpful. Should you have any comments about the book (good, bad, or otherwise), feel free to contact us at the Prentice Hall web page (http://www.prenhall.com), or drop us a note at one of the electronic addresses listed below:

Samuel B. Green (kusbg@ukans.edu)

Neil J. Salkind (njs@ukans.edu)

Using SPSS for Windows

You're probably familiar with how other Windows applications work, and you will find that many SPSS features operate exactly the same way. You know about dragging, clicking, double-clicking, and working with windows. If you don't, you can refer to one of the many Prentice-Hall books that can help. Keep in mind that SPSS 9.X is designed to work with the Windows 95, Windows 98, and Windows 2000 operating systems and will not work with any earlier version of the operating system.

SPSS 9.X takes advantage of Windows special architecture as well as other features such as shortcuts, right-clicking, and mullet-tasking. Throughout *Using SPSS for Windows*, we will assume that you are familiar with Windows and what you need to do concerning file management and the most simple skills, such as using the mouse.

In this first unit, we introduce you to SPSS, beginning with how to start SPSS, and walk you through a tour so that you know some of the most important features of SPSS.

In Lesson 1, "Starting SPSS for Windows," the first of four Lessons in this unit, you will find out how the SPSS Windows group is organized and how you start SPSS.

In Lesson 2, "The SPSS Main Menus and Toolbar," we introduce you to the opening SPSS window, point out the various elements in the window, and explain what they do. The main menus in the SPSS window are your opening to all the SPSS features you will learn about in using SPSS for Windows. We also introduce you to the toolbar, a collection of icons that perform important tasks with a click of the mouse.

Lesson 3, "Using SPSS Help," introduces you to SPSS online help. If you've ever used another Windows application, you know how handy it is to have this type of help immediately available and how it can get you through even the most difficult procedures.

In the last Lesson in Unit I, "A Brief Tour of SPSS," we provide a simple example of what SPSS can do including simple analysis, the use of the Data Editor, and the creation of a chart. Here we'll whet your appetite for the terrific power and features of SPSS and what is in store for you throughout the book.

Starting SPSS for Windows

After This Lesson, You Will Know

- How to start SPSS
- What the opening SPSS screen looks like

Key Words

- Viewer
- Data Editor

With this lesson you will start your journey on learning how to use SPSS for Windows (or SPSS), the most powerful and easiest-to-use Windows-based data analysis package available.

Keep in mind that throughout these lessons we expect you to work along with us. It's only through hands-on experiences that you will master the basic and advanced features of this program.

Starting SPSS

TIP

To place SPSS on the Windows Start menu, open the Explorer, locate the SPSS executive file (spss.exe), and drag and drop it on to the Start menu.

Like other Windows-based applications, SPSS can be organized on the Start menu as you see in Figure 1 (at the top of page 3).

This group was created when you first installed SPSS. To start SPSS, follow these steps:

1. Click Start → Programs → SPSS 9.0 for Windows icon. When you do this, you will see the SPSS opening screen as shown in Figure 2 (at the bottom of page 3).

The SPSS Opening Window

As you can see in Figure 2, the SPSS opening window is the **Data Editor**. This is where you enter data you want to use with SPSS. Although you cannot see it when SPSS first opens, there is another open (but not active) window as well. This is the **Viewer**. The Viewer displays

Figure 1. SPSS on the Start menu.

Figure 2. The SPSS opening screen.

statistical results and charts that you create. An example of the Viewer window is shown in Figure 3. As you will see in Lesson 4, you create a data set in the Data Editor, then, once the set is analyzed or graphed, you examine the results of the analysis in the Viewer.

Figure 3. The Viewer window.

If you think the Data Editor is similar to a spreadsheet in form and function, you are right. In form, it certainly is, since the Data Editor consists of rows and columns just like in Excel and Lotus 1-2-3. Values can be entered and then manipulated. In function as well, the Data Editor is much like a spreadsheet. Values that are entered can be transformed, sorted, rearranged, and more. In addition, SPSS can use formulas, as you will learn in Lesson 12.

As you will learn in Lesson 10, one of the many conveniences of SPSS is its ability to import data from a spreadsheet accurately and efficiently. This ability makes SPSS particularly well suited and powerful for further analysis of data already in spreadsheet form.

Unlike the previous version of SPSS, these are the only two windows you need to know about. Once an analysis is completed, the Viewer will allow you to examine the results of an analysis, the graph that you might have created, notes that SPSS generates about the procedure, and a title. You will see examples later in this unit.

The SPSS Main Menus and Toolbar

After This Lesson, You Will Know

- Each of the SPSS main menus and what the commands on the menus do
- The icons on the toolbar

Key Words

- Data menu
- Edit menu
- File menu
- Graphs menu
- Open dialog box
- Analyze menu
- Transform menu
- Utilities menu
- View menu
- Toolbar
- Status Bar

Menus are the key to operating any Windows application, and that is certainly the case with SPSS. Its 10 main menus (including the standard Window and Help menus) provide access to every tool and feature that SPSS has to offer. In this lesson, we will review the contents of each of these menus and introduce you to the toolbar, a set of icons that takes the place of menu commands. The icons make it quick and easy to do anything, from saving a file to printing a chart.

The SPSS Main Menus

SPSS comes to you with 10 main menus, as you see in the opening screen in Figure 2 (at the bottom of page 3). If you have used any Windows applications in the past, menu names such as File and Edit are surely familiar.

On the other hand, SPSS is SPSS since it has many unique features and tools. While you think you may know all about the File menu and what options are available on it, stick with us through the rest of this lesson to see exactly what the File menu, and the other nine menus, can do for you.

5

TIP

Want to set the number of files that SPSS lists on the File menu? Click Edit → Options and change the value limiting the number of names.

The File Menu

The purpose of the **File menu** (Figure 4) is to work with files. Using the options on this menu, you create new files, open existing ones, save files in a variety of formats, display information about a file, print a file, and exit SPSS. The File menu also lists the last few documents that were accessed, so you can quickly return to a previous document.

File	
New	▶
Open...	Ctrl+O
Database Capture	▶
Read ASCII Data	▶
Save	Ctrl+S
Save As...	
Display Data Info...	
Apply Data Dictionary...	
Print...	Ctrl+P
Stop Processor	Ctrl+Alt+P
1 Chapter 4 Data Set 1	
2 Employee data	
3 C:\WINDOWS\Start Menu\Cpw	
4 c:\windows\TEMP\~spssocn.cht	
5 Figure 4.11	
6 Figure 4.12	
7 Figure 4.12	
8 50 values Excel 4.0	
9 Chapter 6 Data Set 1	
Exit	

Figure 4. The File menu.

For example, when it comes time to start working with the file named Teacher Scale Results, you would select Open from the File menu and then select the file name from the **Open** dialog box. You will learn more about this process in Lesson 7.

The Edit Menu

When it comes time to cut or copy data and paste it in another location in the current, or another, data file, you will go to the **Edit menu**. You will also seek out options on the Edit menu to search for data or text, replace text, and set SPSS preferences (or default settings). All these activities and more are found on the Edit menu in Figure 5.

Edit	
Undo	Ctrl+Z
Cut	Ctrl+X
Copy	Ctrl+C
Paste	Ctrl+V
Clear	Del
Find...	Ctrl+F
Options...	

Figure 5. The Edit menu.

TIP

When items on a menu are dimmed, it means they are not available.

For example, if you wanted to find what Mary Jones scored on test 1, you could search for "Mary Jones" and then read across the file to find her score on the variable named test 1. You would use the Find command on the Edit menu to search for that information.

The View Menu

Here's a chance to customize your SPSS desktop. Using various commands on the **View menu**, you can choose to show or hide the toolbar, **Status bar**, and grid lines in the Data Editor window, change fonts, and use Value Labels. You can see these commands in Figure 6.

Figure 6. The View menu.

For example, if we wanted to hide the toolbar, we would be sure that the toolbar option is not checked on the View menu.

The Data Menu

Variables and their values are the central element in any SPSS analysis, and you need powerful tools to work with variables. You have them on SPSS. On the **Data menu** you see in Figure 7, you can see commands that allow you to define and sort variables, work with templates, go to a specific case, merge and aggregate files, and weigh cases as you see fit.

Figure 7. The Data menu.

For example, if we want to assign a label to a variable such as gender, it will read as "male" or "female" rather than 1 or 2 in the Data Editor. The value of 1 or 2, however, is maintained as the value of the gender variable even though words appear in the cells.

The Transform Menu

There will be times when a variable value needs to be transformed or converted to another form or another value. That's where the commands on the **Transform menu** you see in Figure 8 (at the top of page 8) come in handy. On this menu, you will find commands that allow you to compute new values, create a set of random values, recode values, replace missing values, and do more.

For example, you could easily compute a new variable that represents the mean of a set of items using the Compute command on the Transform menu.

Figure 8. The Transform menu.

The Analyze Menu

Here's the meat-and-potatoes menu! As you can see in Figure 9, there are 16 different options on the **Analyze menu** that lead to almost any statistical analysis technique you might want to use. These range from a simple computation of a mean and standard deviation to time series analysis and multiple regression.

Figure 9. The Analyze menu.

For example, if you wanted to determine if there is a significant difference between the average rating that Professor 6 received on a teaching evaluation form versus the average rating received by Professor 4, you could look to the Compare Means option on the Analyze menu.

The Graphs Menu

Want to see what those numbers *really* look like? Go to the **Graphs menu** where you can create bar, line, area, and some 15 other graphs. Graphs make numbers come alive, and you should pay special attention to Unit 4, where we show you how to create, edit, and print them. Take a look at Figure 10 (at the top of page 9) to see what graph options are available.

For example, if you want to see test scores as a function of gender, a bar graph (on the Graphs menu) could do it quite nicely.

The Utilities Menu

Here you can find out information about variables and files, and you can define and use sets of variables. You can see these options in Figure 11 (on page 9) on the **Utilities menu**.

For example, the File Info option (for File Information) on the Utilities menu can tell us that the file named *Teacher Scores* contains 50 cases and 8 variables.

Figure 10. The Graphs menu.

Figure 11. The Utilities menu.

The Window and Help Menus

These two menus function much like any other Windows application menus. The **Window menu** helps you switch from one window to another and minimize the SPSS Data Editor or Viewer. The Help menu, as seen in Figure 12, provides online help. We will focus on the Help menu in the next lesson.

Figure 12. The Help menu.

The SPSS Toolbar and Status Bar

What's the easiest way to use SPSS? Clearly, through the use of the **toolbar**, the set of icons that are underneath the menus. You can see the Data Editor toolbar in Figure 13 (at the top of page 10) and a description of what each icon does in Table 1 (on page 10). Each icon represents a command on a menu. Click on the icon, and the command is performed. So, instead of going to the Utilities menu to select variables, you can just click on the Variables icon on the toolbar.

Want to know what an icon on the toolbar does? Just place the mouse pointer on it, and you'll see a brief discussion of its function.

Figure 13. The Data Editor toolbar buttons.

Different screens have different toolbars. For example, as you will see in Lesson 15, when you create a chart, a new set of icons becomes available on the toolbar.

Table 1

Toolbar Icons

Icon	Title	What it does
	Open	Opens an already created file
	Save	Saves a new or already created file
	Print	Prints a file
	Dialog Recall	Recalls the last used dialog box
	Undo	Undoes a change in formatting or data entry
	GoTo Chart	Goes to a named chart
	GoTo Case	Goes to a numbered case
	Variables	Provides information about a variable
	Find	Finds a record
	Insert Case	Inserts a case in the data file
	Insert Variable	Inserts a new variable into the data file
	Split File	Splits a file along some defined variable
	Weight Cases	Weights cases
	Select Cases	Selects a set of cases using a certain criterion
	Value Labels	Turns labels on and off
	Use Sets	Creates sets of variables

TIP

If you are performing an analysis and nothing seems to be happening, look in the Status Bar before you panic and conclude that SPSS or Windows has locked up. Large numbers and complex analyses often take computer resources and time to complete.

Another useful tool is the Status Bar located at the bottom of the SPSS window. Here, you can see a one-line report as to what activity SPSS is currently involved in. Messages such as "SPSS Processor is ready" tell you that SPSS is ready for your directions or input of data. Or, "Running Means …" tells you that SPSS is in the middle of the procedure named Means.

The Data Files

An important part of learning how to use SPSS and using this book, *Using SPSS for Windows*, is using the sample files included on the student disk. Throughout Part I of the text, titled "Introducing SPSS," we will use two separate sets of data to illustrate various SPSS features, such as entering and working with data. There is a detailed description of each of these files shown in Appendix A.

The Crab Scale File

The first data set is a collection of scores on the Crab Scale and some biographical information for 10 college professors who completed a measure of crabbiness. Table 2 gives a summary of the variables, their definition and their range of values.

Table 2

Crab Scale Summary

Variable	Definition	Range
id_prof	professor's identification number	1 through 10
sex_prof	professor's gender	1 or 2
age	professor's age	33 through 64
rank	professor's rank	Assistant, Associate, or Full Professor
school	professor's school	Liberal Arts, Business School
crab1	score on item 1 on the Crab Scale	
crab2	score on item 2 on the Crab Scale	
crab3	score on item 3 on the Crab Scale	
crab4	score on item 4 on the Crab Scale	
crab5	score on item 5 on the Crab Scale	
crab6	score on item 6 on the Crab Scale	

The Crab Scale includes the following six items:

1. I generally feel crabby if someone tries to help me.
2. I generally feel happy when I watch the news.
3. I generally feel crabby when I watch mothers and fathers talk baby talk to their babies.
4. I generally feel happy when I am able to make sarcastic comments.
5. I generally feel crabby when I am on a family vacation.
6. I generally feel happy when I am beating someone at a game.

A teacher responds to each item on the following 5-point scale:

1. Totally agree
2. Agree
3. In a quandary
4. Disagree
5. Vicious lies

The Crab Scale yields two scores:

1. *The Cross-Situational Crab Index:* This index tries to assess whether individuals refuse to be happy regardless of the situation.
2. *The True Crab Scale:* This index attempts to assess whether an individual is acting in a true crablike fashion: crabby when confronted with a pleasant stimulus and happy when confronted with an unpleasant stimulus.

Items 1 through 6 are summed to yield a total score. For the Cross-Situational Crabbiness Index, all scores are summed together. Items 2, 4, and 6 are happiness items, and the scores on these items must be reversed so that higher scores indicate more crabbiness, as shown at the top of page 12.

Original Scoring	Recoded Scoring
1	5
2	4
3	3
4	2
5	1

You can see the actual set of data in Appendix A. This data file is saved on your SPSS student disk as Crab Scale Results.

The Teacher Scale File

No teacher escapes being rated by students. The second set of data we will deal with in Part I of *Using SPSS for Windows* is a set of responses by students concerning the performance of these 10 professors.

The second data set is a collection of scores on the Teacher Scale and some biographical information for 50 students who completed the Teacher Scale. Scores on the Teacher Scale that make up this sample file are also shown in Appendix A. They are contained on the student disk under the file name Teacher Scale Results.

Table 3 shows the biographical information we collected on each student and their responses to the 5-point scale. We will be using them in examples throughout this part of *Using SPSS for Windows*.

Table 3
Teacher Scale Summary

Variable	Name	Range
id_stud	student's identification number	1 through 50
id_prof	professor's identification number	1 through 5
sex_stud	student's gender	1 or 2
teacher1	score for item 1 on the Teacher Scale	1 through 5
teacher2	score for item 2 on the Teacher Scale	1 through 5
teacher3	score for item 3 on the Teacher Scale	1 through 5
teacher4	score for item 4 on the Teacher Scale	1 through 5
teacher5	score for item 5 on the Teacher Scale	1 through 5

The Teacher Scale contains the following five items:

1. I love that teacher.
2. My teacher says good stuff.
3. The teacher has trouble talking.
4. The teacher is a jerk.
5. My teacher made the boring lively, the unthinkable thinkable, the undoable doable.

Items 3 and 4 must be reversed so that higher scores indicate effectiveness as follows.

Original Scoring	Recoded Scoring
1	5
2	4
3	3
4	2
5	1

After This Lesson, You Will Know

- About the contents of the SPSS Help menu
- How to use the F1 function key for help
- What Help options are available
- How to use the Find option to search for particular words

Key Words

- Ask Me
- Contents
- F1 function key
- Find
- Help menu
- Index
- SPSS Help
- Topics

If you need help, you've come to the right place. SPSS offers help that is only a few mouse clicks away. It is especially useful when you are in the middle of creating a data file and need information about a specific SPSS feature. Help is so comprehensive that even if you're a novice SPSS user, **SPSS Help** can show you the way.

How to Get Help

You can get help in SPSS in several ways. The easiest and most direct is by pressing the **F1 function** key or by using the **Help menu** you saw in Figure 12.

- As you can see, there are eight options on the Help menu.
- **Topics** lists the topics for which you can get help. You can click on any one of these.
- Tutorial takes you through a step-by-step tutorial for major SPSS topics.

- SPSS Home Page uses your Internet connection to take you to the home page of SPSS on the Internet. Syntax Guide provides you with help using SPSS' powerful syntax feature.
- Syntax Guide, which provides you with information on SPSS programming language
- Statistics Coach walks you through the steps you need to determine what type of analysis you want to conduct.
- **Ask Me** uses a natural language tool to answer questions that you ask SPSS.
- About ... tells you the version of SPSS that you are currently using.
- Register Product ... helps you register your copy of SPSS.

Using the F1 Function Key

The F1 function key is a quick way to get help, but it only opens the **Help Topics** dialog box you see in Figure 14. Here, you can click **Contents, Index, Find** or **Ask Me**.

Figure 14. The Help Topics dialog box.

Using the Topics Option

The Topics option on the SPSS Help menu provides an alphabetical listing of help topics by Contents, an Index option, the Find option, and Ask Me.

Using the Contents Option

The Contents tab presents the major headings for help. Double-clicking on any one provides a list of possible topics that you might want to consult for the help you need. For example, if you want help on how to compare the means of two samples, you would follow these steps:

1. Press **F1**.
2. Click the **Contents**.
3. Double-click **Statistical analysis**, and you will see a list of the topics within this general heading.

4. Double-click the topic labeled **Compare Means**.
5. Double-click the topic labeled **Independent-Samples T Test** procedure. You will see Help, as shown in Figure 15.

Figure 15. Using the Contents tab to get help.

Other tabs in the Help Topics dialog box are as follows:

- The Index tab, when clicked, lists all the SPSS topics in alphabetical order
- The Find tab, when clicked, allows you to search for a topic on which you need help.
- The Ask Me tab, when clicked, requires you to ask a question, and SPSS will find help on that topic if it understands your query.

What can the various Help menu options do for you? Here is a summary and a brief tour: Once you find help on the subject you want (such as information about the mean), you can click on the Options button in the Help window (or right-click anywhere in the window) and perform a variety of tasks. For example, you can annotate the Help screen with your own information, copy the Help content to the clipboard, print out the content of the Help menu, change the size of the fonts of the Help windows, or change the position of Help on the screen.

Using the Index Option

The Index tab provides an alphabetical listing of all the topics in SPSS. To find help on a particular topic, follow these steps. For example, the numbered list on top of page 16 shows how you would use the Index option to find help on means.

1. Click **Help → Topics**.
2. Click the **Index tab**.
3. Type **mean**.

As you enter the letters of the term for which you need help, SPSS Help tries to identify the topic listing. As you can see in Figure 16, help is available. Double-clicking on the index entry "mean," or clicking the Display button, produces additional topics. They require you to double-click once again for the actual help. In Figure 17, you can see the definition of the mean, one of the options available in the Help window.

Figure 16. Identifying the topic for help in the Help Index.

Figure 17. Defining the term mean.

Using the Find Option

What if you can't find a term in the Index, but you need help anyway? The Find option in the Help Topics dialog box, as you see in Figure 18 (at the top of page 17), allows you to enter any words that may be part of a Help screen rather than just a category. In effect, you are searching all the words in all the topics.

For example, let's use the Find option and the term "population" and see what SPSS delivers. Follow these steps. If the Help window is opened, close it now.

1. Press **F1**.
2. Click the **Find** tab.
3. Type "population," and SPSS returns a list of topics for which the word is relevant. In Figure 18, you can see the 40 topics related to the word "population" for which you can get additional help. Just double-click on any of the items.

Figure 18. Using Find for help on a particular topic.

SPSS Find is very sensitive to what words you select. For example, if you need help on the word "mean," SPSS will turn up lots of references since the word (as written) is the most general. The word "Mean," however, is more specific, and the word "MEAN" even more so (since MEAN is the specific procedure in SPSS syntax). If you know exactly what you're looking for, you can be specific, but be careful because specificity can cause you to miss what you are looking for if you are not sure of your topic's exact terminology.

Using Ask Me

The Ask Me option allows you to "ask" SPSS a question, and it will provide possible topics that might contain an answer. The major problem with this option is that it generally provides a very large host of topics (much like the Index option) and does not take into account the context within which the topic appears.

Options in Any SPSS Help Window

Within any one SPSS Help window, there are various other options you can use. The Contents and Index options you already know about. All of these are not always available.

- The **Contents** button returns you to the list of topics in Help (see Figure 14).
- The **Index** button returns you to the Index (see Figure 16).
- The **Back** option takes you back to the previous Help screen.
- The **Print** option prints out the contents of the Help window.
- The **Options** option provides the various options mentioned earlier in this lesson, such as copy and annotate.
- The **How To** option provides a step-by-step description of how to perform the procedure.
- The **Syntax** button provides the actual syntax or SPSS language to perform a particular technique. These language commands can then be cut and pasted into a syntax window.
- The **Also** option provides additional topics.

A Brief SPSS Tour

After This Lesson, You Will Know

- How to open a file
- Some of the basic functions that SPSS can perform

Key Words

- Fonts
- Open

In the first three lessons of *Using SPSS for Windows*, you learned how to start SPSS, took a look at the SPSS main menus, and found out how to use SPSS Help. Now, sit back and enjoy a brief tour of SPSS activities. Nothing fancy here. Just creating some new variables, simple descriptions of data, a test of significance, and a graph or two. What we're trying to show you is how easy it is to use SPSS. We will spend all of Part II of *Using SPSS for Windows* concentrating on exactly how to use SPSS' analytic procedures.

Opening a File

You can enter your own data to create a new SPSS data file, use an existing file, or even import data from such applications as Microsoft Excel into SPSS. Any way you do it, you need to have data to work with. In Figure 19 (at the top of page 19), you can see we have a screen full of data, part of the Teacher Scale Results file mentioned earlier and available on the disk that accompanies this book. We opened it using the **Open** option on the File menu.

If you use a spreadsheet application, then the structure of the data file appears familiar; it has rows and columns, with cases for rows and variables for columns.

Working with Appearance

Everyone has his or her preference on how things look. As you can see in Figure 19, the data are listed in a sans serif font named Arial, which is 10 points in size. For whatever reason, you may want to select another font and change the style in which the values or headings appear.

Figure 19. An open SPSS file.

Simply by using the **Fonts** option on the View menu, we changed the font to Times Roman 10 point. We also used the Grid Lines option on the View menu to turn off the grid lines. The data file now appears as shown in Figure 20.

Figure 20. Working with fonts, sizes, and styles with grid lines turned off.

Creating a New Variable

As you know, the Teacher Scale is a five-item measure of teacher effectiveness. Let's assume that we want to compute a new variable that is the average of the five items, so that each student's ratings have an average score.

Figure 21. The new variable, average, created using the Compute option.

To create a new variable, we use the Compute option on the Transform menu. The finished result (the new variable named average) is shown in Figure 21 (above).

A Simple Table

Now it's time to get to the reason why we're using SPSS in the first place, the various analytical tools that are available. First, let's say we want to know the general distribution of males and females. That's all, just a count of how many males and how many females are in the total sample.

In Figure 22 (at the top of page 21), you can see an output window that provides exactly the information we asked for, which was the frequency of the number of males and females. We used the Frequencies option on the Summarize menu (under the main menu Statistics) to compute these values. We then told SPSS all we wanted was a frequencies count. We could have computed several other descriptive statistics, but just the count is fine for now. Here's your first look at real SPSS output, contained in the Viewer window.

Guess what? With just another few clicks, we can create the bar chart you see in Figure 23 (at the top of page 22). This graph also shows the special graphing tools on the toolbar in the SPSS Chart Editor. There are lots of ways to jazz up this graph, many of which we will discuss in Lesson 16.

Frequencies

Statistics

Sex of Student

N	Valid	50
	Missing	0

Sex of Student

		Frequency	Percent	Valid Percent	Cumulativ e Percent
Valid	Male	28	56.0	56.0	56.0
	Female	22	44.0	44.0	100.0
	Total	50	100.0	100.0	

Figure 22. The Viewer window showing the results of a simple descriptive analysis.

A Simple Analysis

Let's see if males and females differ in their average Teach scores. This is a simple analysis requiring a t test for independent samples. You may already know about this procedure from another statistics class you have had, or it may be entirely new. The procedure is a comparison between the mean for the group of males and the mean for the group of females.

In Figure 24 (at the bottom of page 22) you can see a partial summary of the results of the t test. Notice that the listing in the left pane of the Viewer now shows the Frequencies, Graph, and T-Test procedures listed. To see any part of the output, all we need to do is click on that element, in the left pane of the Viewer, as we did with Frequencies. When SPSS produces an output window, you almost always will have to scroll to see the entire output.

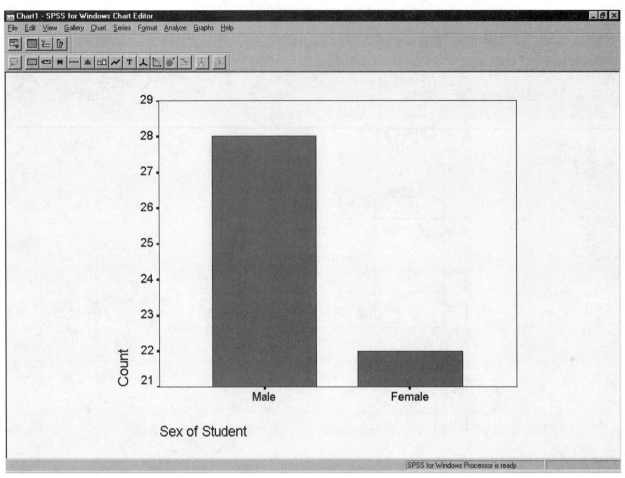

Figure 23. A simple bar chart.

Figure 24. The results of an independent-samples t test.

Creating and Working with Data Files

You've been introduced to SPSS and what SPSS offers. Now it's time to learn how to work with data that you use to create SPSS data files. The six lessons in this unit will cover important issues such as defining variables, entering and editing data, inserting and deleting cases and variables, selecting, cutting and pasting data, printing SPSS documents, exiting an SPSS data file, and importing and exporting SPSS data.

These crucial skills lay a foundation for Part II of *Using SPSS for Windows*, where you will learn how to use SPSS procedures. Read through these six lessons and be sure to work through each step.

Defining Variables

After This Lesson, You Will Know

- How to create a data file
- How to define an SPSS variable
- How to work with variable types, labels, missing values, and column format
- How to define Column Format dialog box
- How to define Labels dialog box
- How to define Variable Type dialog box

Key Words

- Cell
- Column
- Data file
- Row
- Variable information bar

H ere's where all the work begins, with the entry of data into the SPSS spreadsheetlike structure. When you first open SPSS, the Data Editor window is labeled Untitled - SPSS Data Editor, and it's ready for you to enter variables as well as cases.

The Data Editor Window

TIP

SPSS allows you to have only one Data Editor window open at a time. Unlike other Windows applications, the only open file is also the active one.

If you are a regular user of a spreadsheet such as Excel or Lotus 1-2-3, then you are familiar with the terminology that follows, because the SPSS Data Editor follows a very similar design. If you are not a spreadsheet user, pay special attention to what follows because it will provide a foundation for many of the ideas and practices that come later in *Using SPSS for Windows*.

All Data Editor windows consist of several important elements, as labeled in Figure 25 (at the top of page 25).

A **row** is a horizontal collection of information that represents a case. For example, in Figure 25 each case is represented by an identification number for a professor.

A **column** is a vertical collection of information that represents a variable. For example, in

Figure 25. The Data Editor window showing a data file.

Figure 25 age in years is a variable. Usually, but not always, there is a value entered for each variable in a **data file**.

A **cell** is where a row and a column intersect. It is where the value of a particular variable for a particular case is entered. For example, the score for Professor 6 on the first item of the Crab Scale is 2.

All the rows, columns, and data entered in the cells make up a data file, a collection of variables and cases. In Figure 25, you can see the data file saved as Crab Scale Results.

SPSS' Data Editor is useful for smaller data sets. But if you have lots of data manipulation to do, such as sorting of variables and reordering, you might want to use a spreadsheet such as Excel or a database application such as Access and the import the data (see lesson 10) into SPSS. Besides, SPSS is limited by 8 character label names. These other applications are not.

Creating a New Data Window

Data in an SPSS data file are organized as variables for at least one case. Even if we had demographic information and crabbiness ratings for only one professor, Crab Scale Results would still be a data file.

Our first step in the creation of a new data file is the definition of variables. Before we do that, we must first create a place for those variables, a new data window. Here's how.

1. **Click File → New → Data**. When you do this, you will see a new data window like the one you see in Figure 25 but without any values entered in the cells. The window is maximized. Variables are unnamed, with each column label being "var" and dimmed because the variables are undefined. If you already have a Data Editor window open and variables defined and you try to create a new one, SPSS will ask you if you want to save the existing Data Editor file.

Defining Variables

SPSS can't work unless variables are defined and data is entered in the Data Editor. You can have SPSS define the variables for you, or, preferably, you can do the defining yourself. Doing it yourself offers much more control over the way things look and work.

Having SPSS Define Variables

Now that the new data window is open, you can do one of two things. The first is to enter data into any cell in the Data Editor and press the Enter key (which is the standard way of entering data). For example, you could enter the value 87 in row 1, column 1. Since SPSS must have a variable name to work with, SPSS will automatically name the variable VAR00001. If you did this in row 1, column 5, then SPSS would name the variable VAR00005 and also number the other columns sequentially, as you see in Figure 26.

Figure 26. SPSS will automatically name variables as you enter data in cells.

Note also that right below the main menu in the upper left-hand corner of the Data Editor is an indicator of what cell is being highlighted. For example, in Figure 26, you can see that 1:VAR00005 represents row 1, variable 5.

Custom Defining Variables

When getting started with a new data file, custom definition should be your choice because it allows for much greater flexibility, such as

- providing your own names for variables,
- providing descriptive labels, and
- assigning special formats such as text or date or time.

To define a variable name, follow these steps. Be sure you are in a new Data Editor window.

1. Highlight the column you wish to represent the variable. It's best to start with column 1.
2. Click **Data → Define Variable**. When you do this, you will see the **Define Variable** dialog box, as shown in Figure 27.

As you can see, SPSS automatically assigns the name VAR00001 in the Variable Name text box.

Figure 27. The Define Variable dialog box.

3. Enter a name for the variable. In our example, we are going to use id_prof (variable 1 in the data set you saw in Figure 25). The name you assign to a variable cannot have more than eight characters.

As you can see in Figure 27, the default settings are for the variable to be numerical, to have no label, to have no missing values, and to be right-aligned. Given no other information, these settings are what SPSS assigns. The default settings, however, can easily be changed by clicking on any one of the four buttons in the Change Settings area of the Define Variable dialog box. The buttons are Type, Labels, Missing Values, and Column Format.

Defining Variable Types

If you click the Type button, you see the **Define Variable Type** dialog box. Its variable definitions include numeric (e.g., 3435.45), comma (e.g., 3,435.45), dot (e.g., align) (e.g., 3.43545), scientific notation (e.g., 3.4E+03), date (e.g., 12-FEB-1996), dollar (e.g., $3,435.45), custom currency (as you design it), or a string (such as William).

Once you define a variable type, you can always go back and change it. Just select the variable and then select Define Variable from the Data menu. You can also set column width and number of decimal places.

Defining Variable Labels

If you click the Label button, you see the **Define Labels** dialog box, as shown in Figure 28.

Figure 28. The Define Labels dialog box.

Why would you want to change the label of a variable? In general, it makes more sense to work with numbers than with string or alphanumeric variables in an analysis. In other words, values such as 1 for assistant professor, 2 for associate professor, and 3 for full professor provide more information than the actual text that describes the levels of the variable named rank.

Just the same, it sure is a lot easier to look at a data file and see words rather than numbers. Just think about the difference between a data file with numbers representing various levels (such as 1, 2, and 3) of a variable and the actual values (such as assistant professor, associate professor, or full professor). The Labels option in the Define Variable dialog box allows you to enter values in the cell, but what you will see are value labels.

If you take a look at Figure 29, you can see that the label in the highlighted cell reads as Assistant Professor, but the actual value (shown in the **variable information bar**) reads as 1.

Figure 29. A label and the true value represented in a cell.

Changing Variable Labels

To assign or change a variable label, follow these steps:

1. Click **Data → Define Variable**.
2. Click **Labels**.
3. Enter a name for the variable in the Variable Label text box.
4. Press the Tab key to move to the Value Label text box.
5. Enter a value for the variable. This is what will appear in the data file window, such as 1, 2, or 3 in our example in Figure 29.
6. Enter the value label for the value.
7. Click **Add**. Now, the same steps need to be taken to apply a label to Associate Professor and Full Professor.
8. Click **Continue**. When you finish your business in the Define Labels dialog box (as shown in Figure 30), click **OK**, and the new labels will take effect.

Figure 30. Assigning labels to values.

Defining Missing Values

If you click the Missing Values button in the Define Variable dialog box, you can tell SPSS how to deal with the missing values that you specify.

The **No missing values** option treats all values as being valid, such that no missing values are present in the data file. The **Discrete missing values** option allows you to enter up to three values for a missing variable. The **Range of missing values** option allows you to define a range and include high and low values as missing. Finally, the **Range plus one discrete missing value** option will identify as missing all the values between the low and high values you identify, plus one additional value outside the range.

Working with Column Format

If you click the Column Format button in the Define Variable dialog box, you will see the **Define Column Format** dialog box shown in Figure 31. Here you can do two important things to change the appearance of data.

Figure 31. The Define Column Format dialog box.

The first is the width of the data column, which can range from 1 to 256 characters. Second, you can align cell entries left, right, or center. As you can see in Figure 31, the default width is 8 characters, and the default alignment is right. As with any other change you want to make, you must first highlight the variable to be changed. Then you can change the width of a column (that contains the variable) or the way that cell entries are aligned. You should keep in mind that larger fonts take up more space and will need wider columns to show all the information.

You cannot change the width of more than one variable at a time through the Define Column Format dialog box, but you can do that through the Templates option on the Data menu. Here's how.

1. Select the contiguous columns for which you want to change the width.
2. Click **Data → Templates**.
3. Click the **Column Format** check box.
4. Click **Define>>**.
5. Click the **Column Format** button.
6. Enter the new value in the Column Width text box.
7. Click **Continue**.
8. Click **OK**.

You can also change the width of any one column by dragging the line that separates columns to the left or right. Once you release the mouse, the column width will be changed. While imprecise, this technique is certainly fast! You can see how we did that in Figure 32, where we increased the rank column size. Note that the mouse pointer takes on the shape of a double pointed arrow when it is placed on the column border.

	id_prof	sex_prof	age	rank	school	crab1	crab2	crab3	crab4	crab5	
1	1.00	Male	33.00	Assistant Professor	Liberal Arts	2.00	3.00	3.00	3.00	2.00	
2	2.00	Male	58.00	Full Professor	Liberal Arts	5.00	3.00	4.00	3.00	5.00	

Figure 32. Dragging the column border to increase the column width.

Entering and Editing Data

After This Lesson, You Will Know

- How to enter data into an SPSS Data Editor window
- About editing data in SPSS

Key Words

- Active cell
- Save File As dialog box
- Save Data As dialog box

You just learned how to define a set of variables. Now it's time to enter data that correspond to the set of variables. We'll also learn how to edit data. The file that you will create is already on your SPSS work disk and is named Lesson 6 Data File 1. It consists of 10 cases and three variables (id, sex, and test1), and you can see what it looks like in Figure 33 (at the top of page 31).

Getting Ready for Data

Let's start at the beginning. First, we'll define each of the three variables in the data file you see in Figure 33. Start with an empty Data Editor window.

1. Click column 1, row 1.
2. Click **Data → Define Variable**.
3. Type **id**.
4. Click **OK**.
5. Repeat this same procedure for the variables named sex and test1. Three columns should be labeled and ready for data.

Entering Data

Entering data into the Data Editor window and creating a data file is as simple as entering data in a spreadsheet or creating a table using a word processor. You just place the cross-hair-shaped cursor in the cell where you want to enter data, click, and type away. Let's enter data for the first case.

File Edit View Data Transform Analyze Graphs Utilities Window Help

1:id |1

	id	sex	test1	var	var	var	var	var	var	var	var	v
1	1.00	1.00	45.00									
2	2.00	2.00	43.00									
3	3.00	2.00	44.00									
4	4.00	1.00	66.00									
5	5.00	2.00	56.00									
6	6.00	2.00	75.00									
7	7.00	2.00	45.00									
8	8.00	2.00	67.00									
9	9.00	1.00	57.00									
10	10.00	1.00	68.00									
11												
12												
13												
14												
15												
16												
17												
18												
19												
20												
21												

SPSS for Windows Processor is ready

Figure 33. A simple data file.

1. Place the cursor on row 1, column 1.
2. Click once. The cell borders of the individual cell in the data file will be outlined.
3. Type **1** for id
4. Press **Tab** to move to the next variable in the current case. You can also press the down arrow (↓) key. If you want to move to the next cell in the column, press the Enter key. SPSS will enter the value 1.00 since the default format is two decimal places. The next cell in the row will then be highlighted. You'll notice that as you enter values into cells in the Data Editor the value appears in the data entry information bar right above the column headings.

> **TIP**
>
> If you press the Enter key after entering a variable, the next cell in the column will be highlighted.

The cell in the Data Editor that is highlighted and that shows the value in the information bar is the **active cell**. In Figure 34 the active cell has a value of 1.

Figure 34. Entering the first data point in the Data Editor.

5. Type **1**.
6. Press the tab key to move to the column labeled "test 1." The Shift+Tab key combination moves one cell to the left.
7. Type **45**. To get to the next case, press the Home key and the down arrow (↓) key. Compare your Data Editor to the one you see in Figure 33 to be sure you are entering data in the correct locations.
8. Continue entering data in the Data Editor until all the data you see (all 10 cases) in Figure 33 are entered.

If you make an error, just backspace. Or, just don't worry about it! You will learn how to correct such errors in the next section in this lesson.

Editing Data

Editing data in a data file is simply a matter of locating the data you want to edit and then changing them. There are several techniques you can use to do this including a simple click and edit or cutting and pasting. You'll learn about them all in this part of the lesson.

Changing a Cell Value

Let's say that you want to change the value of test1 for case 3 from 44 to 54. You made an error in data entry and want to correct it. Here's how.

1. Click on the cell you want to change, which in this case is the cell in test1, case 3 with a value of 44. When you click on the cell, its value will appear in the data information bar or the cell editor area.
2. Type **54**. As you begin typing the new value, it replaces the old one.
3. Press **Enter**. The new value is now part of the data file.

Editing a Cell Value

You can also edit an existing value without replacing it. For example, you may want to change the test1 value for case 1 from 45 to 40, and you just want to change the last digit rather than replace the entire value. Here's how.

TIPS

Until you press the Enter key or move to another cell, the value of a cell is not locked in.

How often should you save? You should save after a set amount of work (either time or pages worth). One general rule is to save as often as necessary so that you can easily recreate any work you might lose between saves—every time you finish entering 10 cases or after 30 minutes of work might be a good starting guideline.

1. Click the cell containing the value you want to edit. In this case it is the cell for test1, case 1, which contains the value 45. When you click in the cell, cell values are highlighted and appear in reverse video as with any Windows application.
2. Click to the right of the last digit in the data entry information bar. A blinking horizontal line will appear in the cell editor following the last digit of the cell entry.
3. Backspace once to delete the 5.
4. Type **0**.
5. Press **Enter** or move to another cell. The new value is now part of the data file.

If you wanted to change a value such as 4565 to 4665, you would use the mouse pointer to insert the blinking cursor between the first 5 and the 6, press the backspace key once, and then enter the new value. If you wanted to insert a value in an existing one (such as changing 198 to 1298), you would place the cursor where you want the new values to be inserted and just enter them.

Saving a Data File

This is the easiest operation of all, but it may be the most important. As you know from your experience with other applications (be they Windows-based or otherwise), saving the files that you create is essential. First, saving allows you to recall the file to work on at a later time. Second, saving allows you to back up files. Finally, you can save a file under a new name and use the copy for a purpose different from the original purpose.

Don't wait to save until your data file is entered and you are sure there are no errors. Why should you save a file before it is entered exactly as you want it? Good question. It's a matter of being "safe rather than sorry."

When you are creating a data file document (and before you save it for the first time), the only "copy" of it is stored in the computer's memory. If, for some reason, the computer malfunctions or the power (and the computer) goes off, whatever is stored in this temporary memory will be lost. It literally disappears, whether it is a data file with three variables and 10 cases or 300 variables and 10,000 cases. Save data files as you work!

Before saving a file for the first time, however, the first order of business is deciding on a name for the file.

Naming a File

To save a data file, you must assign a unique file name to it. For example, if you were to name a file "data" you might find it confusing, because you will surely be creating more than one file, and "data" describes virtually all of them! Also, should you try to save a file to a directory containing an identically named file with different contents, the new file will overwrite the original file. You lose the original file. For these reasons, use a name that describes the contents of the data file. SPSS also automatically attaches the .sav extension, although you can assign any extension you want.

With Windows 95, file names can be up to 225 characters long, so you shouldn't have any difficulty being sufficiently descriptive, although being wordy has problems, too. Try to find a middle ground between describing the file and not having a name so long that it can't easily fit on the screen.

Saving a File

To save the data document that is active (which has the data you entered, as you saw in Figure 32), follow these steps:

1. Click **File → Save**. When you do this, you will see the **Save Data As** dialog box as shown in Figure 35.

Figure 35. The Save Data As dialog box

2. Select the directory in which you want to save the data. If you are saving to a hard drive and you are working in a computer lab, be sure you have permission. If you are saving to a floppy disk, select drive a or drive b.
3. Enter the file name you want to use in the File Name text box to save the data that has been entered. We used Lesson 6 Data File 1.
4. Click **OK**.

You can have Windows hide file extensions by going to the Explorer, right clicking, selecting properties and asking Windows to hide extensions.

Unlike other Windows applications, you must first enter data before you can save the data as an SPSS file. SPSS will not let you save a blank Data Editor window.

The data you entered will then be saved as a data file, and the name of the file will appear in the title bar of the Data Editor window. The next time you select Save Data from the File menu, you will not see the Save Data As dialog box. SPSS will just save the changes under the name you originally assigned to the data file. And remember, SPSS will save the data in the active directory. In most cases, that will be the same directory that contains SPSS, a situation you may or may not want.

The Save As option on the file menu allows you to save a file under another name or under another format. For example, if you select the Save As options, you can select from such formats as Excel and Lotus 1-2-3—very handy for exporting your SPSS file to another application.

Opening a File

Once a file is saved, you have to open or retrieve it when you want to use it again. The steps are simple.

1. Click **File → Open**, and you will see the **Open File** dialog box as you see in Figure 36.

Figure 36. The Open File dialog box.

2. Find the file you want to open, and highlight it.
3. Double-click on the file name to open it or Click **OK**.

Saving a File in a New Location

You can easily select any other location to save a file. Perhaps you want to keep the application and data files separate. For example, many SPSS users have a separate directory for each project. That way, files from different projects don't get mixed together. Or, you may want to save a file to a floppy disk and then take the disk home for safekeeping.

Here's how to save a file to another location:

1. Click **File → Save As**. You'll see the **Save Data As** dialog box shown in Figure 37 (at the top of page 35).
2. Enter the name of the file in the File Name text box.
3. In the Save In section of the Save As dialog box, click the directory where you want the file saved. For example, if you want to save the file to a disk in drive B, click [-b-].
4. Click **OK**, and the file is saved to the new location.

You can save to any location by clicking a series of drives and directories.

Figure 37. The Save Data As dialog box.

Inserting and Deleting Cases and Variables

After This Lesson, You Will Know

- How to insert and delete a case
- How to insert and delete a variable
- How to delete multiple cases and variables

Key Words

- Insert
- Delete

More often than not, the data you first enter to create a data file need to be changed. For example, you may need to add a variable or delete a case. You learned in the last lesson how to enter and edit data and then save all the data as a data file. But the simple editing may not be enough.

There are times when you want to add one or more cases, or even an entirely new variable, to a data set. A subject might drop out of an experiment and you may choose to delete a case, or for measurement or design reasons an entire variable may no longer be useful and need to be deleted from a data file. In this lesson, we will show you how to insert and delete both cases and variables.

The SPSS file we'll work with in this lesson is shown in Figure 38 (at the top of page 37). It contains three variables (age in years, social class, and preference for soft drink) and five cases, and it is saved on the student disk as Lesson 7 Data File 1.

Inserting a Case

TIP

When inserting a case, you can select any cell in the row above which you want to insert the case.

Notice in Figure 38 that the cases are sorted by age in ascending order from the youngest subject (aged 44) to the oldest subject (age 67). Let's say we want to add a new case. We'll place it between the second and third cases.

1. Select a cell in the row above which you want to **insert** the new case. In this example, it is row 3 since we want the new case to appear right above row 3. You can select any cell in the row.

Figure 38. A sample file of cases and variables.

2. Click **Data → Insert Case**, or click the **Insert Case** button on the toolbar. As you can see in Figure 39, an entire new row opens up, providing room to enter the data for the new case.

Figure 39. Inserting a new case.

You'll notice that when you add a case, dots appear in the blank cells indicating that there are missing data. Now you can enter the data that make up the new case. Enter any data you want.

Inserting a Variable

Now let's say that you need to add an additional variable to the data file. For example, you want to add the variable weight in pounds so that it appears before the variable labeled "pref," for preference.

1. Select a cell in the column to the right of where you want to insert the new variable. We selected a cell in column 3 (labeled pref) since we want to insert a new variable just to the left of pref.
2. Click **Data → Insert Variable**, or click the **Insert Variable** button on the toolbar. As you can see in Figure 40 (at the top of page 38), an entire new column opens up providing room to enter the data for the new variable. As you can also see, the new variable is automatically named by SPSS as VAR00001.

TIP

When inserting a variable, you can select any cell in the column to the right of which you want to insert a variable.

Figure 40. Inserting a new variable.

You'll notice that when you add a variable, dots appear in the blank cells, indicating that there are missing cases. You can define the variable (we named it weight) and enter the data for each case. The data file with a new case and variable added, and with data added as well, appears in Figure 41.

Figure 41. Adding a new case, a new variable, and data to a data file.

Deleting a Case

Now it comes time to learn how to **delete** a case that you no longer want to be part of the data file. For example, let's delete the fourth case in the data file you now see in Figure 41.

1. Click on the case number (not any cell in the row) to highlight the entire row as you see in Figure 42 (at the top of page 39).
2. Click **Edit** → **Clear**. You can also press the **Del** key, or right-click and click **Clear**, and the case will be deleted. As you probably know from other Windows applications, there is usually an Undo command on the Edit menu that undoes the last action.

Figure 42. Selecting a case or row to be deleted.

Deleting a Variable

We're sure you know what's next, deleting a variable. Needing to delete a variable is probably a rare occurrence; you would have thought through your data collection procedures well enough to avoid collecting data you don't need. Nonetheless, the situation does arise.

For example, perhaps you find out after the fact that data you collected (such as social class) are confidential and cannot be used. You therefore need to delete the variable across all cases. Here's how.

1. Click on the variable or column to highlight the entire column.
2. Click the **Edit → Clear**. You can also press the **Del** key, and the variable will be deleted, or right-click and click **Clear**. The data file with the deleted case and variable is shown in Figure 43.

TIP

To delete more than one case or more than one variable, drag over all the cases or variables you want to delete and then press the Del key.

Figure 43. Data file after deleting a variable.

Selecting, Copying, Cutting, and Pasting Data

After This Lesson, You Will Know

- How to select data
- How Cut and Copy and Paste can be used in a data file
- How to cut and paste data
- How to copy and paste data
- What the clipboard does, and what its limitations are

Key Words

- Buffer
- Clipboard
- Copy
- Cut
- Paste

This last lesson on editing a data file has to do with some Windows techniques that you may already be familiar with: selecting, cutting, copying, and pasting. In fact, these simple operations can save you time and trouble, especially when you want to move the value of one or more cells from one location to another, or to repeat columns or rows.

Copying, Cutting, and Pasting

With the **Cut**, **Copy**, and **Paste** tools located on the Edit menu, you can easily move cell entries (be it one or more cells) from one part of a data file to another part of the same data file. You can also move cell entries from one data file to another entirely different data file or even to another Windows application!

In general, the steps you take to cut or copy and paste are as follows:

1. Select the data you want to cut or copy by dragging over the data with the mouse pointer. It can be an individual cell, row, column, or more than one row or column. Rows and columns can also be selected by clicking on them at the top (for a column) or at the left (for a row). A range of cells defines a rectangular- or square-shaped set of cells.

2. Click **Edit → Cut** or **Copy**. Unfortunately, unlike in other Windows applications, there are not cut, copy, and paste buttons on the toolbar.
3. Select the destination, or target cell, where you want the data pasted. The destination, or target cell, you select will act as the upper left-hand anchor if you are cutting or copying more than one cell.
4. Click **Edit → Paste**.

The selected data will appear in the new location. Here is an example of cutting and pasting and copying and pasting. The data that we're using, which you see in Figure 44, is contained in the file named Lesson 8 Data File 1 on the student disk. It consists of five cases of three variables (weight in pounds, height in inches, and strength ranking).

Figure 44. A file for practicing cutting, copying, and pasting.

Selecting Data

Before you can cut, copy, or paste anything, you first have to select what you want to cut or copy. This is no big deal, and you are probably used to the most direct way of selecting data, which is through the drag technique. For example, if you want to select a particular section of a data file, just drag the mouse pointer over that section.

Thus, any data, case, or variable can be selected by just dragging over the information using the mouse. What if you're not a mouser? Not to worry. Here's an easy-to-use summary (Table 4) that will tell you how to use the keyboard to select any amount of text you want.

Table 4

Keyboard Strokes for Selecting

To select	Use these keys
one cell down	↓ or the Enter key
one cell up	↑
one cell to the right	→
one cell to the left	←
the first cell in a case	Home
the last cell in a case	End
the first case in a variable	Ctrl + ↑
the last case in a variable	Ctrl + ↓
an entire case	Shift + Space
an entire variable	Ctrl + Space
a block of cells	Shift + ↑ or ↓ or ← or →

Cutting and Pasting

Data are cut from a data file when you want to remove them from their original locations and paste them into another location.

Here's an example of cutting data to rearrange the order in which variables appear. We'll be showing you this activity in Figures 45 and 46 where part of the data file is be copied to a new location. Specifically, we'll move the height variable so that it is after strength.

1. Select the data you want to cut as you see in Figure 45. In this example, we are selecting the variable (and not just the data in that column) named height. Remember, when data are cut, they disappear from the original location. When you select, be sure to click on the variable name.

Figure 45. Cutting and pasting text within the same data file.

2. Click **Edit** → **Cut**, or right-click **Cut**. When you do this, the variable height disappears from the Data Editor.
3. Move the insertion point to the location where you want to insert, or paste, the data. Click at the top of the column where the new variable name will appear so you highlight the entire column.
4. Click **Edit** → **Paste**, or right-click **Paste**. The data that were cut will then appear as you see in Figure 46. This is a pretty efficient way of getting data from one place to another.

Figure 46. Cutting and pasting text within the same data file.

This is an example of cutting and pasting text within the same data file. Should you want to cut and paste between data files, the process is much the same. Here are the general steps.

1. Select the data you want to cut and paste.
2. Click **Edit → Cut**.
3. Open a new data file or the one into which you want the data pasted.
4. Move the insertion point to the location where you want to insert, or paste, the data.
5. Click **Edit → Paste**. Data will appear in the new location.

In Figure 47, you can see the results of cutting all the data seen in Figure 44 and pasting them into a Windows Word Pad document along with some other text. Notice that only the data and not the column headings are transferred.

Figure 47. Exporting SPSS data to another application.

Copying and Pasting

Copying data is not much different from cutting data, except that the data remain in their original locations. Copying is the ideal tool when you want to duplicate data within a document or between documents.

For example, the weight, strength, and height data may be part of one data file, and you want to copy only the first two variables (weight and strength) to a new data file. You will add additional variables and cases to the new file, but you want to preserve the original.

The steps for copying and pasting are basically the same as cutting and pasting except for one different command. Here are the steps.

1. Select the data you want to copy. Remember, when data is copied, the data remains where it was originally located.

2. Click **Edit** → **Copy**, or right-click **Copy**.
3. Move the insertion point to the target cell where you want to insert or paste the copied data.
4. Click **Edit** → **Paste**, or right-click **Paste**. The data that were copied will then appear.

A good use of copy and paste would be to copy data from a master data file that you want to use over and over, don't want to change, and need to borrow from in the future. Using copy and paste will leave the master document intact while you copy what you need.

Where Copy or Cut Data Go

TIP

Want to paste the same data in several locations? Just continue to select the Paste option from the File menu or the right-click menu.

What happens to data that you cut or copy? When you cut or copy data, they are placed in a buffer, an area reserved for temporary memory. This **buffer** is called the **clipboard**. The data are retrieved from the buffer when you select Paste. In fact, whatever information is in the buffer stays there until it is replaced with something else.

For this reason you can paste the contents of the buffer into documents over and over again until something new has been cut or copied, replacing what was in the buffer. That's why the Paste button is always darkened (or active) since it's ready to paste whatever is in the buffer.

Want to see the contents of the clipboard? Here's how.

1. Click **Start** → **Programs** → **Accessories** → **Clipboard Viewer**. As Figure 48 shows, you'll see the current contents of the clipboard. In this case, it's still the three columns of data that were cut from Figure 44.

Figure 48. Viewing the contents of the clipboard.

It's useful to remember some things about the clipboard.

First, this buffer can hold only one thing at a time. As soon as you cut or copy something new, the new data replace whatever was first in there.

Second, when you quit SPSS, the contents of the clipboard disappears. The clipboard is a temporary place.

Printing and Exiting an SPSS Data File

After This Lesson, You Will Know

- How to print a data file
- How to print a selection from a data file
- How to print output from an analysis or a chart

Key Word

- Print dialog box

Once you've created a data file or completed any type of analysis or chart, you probably will want to print a hard copy for safekeeping or for inclusion in a report or paper. When your SPSS document is printed and you want to stop working, it's time to exit SPSS. You probably already know the way to exit an application is not by turning off the computer! Rather, you need to give your application (and Windows 95) time to do any necessary housekeeping (closing and ordering files, and so forth). In this lesson, we will show you how to print and safely exit SPSS.

Printing with SPSS

Printing is almost as important a process as editing and saving data files. If you can't print, you have little to take away from your work session. You can export data from an SPSS file to another application, but getting a hard copy right from SPSS is often more timely and more important.

In SPSS, you can print either an entire data file or a selection from that file. We'll show you how to do both.

Printing an SPSS Data File

Let's begin with data files. It's simple to print a data file.

1. Be sure that the data file you want to print is the active window.
2. Click **File → Print**. When you do this, you will see the **Print** dialog box shown in Figure 49 (at the top of page 46).

> **TIP**
>
> You can also click on the Tip icon on the toolbar to get the Print dialog box.

Figure 49. The Print dialog box.

As you can see, you can choose to print the entire document or a specific selection (which you would have already made in the Data Editor window), and increase the number of copies from 1 to 99 (that's the limit).

3.   Click **OK** and whatever is active will print.

Look at the printed output in Figure 50, and then read the comments below.

E:\SPSS for Windows\SPSS Data Disk Files\Student Disk Files\Lesson 9\Lesson 9 Data File 1.sav

	weight	height	strength
1	132	68	5
2	155	71	4
3	215	76	1
4	165	72	2
5	178	71	3

1-1

Figure 50. Some SPSS output.

First, you can see the title of the name assigned to the data file at the top of the page, including the complete path. In this case, it's E:\SPSS for Windows\SPSS Data Disk Files\Student Disk Files\Lesson 9\Lesson 9 Data File 1.sav. This is a (cumbersome, but) convenient reminder of what's being printed.

Second, a footer (1-1) is automatically assigned to the page.

Third, the default is to print gridlines. If you do not want the grid lines to print, click Grid Lines from the View menu (so it is not checked) and the grid lines will not appear, either on screen or on the hard copy. If you want value labels printed, then select Value Labels from the View menu, and those labels will appear in cells, rather than the actual value you entered.

Finally, the default for the orientation is to print in Portrait, which means the short edge of the paper is horizontal. If you want to switch to Landscape, you have to select Setup from the Print dialog box and then click Landscape. Our advice is to use the Landscape orientation if in doubt, since most data files contain more variables than can fit in the Portrait orientation.

Printing a Selection from an SPSS Data File

Printing a selection from a data file follows exactly the steps that we listed for printing a data file, except that in the Print dialog box, you select the portion you want to print and click on the Selection option in the Print dialog box. The steps are shown at the top of page 47.

1. Be sure that the data you want to print is selected (using the techniques we discussed in the last lesson).
2. Click **File → Print** or click the **Print icon** on the toolbar. When you do this, you will see the **Print** dialog box.
3. Click Selection if it is not already selected.
4. Click **OK**, and whatever you selected will be printed.

Printing from the Viewer Window

When you complete any type of analysis in SPSS or create a chart, the results appear in a Viewer window, as you first saw in Figure 3. To print the output from such a window, follow exactly the same procedures as you did for printing any data file. The only difference is that instead of a Print dialog box that contains the name of the data file, you will see a Print dialog box like that in Figure 51.

Figure 51. The Print dialog box.

Clicking OK in the Print dialog box will print all the contents of the Viewer. To print a selection from the Viewer, first make the selection by either clicking on the actual material in the right-pane of the Navigator, or clicking on the name of the material you want to print in the left pane of the Viewer. Then select the Print option from the File menu and click Selection in the Print dialog box. If the Selection option is dimmed in the Print dialog box, it means that you didn't make a selection and, therefore, cannot print it.

We will discuss printing graphs in Unit 4.

Exiting SPSS

How do you end your SPSS session and close up shop for the day? Easy.

1. Click **File → Exit SPSS**. SPSS will be sure that you get the chance to save any unsaved or edited windows and will then close.

Exporting and Importing SPSS Data

After This Lesson, You Will Know

- How to export a data file to another application
- How to export a chart to another application
- How to import data from another application

Key Words

- Export
- Import

You already know how to open an SPSS data file by selecting Open from the File menu, locating the file, and clicking OK. But what if you created a file in another application, such as Excel or Lotus 1-2-3 or Word for Windows, and want to use that file as a data file in SPSS? Or what if you want to use an SPSS data file or a chart in a report you created with Word for Windows? Does that mean reentering all the data? Not at all. SPSS lets you export and import data, and in this lesson you will learn how to do both.

Exporting and Importing Data

When you **export** an SPSS data file, you are sending it to another application. It may be a Windows application, a DOS application, or an OS/2 application. Just as one country exports products to other countries, so you are exporting data from SPSS to another application.

When you **import** data from another application, you are going to use it with SPSS. It may be a file created in Word or Excel or dBase. Just as one country imports products from other countries, so you are importing data from another application to SPSS.

In general, the more commercially popular an application is, the more different types of data it supports. For example, Word can translate more than 30 different data formats. SPSS was designed for a more narrow audience than such a popular word processor, so fewer applications can directly read SPSS files. With the increasing popularity of SPSS and with the release of version 9.X however, SPSS is more compatible with other applications than ever before.

Exporting Data

Here's just the situation where you would be interested in exporting data. You have been using SPSS to analyze data, and you want to use the results of the analysis in another application. To do so, you want to export data from SPSS. Let's go through the steps of both exporting data, exporting an analysis of that data, and exporting a chart.

Why might you want to export data? One good example is when you want to create an appendix of the raw data used in the analysis. You could just print the data file. As you remember, SPSS is limited in that you cannot use more than eight characters to name a variable or change the height of rows (or cases). You, however, want longer variable names or taller rows. So, you'll export the data to Microsoft Excel, which has much greater flexibility in formatting. And since you are writing your report in Microsoft Word for Windows, an Excel-generated appendix is completely compatible.

The first and most important thing to remember about exporting data to another application is the SPSS data must be saved in a format that the other application can understand. Fortunately, SPSS can save data files under a wide variety of formats. Just by examining Table 5, you can get a general idea as to what applications data files can be exported to. The SPSS data file must be saved using the appropriate extension for the application you are exporting to.

Table 5

Application Extensions

Application	Extension
SPSS/PC+	.sys
SPSS Portable	.por
Tab Delimited	.dat
Fixed ASCII	.dat
Excel	.xls
1-2-3 Release	.wk3
Sylk	.slk
dBase	.dbf

Let's go through some examples, beginning with exporting the file we named Teacher Scale Results to Excel for Windows.

1. Be sure the data file you want to export is active.
2. Click **File → Save As**.
3. In the "Save as type" area type scores, select the format used by the application you are exporting to, as you can see in Figure 52 (at the top of page 50). When you make the selection, the file extension changes. In this example, it would be .xls (for Excel). Be sure to provide a name for the new file. In this case, it is scores, and the file will be saved as scores.xls.
4. Click **OK**. A new file is created under the file name scores.xls, which can now be read by Excel.
5. Open Excel.
6. In Excel, click **File → Open**.
7. Open the new exported file. Excel displays the file as shown in Figure 53 (at the top of page 51).

What if the application you want to export data into is not listed in the above table? Almost every application can read Tab Delimited or Fixed ASCII data. For example, let's say you wanted to export an SPSS data file into Word for Windows (which saves files with a .doc extension).

Figure 52. Selecting a format for exporting an SPSS data file.

TIP

When SPSS exports a data file, it saves the export file, but you still see the original data in the active SPSS window.

You could save it as a Tab Delimited file, and then have Word read it, as we did in Figure 54 (on page 51). Now, it "ain't purty," but the information is all there. With some changing of font size and spacing, it could appear quite nice and fit well into any document.

Exporting a Chart

SPSS has some pretty terrific charting features. You saw what an SPSS chart looks like in Lesson 4, and you'll learn more about them later in Part I of *Using SPSS for Windows*. It won't be uncommon for you to need to create a chart and export it into another application. Let's export a graph into a Word file.

1. Create the graph you want to export. Be sure it is active.
2. Click on the actual graph in the right pane of the Viewer. When the graph is selected and ready to be exported, it will be surrounded with a thin black line.
3. Click **Edit → Copy**, or right-click, and click then **Copy** or **Copy objects** (depending upon the application).
4. Open the application into which you want to export the chart. In this example, the application is Word.
5. Click **File → Paste** or **Paste Special** (depending upon the application), or right-click, and then click **Paste**. The chart should appear in the new document as you see in Figure 55 (at the top of page 52).

Microsoft Excel - scores

	A	B	C	D	E	F	G	H
1	ID_STUD	ID_PROF	SEX_STUD	TEACHER1	TEACHER2	TEACHER3	TEACHER4	TEACHER5
2	80761	1	1.00	4.00	4.00	2.00	1.00	3.00
3	22920	1	1.00	5.00	4.00	2.00	1.00	3.00
4	84768	2	1.00	4.00	3.00	3.00	2.00	3.00
5	89225	2	1.00	3.00	3.00	3.00	1.00	4.00
6	94354	3	1.00	3.00	5.00	1.00	2.00	3.00
7	40351	4	1.00	2.00	4.00	2.00	2.00	2.00
8	62034	4	1.00	2.00	4.00	2.00	2.00	4.00
9	26841	5	1.00	2.00	4.00	2.00	1.00	3.00
10	13691	5	1.00	2.00	3.00	1.00	3.00	2.00
11	70386	6	1.00	3.00	4.00	2.00	3.00	5.00
12	45176	6	1.00	5.00	4.00	1.00	1.00	4.00
13	29627	6	1.00	2.00	4.00	2.00	1.00	4.00
14	24824	6	1.00	1.00	5.00	2.00	2.00	4.00
15	39986	7	1.00	5.00	5.00	2.00	1.00	5.00
16	77974	7	1.00	5.00	4.00	2.00	1.00	4.00
17	38396	7	1.00	5.00	5.00	2.00	1.00	5.00
18	78665	7	1.00	4.00	3.00	2.00	1.00	3.00
19	20227	7	1.00	4.00	5.00	1.00	1.00	5.00
20	66298	8	1.00	5.00	5.00	1.00	1.00	3.00
21	27423	8	1.00	5.00	5.00	1.00	1.00	4.00
22	79359	8	1.00	5.00	5.00	1.00	1.00	5.00
23	66513	8	1.00	5.00	5.00	1.00	1.00	5.00
24	28796	9	1.00	2.00	4.00	4.00	3.00	1.00
25	67564	9	1.00	3.00	3.00	4.00	4.00	1.00
26	35598	9	1.00	3.00	3.00	2.00	1.00	2.00
27	77823	10	1.00	5.00	5.00	2.00	1.00	5.00
28	34850	10	1.00	5.00	5.00	1.00	2.00	5.00
29	54217	10	1.00	3.00	5.00	1.00	1.00	4.00
30	82104	1	2.00	4.00	5.00	2.00	1.00	2.00
31	22466	1	2.00	5.00	3.00	1.00	2.00	4.00
32	75812	1	2.00	3.00	5.00	2.00	1.00	3.00
33	87172	2	2.00	3.00	4.00	1.00	2.00	3.00
34	98221	2	2.00	3.00	3.00	2.00	3.00	2.00

Figure 53. An Excel file showing data that we exported from SPSS.

Microsoft Word - Data in Word Format

```
ID STUD     ID PROF     SEX STUD     TEACHER1     TEACHER2     TEACHER3     TEACHER4
     TEACHER5

80761 1     1      4      4      2      1      3

22920 1     1      5      4      2      1      3
```

Figure 54. Reading a tab delimited file.

Exporting the Results of SPSS Output

Here's the situation. You've just done an analysis of variance using SPSS, and you want to export the results of that analysis into another document. In effect, output is treated just like text. It can be cut or copied and pasted, and exporting output is identical to what you just did with a chart.

Why retype all that information when you can just paste it right in? Here's how.

1. Run the analysis you want.
2. Right click on the output you want to export in the right pane of the Viewer.

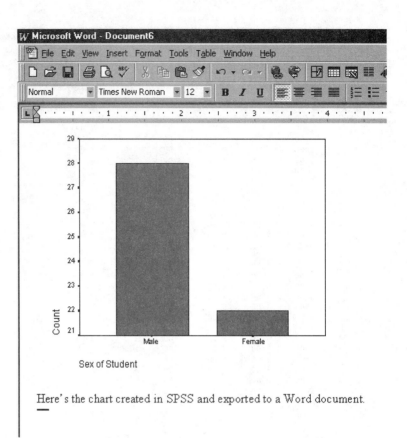

Here's the chart created in SPSS and exported to a Word document.

Figure 55. Exporting a graph created in SPSS to a Word document.

3. Click **Edit → Copy**, or right-click, then click **Copy** or **Copy objects** depending upon the application.
4. Open the document into which you want to paste the output.
5. Click **Edit → Paste**, or right-click, and then click **Paste**.

Here's an important caution, however. If you copy results as an object, then you will not be able to edit it in the new application. An object is a bit-mapped image, much like a picture. If you simply copy them (and not use the Copy objects option), the data will be exported as text and you can edit it, but it will lose it's original format. The best advice? Make your SPSS results to be exactly as you would like them to appear and then copy them as an object.

Importing Data

Here's the situation. You are a user of Excel or Lotus 1-2-3 or QuattroPro, and you've entered your data into one of these spreadsheets. Or perhaps you choose to enter your data into one-of the many word processors available, such as Word for Windows, or Ami Pro. Now you want to analyze the data using SPSS.

This might be the situation if you did not have access to SPSS when it came time to enter the original data or if you just feel more comfortable using some other application to enter data.

1. Click **File → Open**.
2. Locate the file you want to import, highlight it, and then click **OK**. When you do this, you will see the data in the SPSS Syntax Editor window, as shown in Figure 56 (at the top of page 53). You can now use these data as you would those in any SPSS data file.

Figure 56. Imported data in an SPSS window.

Just as you can export from SPSS to other applications, so you can import from a variety of different applications. A word of caution, however. Even though SPSS can read certain file formats (such as .xls for Excel files), it does not mean that SPSS can read the latest version of Excel. For example, the current version of SPSS (9.X) cannot read the latest version of Excel files. So, before you start entering loads of data to import, check to see if it's even possible.

The most important thing to remember about exporting and importing is finding the right format. You need to save a file in the right format so it can easily be exported or imported. Almost any set of data can be imported and exported as an ASCII file. When you want the data to remain intact as far as format and such, you'll have to look for a different format and experiment to see which format works best. At the very least, you should be able to simply select the data and import or export it to and from SPSS using the Copy and Paste commands available on the main menu and when you right-click.

TIP

You can also import ASCII data into SPSS by selecting Read ASCII Data from the File menu and then selecting the file.

Working with Data

In the last two units you learned the basics of SPSS, including how to start and exit the program and how to create a data file, including editing that data, printing it, and working with the importing and exporting features of SPSS. Our next step, and the focus of this unit, is to work with SPSS data so their final form best meets your particular data analysis needs. With that in mind, we will show you how to find data, recode it, sort a set of cases, and merge and split files.

Finding Values, Variables, and Cases

After This Lesson, You Will Know

- How to find variables, cases, and values
- How to find text

Key Words

- Case
- Case sensitive
- Go To Case dialog box
- Search for Data dialog box
- Value
- Variable
- Variables dialog box

Just imagine you have a data file that contains 500 cases and 10 variables. You know that the entry for age (one of the 10 variables) for case 147 was entered incorrectly. You can either scroll down to find that case or use one of the many find tools that SPSS provides. We'll go through those tools and how to use them in this lesson.

Finding Things

Before we begin showing you how to find things, let's pause for a moment to distinguish among variables, cases, and values. Even if we've covered some of this before, it's a good idea to see all of it in one place.

A **value** (also called a cell entry) is any entry in a cell, or the intersection of a row and a column. Values can be numerical such as 3, 56.89 or $432.12, or alphanumerical or text such as Sam, Sara, or Julie.

A **variable** is something that can take on more than one value. Age, weight, name, score on test1, and time measured in seconds are all variables. Variables are defined in SPSS by columns.

A **case** is a collection of values that belong to a unique unit in the data file, such as a person or a teacher or a school. Cases are defined in SPSS by rows.

With a small data file, you can just eyeball what is on the screen to find what you need. With a large data file, however, you could spend a good deal of time trying to find a case or variable, and even more time trying to find a particular value. If you have 10 variables and 500 cases and no missing data, you have 5,000 cell entries (all of which are values). Trying to find a particular one could take all day! Thus, the SPSS features that can find variables, cases, and values are most welcome.

Finding Variables

For the example in this lesson, we'll use the data file named Crab Scale Results on the student disk. Open that file now. We'll find the variable named rank.

1. Make sure the data file that contains the variable you want to find is active.
2. Click **Utilities** → **Variables**. When you do this, you will see the **Variables** dialog box, as shown in Figure 57.

Figure 57. The Variables dialog box.

3. Click **Rank**. The Variables dialog box provides a good deal of information about the variable, including its name, label, type, missing values that are included, and value labels (Assistant Professor, etc.).
4. Click **Go To**, and SPSS will highlight the column containing the variable, as you see has been done in Figure 58.

Figure 58. Finding the variable in a data set.

You're now ready to perform any type of operation on that variable, such as working with labels, transformation, recoding, and more.

Finding Cases

Now that you know how to find any variable in a data file, it's time to see how you can find any case. In the Crab Scale Results example, let's assume that you need to locate case 8. You can do that by scrolling through the data file, which is simple enough. If the cases number in the hundreds, however, it's not so simple a task. To save you time and trouble, SPSS finds cases like this.

1. Click **Data → Go To Case**. When you do this, you will see the **Go To Case** dialog box, as shown in Figure 59.

Figure 59. The Go to Case dialog box.

2. Type **8**.
3. Click **OK**. SPSS will highlight the case corresponding to the number you entered, for whatever column or variable the cursor is currently located in. For example, if we just found the variable named rank and then (as a separate operation) located case 8, the highlighted cell would be the rank for case 8, which is Assistant Professor.

Finding Values

Finding values is the most useful of all the search tools, but in one important way it also is the most limited. It's the most useful because any data file has more values than it does variables or cases. It's the most limited because it can only search for a value within one variable.

For example, let's say we want to find the case with an age value of 36.

1. Click the column labeled age. You may highlight any cell in the variable (or column) in which you want to search for the value, such as age.
2. Click **Edit → Find**. When you do this, you will see the **Search for Data in Age** dialog box, as you see in Figure 60.

Figure 60. Searching for a value.

TIP

Any search operation requires you to enter the search information in a dialog box, which may block your view of the data editor. You'll have to move the dialog box to view the results of the search. Do this by dragging on the title bar.

3. Type **36**. You can search either forward or backward through the variable. If you highlighted the first cell in the column, you cannot search backwards since there's no place to go.
4. Click **Search Forward** to search forward through the variable or Search Backward to search backward through the variable. SPSS will highlight the value when it is found. If SPSS cannot find the value, you will get a Not Found message.

TIP

Not found does not mean "does not exist." It may mean you are searching in the wrong direction.

Be careful where you begin searching and whether you search forward or backward. You'll get the Not Found message when SPSS finishes searching entirely through the variable in the direction you indicated; SPSS won't start the search over again. For example, if you are in the next-to-last case and want to search for the value 45 in the Crab Scale Results file, SPSS will not find it if the value is in an earlier case unless you search backward. Perhaps the next version of SPSS will be capable of searching through the entire file.

You can also use the Search for Data option to search for values entered as numbers but appearing as text. For example, if you wanted to find the first occurrence of Female in the variable named sex_prof, you would do as follows:

1. Highlight any cell in the variable (or column) named sex_prof.
2. Click **Edit → Find**.
3. Type **Female** in the **Search for Data** dialog box.
4. Click **Search Forward**. SPSS will highlight the first occurrence of the value Female.

If you remember correctly, the value Female was not originally entered in the cell. Instead, the value 2 was entered, and through the definition of the variable the label Female was assigned to that value. If you searched for the value 2 in the same column (sex_prof), SPSS would stop on all occurrences of what you now read as Female. That's because SPSS is looking for *data*, and not necessarily for numbers or text, and Female and 2 are both data. And, if you entered the value female, SPSS would find Female as well, since it looks for whatever it can find that corresponds to what you enter in the Search for Data dialog box.

If you want to search for a string and you don't care about upper case and lower case (so Doctor and doctor are considered by SPSS to be the same), then you can click in the Ignore case of text in the strings check box. If you want the search to be **case sensitive** (where upper and lower case letters are distinguished from one another), then be sure the Ignore case of text in strings box is checked.

Recoding Data and Computing Values

After This Lesson, You Will Know

- How to recode data and create new variables
- How to compute new values
- How to recode into Same Variables dialog box
- How to recode into Same Variables: Old and New Values dialog box

Key Words

- Compute
- Compute Variable dialog box
- Formula
- Function
- Recode

There are often situations where you need to take existing data and convert them into a different variable, or to take existing variables and combine them to form an additional variable. For example, you may want to **compute** the mean or standard deviation for a set of variables and enter those values in a separate variable in the data file. Or you may want to **recode** data so that, for example, all values of 10 or greater equal 1, and all values less than 10 equal 0. Your needs for transforming or recoding data will depend on the nature of your data and the purpose of your analysis. In either case, SPSS provides some easy-to-use and powerful tools to accomplish both tasks, which we will show you in this lesson.

Recoding Data

You can recode data in one of two ways. First, you can recode a variable to create a new variable. Or you can recode a variable and modify the variable that has already been entered. In this lesson you will use the data saved in the file named Crab Scale Results on the student disk.

As you may remember, the Crab Scale includes the following 6 items:

1. I generally feel crabby if someone tries to help me.
2. I generally feel happy when I watch the news.

3. I generally feel crabby when I watch mothers and fathers talk baby talk to their babies.
4. I generally feel happy when I am able to make sarcastic comments.
5. I generally feel crabby when I am on a family vacation.
6. I generally feel happy when I am beating someone at a game.

Each item is ranked on the following 5-point scale.

1. Totally agree
2. Agree
3. In a quandary
4. Disagree
5. Vicious lies

Since some of the crabbiness items (2, 4, and 6) are reversed, these items need to be recoded. For example, if someone totally agrees (a value of 1) with item 2, it means they are happy when they watch the news. Since we are measuring crabbiness and since the lower the score the more crabby someone is, the accurate scoring of this item should be reversed, as shown in Table 6.

Table 6

Reversed Crab Scale Scores

Original response	Recorded response
1	5
2	4
3	3
4	2
5	1

Here's how to do just that.

1. Be sure the file named Crab Scale Results is active.
2. Click **Transform** → **Recode** → **Into Same Variables**, since we want the transformed variable to replace the values in the current variable that is being transformed. You should see the **Recode into Same Variables** dialog box, as shown in Figure 61.

Figure 61. The Recode into Same Variables dialog box.

3. Double-click **crab2** to move the variable into the Variables text box.
4. Click the **Old and New Values ...** button, and you will see the **Recode into Same Variables: Old and New Values** dialog box, as shown in Figure 62.

Figure 62. Recoding old values into new ones.

5. Type **5** in the Value area under Old Values.
6. Type **1** in the Value area under New Values.
7. Click **Add**. The variable is added to the Old --> New box, as you see in Figure 63. When SPSS encounters a 5 for variable 2, it will recode it as a 1.

Figure 63. Recoding a variable from one value to another.

8. Click **Continue**, and you will be returned to the Recode into Same Variables: Old and New Values dialog box.
9. Click **OK**, and the actual values entered in the cells will change according to the way in which they were recorded. For example, if someone responded with a 5 to item 2 on the Crab Scale (as was the case for Professor 3), the recorded value would be 1.

To recode more than one variable at a time (such as items 2, 4, and 6), just add all of them to the Numeric Variables box in the Recode into Same Variables dialog box.

Computing Values

Computing a value means taking existing data and using them to create a new variable in the form of a numeric expression.

To show you how to do that, we will compute a total score for any one individual on the crabbiness scale based on a custom **formula**. To do this, we will simply add together the scores for variables crab1 through crab5. Keep in mind that SPSS comes with 70 predesigned **functions** (a predesigned formula) that will automatically perform a specific computation.

For example, we could tell SPSS to compute a new variable that is the addition of items crab1, crab2, crab3, crab4, and crab5. Or, we could use the SUM function that SPSS provides to accomplish the same end. We'll show you how to do both.

Creating a Formula

Let's create a formula that will add together the values of all five crabbiness items.

1. Click **Transform → Compute**. When you do this, you will see the **Compute Variable** dialog box, as shown in Figure 64.

Figure 64. The Compute Variable dialog box.

2. Click the **Target Variable** text box and enter the name of the new variable to be created. We named it tot_crab, which is the sum of items 1 through 6 on the Crab Scale.
3. Click the **Numeric Expression** text box.
4. Click **crab1**, the first variable you want to include in the formula.
5. Click the ► to add it to the Numeric Expression text box.
6. Type +.
7. Continue adding variables and using the + key to add them together. The completed formula looks like this.

crab1+crab2+crab3+crab4+crab5+crab6

8. Click **OK**. As you can see in Figure 65 (at the top of page 63), the variable named tot_crab was added to the existing data file.

Figure 65. The newly computed variable.

For example, the tot_crab score for case 1 is 16, the simple addition of all the crab items (appropriately recoded, we might add!). If you wanted the average, you could just edit the formula in the Numeric Expression text box to read as

$$(crab1+crab2+crab3+crab4+crab5+crab6)/6$$

In fact, you can perform any type of mathematical computation you see fit.

Using a Function

Functions are predesigned formulas. So instead of

$$crab1+crab2+crab3+crab4+crab5+crab6$$

you can enter

$$SUM(crab1,crab2,crab3,crab4,crab5,crab6)$$

which will accomplish the same thing.

There are more than 70 different functions including arithmetic functions, statistical functions, distribution functions, logical functions, date and time functions, cross-case functions, and string functions. It's beyond the scope of *Using SPSS for Windows* to go into each type and provide examples.

Regardless of how complex or simple functions are, they are all used the same way. We'll show you how to use one of the most simple functions, SUM, which adds a group of values together.

1. Click **Transform** → **Compute**. If the dialog box is not clear, click Reset.
2. Type **tot_crab** in the Target Variable text box.
3. In the **Functions** text box, find the function you want to use. You can type the first letter of the function (which would be "s" in the case of SUM) and SPSS will take you to the first function beginning with that letter.
4. Double click on the function to add it to the Numeric Expression: text box.
5. Double click **crab1** to add it to the formula.
6. Continue adding variables by double clicking them or by typing their names. The finished dialog box appears in Figure 66 (at the top of page 64). Notice there are no "+" signs, but commas that separate the variables in the formula expression.
7. Click **OK** and the new variable is created.

Figure 66. A completed formula.

An alternative to typing in each variable in the list is to use the "to" operator. Instead of crab1,crab2, … through crab6, you could type crab1 to crab6, as you see in Figure 67. You'll see the same result.

Figure 67. Adding a new variable using the Compute option.

Sorting, Transposing, and Ranking Data

After This Lesson, You Will Know

- The differences among sorting, transposing, and ranking data
- How to sort cases on one or more than one variable
- How to transpose a data file
- How to rank data

Key Words

- Data
- Rank
- Sort Cases
- Transpose

As you have seen in the last few lessons, working with **data** includes importing, transforming, and recoding data. Working with data also involves sorting, transposing, and ranking data, techniques every SPSS user needs to know to create a data file that exactly fits data analysis needs. We'll look at each of these techniques in this lesson.

Sorting Data

The first of the three data tools is sorting. Sorting data involves reordering of data given the value of one or more variables. Sorting is an invaluable tool when it comes to organizing information.

For example, if you wanted the data for the Crab Scale Results organized by the variable named rank, you would sort on that variable. If you wanted to sort on more than one variable, you can do that easily as well, such as a sex within rank sort.

Sorting Data on One Variable

Sorting data is as simple as identifying the variable on which you want to sort and directing SPSS to sort.

1. If it is not already opened, open Crab Scale Results.
2. Click **Data → Sort Cases**. When you do this, you will see the **Sort Cases** dialog box, shown in Figure 68.

Figure 68. The Sort Cases dialog box.

3. Double click **Rank** to move rank from the variable list to the **Sort by:** text box. The Ascending that appears next to rank in the sort box means that the variable will be sorted in ascending order.
4. Select whether you want to sort in ascending or descending order.
5. Click **OK**.

In Figure 69, you can see the data sorted by rank. After the sort, assistant, associate, and full professors are grouped together. As you can see, when alphanumeric information is sorted in ascending order, the sort is from A to Z.

Figure 69. The Crab Scale Results file sorted on rank.

Sorting Data on More Than One Variable

Sorting data on more than one variable follows exactly the same procedure as the one just outlined, except that you need to select more than one variable to sort on. SPSS will sort in the order they appear in the Sort by list in the Sort Cases dialog box. For example, if you want to sort on gender within rank, then rank should be the first selection in the Sort Cases dialog box and gender (sex_prof) would be the second, as you see in Figure 70 (at the top of page 67).

Figure 70. The Sort Cases dialog box when sorting on more than one variable.

1. Click **Data → Sort Cases**.
2. Click **Rank** to move rank from the variable list to the Sort by: text box, as you see in Figure 70.
3. Select whether you want to sort in ascending or descending order.
4. Double click Sex of Teacher to move sex_prof from the variable list to the Sort by text box.
5. Select whether you want to sort in ascending or descending order.
6. Click **OK**. The completed sort is shown in Figure 71.

Figure 71. Sorting by sex within rank.

As you can see in Figure 71, the cases have been sorted on the variable named rank, such that assistant, associate, and full professors are grouped together, and within rank they are sorted on sex_prof. Also note that in Figure 71, the sorting on sex_prof is according to the values in the cells (1 for male and 2 for female) and not the labels. If it were sorted according to the labels, then the sort would be with females first since ascending order for text is A through Z.

TIP

When you want to use a procedure using the same dialog box, use the Recall dialog box button on the toolbar and select the dialog box you want to use.

Transposing Cases and Variables

As you already know, an SPSS data file is constructed with cases represented by rows and variables represented by columns. This is the way that most data are entered in any type of data collection form, including spreadsheets and other data collection applications.

There may be occasions, however, where you want cases listed as columns and variables listed as rows. In other words, you want variables and cases transposed. This is most often the case when you are importing data (see lesson 10) from a spreadsheet where the data were not entered as cases (rows) and variables (columns). Now that you've imported the data, you want to switch them to fit the conventional SPSS format. Here's how to do it.

1. Click **Data → Transpose**.
2. In the Transpose dialog box, double click the variable name to insert the variable in the Variables text box.
3. Repeat steps 2 and 3 until all the variables that you want to become cases have been entered.
4. Click **OK**. All the variables that were not transposed will be lost, so if you transpose either all the variables in the data file or just some, the ones you don't will not appear after the operation is performed.

Ranking Data

The final data manipulation technique we will deal with is ranking data. Let's say that we used the Compute feature (on the Transform menu) to create a sum of all Crab scores as we did earlier (see Figure 67, on page 64).

Now let's say that we are not interested in the absolute value of the Crab score, but rather in the relative rank of professors according to their Crab score. Here's how to do it.

1. If you have not done so already, create a new variable (using the Compute command on the Data menu) named tot_crab, a total of all six crab item scores.
2. Click **Transform → Rank Cases**. You'll see the **Rank Cases** dialog box, as shown in Figure 72.

Figure 72. The Rank Cases dialog box.

3. Click on **tot_crab**.
4. Click on the ▶ to move the variable into the Variable(s): text box.
5. Click on the Largest value button in the Assign Rank 1 to area.

6. Click **OK**, and a new variable, named rtot_cra, will be created, as you see in Figure 73, reflecting the ranking of all cases on the variable tot_crab. Cases 2 and 4 have the same tot_crab score (13), and, therefore, the same rank (5.5).

	tot_crab	sum	rtot_cra
1	16.00	16.00	4.000
2	13.00	13.00	5.500
3	9.00	9.00	10.000
4	13.00	13.00	5.500
5	12.00	12.00	7.500
6	20.00	20.00	3.000
7	23.00	23.00	2.000
8	24.00	24.00	1.000
9	10.00	10.00	9.000
10	12.00	12.00	7.500

Figure 73. Ranking on a computed variable.

If you select more than one variable on which cases will be ranked, then a separate and new variable will be created for each one of those, and the relative rankings will be listed as well.

Splitting and Merging Files

After This Lesson, You Will Know

- How to split a file
- How to merge more than one file and more than one case

Key Words

- Add Cases from … dialog box
- Add Cases: Read File dialog box
- Add Variables from … dialog box
- Add Variables: Read File dialog box
- Merge
- Split
- Split File dialog box

The last skills you need to master before you move on to creating and working with SPSS charts are how to split and merge files. When you **split** a file, you are dividing it into two new files for separate analysis. When you **merge** files, you are combining two files using the same variable or variables, or the same cases using different variables. In this lesson, we'll look at how to do each of these.

Why Split?

Throughout this first part of *Using SPSS for Windows*, you have used the Crab Scale Results and Teacher Scale Results to perform simple and complex procedures. We'll use the file named Teacher Scale Results to demonstrate how to split a file.

In general, you split a file when you want to create two separate files, both having at least one variable in common. Creating two separate files might be a choice if you want to produce individual listings of data or prepare data in a way that a particular section, split or organized using a particular variable, can be cut or copied.

For example, in this lesson we will split the Teacher Scale Results file using the variable named sex_stud into two separate files. One file will be named Sex Males, and the other will be

Sex Females. Then we can do analysis of variance or regression on the separate files. If we did not split Teacher Scale Results, we could generate simple descriptive statistics using sex_stud as a categorical variable and could get means and standard deviations of each score for males and for females in the same analysis. SPSS is not powerful enough, however, for us to perform more sophisticated analyses such as regressions only on males without splitting the file.

Splitting a File

Splitting a file is not a particularly difficult process. In fact, it's only a matter of selecting the appropriate SPSS command then the variable based on which you want to split.

For example, for the Teacher Scale Results we'll split on sex_stud by following these steps:

1. Click **Data → Split File**. When you do this, you will see the **Split File** dialog box, as shown in Figure 74.

Figure 74. The Split File dialog box.

2. Click **Organize output by groups** since you are presumably splitting the files to create data for two separate analyses.
3. Double click **sex_stud**.
4. Click **OK**. The file will then be organized such that all male students are grouped together as are all female students.

Once the split is completed, SPSS will not create two physically separate files. Rather, for the rest of the SPSS session, SPSS will perform every procedure as if the file was physically split into two separate files. A simple descriptive analysis results in descriptive statistics for both males and females.

For example, if you calculate simple descriptive statistics on the variable named Teacher1, then you will get separate output for both males and females without having to identify an independent variable named sex_stud. The results of such an analysis are shown in the Viewer in Figure 75 (at the top of page 72). Notice that the analysis was automatically done for both males and females.

Any analysis is performed on each split of the file. For example, if you split on sex_stud (2 levels) and id_prof (10 levels), you would have 20 different descriptive analyses.

→ Descriptives

Sex of Student = Male

Descriptive Statistics[a]

	N	Minimum	Maximum	Mean	Std. Deviation
TEACHER1	28	1.00	5.00	3.6429	1.3113
Valid N (listwise)	28				

a. Sex of Student = Male

Sex of Student = Female

Descriptive Statistics[a]

	N	Minimum	Maximum	Mean	Std. Deviation
TEACHER1	22	1.00	5.00	3.1818	1.0970
Valid N (listwise)	22				

a. Sex of Student = Female

Figure 75. A simple analysis on a split file.

Merging Files

Merging files is just as useful as splitting files. Files can be merged, or combined, in two different ways.

First, you can combine two files that contain the same variable or variables but different cases. This would be the setting if more than one researcher were collecting data on the same variables but for different cases (or subjects), and you need to combine the two data files. For example, the Teacher Scale Results survey could have been administered to more than one group of students, and we eventually might want to combine the results of each administration.

Second, you can combine two files that contain different variables but the same cases. For example, you might be having one person collect data using a certain sample and then another person collecting a different set of data on the same sample. Then you want these two combined. Let's look at these possibilities.

Merging Same Variables and Different Cases

In this example, we are going to combine, merge, or add (your choice of words) a new set of five cases of Teacher Scale data to the existing file named Teacher Scale Results. You can see the new data in Figure 76 (on page 73). These data are saved as Teacher Scale Results—Additional Data on your data disk.

In this example one researcher collected data on 50 students, and another researcher collected data on five students. The Teacher Scale Results should be open.

1. Click **Data → Merge Files**, then click **Add Cases**. When you do this, you will see the **Add Cases: Read File** dialog box, as shown in Figure 77 (on page 73). This looks like an Open or a Save dialog box, and in a sense you are opening a new file and merging it with another.

2. Select the file to which you want to add cases. In this example, the file name is Teacher Scale Results—Additional Data. You are adding the additional data of five cases to the file that contains 50 cases.

TIP

It is critical that each file be sorted on the same merged variable.

3. Click **Open**, and you will see the **Add Cases from ...** dialog box, as shown in Figure 78.

Figure 76. Cases that will be added to the Teacher Scale Results file.

Figure 77. The Add Cases: Read File dialog box.

Figure 78. The Add Cases from dialog box.

4. Click **OK**, and the file named Teacher Scale Results—Additional Data is added to the file named Teacher Scale Results, and the total file now has 55 cases (50 cases from Teacher Scale Results—Additional Data and 5 from Teacher Scale Results—Additional Data).

Merging Different Variables and Same Cases

Now we have the example where you have two files that contain a different set of variables for the same cases. For example, we want to combine the Teacher Scale Results—Additional Data and Crab Scale Results files where the common variable is id_prof.

What SPSS will do in this case is combine cases in the Teacher Scale Results file with cases in the Crab Scale Results file, using the variable named id_prof as a common link.

1. Click **Data → Merge**, then click **Add Variables**. You will see the **Add Variables: Read File** dialog box.
2. Select the file to which you want to add this set of cases. In this example, the file name is Crab Scale Results.
3. Click **Open** and you will see the **Add Variables from …** dialog box, as shown in Figure 79. As you can see, SPSS has already identified that id_prof is common to the two files and has listed it in the Excluded Variables area.

Figure 79. The Add Cases from dialog box.

4. Click **OK**.

The result of this merging, shown in Figure 80 (at the top of page 75), is a file larger than either of the two files that share the variable named id_prof. If you recall the file named Teacher Scale Results, you will see it does not contain any demographic information, such as gender or age, but the merged file including Teacher Scale information does, since it was merged with the Crab Scale data.

Figure 80. Merging two files.

Working with SPSS Charts and Output

A picture surely is worth a thousand words, and nowhere is this more true than with numbers. You could look at a set of data all day long and not really see what the nature of the relationship is between variables until a graph or a table is created. In this last part of introducing you to SPSS basics, we will go through the steps of creating a chart and modifying one. Then we will provide an overview of a new SPSS feature, pivot tables, and how they work, plus some tips on using the Output Navigator window.

Creating an SPSS Chart

After This Lesson, You Will Know

- How to create a simple line chart
- About some of the different charts that you can create with SPSS

Key Words

- Area chart
- Bar chart
- Define Simple Line: Values of Individual Cases Dialog box
- Line Charts dialog box
- Pie chart

S PSS offers you just the features to create charts that bring the results of your analyses to life. In this lesson, we will go through the steps to create several different types of charts and provide examples of different charts. In Lesson 16, we'll show you how to modify a chart by adding a chart title, adding labels to axes, modifying scales, and working with patterns, fonts, and more. One note of caution: Throughout this unit of *Using SPSS for Windows*, we'll use the words graph and chart interchangeably.

Creating a Simple Chart

The one thing that all charts have in common is that they are based on data. Although you may import data to create a chart, in this example we'll use the data you see here to create a line chart of test scores by grade. These data are available on the student disk in the file named Lesson 15 Data File 1.

Grade	Score
1	45
2	56
3	49
4	57
5	67
6	72

Creating a Line Chart

The steps for creating any chart are basically the same. You first enter the data you want to use in the chart, select the type of chart you want from the Graph menu, define how the chart should appear, and then click OK. Here are the steps we followed to create the chart you see in Figure 81.

Graph

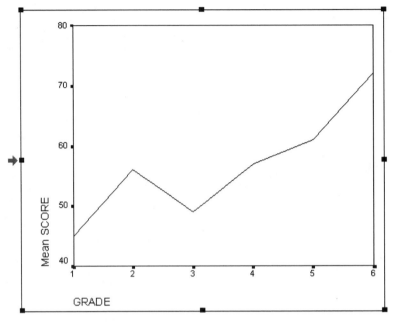

Figure 81. A simple SPSS chart.

1. Enter the data you want to use to create the chart.
2. Click **Graphs → Line**. When you do this, you will see the **Line Charts** dialog box, as shown in Figure 82.

Figure 82. Defining a line graph.

TIP

Charts can be easily copied (use the Edit menu) and pasted into other Windows applications.

3. Click **Simple**.
4. Click **Values of individual cases**.
5. Click **Define**. When you do this, you will see the **Define Simple Line: Values of Individual Cases** dialog box, as shown in Figure 83 (at the top of page 79).

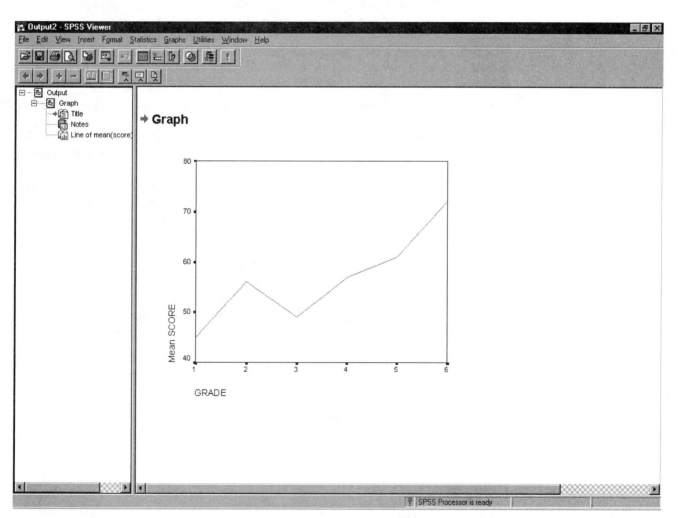

Figure 83. Defining the type of line in a chart.

6. Click **grade**, click **Variable** in the **Category Labels** area, and then click ▶ .
7. Click **score**, and then click ▶ to move the variable to the **Line Represents** area.
8. Click **OK**, and you see the chart in the Output Navigator, as shown in Figure 84.

Figure 84. A simple line graph in an Output Navigator window.

This is the default chart with no additions, changes, or edits. (See Lesson 16.)

Saving a Chart

A chart is only one possible component of the Output Navigator window. The chart is not a separate entity that stands by itself and cannot be saved. To save a chart, you have to save the entire contents of the Output Navigator. To do so, follow these steps:

1. In the Output Navigator window, click **File → Save**.
2. Provide a name for the Output Navigator window.
3. Click **OK**. The Output Navigator is saved under the name that you provide with an .spo extension. If you want to open this file later, you have to select this extension from the Files of type drop-down menu.

Printing a Chart

There are several ways to print a chart. The first way is to print from the Output Navigator by selecting the chart and then selecting Print.

1. Be sure that the chart you want to print is in the active Output Navigator window.
2. Click on the chart so that it is selected.
3. Click **OK**. The chart will be printed.

If you want to print only a part of the Output Navigator window, first select the element by clicking on it once and then select **File → Print**, click Selection and OK.

Different SPSS Charts

SPSS offers 17 different types of chart (all of which you can see samples of at Chart → Gallery). While some types of chart may be used in lieu of others, each has its own purpose. The purpose depends on the type of data being charted as well as the research question being asked. It's beyond the scope of this book to detail each chart and all the possible combinations, but you should see how some of the simple charts appear.

Following are examples of some of these simple charts. Keep in mind that there is an almost infinite number of variations of the charts you can create using SPSS. You'll learn about modifying charts in Lesson 16. All sample charts that follow appear as they are first created, with no modification.

The Bar Chart

A **bar chart** represents values as separate bars with each bar corresponding to the value in the Data Editor. Bar charts are often used because they are easy to understand and require little attention to detail. In Figure 85 (at the top of page 81), you can see an example of a bar chart of the number of males and females.

The Area Chart

An **area chart** represents the proportions of the whole that each data point contributes. In Figure 86 (on page 81), you can see an example of average product preference as a function of earning power (high, moderate, and low).

The Pie Chart

The **pie chart** is a circle divided into wedges, with each wedge representing a proportion of the whole. Pie charts provide a clear picture of the relative contribution that a data point makes to the overall body of information. In Figure 87 (at the top of page 82), you can see a pie chart for expenses (rent, insurance, and miscellaneous).

Graph

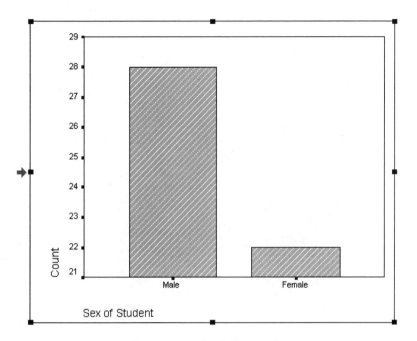

Figure 85. A simple bar graph.

Graph

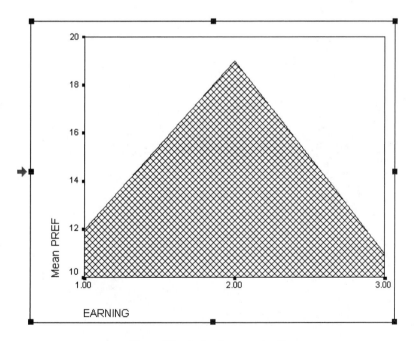

Figure 86. A simple area chart.

Graph

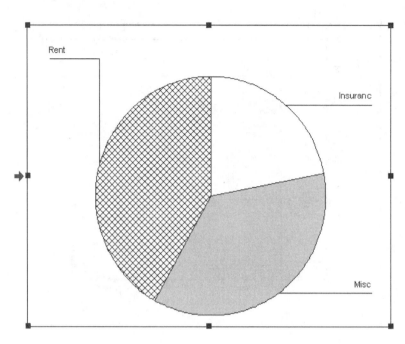

Figure 87. A simple pie chart.

Keep in mind that when you first create a chart, all the SPSS defaults are used. You can easily change type size and font and many other characteristics. You will learn how to do that in the next lesson.

Enhancing SPSS Charts

After This Lesson, You Will Know

- How to modify chart elements, including titles, axes, colors, and patterns

Key Words

- Category Axis
- Category Axis dialog box
- Colors dialog box
- Patterns dialog box
- Pattern dialog box
- Scale Axis
- Scale Axis dialog box
- SPSS Chart Editor
- Text Styles dialog box
- Titles dialog box

A picture might be worth a thousand words, but if your pictures or charts don't say what you want, what good are they? Once you create a chart, as we showed you in the last lesson, you can finish the job by editing the chart to reflect exactly your meaning. Color, shapes, scales, fonts, text, and more can be altered, and that is what you'll do in this lesson. As you can see in Figure 88, we'll be working with the line chart that was first shown to you in Figure 81. Only in this case we've made all the modifications.

Modifying a Chart

The first step with the modification of any chart is to double-click on the chart in the right pane of the Output Navigator to access the **SPSS Chart Editor** and then click the maximize button on the Application title bar. As you can see in Figure 88 (at the top of page 84), there is a Chart toolbar containing a set of buttons across the top of the chart. In Figure 89 (also on page 84), you can see each button better and what each represents.

TIP

A single-click on a chart element selects it. A double-click on a chart element activates it and opens the Chart Editor.

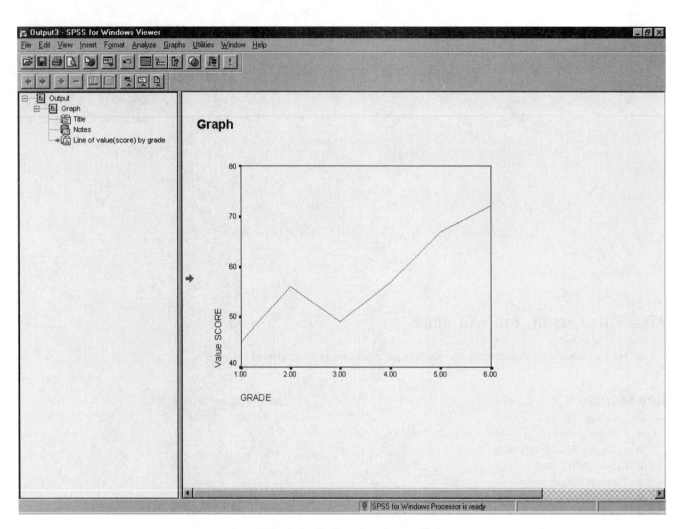

Figure 88. A simple line chart for modifying.

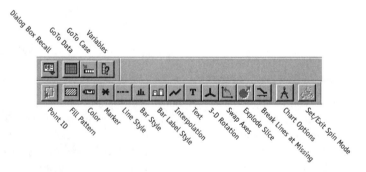

Figure 89. The toolbar buttons in the Chart Editor window.

One cautionary note before we begin. The most basic reason for modifying a chart should be to increase the chart's ability to communicate your message. If you get caught up in Chart Junk (a close cousin to Font Junk), you'll have a mess on your hands. Modify to make better, not to show your reader that you know how to use SPSS.

One instructional note before we begin. The general strategy for changing an element in a chart, such as you see in Figure 88, is to select the chart element and then make the change. You select a chart element much as you select any Windows element, by clicking. If you single-click, you then must select the menu command for the item you want to change. If you double-click in some cases, you will go immediately to the dialog box in which you can make the change.

Working with Titles and Subtitles

Our first task is to enter the title and a subtitle for the chart you see in Figure 88.

1. Click **Chart → Title**. When you do this, you will see the **Titles** dialog box, as shown in Figure 90.

Figure 90. The Titles dialog box.

2. Type **Score by Grade** in the Title 1 section.
3. Press the Tab key.
4. Type **9/25/98** in the Title 2 section.
5. Click **Center** from the drop-down menus for justification of the title and subtitle.
6. Click **OK**.

The title and subtitle (if you entered one) appear as elements on the chart. If you want to edit a title or a subtitle, just be sure that the chart is active and select Title from the Chart menu.

Working with Fonts

Now it's time to work with the font used to represent any text in the chart. You can do this one of two ways, with each way yielding the same dialog box used to change fonts.

1. Select the area of the chart containing the font you want to change. When you select text, it appears with a solid line around it. In this example, we selected the title of the chart.
2. To select a new font and size, you can either select Text from the Format menu or click on the Text button on the toolbar. When you do either of these, you will see the **Text Styles** dialog box, shown in Figure 91.

Figure 91. The Text Styles dialog box.

3. Select the font and size you want to use.
4. Click **Apply**, and the font will change in the chart. The Text Styles dialog box will remain on the screen until you close it. That way you can make several text style changes without having to reselect the Text Styles dialog box.

The font size was set at 14 point for the first title and 12 point for the second title. The font used was Book Antigua for both title elements. You cannot highlight more than one text area at a time, so you have to highlight each one and then select the font you want to use.

Working with Frames

SPSS, by default, places a frame around the top and right side of the chart, an inside frame. And if you want, it can also place a frame around the entire chart, called an outside frame. To include or exclude an inner and outer frame, select the option (Inner Frame or Outer Frame or both) from the Chart menu. The graph's inner frame was removed, making for a less cluttered appearance.

Working with Axes

The X and Y axes provide the calibration for the independent (usually the X axis) variable and the dependent (usually the Y axis) variable. SPSS names the Y axis the **Scale Axis** and the X axis the **Category Axis**. Each of these axes can be modified in a variety of ways. To modify either axis, double-click on the title of the axis.

How to Modify the Scale (Y) Axis

For example, to modify the Y axis, follow these steps:

1. Double-click on the label (Value SCORE) of the axis, and not the axis itself.
   When you do this, you will see the **Scale Axis** dialog box, as shown in Figure 92.

Figure 92. The Scale Axis dialog box.

2. Select the options you want from the Scale Axis dialog box. In the example you see in Figure 88, we changed the label Value Score to Score and centered the axis title. We could have done several other things, such as changing the range of the scale (which is 40 to 80 based on data values of 45 and 72) and working with major divisions and minor divisions.

Working with the Category (X) Axis

Working with the X axis is no more difficult from working with the Y axis. Here's how the X axis was modified.

1. Double-click on the label of the X axis. The **Category Axis** dialog box opens. It is very similar to the Scale Axis dialog box you see in Figure 92.
2. Select the options you want from the Category Axis dialog box. We centered the axis title.

Working with Legends

A legend provides information about the elements within a chart. For example, in Figure 88 you can see the line chart has a legend defining what the line represents. If you select Legend from the Chart menu or double-click on the legend, you can assign a title to the legend, and change the location and justification of the legend.

Working with Patterns and Colors

Time to have some fun (and be practical besides). When SPSS creates a chart, and if you have a color monitor, it assigns different colors or symbols to different elements in a chart. We'll use two tools, one to work with patterns and one to work with colors. We'll use a simple bar chart, as shown in Figure 93, as an example.

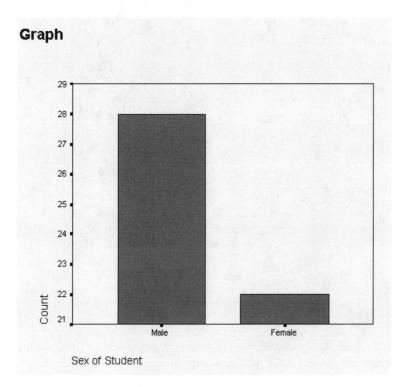

Figure 93. A simple bar chart.

Changing Patterns

To change the patterns of any element in a chart, follow these steps:

1. Double-click to open the Chart Editor.
2. Click on the chart element you want to select. When you select a chart element, handles are placed on the edges of all the elements that are identical. In this case, we will click on one of the bars and all the bars are selected.
3. Click on the **Pattern** button or click **Format**, and you will see the **Pattern** dialog box shown in Figure 94.

Figure 94. The Pattern dialog box.

4. Click on the pattern you want to use.
5. Click **Apply**, and the pattern used in the bars will change. In the bar chart you see in Figure 95, the hatched pattern was used for the Sex of Student variable.

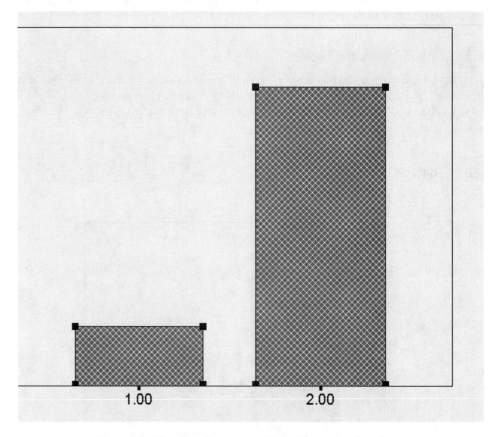

Figure 95. Changing the pattern of an element in a bar chart.

Now that the patterns are straight, we have one more step. We will eliminate the color from the bars since printing on color (your printer will see the colors as being black or a shade of gray) uses lots of toner.

Changing Colors

To change the color of any element in a chart, follow these steps:

1. Click on the chart element you want to select.
2. Click on the **Color** button, or click **Format** → **Color**. When you do this, you will see the **Colors** shown in Figure 96.

Figure 96. The Colors dialog box.

4. Select the color you want to use to fill the bar, which in our example is white.
5. Click **Apply**.
6. Select the color you want to use (if any) for the border of the bar, which in this example is black.
7. Click **Apply**.

Setting Chart Preferences

Now that you know something about creating and modifying charts, you should know there are certain default settings that you can set before you create a chart. They allow you to choose a particular format for viewing your charts. These settings, shown in Figure 97, allow you to set the following visual elements:

TIP

You can set the Chart (and other) defaults you want to use in the Options dialog box at Edit → Options.

- the font used in the chart
- the nature of how items are filled with patterns or colors
- the height to width ratio of the chart
- the presence of a frame (inside and/or outside)
- the presence of grid lines

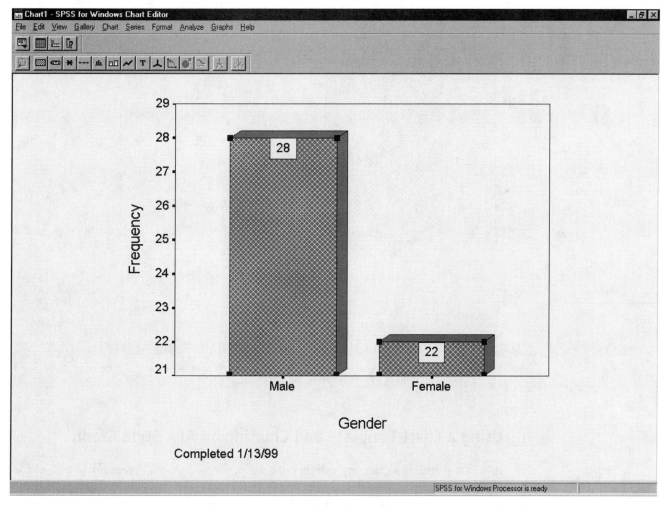

Figure 97. Setting chart preferences.

For example, if you want the initial chart to use Times Roman as a font, specify it in the SPSS Options dialog box you access through the Edit menu in the Chart Editor.

Getting Fancy

Before we finish with this bar chart and with your introduction to SPSS charts, let's add just a few more things to jazz up the bar chart.

First, let's make it appear 3-dimensional. Click on the Bar Styles button on the toolbar and then click on the 3-D icon. Let's change the depth to 10%. Then we'll click on the Bar Label Styles button and place the corresponding Y axis value at the top of each bar. Both of these changes are simple and increase the informative nature of the chart. We even changed the color of the 3-D effect shadow to gray. Our finished bar chart, which appears in Figure 98, also includes some changes in labels and frames and a new footnote.

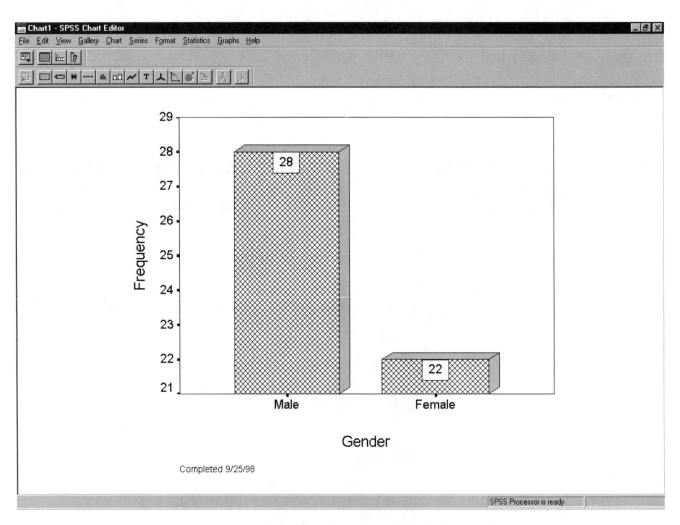

Figure 98. A finished bar chart.

Using a Chart Template and Creating an APA Style Graph

If you are preparing a chart or graph for publication, you will want it to conform to the style detailed in the *Publication Manual of the American Psychological Association*. Such style characteristics are spelled out in the manual and shown in Figure 99 (at the top of page 91).

As you can see, the chart has no title. The title belongs as a caption in the manuscript under the chart. SPSS provides no option for chart captions.

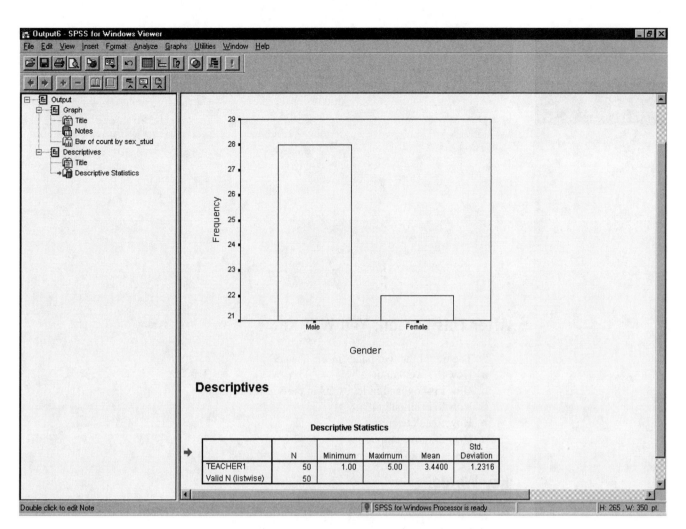

Figure 99. A chart prepared according to APA style guidelines.

If you intend to create charts according to APA guidelines, you should create a chart template. That way, when you create a new chart, all you need to do is apply the chart template, and the formatting (such as centered axes titles and 12-point size titles) will be automatic. To create a chart template, follow these steps:

1. Once you complete a chart that fits your style needs, click **File → Save Chart Template**.
2. Enter a name for the template. The template will automatically have an .sct extension.
3. Click **Save**. The chart template will be saved.

To use a chart template once it has been created, follow these steps:

1. After clicking the **Define** button when creating a chart, click the **Template** check box.
2. Using the Use Template from File dialog box, locate the template that you want to use.
3. Click **OK**.

Lesson 17

Using the Viewer

After This Lesson, You Will Know

- The use of the two panes in the Viewer
- How to save output
- How to show and hide results in the Viewer window
- How to print output
- How to delete output
- How to move output

Key Words

- Contents pane
- Outline pane

When you complete any type of procedure in SPSS, be it the creation of a simple chart or the results of a complex analysis, the output appears in the Viewer. The Viewer is a separate SPSS screen that lists all operations performed on a set of data in the order in which they were completed.

For example, in Figure 100 (at the top of page 93), you can see that two different types of analysis were done; the first was a simple description of the data (Descriptives) and the second was the creation of a bar chart (Graph).

As you can see, the screen is titled Output2 - SPSS Viewer, since it is the second Viewer window created during this work session. Until you save the contents of the Viewer using a new name, the Viewer window will keep the name that SPSS assigned when it was first created. Unless named by you, the names automatically assigned are Output1, Output2, etc.

The Viewer consists of two panes. The **Outline pane** on the left side of the Viewer and the **Results pane** on the right side of the Viewer.

The **Outline pane** lists in outline form all the analyses that have been completed. The **Contents pane** contains the results of the analyses. For example, in Figure 100, you can see an outline in the left pane of what is contained in the right pane. In the right pane, you find labels for the output (such as Descriptives) along with the corresponding table. In any Outline pane, you will find names of tables or charts, the table or chart, and notes that accompany the generation of the table or chart. For now, we'll show you how to save Viewer output, print it, delete elements in the Viewer, and move the elements around so the output best fits your needs.

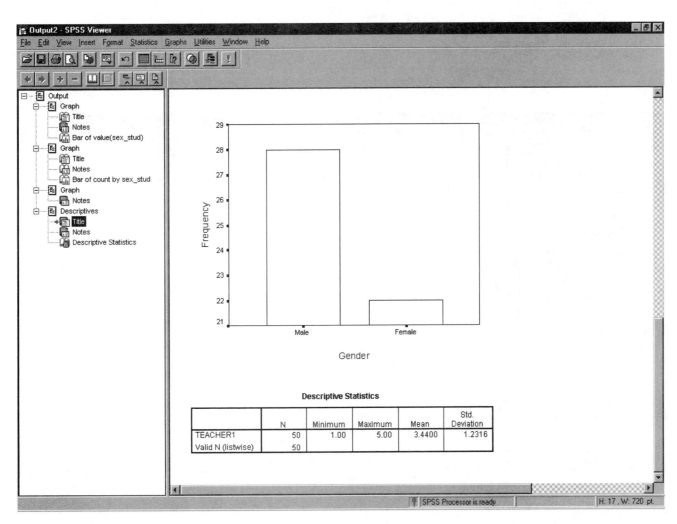

Figure 100. The Viewer window.

Saving Output

Once output is generated, you will probably want to save it for later use or even to add it to another work session. To save output from the Viewer, follow these steps:

1. Click **File → Save**.
2. Provide a name for the output.
3. Click **OK**. The output will be saved using the file name that you provided, along with the .spo extension. When you want to open the Viewer you saved, you will have to specify the .spo extension in the File Type drop-down menu in the SPSS Open dialog box.

To Selectively Show and Hide Results

You can choose to show or hide any results that appear in the Viewer window. You may generate results that you want to hide while you print out others, a convenient way to be selective as you focus your discussion of the results.

To hide a table or chart without deleting it, follow these steps:

1. Click on the item in the Outline pane.
2. Click **View → Hide**.

TIP

The red arrow in the Outline or Results pane indicates which element in the Viewer is active.

For example, in Figure 101, you will see that the title of the procedure Descriptives (which appears in Figure 100) in the Contents pane was hidden. Although it is not deleted, it no longer appears in the Results pane. But, as you can see in Figure 101, it still appears in the Outline pane of the Viewer window.

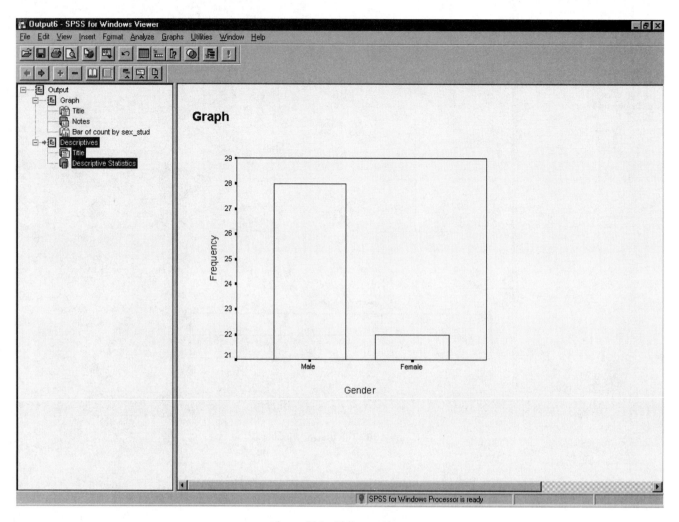

Figure 101. Hiding output.

To show a table or chart once it has been hidden, follow these steps:

1. Click on the item in the Outline pane.
2. Click **View → Show**. The item reappears in the Contents pane.

You'll want to hide and show output as you decide what you want to appear in a hard copy of the Viewer.

Printing the Contents of the Viewer Window

To print the contents of the Viewer, follow these steps:

1. Click **File → Print**.
2. Click **OK**. All the tables and charts in the Viewer will be printed.

Printing a Selection from the Viewer Window

To print a specific selection from the Viewer window such as a table or a chart, follow these steps:

1. Click on the table, chart, or both that you want to print in the Viewer window. You can select more than one element. Hold down the Shift or Ctrl key when you click multiple elements.
2. Click **File → Print**.
3. Click **Selection → OK**. The element or elements you selected will be printed.

Any element surrounded by a black line is selected and will print. You can select as many elements as appear in the Contents pane to print at once.

Deleting Output

To delete output from the Viewer, follow these steps:

1. Click on the output you want deleted, either in the Outline or Contents pane of the Viewer window.
2. Click **Edit → Delete**, or press the **Del** key.

TIP

If you accidentally delete an element, don't do anything else before you click Edit → Undo to restore your work.

Moving Output

Although the output in the Viewer window appears as it was created, you can change the order in which it appears. To change the order, do the following.

In the Outline pane of the Viewer, drag the icon representing the output to its new location.

For example, in Figure 102, you can see that the element titled Descriptive Statistics is being moved to the place above the element titled Notes and below Title. You can see how the Outline appears after the move in Figure 103. Remember that the order in which elements appear in the Outline pane directly reflects their order in the Results pane.

Figure 102. Moving Viewer elements.

Figure 103. After the move.

Working with SPSS Procedures
Creating Variables

In Part I of *Using SPSS for Windows*, you learned how to use the program to perform basic data entry and manipulation, create and edit graphs, and create and work with tables. Part II of the book moves beyond these basic techniques into discussions of many statistical procedures that are available in SPSS.

Part II consists of 27 lessons. Each lesson presents a topic—from simple analyses, such as descriptive statistics for quantitative variables and one-sample *t* tests, to more complex analyses, such as two-way analysis of variance, multiple regression, and factor analysis. It should be noted that the terms used by SPSS for various types of analyses may be different from the terms used in many textbooks and classes. For example, the statistical test for the difference between two related means is often called *matched-samples t test* or a *correlated-samples t test*. SPSS calls it *paired-samples t test*.

Part II includes applications and homework exercise problems to illustrate how to conduct various statistical procedures. Because of the simplified nature of the application presentations, the APA results sections are much briefer and less complex than those published in research journals.

Lessons are divided into several major sections that show you when and how to apply the different statistical procedures and how to analyze and interpret their results. Lessons may not include all nine of these sections.

- Each lesson begins with a section that introduces the statistical procedure and describes how to structure the SPSS data file to conduct the procedure.
- "Applying the [Procedure]" illustrates the research designs and situations associated with the procedure.
- "Understanding the [Procedure]" provides the underlying assumptions of the procedure and additional pertinent information
- "The Data Set" section describes the variables in the application data set used to illustrate the statistical procedure and presents research questions that will be addressed by the statistical analyses. The data sets for the examples are on the student disk and are labeled in the general format of "Lesson? Data File?" where the lesson number is substituted for the first question mark and the data set number is substituted for the second question mark.
- "Conducting the [Procedure]" describes all of the steps required to conduct the statistical analysis using SPSS for Windows. In most cases, we choose analysis options that have relatively broad applicability. However, some options may need to be modified to meet the needs of the data analysis. We also present selected SPSS output and discussion of the output for each analysis in this section. Because it is not necessary to view all of the SPSS output to understand the procedure being discussed, we present abridged output for many analyses.
- "Using SPSS Graphs to Display the Results" demonstrates various graphical techniques that might be used in reporting results. Each graph we present has

been edited to be consistent with the recommendations in the *Publication Manual of the American Psychological Association*. Therefore, the graph you see in your output may look somewhat different from the graph we present in the book. We present graphs in this form so you can see how to present graphs for publication.

- The purpose of the next section, either "Writing an APA Results Section" or "Writing an APA Participants Section," is to provide actual models of results and participant sections in APA manuscript format.
- "Alternative Analyses" describes related statistical procedures that may be used instead of the particular procedure described in the lesson.
- Homework problems are given in the "Exercise" section. The data needed to complete the exercises at the end of each lesson are in the data files on the student disk labeled "Exercise Files."

Many statistical procedures in Part II are extremely complex, and we cannot provide the in-depth understanding that a textbook or a statistics class can provide. We strongly recommend that you consult textbooks on any statistical procedures you are unfamiliar with before conducting analyses using those procedures.

Many procedures in the lessons require multiple tests. In these cases, we illustrate how to control for Type I error across the multiple tests using one of three procedures. Step-by-step procedures for each method are described in Appendix B.

In Unit 5, the first unit of Part II, we discuss how to create variables and how to compute and interpret descriptive statistics. In the first lesson of Unit 5, we describe how to create new quantitative and qualitative variables from existing variables (e.g., overall scale scores from item scores). In the next lesson, we illustrate how to summarize the results on qualitative variables using tabular and graphical displays. In the last lesson of the unit, we discuss how to describe the results on a quantitative variable, overall and within levels of a qualitative variable. We also explain how to determine percentile ranks associated with scores on a quantitative variable.

Because the objective of Unit 5 is to understand how to conduct descriptive statistics and excludes inferential techniques, we have developed applications aimed at describing research participants rather than answering research questions. We discuss applications for answering research questions in Units 6 through 10 of Part II.

Summarizing and Describing Data

Before conducting the statistical analyses described in later lessons, it is important to know how to create the variables that you might analyze. In this lesson, we will present methods for developing an overall scale from a set of quantitative variables that assess the same dimension. The quantitative variables that are combined together may have the same or different metrics. We will also learn how to create a qualitative variable from one or more quantitative variables.

Quantitative variables have the same metric if they are measured on the same response scale (e.g., items responded to on a 5-point scale with the same verbal anchors). In creating an overall scale from quantitative variables with the same metric, we may need initially to reverse scale some variables. We reverse scale variables that are in the opposite direction of the dimension that we are interested in assessing. For example, items that assess self-esteem may be worded to reflect high self-esteem, such as "I feel good about myself," or low self-esteem, such as "I do not think I am a good person." To create a meaningful overall self-esteem scale, we have to reverse scale the item representing low self-esteem so that higher values on it reflect higher levels of self-esteem. After reverse scaling variables that are in the opposite direction of the dimension of interest, we sum all variables, those that were reverse-scaled and those that were not. For our self-esteem example, we add together the reverse-scaled low self-esteem item with the high self-esteem item. We discuss in this lesson how to reverse-scale variables and how to combine variables to create overall scores with or without missing data.

A similar strategy is required for creating an overall scale from variables with different metrics. Because the variables have different metrics, we standardize them by converting them to z-scores before creating an overall scale. For example, before summing across three different personality measures, a self-report measure, a behavioral observation, and a teacher rating, we convert the scores on the three measures to standardized scores. We explain in this lesson how to transform scores on variables with different metrics to z-scores, how to reverse-scale z-scored variables, and how to combine them to create overall scores. Although we create overall scores by computing total scores, the techniques can be easily adapted to develop overall scores by calculating mean scores.

For some analyses, you may want to create a qualitative or categorical variable from one or more quantitative variables. We can divide a single quantitative variable into categories. For example, we might categorize a quantitative variable measuring stress into three categories: low-, medium-, and high-stress categories. Qualitative variables may also be created by categorizing two or more quantitative variables. For example, we could form a four-category variable from two quantitative variables—performance IQ and verbal IQ.

1. Low performance and low verbal IQ
2. Low performance and high verbal IQ
3. High performance and low verbal IQ
4. High performance and high verbal IQ

Applying Methods for Creating Variables

We will demonstrate initially how to create overall scores from variables of particular types:

- Variables that have the same metric and require no reverse-scaling
- Variables that have the same metric and require reverse-scaling for one or more of the variables
- Variables that have different metrics and require no reverse-scaling
- Variables that have different metrics and require reverse-scaling for one or more of the variables
- Variables that have missing data

Next we will show how to create a qualitative variable from

- A single quantitative variable
- Multiple quantitative variables

We demonstrate all seven applications for creating new variables from existing ones with the following example study.

Casey gains the cooperation of 40 women college students to participate in his study. All participants gained at least 10 pounds their first year in college. He is interested in their eating habits and their feelings about eating during their second year of college. Casey asks the students to complete three scales at the beginning of their second year: the Positive Body Image (PBI) scale, the Positive Attitude toward Eating (ATE) scale, and the Overeating Guilt (OG) scale. In addition, he asks students to make ratings about their hunger on four consecutive days during the first month of their sophomore year. Finally, at the end of their sophomore year, they estimate the number of days they skipped lunch or dinner during a typical month of their second college year and the proportion of days that they were on diets. Casey enters the data from the 6 items of the PBI, the 5 items of the ATE, the 8 items of the OG, the 4 ratings of daily hunger, and the 2 eating habit measures. Accordingly, Casey's SPSS data file contains 40 cases and 25 variables.

The Data Set

All seven applications use the data set named *Lesson 18 Data File 1* on the student disk. Table 7 (at the top of page 101) shows the variables in the data set.

Creating Variables

In this section, we demonstrate how to create scales for seven applications.

Creating an Overall Scale from Variables with the Same Metric and No Reverse Scaling

Casey wants to compute scores on the Positive Attitude toward Eating (ATE) scale. Higher scores on all five items indicate positive feelings toward eating, and therefore, none of the items requires reverse scaling. Casey creates a total scale score by summing across all five items.

Table 7
Variables in Lesson 18 Data File 1

Variable	Definition
skipmeal	Estimated number of days skipped lunch or dinner during a typical month of sophomore year
dietdays	Estimated proportion of days on diet during sophomore year
hunger1 to hunger4	Ratings of hunger on four consecutive days during first month of sophomore year. Participants indicated their hunger on a 0-to-100 scale, with 0 = no hunger during entire day and 100 = voracious during entire day. A missing score was assigned if participant failed to submit rating via e-mail at the end of a day.
pbi01 to pbi06	Six-item Positive Body Image (PBI) scale, completed at beginning of sophomore year. Participants respond on a 5-point scale, with 1 = totally disagree to 5 = totally agree.
	1. I dislike the size of my waist.*
	2. I have a good-looking body.
	3. I hate my thighs.*
	4. I like the firmness of my abdominal muscles.
	5. I dislike the size of my hips.*
	6. I like how I look.
ate01 to ate05	Five-item Positive Attitude toward Eating (ATE) scale, completed at beginning of sophomore year. Participants indicate how they feel about eating on a 3-point scale (−1 = negative feeling; 0 = neutral feeling; 1 = positive feeling).
	1. Eating desserts
	2. Eating at fast food restaurants
	3. Eating snacks
	4. Eating appetizers
	5. Eating breakfast
og01 to og08	Eight-item Overeating Guilt (OG) scale, completed at beginning of sophomore year. Participants indicate how they feel after overeating by specifying their agreement with statement on a 5-point scale, with 1 = totally disagree to 5 = totally agree.
	1. I feel like I am a weak person.
	2. It is not a big deal.*
	3. I am not upset with myself.*
	4. I hate myself.
	5. I feel like I have no self-discipline.
	6. I feel absolutely nauseous.
	7. I feel ok about myself.*
	8. I do not feel guilty.*

*Higher scores on these items represent lower scores on scale.

To create an overall ATE scale score, follow these steps:

1. Click **Transform**, and click **Compute**.
2. Type **ate** in the Target Variable text box.
3. In the Functions box, scroll down until you find an expression that says SUM(numexpr,numexpr ...). Highlight the expression and click ▲ to move it to the Numeric Expression text box.
4. In the Numeric Expression text box, highlight the two question marks in the SUM(?,?) expression by dragging your mouse across them.
5. Hit the Delete key to remove the question marks.
6. Click **ate01** and click ▶ to move it to the Numeric Expression text box.
7. Type a comma after ate01.

8.   Repeat Steps 6 and 7 for **ate02**, **ate03**, **ate04**, and **ate05**. Do not type a comma after ate05. Figure 104 shows the Compute Variable dialog box after completing Step 8.

Figure 104. Compute Variable dialog box for creating ATE scale scores.

9.   Click **OK**. SPSS will return you to the Data Editor where you can see your new variable, ate.

Creating an Overall Scale from Variables with the Same Metric and Reverse Scaling

Casey wants to compute overall scores on the Positive Body Image (PBI) scale, such that higher PBI scale scores represent a positive body image. Three PBI items (pbi02, pbi04, and pbi06) are worded so that a higher item score represents a positive body image. The other three items (pbi01, pbi03, and pbi05) are worded so that higher item scores indicate a negative body image and, consequently, need to be reverse scaled before the six PBI items are summed to create overall PBI scale scores.

Reverse Scaling

To reverse scale pbi01, pbi03, and pbi05, follow these steps:

1.   Click **Transform**, click **Recode**, then click **Into Same Variables**.
2.   In the Recode into Same Variables dialog box, click on **pbi01** hold down the Ctrl key, and click **pbi03** and **pbi05**. Click ► to move them to the Numeric Variables box.
3.   Click **Old and New Values**.
4.   Within the Old Value area, click **Value** if not chosen. Type **1** in the text box to the right of Value.
5.   Within the New Value area, click **Value** if not chosen. Type **5** in the text box next to Value.
6.   Click **Add**.
7.   Repeat for each of the remaining four values, changing 2 to 4, 3 to 3, 4 to 2, and 5 to 1. Make sure you click **Add** after each new value.
8.   Click **Continue**.
9.   Click **OK**.

These three items are now scaled in the appropriate direction. You are ready to compute PBI scale scores.

Computing Total Scale Scores

To compute PBI scale scores, follow these steps:

1. Click **Transform**, and click **Compute**.
2. Click **Reset** to clear the dialog box.
3. Type **pbi** in the Target Variable text box.
4. In the Functions box, scroll down until you find an expression that says SUM(numexpr,numexpr ...). Highlight the expression and click ▲ to move it to the Numeric Expression text box.
5. In the Numeric Expression text box, highlight the two question marks in the SUM(?,?) expression by dragging your mouse across them.
6. Hit the Delete key to remove the question marks.
7. Type **pbi01 to pbi06** between the parentheses in the Numeric Expression text box. Figure 105 shows the Compute Variable dialog box after completing Step 7.

Figure 105. Compute Variable dialog box for creating an overall PBI scores.

8. Click **OK**. SPSS will return you to the Data Editor where you can see your new variable, pbi.

Creating an Overall Scale from Variables with Different Metrics and No Reverse Scaling

Casey wishes to create an index of restrictive eating (IRE) by combining the skipmeal and the dietdays variables. For the skipmeal variable, students estimated the number of days they skipped lunch or dinner. For the dietdays variable, students estimated the proportion of days they were on diets. The two variables have different metrics (number of days and proportion of days) and, accordingly, cannot simply be summed together. One solution is for Casey to transform the two variables into z-scores to create a comparable metric and then to sum the z-scores to create an overall index of restrictive eating.

Creating Standardized Scores

The first step is to standardize the metric on the two restrictive eating variables so that they can be summed together.

1. Click **Analyze**, click **Descriptive Statistics**, then click **Descriptives**.
2. In the Descriptives dialog box, hold down the Ctrl key and click **skipmeal** and **dietdays** to select them.

3. Click ► to move them to the Variable(s) box.
4. Click **Save standardized values as variables**.
5. Click **OK**.
6. Click **Window** and click **Lesson 18 Data File 1** to return to the Data Editor where you can see two new variables, zskipmea and zdietday, shown in Figure 106.

	zskipmea	zdietday
1	.20053	-1.50761
2	2.42861	-.73589
3	.20053	1.35878
4	-.69071	-1.06663
5	-1.13632	.25632
6	1.53738	-.73589
7	.86895	.03583

Figure 106. Z-scored variables in the Data Editor.

Computing Total Scale Scores

Now you can compute overall IRE scores by following these steps:

1. Click **Transform**, and click **Compute**.
2. Click **Reset** to clear the dialog box.
3. Type **ire** in the Target Variable text box.
4. In the Numeric Expression text box, type the following expression: SUM(zskipmea,zdietday). Figure 107 shows the Compute Variable dialog box after completing Step 4.

Figure 107. Compute Variable dialog box for creating IRE scores.

5. Click **OK**. SPSS will return you to the Data Editor where you can see your new variable, ire.

Creating an Overall Scale from Variables with Different Metrics and Reverse Scaling

Casey believes that both items from the Positive Attitude toward Eating (ATE) scale and from the Overeating Guilt (OG) scale assess positive emotional reaction to eating. He would like to combine them together to create a positive emotional reaction to food (PERF) index. However, the items from the two scales have different metrics. The ATE items describe eating activities and ask individuals to give their emotional response on a −1 to +1 scale, while the OG items are statements about how they feel after overeating and ask individuals to indicate whether they agree with these statements. Consequently, the item scores from the two scales have to be transformed to z-scores so that they have comparable metrics. In addition, higher scores on 4 of the 13 items (items: og01, og04, og05, og06) reflect negative feelings rather than positive feelings and need to be reverse scaled. Given items have been transformed to z-scores, Casey can reverse scale these four items by multiplying them by −1 (making positive values negative and negative values positive). Now, Casey can sum the 13 transformed items to yield PERF index scores.

Creating Standardized Scores

Follow these steps to create standardized scores:

1. Transform the items for the ATE scale (ate01 to ate05) and the Overeating Guilt scale (og01 to og08) to z-scores. To transform these items, follow the procedure (Steps 1–5) described in the previous section for "Creating standardized scores" in "Creating an Overall Scale from Variables with Different Metrics and No Reverse-Scaling." The names for the z-scaled items are zate01 to zate05 and zog01 to zog08.

Reverse Scaling Standardized Scores

To reverse-scale the z-scored OG items zog01, zog04, zog05, and zog06, follow these steps:

1. Click **Transform**, and click **Compute**.
2. Click **Reset** to clear the dialog box.
3. Type **zog01** in the Target Variable text box.
4. In the Numeric Expression text box, type the following expression: **−1 * zog01**. Figure 108 shows the Compute Variable dialog box after completing Step 4.

Figure 108. Reverse scaling a z-scored variable.

5. Click **OK**.
6. Click **OK** in response to the Change Existing Variable prompt.
7. Repeat steps 1 through 6 to reverse-scale **zog04**, **zog05**, and **zog06**.

Creating Total Scale Scores

To compute an overall PERF index scores, follow these steps:

1. Click **Transform** and click **Compute**.
2. Click **Reset** to clear the dialog box.
3. Type **perf** in the Target Variable text box.
4. In the Numeric Expression text box, type SUM(zate01 to zate05) + SUM(zog01 to zog08). Figure 109 shows the Compute Variable dialog box after completing Step 4.

Figure 109. Compute Variable dialog box for creating PERF index scores.

5. Click **OK**. SPSS will return you to the Data Editor where you can see your new variable, perf.

Creating an Overall Scale from Variables with Missing Data

Casey wishes to create a total hunger score from his four daily hunger ratings (hunger1 to hunger4). The four ratings have the same metric and are all scaled in the same direction and, therefore, do not need to be reverse scaled. However, some students are missing one or more daily hunger ratings. Casey decides to create total hunger scores for students who completed at least 3 of the 4 daily hunger ratings. For students with no missing ratings, he creates total scores by simply summing the four ratings. For students with one missing rating, he takes the mean of the three nonmissing ratings and multiplies by four to create a total-like score. In effect, this procedure is equivalent to substituting the mean of the nonmissing ratings for the missing rating and summing the three nonmissing ratings and the substituted value for the missing rating.

To create an overall hunger variable, follow these steps:

1. Click **Transform** and click **Compute**.
2. Click **Reset** to clear the dialog box.
3. Type **hunger** in the Target Variable text box.

4. In the Functions box, scroll down until you find an expression that says MEAN(numexpr,numexpr …). Highlight the expression and click ▲ to move it to the Numeric Expression text box. The first question mark will be highlighted.
5. Click **hunger1** and click ▶ to move it to the Numeric Expression text box.
6. Move your cursor to the other side of the comma.
7. Click **hunger2** and click ▶ to move it to the Numeric Expression text box.
8. Type a comma after **hunger2**.
9. Repeat Steps 6, 7, and 8 for **hunger3** and **hunger4**. Do not type a comma after **hunger4**.
10. Delete the extra question mark.
11. Place your cursor between MEAN and the first parentheses and click. Type **.3**. This tells SPSS that you must have at least three nonmissing data scores for it to compute a mean score for an individual.
12. Type **4 *** in front of MEAN.3(hunger1,hunger2, hunger3, hunger4) to multiply the mean score times 4, the number of variables in the parentheses. This multiplication process produces a total-like score. Figure 110 shows the Compute Variable dialog box after completing Step 12.
13. Click **OK**. SPSS will return you to the Data Editor where you can see your new variable, hunger.

Figure 110. Creating an overall hunger variable with missing data.

For all cases but one, overall hunger scores were computed. However, for Case 2, there is no overall hunger score because that individual has scores on only two of the daily hunger ratings rather than the three required.

Warning! This method could be used for a wide range of applications. When faced with missing data, a researcher could create total scores by taking the mean of the nonmissing items, given participants responded to at least some number of them, and then multiply the mean by the number of items. For example, a researcher could create a total score for 20 items by taking the mean of the nonmissing items, given participants responded to at least 10 items, and then multiply the mean by 20 (e.g., 20*mean.10(item01 to item20). However, we do not recommend general use of this method. The method should be used only if all items are equivalent to each other, the missing values are completely missing at random, and the mean is based on a high percentage of items with nonmissing values.

Categorizing a Single Quantitative Variable

Casey is interested in categorizing students into those who have negative feeling about eating and those who have nonnegative feeling about eating. He assigns labels of negative and nonnegative based on the students' scores on the Positive Attitude toward

Eating (ATE) scale. Students who score less than 0 on the ATE are classified as negative eaters (eatcat = –1), and those who score 0 or higher are classified as the non-negative eaters (eatcat = 1).

To create this categorization, follow these steps:

1. Click **Transform**, click **Recode**, then click **Into Different Variables**.
2. Click **ate**, then click ▶ to move it to Input Variable -> Output Variable text box.
3. Move your cursor to the Name text box in the Output Variable area, and type **atecat**.
4. Click **Change**. Figure 111 shows the Recode into Different Variables dialog box after completing Step 4.

Figure 111. Recode into Different Variables dialog box.

5. Click **Old and New Values**.
6. Click **Range: Lowest Through** in the Old Value Range area.
7. Type **–1** in the text box after Through.
8. Type **–1** in the Value text box in the New Value area.
9. Click **Add**.
10. Click **All other values** in the Old Value area.
11. Type **1** in the Value text box in the New Value area.
12. Click **Add**.
13. Click **Continue**.
14. Click **OK**. SPSS will return you to the Data Editor where you can see your new variable, atecat.

Creating a Qualitative Variable from Two Quantitative Variables

Casey wishes to categorize his sample into four groups based on their Positive Body Image scores (pbi) and Positive Attitude toward Eating scores (ate).

- *Individuals with positive body images and positive attitudes toward eating*
- *Individuals with positive body images and nonpositive attitudes toward eating*
- *Individuals with nonpositive body images and positive attitudes toward eating*
- *Individuals with nonpositive body images and nonpositive attitudes toward eating*

He selects the midpoint value on each scale to differentiate among students who fall into these four categories. For the PBI, the midpoint on the 1-to-5 response scale for any one item is 2.5, and there are 6 items; therefore, the PBI scale midpoint is 15 (= 2.5 x 6). Similarly, for the ATE, the midpoint on the response scale for any one item is 0, and there are 5 items; therefore, the ATE scale midpoint is 0 (= 0 x 6). Casey creates a variable called catfood that classifies a student as having

- *a positive body image and a positive attitude toward eating (catfood = 1)*
- *a positive body image and a nonpositive attitude toward eating (catfood = 2)*
- *a nonpositive body image and a positive attitude toward eating (catfood = 3)*
- *a nonpositive body image and a nonpositive attitude toward eating (catfood = 4)*

To create the catfood variable, follow the steps for creating each of the four categories. To create a category for students with positive body images and positive attitudes toward eating, follow these steps:

1. Click **Transform**, and click **Compute**.
2. Click **Reset** to clear the dialog box.
3. Type **catfood** in the Target Variable text box.
4. In the Numeric Expression text box, type **1**.
5. Click **If**.
6. In the Compute Variable: If Cases dialog box, click **Include if case satisfies condition**.
7. In the text box below Include if case satisfies condition, type **pbi > 15 & ate > 0**. Figure 112 shows the Compute Variable: If Cases dialog box with the appropriate command.

Figure 112. Compute Variable: If Cases dialog box.

8. Click **Continue**.
9. Click **OK**.

To create a category for students with positive body images and nonpositive attitudes toward eating, follow these steps:

1. Click **Transform**, and click **Compute**.

2. In the Numeric Expression text box, type **2**.
3. Click **If**.
4. In the text box below Include if case satisfies condition, type **pbi > 15 & ate <= 0**.
5. Click **Continue**.
6. Click **OK**.
7. Click **OK** in response to Change Existing Variable? prompt.

To create a category for students with nonpositive body images and positive attitudes toward eating, follow these steps:

1. Click **Transform**, and click **Compute**.
2. In the Numeric Expression text box, type **3**.
3. Click **If**.
4. In the text box below Include if case satisfies condition, type **pbi <= 15 & ate > 0**.
5. Click **Continue**.
6. Click **OK**.
7. Click **OK** in response to Change Existing Variable? prompt.

To create a category for students with nonpositive body images and nonpositive attitudes toward eating, follow these steps:

1. Click **Transform**, and click **Compute**.
2. In the Numeric Expression text box, type **4**.
3. Click **If**.
4. In the text box below Include if case satisfies condition, type **pbi <= 15 & ate <= 0**.
5. Click **Continue**.
6. Click **OK**.
7. Click **OK** in response to Change Existing Variable? prompt. SPSS will return you to the Data Editor where you can see your new variable group.

Exercises

The data for the Exercises 1 and 2 are in the data set named *Lesson 18 Exercise File 1* on the student disk. The data are from the following research problem:

Marion collected questionnaire data from 12 students concerning their attitudes toward math. The students responded to three attitudinal items on a 5-point scale, with 1 = totally disagree to 5 = totally agree. Table 8 shows the three items.

Table 8
Math Attitude Items

Variable	Definition
item1	I like my mathematics classes.
item2	I find math to be a positive challenge.
item3	I am fearful of math.

1. Reverse-scale the values for item3 (1=5, 2=4, 3=3, 4=2, 5=1).
2. Compute a scale called mathatt by taking the mean across the three attitudinal items with nonmissing values and multiplying that mean score by 3 to get a total-like score. Compute this score so that if any case has more than one missing value, mathatt will show a missing value for that case.

The data for the Exercises 3 through 5 are in the data set named *Lesson 18 Exercise File 2* on the student disk. The data are from the following research problem:

Susan is interested in how much coffee people drink at work. To answer this question, she has 10 individuals record the number of cups of coffee they drink daily at work for four days. She also collects an index of job stress and each person's age. The data file contains the four variables concerning coffee drinking (day1 through day4), the job stress variable (jobstres), and the age variable (age). There are no missing data in this data set.

3. Create a categorical age variable named agecat with three age categories, 20–29, 30–39, and 40 and beyond.
4. Create a categorical job stress variable named jobcat with two categories, 1 (jobstres score less than or equal to 21) and 2 (jobstres score greater than 21).
5. Create a new variable called group with four categories based on low and high amounts of coffee drinking and low and high degree of job stress. When creating your new variable, split the sample into low and high amounts of coffee drinking based on the total amount of coffee drinking, such that individuals who drink less than 5 cups of coffee are considered low and those who drink 5 or more cups are considered high.

The data for the Exercises 6 through 8 are in the data set named *Lesson 18 Exercise File 3* on the student disk. The data are from the following research problem:

Matt is interested in negative peer interaction in preschoolers. He collects data on 20 preschoolers. He has three measures: (1) a teacher rating of prosocial behavior with peers, (2) behavioral observations of the number of aggressive acts against peers per hour, and (3) peer reports of aggression. He wants to combine his three measures into a single measure of negative peer interaction. There are no missing data in this dataset.

6. Transform the scores for the three variables into z-scores.
7. Reverse-scale the prosocial rating so that higher values reflect negative peer interaction.
8. Create an overall negative peer interaction score.

Univariate Descriptive Statistics for Qualitative Variables

Qualitative or categorical variables are those whose values represent mutually exclusive categories with no quantitative meaning, such as gender, race, or religious preference. In this lesson, we focus on methods for describing qualitative variables using the Frequencies procedure. These methods can also be used to describe a variable with ordinal, interval, or ratio data if the variable has a limited number of values.

The Frequencies procedure in SPSS can be used to describe one or more qualitative variables. It allows us to determine the frequencies or percentages for categories of a variable as well as the mode, a measure of central tendency. In addition, Frequencies can be used to depict qualitative data graphically in charts such as bar charts and pie charts.

Applying Frequencies to Describe Qualitative Variables

We will discuss applications of Frequencies for three types of variables:

- Qualitative variables with two categories
- Qualitative variables with a moderate number of categories
- Qualitative variables with many categories

Qualitative Variables with Two Categories

Linda has collected data on the gender of her research participants. There are 120 participants in her study. She wants to know the percentages of men and women in her sample.

Qualitative Variables with a Moderate Number of Categories

Linda also has collected information on the ethnic status of the participants in her study. Her ethnicity variable consists of five categories: White, Hispanic, Black, Asian, and Native American. Again she is interested in the percentages or frequencies of research participants in these categories.

Qualitative Variables with Many Categories

Finally, Linda has collected data on the occupations of the participants. The occupational variable consists of 10 categories with each value representing a different job description. She is interested in obtaining the frequencies or percentages of participants in the 10 job categories.

Understanding Frequencies and Statistical Indices for Qualitative Variables

Frequency distributions are tabular or graphical presentations of data that show each category for a variable and the frequency of the category's occurrence in the data set. Percentages for each category are often reported instead of, or in addition to, the frequencies.

The mode is the measure of central tendency associated with a qualitative variable. The mode is the most frequently occurring score or category in a data set. Distributions of variables may be unimodal (one category appears more frequently than others), bimodal (two scores or categories occur most frequently), or multimodal (more than two categories occur most frequently).

The Data Set

The data for this lesson involve the three applications described earlier and are in the data file named *Lesson 19 Data File 1* on the student disk. The variables in the data file are shown in Table 9.

Table 9
Variables in Lesson 19 Data File 1

Variables	Definition
gender	A qualitative variable that indicates the gender of the participants with the following categories: 1 = Men 2 = Women
ethnic	A qualitative variable that indicates the ethnic group of the participants with the following categories: 1 = Black 2 = Hispanic 3 = Asian 4 = White 5 = Other
job	A qualitative variable that indicates the job classification of the participants with the following categories: 1 = Clerical 2 = Management 3 = Maintenance 4 = Academic 5 = Professional 6 = Self-Employed 7 = Medical 8 = Skilled 9 = Military 10 = Unemployed

The Research Question

For descriptive statistics, there is no research question as such. However, Linda is interested in the frequencies or percentages of research participants in each category of her variables.

1. What are the percentages of men and women in the sample?
2. What are the frequencies associated with each ethnic status category?
3. How many participants are in each of the 10 job categories?

Conducting Frequencies to Describe Qualitative Variables

To compute frequencies for the gender, ethnicity, and occupational variables, follow these steps:

1. Click **Analyze**, click **Descriptive Statistics**, then click **Frequencies**. When you do this, you will see the Frequencies dialog box as shown in Figure 113.

Figure 113. The Frequencies dialog box.

2. Hold down the Ctrl key, and click **ethnic**, **gender**, and **job** to select them, then click ▸ to place them in the Variable(s) box.
3. Click **Statistics**. You will see the Frequencies: Statistics dialog box, as shown in Figure 114.

Figure 114. The Frequencies: Statistics dialog box.

4. Under the Central Tendency area, click **Mode**.
5. Click **Continue**.
6. Click **OK**.

Selected SPSS Output for Frequencies

The output for the analysis is shown in Figure 115 (at the top of page 115). The output initially presents the mode for each of the three variables. The tables labeled Ethnic Status, Gender of the Participant, and Job Category show the frequencies (counts) of these variables. In addition, the tables show the percentage of participants in each category. Because the variables are qualitative, the column labeled Cumulative Percent is not meaningful.

Statistics

		Gender of Participant	Ethnic Status	Job Category
N	Valid	120	120	120
	Missing	0	0	0
Mode		2	4	7

Gender of Participant

		Frequency	Percent	Valid Percent	Cumulative Percent
Valid	Men	58	48.3	48.3	48.3
	Women	62	51.7	51.7	100.0
	Total	120	100.0	100.0	

Ethnic Status

		Frequency	Percent	Valid Percent	Cumulative Percent
Valid	Black	20	16.7	16.7	16.7
	Hispanic	24	20.0	20.0	36.7
	Asian	17	14.2	14.2	50.8
	White	51	42.5	42.5	93.3
	Other	8	6.7	6.7	100.0
	Total	120	100.0	100.0	

Job Category

		Frequency	Percent	Valid Percent	Cumulative Percent
Valid	Clerical	13	10.8	10.8	10.8
	Management	5	4.2	4.2	15.0
	Maintenance	7	5.8	5.8	20.8
	Academic	15	12.5	12.5	33.3
	Professional	13	10.8	10.8	44.2
	Self-Employed	13	10.8	10.8	55.0
	Medical	20	16.7	16.7	71.7
	Skilled	13	10.8	10.8	82.5
	Military	12	10.0	10.0	92.5
	Unemployed	9	7.5	7.5	100.0
	Total	120	100.0	100.0	

Figure 115. Summary statistics for the frequencies analysis.

Using SPSS Graphs to Display the Results

Bar charts are often used to display the results of categorical or qualitative variables. Bar charts allow for the visual representation of the frequencies in each category and can be used to display results of variables with a relatively large number of categories. An alternative to the bar chart is the pie chart. Pie charts also present the frequencies or percentages in each category but in a form that can be edited to highlight specific categories. Pie charts are more useful for displaying results of variables that have relatively few categories, in that pie charts become cluttered and difficult to read if variables have many categories.

Creating a Bar Chart

To create a bar chart, follow these steps:

1. Click **Analyze**, click **Descriptive Statistics**, then click **Frequencies**.
2. Click **Reset** to clear the dialog box.
3. Click **job**, then click ► to place it in the Variable(s) box
4. Click **Charts**. You will see the Frequencies: Charts dialog box, as shown in Figure 116 (at the top of page 116).

Figure 116. The Frequencies: Charts dialog box.

5. Click **Bar charts**.
6. Click **Continue**.
7. Click **OK**.

To make the chart more descriptive, we added bar labels to indicate the number of individuals in a specific category. To add bar labels, follow these steps:

1. Double-click on the chart to select it for editing and maximize the chart window.
2. Click **Format**, then click **Bar Label Styles**.
3. Select **Framed**.
4. Click **Apply All**.
5. Click **Close**.

The edited chart appears in Figure 117.

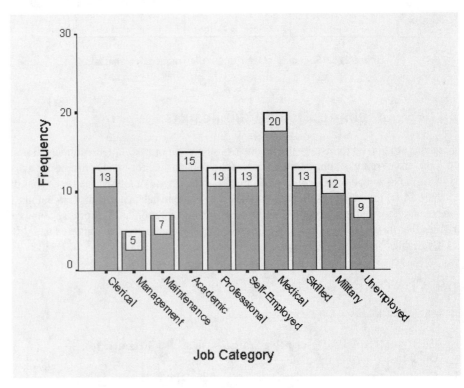

Figure 117. Number of participants in each job category.

We edited the chart to conform to APA standards by centering the axes. In addition, you may want to order the categories on your chart by clicking on the **Series ... Display** option. In the Categories box, you can rearrange your categories by moving them back and forth between the Display and Omit boxes until they are in the desired order (perhaps in descending frequencies) in the Display box.

Creating a Pie Chart

To create a pie chart for the ethnicity variable, follow these steps:

1. Click **Graphs**, then click **Pie**.
2. Click **Summaries for Groups of Cases**.
3. Click **Define**. You will see the Define Pie: Summaries for Groups of Cases dialog box in Figure 118.

Figure 118. The Define Pie: Summaries for Groups of Cases dialog box.

4. Highlight **ethnic** and click ▶ to move it to the Define Slices by box.
5. Click **OK**.

To add percentages to the pie slices, follow these steps:

1. Double-click on the chart to select it for editing and maximize the chart window.
2. Click **Chart**, then click **Options**.
3. In the Pie Chart Options dialog box, click next to **Percents** in the Labels box.
4. Click **Format**.
5. Click on the down arrow next to Position and select **Numbers inside, text outside**.
6. Click **Continue**.
7. Click **OK**. You can see the edited graph in Figure 119 (at the top of page 118).

An APA Participants Section

The sample consisted of 120 participants, approximately half of whom were women ($\underline{N} = 62$), while the rest were men ($\underline{N} = 58$). Figure 119 shows the frequencies and percentages for ethnic status. Approximately 42 percent of the participants were White, and the remaining participants were relatively evenly distributed across Blacks (17%), Hispanics (20%), Asians (14%), and others (7%).

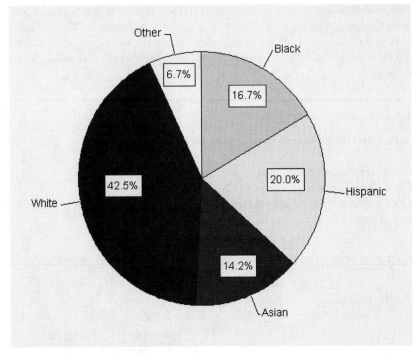

Figure 119. Percentage of participants in each ethnic group.

Table 10 reports the frequencies and percentages associated with the job categories. The most frequently occurring job category was the medical profession, and the least common job category was management.

Table 10

Frequencies and Percentages of Job Categories

Job categories	Frequency	Percentage
Medical	20	16.7
Academic	15	12.5
Self-Employed	13	10.8
Skilled labor	13	10.8
Clerical	13	10.8
Professional	13	10.8
Military	12	10.0
Unemployed	9	7.5
Maintenance	7	5.8
Management	5	4.2

Exercises

Exercises 1 through 4 are based on the following research problem. The data for these exercises can be found in the data file named *Lesson 19 Exercise File 1*.

Ann wants to describe the demographic characteristics of a sample of 25 individuals who completed a large-scale survey. She has demographic data on the participants' gender (two categories), educational level (four categories), marital status (three categories), and community population size (eight categories).

1. Conduct a frequency analysis on the gender and marital status variables. From the output, identify the following:
   a. percent of men
   b. mode for marital status
   c. frequency of divorced people in the sample
2. Create a frequency table to summarize the data on the educational level variable.
3. Create a bar chart to summarize the data from the community population variable.
4. Write a participants section describing the participants in Ann's sample.

Exercises 5 through 7 are based on the following research problem. The data for these exercises can be found in the data file named *Lesson 19 Exercise File 2*.

Julie asks 50 men and 50 women to indicate what type of books they typically read for pleasure. She codes the responses into 10 categories: drama, mysteries, romance, historical nonfiction, travel books, children's books, poetry, autobiographies, political science, and local interest books. She also asks the participants how many books they read in a month. She categorizes their responses into four categories: nonreaders (no books a month), light readers (1–2 books a month), moderate readers (3–5 books a month), and heavy readers (more than 5 books a month). Julie's SPSS data file contains two variables: book, a 10-category variable for types of books read, and reader, a four-category variable indicating the number of books read per month.

5. Create a table to summarize the types of books that people report reading.
6. Create a pie chart to describe how many books per month Julie's sample reads.
7. Write a participants section describing your results on the three variables.

Lesson 20

Univariate Descriptive Statistics for Quantitative Variables

The goal of univariate descriptive statistics is to portray accurately and succinctly data from a variable. When there are only a few values for a quantitative variable (e.g., a variable with a 4-point response scale), we can describe its results very accurately by presenting all its values and their relative frequencies. The relative frequency of a value is the number of times it occurs divided by the total frequency across all values. If a quantitative variable has many values, however, it would be impractical to present all values of the variable and their relative frequencies. Rather, it would be easier to present grouped values and their relative frequencies. The relative frequencies for values or grouped values can be presented in a table or a graph.

Graphical and tabular presentations are not always possible in journals because of space limitations. Thus, data are often summarized using statistical indices. If it were important for readers of an article to understand the distribution of a variable, it would be desirable, nevertheless, to present its distribution using a graph. In general, descriptive statistical indices are presented in the text of a manuscript if there are relatively few variables. If there are a large number of variables to be described, statistical indices for these variables can be presented in a table.

In this lesson, we will focus on two SPSS procedures, Explore and Descriptives, to describe the results of quantitative variables using statistical indices, including measures of central tendency, variability, skewness, and kurtosis. We also will demonstrate how to create charts that visually represent the distributions of variables, including stem-and-leaf plots, boxplots, error bar charts, and histograms. Finally, we will illustrate how to convert raw scores on a variable to z-scores and percentile ranks. Percentile ranks will be computed under conditions when we can and cannot assume that raw scores are normally distributed.

Applying Descriptives to Quantitative Variables

We present applications for describing the results for two types of variables:

- Quantitative variables with few values
- Quantitative variables with many values

We present two additional applications:

- Describing the results on quantitative variables within levels of a qualitative variable
- Computing z-scores and percentile ranks on quantitative variables

Quantitative Variables with Few Values

Joanne has 90 college students complete a four-item Likert scale that assesses study motivation in school. Each item has scores that range from 1 (not at all like me) to 5 (very much like me). Joanne is interested in describing the students' responses. Because there are only a few values for each variable, Joanne will create relative frequency tables to summarize her data.

Quantitative Variables with Many Values

Joanne also collected information on each student's college GPA and high school GPA. Joanne is interested in describing the typical high school and college GPAs of her research participants. To summarize these variables, she will compute various statistical indices to look at the distributions. She also will create graphs to visually display the distributions.

Quantitative Variables within Levels of a Qualitative Variable

Joanne collected information about each student's gender (a qualitative variable). She wants to describe the typical high school and college GPAs (quantitative variables) for men and women separately. To summarize these GPA variables, she will compute statistical indices to assess the characteristics of the GPA distributions for men and for women. Alternatively, she could create graphs that visually display differences in the distributions for men and women students.

Computing Z-Scores and Percentile Ranks on a Quantitative Variables

Joanne is interested in determining where GPA scores for particular individuals lie in relation to all GPA scores. She will convert her GPA scores to z-scores and then to percentile ranks to assess the relative position of these GPA scores. Transforming the z-scores to percentile ranks assumes that the z-scores (and the GPA scores) are normally distributed. In contrast, she could convert her GPA scores directly to percentile ranks and would not have to assume that the GPA scores are normally distributed.

Understanding the Statistics

Descriptive statistics involves summarizing distributions of scores by developing tabular or graphical presentations and computing descriptive statistical indices. You can also describe individual scores within a distribution by converting these scores to percentile ranks.

A frequency distribution gives the frequencies associated with all values of a variable. A simple frequency distribution table can be used to delineate the results of a quantitative variable when it has only a few values. For a variable with many levels, the values are grouped together into intervals of values to create a grouped frequency table. There is no specific interval length that would be appropriate for all grouped frequency tables, but the interval length should be wide enough to summarize the results adequately, yet narrow enough to present the distribution accurately. The current version of SPSS does not provide an easy way to generate a grouped frequency table.

SPSS does allow us to display graphically simple and grouped frequency distributions. Bar charts are useful for depicting the frequencies associated with all values of a variable. In contrast, histograms present frequencies for values grouped into intervals. Stem-and-leaf plots also are used to display graphically a distribution of a quantitative variable. Each score on a variable is divided into two parts, the stem and the leaf. The stem gives the leading digits and the leaf shows the trailing digits. For example, for a score of 40, the stem of 4 represents the 10s place and the leaf of 0 represents the units place.

The distribution of a quantitative variable can also be summarized using statistical indices. Measures of central tendency include the mean, the arithmetic average of a set of scores; the median, the middle value of ranked scores; and the mode, the most frequently occurring score. Indices of variability can also be computed to describe a distribution's variability around a measure of central tendency or, more generally, the spread of scores on a variable. The most common measures of variability are the variance and its square-rooted form, the standard deviation. Skewness reflects the degree to which a variable's scores fall at one or the other ends of the variable's scale. If the majority of the scores fall at the high end of the scale, with relatively few scores at the low end, the distribution is negatively skewed. Conversely, if most scores fall at the low end of the scale, with relatively few scores at the high end, the distribution is positively skewed. The kurtosis of a variable reflects the thickness of the tail regions (relative frequency of scores in both extremes) of a distribution.

Measures of central tendency and variability can also be displayed graphically. With error bar charts, means and standard deviations can be displayed for each quantitative variable. An alternative chart that presents a richer picture is a boxplot. With a boxplot, the line in the middle of a box represents the median score on that variable. The length of the box in the boxplot is the interquartile range or in other words, the bottom and top of the box represent the 25th and 75th percentiles, respectively. Outliers are scores that fall between 1.5 and 3 box lengths, while extreme scores are scores that fall more than 3 box lengths from the lower or upper edge of the box. The whiskers, or the lines at the top and the bottom of the plot that originate from the box, represent the smallest and largest values that are not outliers or extreme scores.

We can also describe where individual scores fall with respect to all scores in a distribution. A score may be converted to a percentile rank, the percent of individuals who have scores that fall at or below the score of interest. Percentile ranks can be computed using one of two methods. One method requires that raw scores first be converted to z-scores and then to percentile ranks based on the normal distribution. This method assumes that the raw scores are normally distributed. The second method requires the computation of percentile ranks directly from raw scores and makes no assumptions about the distribution of raw scores.

The Data Set

The data set for this lesson includes the high school and college GPA data described in the four examples. They are in the data file named *Lesson 20 Data File 1* on the student disk. The variables are presented in Table 11.

Table 11
Variables in Lesson 20 Data File 1

Variables	Definition
hsgpa	High school GPA scores
collgpa	College GPA scores
gender	1 = Men
	2 = Women

Conducting Descriptive Statistics Using the Explore Procedure

Now we will compute statistical indices for a single quantitative variable and for a quantitative variable within levels of a qualitative variable and convert a set of scores to z-scores and percentile ranks.

Computing Descriptive Statistics

To compute descriptive statistics for high school and college GPA scores across the entire sample, follow these steps:

1. Click **Analyze**, click **Descriptive Statistics**, then click **Explore**. You will see the Explore dialog box in Figure 120.

Figure 120. The Explore dialog box.

2. Hold down the Ctrl key, and click **hsgpa** and **collgpa**, then click ▸ to place them in the **Dependent List** box.
3. In the Display box, click **Statistics**.
4. Click the **Statistics** button. You will see the Explore: Statistics dialog box as shown in Figure 121.

Figure 121. The Explore: Statistics dialog box.

5. Be sure **Descriptives** is checked.
6. Click **Continue**.
7. Click **OK**.

Selected SPSS Output for Descriptive Statistics

Your output should have descriptive statistics for both high school and college GPA scores, although we show you only the descriptive statistics for college GPA scores in Figure 122.

Descriptives

			Statistic	Std. Error
College GPA Scores	Mean		2.4871	4.751E-02
	95% Confidence Interval for Mean	Lower Bound	2.3927	
		Upper Bound	2.5815	
	5% Trimmed Mean		2.4930	
	Median		2.5650	
	Variance		.203	
	Std. Deviation		.4507	
	Minimum		1.17	
	Maximum		3.45	
	Range		2.28	
	Interquartile Range		.6200	
	Skewness		-.235	.254
	Kurtosis		.012	.503

Figure 122. Descriptive statistics for college GPA scores.

Computing Descriptive Statistics for a Quantitative Variable within Levels of a Qualitative Variable

To compute descriptive statistics for college and high school GPA scores separately for men and women, follow these steps:

1. Click **Analyze**, click **Descriptive Statistics**, then click **Explore**.
2. Click **Reset** to clear the dialog box.
3. Hold down the Ctrl key, and click **collgpa** and **hsgpa** to highlight them. Then click ▶ to place them in the Dependent List box.
4. Click **gender**, then click ▶ to place it in the **Factor List** box.
5. In the Display box, click **Statistics**.
6. Click the **Statistics** button.
7. Be sure **Descriptives** is checked.
8. Click **Continue**.
9. Click **OK**.

Selected SPSS Output

We present only the descriptive statistics for the college GPA scores for men and for women in Figure 123 (at the top of page 125).

Converting Scores to Z-Scores and Percentile Ranks Not Assuming Normality

To convert the college GPA scores to percentile ranks without assuming they are normally distributed, follow these steps:

1. Click **Transform**, and click **Rank Cases**. You will see the Rank Cases dialog box in Figure 124 (on page 125).
2. Click **collgpa**, then click ▶ to place it in the Variable(s) text box.

Descriptives

Gender				Statistic	Std. Error
College GPA Scores	Men	Mean		2.2533	5.887E-02
		95% Confidence Interval for Mean	Lower Bound	2.1347	
			Upper Bound	2.3718	
		5% Trimmed Mean		2.2679	
		Median		2.2950	
		Variance		.159	
		Std. Deviation		.3993	
		Minimum		1.17	
		Maximum		2.94	
		Range		1.77	
		Interquartile Range		.5975	
		Skewness		-.446	.350
		Kurtosis		-.135	.688
	Women	Mean		2.7316	5.517E-02
		95% Confidence Interval for Mean	Lower Bound	2.6203	
			Upper Bound	2.8429	
		5% Trimmed Mean		2.7307	
		Median		2.6800	
		Variance		.134	
		Std. Deviation		.3660	
		Minimum		2.05	
		Maximum		3.45	
		Range		1.40	
		Interquartile Range		.5775	
		Skewness		.051	.357
		Kurtosis		-.744	.702

Figure 123. Descriptive statistics for college GPA scores for men and for women.

Figure 124. The Rank Cases dialog box.

3. Click **Rank Types**. You will see the Rank Cases: Types dialog box in Figure 125.

Figure 125. The Rank Cases: Types dialog box.

4. Be sure **Rank** is checked.
5. Click **Continue**.
6. Click **OK** and return to the Data Editor.
7. Click **Transform**, and click **Compute**.
8. In the Target Variable text box, type **rcollgpa**.
9. In the Numeric Expression text box, type **(rcollgpa / 90) * 100**. The divisor in the expression is equal to the number of cases in the data set.
10. Click **OK**.

Selected SPSS Output

The percentile ranks of the college GPA scores for the first 10 cases are shown in Figure 126 in the column labeled rcollgpa. To compute percentile ranks for a set of scores, we divided the ranks of scores by the number of possible ranks and then multiply by 100 to obtain percentages. In our example, we have 90 cases. Consequently, to compute percentile ranks, we divided the ranks of the scores by 90 and multiplied by 100.

	hsgpa	collgpa	gender	rcollgpa
1	4.00	1.75	1	6.111
2	1.87	1.48	1	2.222
3	3.85	2.65	2	65.556
4	1.31	2.57	2	51.667
5	2.62	2.93	2	82.778
6	1.91	2.59	2	55.000
7	3.00	2.61	2	57.778
8	2.95	2.67	2	68.333
9	2.92	2.64	2	62.778
10	2.74	3.03	2	88.333

Figure 126. Percentile ranks for college GPA of first 10 cases, not assuming that GPA is normally distributed.

Converting Scores to Z-Scores and Percentile Ranks Assuming Normality

We will now convert scores to z-scores and then create percentile ranks from z-scores, assuming that the scores are normally distributed. To convert the college GPA scores to z-scores, follow these steps:

1. Click **Analyze**, click **Descriptive Statistics**, then click **Descriptives**.
2. In the Descriptives dialog box, click **collgpa**, and click ▸ to move it to the Variable(s) text box.
3. Click **Save standardized values as variables**.
4. Click **OK**.

To create percentile ranks for the z-scored college GPA scores, return to the Data Editor and follow these steps:

1. Click **Transform**, and click **Compute**.
2. Type **gparank** in the Target Variable text box.
3. In the Functions box, scroll down until you find an expression that says **CDF.Normal (q,mean,stddev)**.

4. Highlight the expression, and click ▲ to move it to the Numeric Expression text box.
5. Click **zcollgpa**, and click ▶ to place it in the Numeric Expression text box in place of the first question mark (q).
6. Replace the second question mark (mean) with **0** and the third question mark (std-dev) with **1**. Type * **100** after CDF.Normal(zcollgpa,0,1). Figure 127 shows the numeric expression used to create the percentile ranks.

Figure 127. Compute Variable dialog box for creating percentile ranks.

7. Click **OK**.
8. Click **Window**, and click **Lesson 20 Data File 1** to return to the Data Editor where you can see your new variable, gparank.

The percentile ranks obtained when we made no assumptions about the distribution are not necessarily the same percentile ranks we obtained when we assumed the scores were normally distributed. Table 12 shows the scores and percentile ranks for the first 10 cases in the data set, assuming and not assuming a normal distribution.

Table 12

Percentile Ranks for First Ten College GPA Scores, Not Assuming and Assuming Normality

College GPA	Percentile ranks not assuming normality	Percentile ranks assuming normality
1.75	06	05
1.48	02	01
2.65	66	64
2.57	52	57
2.93	83	84
2.59	55	59
2.61	58	61
2.67	68	66
2.64	63	63
3.03	88	89

You can see that the percentile ranks associated with various college GPAs are not identical. Variables with distributions that are substantially nonnormal will have greater discrepancies between percentile ranks computed using the two methods, and variables with relatively normal distributions will yield similar percentile ranks.

Using SPSS Graphs to Display the Results

Three types of charts are frequently used to display the distribution of scores on a single quantitative variable: the histogram, the stem-and-leaf plot, and the boxplot.

Creating a Histogram

To create a histogram of the college GPA scores, conduct the following steps.

1. Click **Graphs**, then click **Histogram**.
2. Click **collgpa**, then click ▸ to move the variable to the Variable text box.
3. Click **Display normal curve**.
4. Click **OK**. The graph is shown in Figure 128.

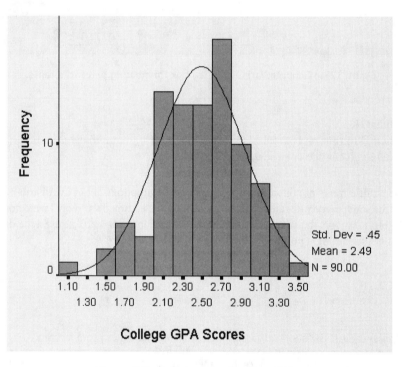

Figure 128. A histogram of college GPAs.

The histogram in Figure 128 has been edited. We changed the scale and the labels on the X and Y axes. In addition, we centered the labels on both axes.

In the social sciences, many researchers think of their quantitative variables as being normally distributed. However, the variables are almost never normally distributed. By imposing the normal curve on the histogram, we can assess visually the degree to which college GPA scores approximate a normal distribution.

Creating a Stem-and-Leaf Plot

A stem-and-leaf plot, like the histogram, effectively communicates the distribution of a variable that has many possible values.

To create a stem-and-leaf plot for the high school GPA scores, follow these steps:

1. Click **Analyze**, click **Descriptive Statistics**, then click **Explore**.
2. Click **Reset** to clear the dialog box.
3. In the Explore dialog box, click **hsgpa**, then click ► to move it to the Dependent List box.
4. In the Display box, click **Plots**.
5. Click the **Plots** button. You will see the Explore: Plots dialog box in Figure 129.

Figure 129. Explore: Plots dialog box.

6. Click the **Stem-and-leaf** box if it does not contain a check.
7. Under Boxplots, click **None**.
8. Click **Continue**.
9. Click **OK**. You can see the stem-and-leaf chart in Figure 130.

High School GPA Scores

High School GPA Scores Stem-and-Leaf Plot

```
Frequency     Stem &  Leaf

   14.00        1 .   00111122333334
   11.00        1 .   56677888999
   15.00        2 .   000000111222234
   22.00        2 .   5555555566666667789999
   11.00        3 .   00001111223
    9.00        3 .   555778889
    8.00        4 .   00000000

Stem width:      1.00
Each leaf:       1 case(s)
```

Figure 130. A stem-and-leaf plot of high school GPA scores.

The stems in the stem-and-leaf plot are the leading digits of each score, and the leaves are the trailing digits of each score. In Figure 130 the first row of the stem-and-leaf plot finds the following digits: 1• 00111122333334. The numeral displayed before the dot is the stem, and the numerals after the dot are the leaves. At the bottom of the plot, SPSS reports the stem width to be 1.0, indicating that the value of the stems represents the units place. Attaching the first leaf of 0 to the stem of 1 produces the score of 1.0; attaching the leaf of 1 to the stem of 1 yields scores of 1.1; and so on. Consequently, the scores displayed in the first row are two 1.0s, four 1.1s, two 1.2s, five 1.3s, and one 1.4. Looking at the data, you can see that there are two values (1.00 and 1.06) summarized as 1.0s and four scores (1.12, 1.14, 1.17, and 1.19) summarized as 1.1s, and so on.

Creating a Boxplot for Different Levels of a Qualitative Variable

An alternative graph that would present a richer picture would be a boxplot. To create a boxplot of the distributions of the college GPA scores by gender, follow these steps:

1. Click **Graphs**, then click **Boxplot**. You will see the Boxplot dialog box in Figure 131.

Figure 131. The Boxplot dialog box.

2. Click **Simple**, then click **Summaries for groups of cases**.
3. Click **Define**. You will see the Define Simple Boxplot: Summaries dialog box in Figure 132.

Figure 132. The Define Simple Boxplot: Summaries dialog box.

4. In the Define Simple Boxplot: Summaries dialog box, click **collgpa**, and click the top ► to move it to the Variable box.
5. Click **gender**, and click the middle ► to move it to the Category Axis box.
6. Click **OK**. The edited graph appears as shown in Figure 133 (at the top of page 131).

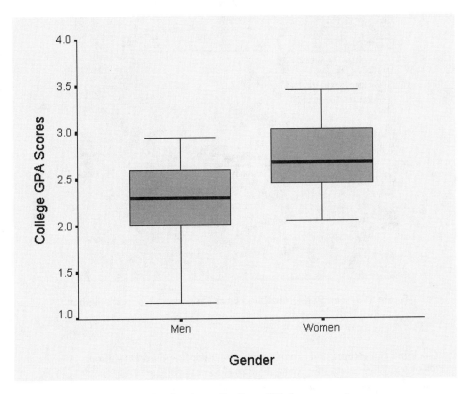

Figure 133. Distributions of college GPA for men and women.

Creating Error Bar Charts

A simple error bar chart involves displaying the means and standard deviations for different variables. To create an error bar chart for high school and college GPA scores by gender, follow these steps:

1. Click **Graphs**, then click **Error Bar**. You will see the Error Bar dialog box in Figure 134.

Figure 134. The Error Bar dialog box.

2. Click **Clustered**, then click **Summaries of Separate Variables**.
3. Click **Define**. You will see the Define Clustered Error Bar: Summaries dialog box in Figure 135 (at the top of page 132).
4. Hold down the Ctrl key and click **hsgpa** and **collgpa**. Click the top ▶ to move them to the Variables box.
5. Click **gender**, and click the second ▶ to move it to the Category Axis box.

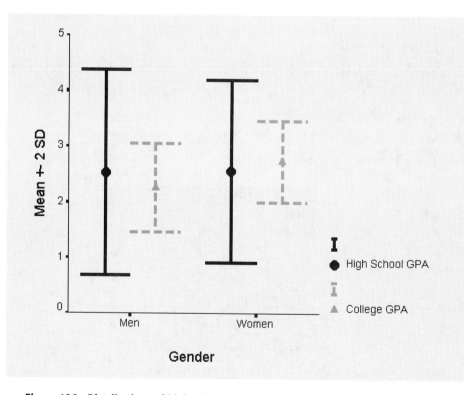

Figure 135. The Define Clustered Error Bar Summaries ... dialog box.

6. Click the Bars Represent down arrow, and click Standard Deviation.
7. The Multiplier box will now be available. Set the Multiplier at **2**.
8. Click **OK**. The chart is shown in Figure 136.

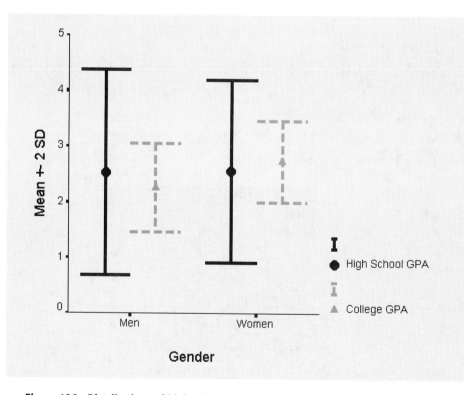

Figure 136. Distributions of high school and college GPA scores for men and women.

Other options could be chosen in the Bars Represent and Multiplier boxes. We chose standard deviation rather than standard error because we are interested in describing the data, not making inferences about it. Also, by setting the multiplier to 2, we can look at two standard deviations around each mean. We used two standard deviations because the error bars would encompass approximately 95% of the scores if they are normally distributed.

Creating Figures in APA Format

In results sections of research papers, figures can provide a visual representation of complex data or statistical results. When presenting figures in a manuscript, describe the figure and its most important features in the text of a results section. The text highlights but does not duplicate the information in the figures.

Here are some guidelines for creating figures in APA format. See the *Publication Manual of the American Psychological Association* (1994) for more detailed information.

1. Figure Numbers:
   - Number all figures consecutively using Arabic numbers (e.g., Figure 1.).
   - Refer to figures in the text by their numbers.
   - Underline the figure number (e.g., <u>Figure 1</u>.).
2. Figure Captions:
   - Figure captions should be brief and explain the content.
   - Capitalize only the first letter of the caption.
   - Do not underline the caption.
3. Axes and Legends:
   - Center the labels on the axes of the graphs.
   - Capitalize the first letter of all important words on the axis labels and in the title of the legend.
   - Capitalize the first letter of the first word of annotations or legend entries.
4. Statistical Symbols:
   - In the caption and in the graph's annotations and legends, underline all statistical symbols except Greek symbols.
5. Footnotes:
   - Content footnotes amplify information in the figure and should communicate a single idea.

An APA Participants Section

We do not present results for the percentile rank analyses in the following participants section because they are not typically reported in manuscripts.

The participants were 46 men and 44 women college students. Table 13 presents the means and standard deviations of high school and college GPAs by gender. The means and standard deviations of high school GPAs were relatively similar for men and for women. However, on the average, women had higher college GPAs than men did.

Table 13

Means and Standard Deviations for College and High School GPA Scores of Each Gender

	Men		Women	
	M	*SD*	*M*	*SD*
High school GPA	2.53	.92	2.55	.82
College GPA	2.25	.40	2.73	.37

Creating Tables in APA Format

In results sections, tables can provide a useful summary of complex data or statistical results. Describe the table and its most important features in the text of your manuscript. The text supplements, not duplicates, the information in the tables.

Here are some guidelines for creating tables in APA format. See the *Publication Manual of the American Psychological Association* (1994) for more detailed information about creating tables.

1. Table Numbers:
   - Number all tables in a document consecutively using Arabic numbers.
   - Refer to tables in the text by their numbers.
   - Do not underline the table number itself (e.g., Table 1).
2. Table Titles:
   - Table titles should be brief and explain the table's content.
   - Capitalize the first letter of each important word in the title.
   - Underline the title of the table. (*Note that words that are underlined in a manuscript will appear in italics when typeset for publication—e.g., the table titles in this book are set in italic.*)
3. Table Columns and Headings:
   - The columns of a table present descriptions of the data (e.g., statistical indices).
   - Provide a heading for each column.
   - Capitalize the first word of headings.
   - Use only horizontal lines to divide the table. Do not use vertical lines to divide columns.
   - Set off headings and major sections of the table with a horizontal line.
4. Abbreviations and Symbols:
   - Abbreviations may be used for statistical indices (e.g., $\underline{M}$ for mean and $\underline{SD}$ for standard deviation).
   - Underline all statistical symbols except Greek symbols.
5. Notes and Footnotes:
   - Notes are used to provide general information, such as the sample size or the significance level obtained for multiple tests (e.g., $\underline{p} < .05$). Notes may be general, specific, or probability notes, and they are presented at the bottom of the table.
   - General notes provide information about the table as a whole and are designated by the word *Note*.
   - Footnotes refer to a specific column, row, or individual entry in the table and are designated with superscripted lowercase letters.
   - Probability notes indicate the level of significance and are designated with asterisks (e.g., $*\underline{p} < .05$ or $**\underline{p} < .001$).

Exercises

The data for the Exercises 1 through 5 are in the data set named *Lesson 20 Exercise File 1* on the Student Disk. The data are from the following research problem.

David collects anxiety scores from 15 college students who visit the university health center during finals week.

1. Compute descriptive statistics on the anxiety scores. From the output, identify the following:
   a. skewness
   b. mean
   c. standard deviation
   d. kurtosis
2. Compute percentile ranks on the anxiety scores assuming that the distribution of scores is normal. What are the scores associated with the percentile ranks of 12, 27, 38, 73, and 88?

3. What are the percentile ranks associated with these scores if you don't assume the distribution is normal?
4. Create a histogram to show the distribution of the anxiety scores. Edit the graph so that most of the normal curve is visible and there are 15 intervals.
5. Based on the histogram and the descriptive statistics, which percentile rank method should you use?

The data for the Exercises 6 through 8 are in the data set named *Lesson 20 Exercise File 2* on the Student Disk. The data are from the following research problem.

Michelle collects questionnaire data from 40 college students to assess whether they have a positive attitude toward political campaigns. She asks them to rate five statements about campaigns on a 5-point Likert scale (1 = disagree to 5 = agree). She also has information on respondents' political party affiliation (politic with 1 = Republican and 2 = Democrat). Table 14 shows the items on the scale.

Table 14

Political Campaign Attitude Items

Variables	Definition
att1	Use of inappropriate tactics in campaign strategies.
att2	Candidates address the issues.
att3	Accurate presentation of candidate's political agenda.
att4	Focus on issues relevant to the average citizen.
att5	Honesty in making campaign promises.

6. Compute total attitude scores from the scores for the five-attitudinal items. The total attitude scores should reflect whether students have a general positive attitude toward campaigning.
7. Compute means on the total attitude scores for the two political parties.
8. Create boxplots showing the distributions of the total attitude scores for the two political parties.

T Test Procedures

Unit 6 examines techniques that use a *t* test to assess hypotheses involving a single mean or differences between two means. The *t* test can be applied to address research questions for designs that involve a single sample, related samples, or independent samples.

Lesson 21 introduces a one-sample *t* test that evaluates whether a mean for a population is equal to a hypothesized test value based on the research hypothesis. Lesson 22 presents a paired-samples *t* test that assesses whether the mean difference between paired observations is significantly different from zero. Then, Lesson 23 deals with an independent-samples *t* test that evaluates whether means for two independent groups are significantly different from each other.

One-Sample T Test

A one-sample *t* test evaluates whether the mean on a test variable is significantly different from a constant, called a test value by SPSS. Each case must have a score on one variable, the test variable.

A major decision in using the one-sample *t* test is in choosing the test value. This test value typically represents a neutral point. Individuals who score higher than the neutral point are given one label, and those who score lower are given a different label. Those who fall exactly on the neutral point are given neither label.

Applying the One-Sample T Test

Various applications of the one-sample *t* test are distinguished by their methods of choosing the test value. The test value may be

- the midpoint on the test variable
- the average value of the test variable based on past research
- the chance level of performance on the test variable

The following are examples for each of the three types of applications.

Test Value as Midpoint of the Test Variable

Dan wants to determine whether students have a negative or a positive view toward current world leaders. He develops the World Leader Scale (WLS), which includes the names of 15 world leaders. He asks 100 students to identify the country that each leader governs and to rate the leader on a scale from 0 to 10, where 0 = a totally worthless leader, 5 = neither a worthless nor a worthy leader, and 10 = a totally worthy leader. A WLS score for a student is the mean rating for the leaders whose countries were correctly identified. Dan conducts a one-sample t test on the 100 WLS scores to determine if the population mean is significantly different from 5. The test value of 5 was chosen because a value less than 5 implies a negative view of world leaders, a score greater than 5 implies a positive view of world leaders, and a value of 5 implies neither a negative nor a positive view of world leaders. Dan's data file for analyzing the results contains 100 cases, one for each student, and one test variable, the WLS scores.

Test Value as the Average Value Based on Past Research

Janet is interested in determining if male adolescents who do not engage in sports are more depressed than the average male adolescent. To test this hypothesis, she obtains Kansas University Depression Inventory (KUDI) scores from 30 adolescent boys who have indicated on a questionnaire that they do not engage in sports outside of school gym classes. The KUDI is a depression measure that was standardized to have a mean of 50 for male adolescents. Janet conducts a one-sample t test on the 30 KUDI scores to determine if the population mean is different from 50. The test value of 50 was chosen because a value less than 50 implies less depression than a typical male adolescent, a value greater than 50 implies more depression than a typical male adolescent, and a value of 50 implies neither less nor more depression than a typical male adolescent. Janet's SPSS data file for analyzing the results contains 30 cases, one for each adolescent, and one test variable, the KUDI scores.

Test Value as the Chance Level of Performance

Lena believes that the Matching Figures Test (MFT), a visual identification task, is too difficult for children who are younger than 5 years old. The MFT consists of 24 items. For each item, a child is shown a picture for two seconds. Five seconds later, the child is asked to select the same picture from a set of three pictures. Lena collects MFT scores on 75 four-year-olds and conducts a one-sample t test on these scores to determine if the population mean is different from chance level. Because the likelihood of a child getting any item correct is one in three, and a child has 24 opportunities to obtain a correct answer, chance level on the MFT is 8 (1/3 times 24). A score less than the test value of 8 implies that 4-year-olds do worse than chance; a score greater than 8 implies that 4-year-olds do better than chance; and a value of 8 implies a score neither below nor above chance level. Lena's SPSS data file for analyzing the results contains 75 cases, one for each child, and one test variable, the MFT scores.

Understanding the One-Sample T Test

The following are the assumptions underlying the one-sample *t* test and an associated effect size statistic.

Assumptions Underlying a One-Sample T Test

There are two assumptions underlying a one-sample *t* test.

Assumption 1: The Test Variable Is Normally Distributed in the Population

With a moderate or larger sample size, the assumption may be violated, and the test will still yield fairly accurate results. Larger sample sizes are required to produce relatively valid results if the population distribution is substantially nonnormal. In most circumstances, a sample size of 30 should be sufficient to yield fairly accurate *p*-values.

Assumption 2: The Cases Represent a Random Sample from the Population, and the Scores on the Test Variable Are Independent of Each Other

The one-sample *t* test will yield an inaccurate *p*-value if the assumption of independence is violated.

Computing an Effect Size Statistic

SPSS supplies all the information necessary to compute an effect size, d, as shown in the following equation:

$$d = \frac{Mean\ Difference}{SD}$$

where the mean difference and standard deviation are reported in the SPSS output. We can also compute d from the t value using the following equation:

$$d = \frac{t}{\sqrt{N}}$$

where N is the total sample size.

A d evaluates the degree that the mean scores on the test variable differ from the test value in standard deviation units. If d equals 0, the mean of the scores is equal to the test value. As d deviates from 0, the effect size becomes larger. Potentially, d can range in value from negative infinity to positive infinity. Regardless of sign, d values of .2, .5, and .8 traditionally represent small, medium, and large effect sizes, respectively.

The Data Set

The data set used in this lesson is named *Lesson 21 Data File 1* on the Student Disk. It represents data from the depression example presented earlier. The single variable in the data set is shown in Table 15.

Table 15
Variables in Lesson 21 Data File 1

Variables	Definition
kudi	Values on the KUDI represent depression scores. Based on previous research, we know that young male adolescents have a mean of 50 on the KUDI. Accordingly, 50 is the test value.

The Research Question

The research question reflects the difference between the mean of the test variable and the test value: Are male adolescents who do not engage in sports more or less depressed than the average male adolescent?

Conducting a One-Sample T Test

To conduct a one-sample t test, follow these steps:

1. Click **Analyze**, click **Compare Means**, then click **One-Sample T Test**. You will see the One-Sample T Test dialog box as shown in Figure 137 (at the top of page 140).
2. Click **kudi**, then click ► to move it to the Test Variable(s) box.
3. Type **50** in the Test Value text box.
4. Click **OK**.

Figure 137. The one-sample T test dialog box.

Selected SPSS Output for the One-Sample T Test

The results of the one-sample *t* test are shown in Figure 138.

One-Sample Statistics

	N	Mean	Std. Deviation	Std. Error Mean
KUDI	30	54.63	10.33	1.89

One-Sample Test

	Test Value = 50					
					95% Confidence Interval of the Difference	
	t	df	Sig. (2-tailed)	Mean Difference	Lower	Upper
KUDI	2.457	29	.020	4.63	.78	8.49

Figure 138. The results of the one-sample t test.

SPSS computes a mean and a standard deviation for the test variable. It also reports the mean difference value, which is the difference between the mean of the test variable and the hypothesized value. The difference between the mean KUDI value of 54.63 and the test value of 50 is 4.63. This difference indicates that male adolescents in the sample on the average were more depressed than the average adolescent.

Using SPSS Graphs to Display the Results

Although graphs are sometimes not included in the results section of a manuscript because of space limitations, graphs should be presented when possible since they convey a rich understanding of the data. Two graphs that can display the data for a one-sample *t* test are the histogram and the stem-and-leaf plot. Lesson 20 presents steps for creating both types of graphs. Figure 139 (at the top of page 141) is a histogram showing the distribution of KUDI scores for the 30 cases.

Figure 139. Distribution of KUDI scores for adolescent boys who do not participate in sports.

An APA Results Section

A one-sample t test was conducted on the KUDI scores to evaluate whether their mean was significantly different from 50, the accepted mean for male adolescents in general. The sample mean of 54.63 (SD = 10.33) was significantly different from 50, t (29) = 2.46, p = .020. The effect size d of .45 indicates a medium effect. Figure 139 shows the distribution of KUDI scores. The results support the conclusion that young male adolescents who do not engage in sports outside of school are somewhat more depressed than average.

Writing an APA Results Section

Here are guidelines for writing results sections for statistical tests that require no follow-up procedures, such as one-sample t tests, correlations, Mann-Whitney U test, or the binomial test.

1. Describe the test, the variables, and the purpose of the test. For example: "A one-sample t test was conducted on the KUDI scores to evaluate whether their mean was significantly different from 50, the accepted mean for male adolescents in general."

2. Report the results of the test.
   - Describe any decisions about test choice that were based on assumptions. For the one-sample t test, we have not considered alternative tests. However, in some future lessons we must choose between more than one test. For example, an independent-samples t test can be conducted based on equal or unequal variances. In writing a results section for an independent-samples t test, you may wish to justify the choice between these two tests.
   - Report the test value and significance level. For our one-sample t test example, it might be "t (29) = 2.46, p = .020." For p-values of .000, report them as "p < .001." Tell the reader whether the test is significant or not.

- Report statistics that allow the reader to make a judgment about the magnitude of the effect. For example, "For the one-sample t test, d = .45."
3. Report the relevant descriptive statistics, such as the mean and standard deviation for the one-sample t test.
   - For a simple analysis, the means and standard deviations can be reported in the text in the form: "M = 54.63, SD = 10.33."
   - Underline all non-Greek statistical symbols as we have done here.
4. Describe and summarize the general conclusions of the analysis. For example: "The results support the conclusion that male adolescents who do not engage in sports outside of school are somewhat more depressed than average."

Exercises

The data for Exercises 1 through 4 are in the data set named *Lesson 21 Exercise File 1* on the Student Data Disk. The data are from the following research problem:

John is interested in determining if a new teaching method, the Involvement Technique, is effective in teaching algebra to first graders. John randomly samples six first graders from all first graders within the Lawrence City School System and teaches them algebra using the new method. Next, the pupils complete an eight-item algebra test. Each item describes a problem and presents four possible answers to the problem. The scores on each item are 1 or 0 where 1 indicates a correct response, and 0 indicates a wrong response. The SPSS data file contains six cases, each with eight item scores for the algebra test.

1. Compute total scores for the algebra test from the item scores. A one-sample t test will be computed on the total scores.
2. What is the correct test value for this problem?
3. Conduct a one-sample t test on the total scores. On the output, identify the following:
   a. mean algebra score
   b. t test value
   c. p-value
4. Given the results of the children's performance on the test, what should John conclude? Write a results section based on your analyses.

The data for Exercises 5 and 6 are in the data set named *Lesson 21 Exercise File 2* on the Student Data Disk. The data are from the following research problem:

As part of a larger study, Dana collected data from 20 college students on their emotional responses to classical music. Students listened to two 30-second segments from "The Collection from the Best of Classical Music." After listening to a segment, students rated it on a scale from 1 to 10, with 1 indicating "Makes me very sad" and 10 indicating "Makes me very happy." Dana computes a total score for each student by summing the student's two ratings (hap_sad). Dana conducts a one-sample t test to evaluate whether classical music makes students sad or happy.

5. Conduct the analyses on these data and write a results section for it.
6. If you have not presented a graph in your results section, create a histogram for the hap_sad scores. Label the graph following APA guidelines.

Paired-Samples T Test

Each case must have scores on two variables for a paired-samples *t* test. The paired-samples *t* test procedure evaluates whether the mean of the difference between these two variables is significantly different from zero. It is applicable to two types of studies, repeated-measures and matched-subjects designs.

For a repeated-measures design a participant is assessed on two occasions or under two conditions on one measure. In the SPSS data file created to conduct a paired-samples *t* test, each participant has scores on two variables. The first variable represents the first score on the measure, and the second variable represents the second score. The primary question of interest is whether the mean difference between the scores on the two occasions (or under the two conditions) is significantly different from zero.

For a matched-subjects design, participants are paired, and each participant in the pair is assessed once on a measure. Each pair of participants is a case in the SPSS data file and has scores on two variables, the score obtained by one participant under one condition and the score obtained by the other participant under the other condition. Again, the primary question for matched-subjects design is the same as for repeated-measures designs: Does the difference between the two means differ significantly from zero?

Applying the Paired-Samples T Test

We discuss four applications of the paired-samples *t* test based on the design of a study.

- Repeated-measures designs with an intervention
- Repeated-measures designs with no intervention
- Matched-subjects designs with an intervention
- Matched-subjects designs with no intervention

Repeated-Measures Designs with an Intervention

Moe wants to assess the effectiveness of a leadership workshop for 60 middle managers. The 60 managers are rated by their immediate superiors on the Leadership Rating Form (LRF), before the workshop and after the workshop. Moe's SPSS data file contains 60 cases, one for each manager, and two variables, LRF before the workshop and LRF after the workshop.

Repeated-Measures Designs with No Intervention

Woody is interested in determining if workers are more concerned with job security or pay. He gains the cooperation of 30 individuals who work in different settings and asks each employee to rate his or her concern about salary level and job security on a scale

from 1 to 10 (1 = no concern and 10 = ultimate concern). Woody's SPSS data file con-
tains 30 cases, one for each employee, and two variables, ratings about concern for
salary level and ratings about concern for job security.

Matched-Subjects Designs with an Intervention

Marilyn is interested in determining if individuals who are exposed to depressed indi-
viduals become sad. She administers the Mood Measure of Sadness (MMS) to 40 stu-
dents and rank-orders their scores. She then pairs students with similar MMS scores.
Students within a matched pair have more similar MMS scores than two students from
different pairs. Marilyn then randomly assigns the two students within each matched
pair to one of two conditions: One student within each pair is exposed to a depressed
individual, and the other person is exposed to an individual who shows no signs of de-
pression. MMS scores (which she calls post-MMS scores) are obtained on the students
after they are exposed to a depressed or nondepressed individual. Marilyn's SPSS data
file contains 20 cases, one for each matched pair of students, and two variables, the
post-MMS scores for the students exposed to the depressed person and the post-MMS
scores for the students exposed to the nondepressed individual.

Matched-Subjects Design with No Intervention

Kristy is interested in investigating whether husbands and wives with infertility prob-
lems feel equally anxious. She obtains the cooperation of 24 infertile couples and then
administers the Infertility Anxiety Measure (IAM) to both the husbands and the wives.
Kristy's SPSS data file contains 24 cases, one for each husband-wife pair, and two vari-
ables, the IAM scores for the husbands and the IAM scores for the wives. Note that in this
study, the participants come to the study as couples or matched pairs, and that the con-
ditions under which the experimenter obtains the IAM scores are the two levels of gen-
der, men and women.

Understanding the Paired-Samples T Test

We next discuss the assumptions and associated effect size statistics for the paired-samples *t* test.

Assumptions Underlying the Paired-Samples T Test

Assumption 1: The Difference Variable Is Normally Distributed in the Population

Difference scores are created by subtracting one of the variables from the other. With a large sample size, the normality assumption may be violated, and the test will still yield relatively valid results. Although a sample size of 30 should be sufficient to yield reasonably accurate *p*-values in many studies, a larger sample size may be required to produce valid results if the population distribution of the difference scores is substantially nonnormal.

Assumption 2: The Cases Represent a Random Sample from the Population, and the Difference Scores Are Independent of Each Other

The paired-samples *t* test will yield inaccurate *p*-values if the assumption of independence is violated.

Computing the Effect Size Statistic for the Paired-Samples T Test

SPSS supplies all the information necessary to compute two types of effect size indices, *d* and η^2 (eta square).

The d statistic may be computed using the following equation:

$$d = \frac{Mean}{SD}$$

where the Mean and the SD (standard deviation) are reported in the output under Paired Differences. d also can be computed from the reported values for t and N (the number of pairs) as follows:

$$d = \frac{t}{\sqrt{N}}$$

The d statistic evaluates the degree that the mean of the difference scores deviates from 0 in standard deviation units. If d equals 0, the mean of the difference scores is equal to zero. As d diverges from 0, the effect size becomes larger. The value of d can range from negative infinity to positive infinity. Regardless of sign, d values of .2, .5, and .8 traditionally represent small, medium, and large effect sizes, respectively.

An eta square (η^2) may be computed as an alternative to d. η^2 ranges in value from 0 to 1. An η^2 of 0 indicates that the mean of the difference scores is equal to zero. In contrast, a value of 1 indicates that the difference scores in the sample are all the same nonzero value (i.e., perfect replication). η^2 can be computed as follows:

$$\eta^2 = \frac{N\,Mean^2}{N\,Mean^2 + (N-1)\,SD^2}$$

or, alternatively, as

$$\eta^2 = \frac{t^2}{t^2 + N - 1}$$

The Data Set

The data set in this lesson illustrates the paired-samples t test that Woody used to study workers' concerns about job security and pay. The data are in the file named *Lesson 22 Data File 1* on the Student Disk and use the variables shown in Table 16.

Table 16
Variables in Lesson 22 Data File 1

Variables	Definition
pay	1 to 10 rating, with higher scores indicating greater concern for salary level
security	1 to 10 rating, with higher scores indicating greater concern for job security

The Research Question

Research questions can be asked about either mean differences or relationships between variables.

1. Mean differences. Are employees more concerned on the average about job security or salary level?
2. Relationship between variables. Is degree of concern related to the job characteristics of pay and security?

Conducting a Paired-Samples T Test

To conduct a paired-samples *t* test, follow these steps:

1. Click **Analyze**, click **Compare Means**, then click **Paired-Samples T Test**. When you do this, you will see the Paired Samples T test dialog box shown in Figure 140.

Figure 140. The Paired-Samples T Test dialog box.

2. Click **pay**. Pay now appears as Variable 1 in Current Selections.
3. Click **security**. Security appears as Variable 2 in Current Selections.
4. Now click on ▸ , and pay - security appears in the Paired Variables box.
5. Click **OK**.

Selected SPSS Output for the Paired-Samples T Test

Partial results of the analysis are shown in Figure 141.

Paired Samples Statistics

		Mean	N	Std. Deviation	Std. Error Mean
Pair 1	PAY	5.67	30	1.49	.27
	SECURITY	4.50	30	1.83	.33

Paired Samples Test

		Paired Differences							
					95% Confidence Interval of the Difference				
		Mean	Std. Deviation	Std. Error Mean	Lower	Upper	t	df	Sig. (2-tailed)
Pair 1	PAY - SECURITY	1.17	2.26	.41	.32	2.01	2.827	29	.008

Figure 141. Partial results of the paired-samples t test.

The mean difference between pay and security (1.17) is equal to the mean for pay minus the mean for security (5.67 - 4.50) and is shown under Paired Differences. Because the mean difference is a positive value, the *t* value is also positive. The difference between the two means is computed based on the alphabetic ordering of the two variables. The variable that is second alphabetically is subtracted from the first.

Using SPSS Graphs to Display the Results

Graphs are useful for illustrating not only the differences between means but also the overlap of the two distributions. For the paired-samples *t* test, error bar charts, boxplots, and histograms of the difference scores can be used. In Figure 142, we present the results of the pay and security ratings with boxplots. To create these boxplots, follow these steps:

1. Click **Graphs**, then click **Boxplot**.
2. Click **Simple**, then click **Summaries of separate variables**. Click **Define** in the Boxplots dialog box.
3. Hold down the Ctrl key, click **pay** and **security**, and click to move them to the Boxes Represent.
4. Click **OK**. The edited graph appears in Figure 142.

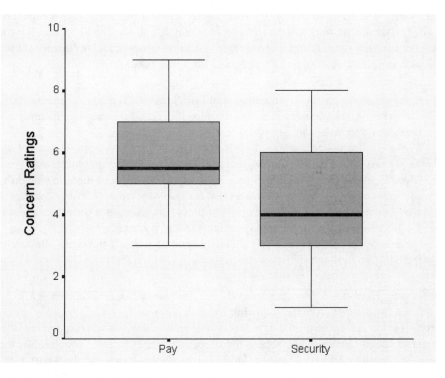

Figure 142. Boxplots of pay and security ratings.

An APA Results Section

A paired-samples $\underline{t}$ test was conducted to evaluate whether employees were more concerned with pay or job security. The results indicated that the mean concern for pay ($\underline{M}$ = 5.67, $\underline{SD}$ = 1.49) was significantly greater than the mean concern for security ($\underline{M}$ = 4.50, $\underline{SD}$ = 1.83), $\underline{t}$ (29) = 2.83, $\underline{p}$ = .008. The standardized effect size index, $\underline{d}$, was .52, a moderate value. The mean difference was 1.17 points between the two 10-point Likert ratings for pay and security, although there was considerable overlap in the distributions for the two ratings, as shown in Figure 142.

Alternative Analyses

Data for a paired-samples t test can be analyzed using a repeated-measures analysis of variance (see Lesson 28). The paired-samples t test and the repeated-measures ANOVA yield identical results in that the p-values associated with the two tests are always the same. The advantage of the repeated-measures ANOVA over the paired-samples t test is that the former computes the effect size statistic, η^2 (labeled Eta Squared).

Data for a paired-samples t test may be analyzed using nonparametric procedures (see Lesson 43). Nonparametric procedures may be considered if the population distribution of the difference scores is not normal.

Exercises

The data for Exercises 1 through 5 are in the data set named *Lesson 22 Exercise File 1* on the Student Data Disk. The data are from the following research problem.

Mike, a developmental psychologist, wants to know if overall life stress increases or decreases as working women grow older. He obtains scores on the ILS (Index of Life Stress) from a group of 100 working women when they are 40 years of age. He is able to obtain a second ILS from 45 of these women at age 60 to assess whether they felt significantly more or less stress as they grew older. The ILS consists of two scores, interpersonal life stress and occupational life stress. The two scores combine to form an index of overall life stress. The SPSS data file contains 45 cases, one for each woman, and four variables, their interpersonal and occupational life stress at age 40 and their interpersonal and occupational life stress at age 60.

1. Compute scores to obtain a total Index of Life Stress (ILS) at age 40 and age 60.
2. Compute a paired-samples t test to determine if overall life stress significantly increases or decreases with age.
3. Create a difference variable to show the changes in life stress from 40 years of age to 60 years of age. Create a histogram to show these changes graphically.
4. Mike decides that an overall ILS does not adequately reflect changes in women's life stress over time. He hypothesizes that occupational stress probably declines as women get older, while interpersonal life stress may increase or stay the same. Conduct paired-samples t tests to evaluate these hypotheses.
5. Write a results section based on your analyses in Exercises 1 through 4. Be sure to include graphical and statistical descriptions in your results.

The data for Exercises 6 through 8 are in the data set named *Lesson 22 Exercise File 2* on the Student Disk. The data are from the following research problem.

Kristy is interested in investigating whether husbands and wives who are having infertility problems feel equally anxious. She obtains the cooperation of 24 infertile couples. She then administers the Infertility Anxiety Measure (IAM) to both the husbands and the wives. Her SPSS data file contains 24 cases, one for each husband-wife pair, and two variables, the IAM scores for the husbands and the IAM scores for the wives.

6. Conduct a paired-samples t test on these data. On your output, identify the following:
    a. mean IAM score for husbands
    b. mean IAM score for wives
    c. t test value
    d. p-value
7. Write a results section in APA style based on your output.
8. If you did not include a graph in your results section, create a boxplot to show the differences between husbands' and wives' IAM scores.

Independent-Samples T Test

The independent-samples *t* test evaluates the difference between the means of two independent groups. With an independent-samples *t* test, each case must have a score on two variables—the grouping variable and the test variable. The grouping variable divides cases into two mutually exclusive groups or categories such as gender (men or women), while the test variable defines each case on some quantitative dimension such as verbal comprehension. The *t* test evaluates whether the mean value of the test variable for one group differs significantly from the mean value of the test variable for the second group.

Applying the Independent-Samples T Test

Independent-samples *t* tests are used to analyze data from different types of studies.

- Experimental studies
- Quasi-experimental studies
- Field studies.

We will illustrate the three types of studies.

Experimental Study

Bart is interested in determining if individuals talk more when they are nervous. To evaluate his hypothesis, he obtains 30 volunteers from undergraduate classes to participate in his experiment. He randomly assigns 15 students to each of two groups. Next, he schedules separate appointments for every student. When students in the first group arrive for their appointments, they are told that in 10 minutes they will be asked to describe how friendly they are by completing a true-false personality measure. In contrast, students in the second group are told that in 10 minutes they will be asked a set of questions by a panel of measurement specialists to determine how friendly they are. In both groups, the conversations between the students and the experimenter are recorded for 10 minutes. During this 10-minute period, the experimenter makes prescribed comments if no conversation occurs within a 1-minute time interval and responds to student questions with a brief response such as yes or no. The percent of time that each student talks during the 10-minute period is recorded. Bart's SPSS data file includes a grouping variable and a test variable for 30 cases. The grouping variable distinguishes between the low-stress group, whose members anticipate completing a personality measure, and the high-stress group, whose members anticipate questions from a panel of measurement specialists. The test, or dependent, variable is the percent of time that each student talks during the 10-minute period.

Quasi-Experimental Study

Mike is interested in assessing whether college students are more likely to argue about their test results with men professors or with women professors. He restricts the sample to professors who teach subjects commonly taught by both men and women, such as history, social work, psychology, education, English, and foreign languages. Mike obtains the permission of 20 men and 20 women professors to observe their classes the day they return graded midterm exams. In each class, Mike records the proportion of students who complain about some aspect of the midterm and how it was graded. Mike's SPSS data file includes both a grouping variable and a test variable for 40 cases. The grouping variable distinguishes between men and women professors, while the test variable is the proportion of students who complained about the midterm.

Field Study

Elaine is interested in determining if men prisoners who are classified as depressed eat less of their meals than those prisoners who are not classified as depressed. Of the 500 prisoners who volunteer for the study, 50 prisoners are classified as depressed. Elaine then randomly samples 50 prisoners from the nondepressed prisoners for use as a comparison or control group. She then monitors for a week the amount of each meal eaten by the 100 participants. To determine the amount of each meal eaten, she weighs their plates before and after each meal. At the end of the week, she computes the proportion of food that was eaten by each prisoner during the week. Elaine's SPSS data file includes both a grouping and a test variable for 100 cases. The grouping variable for the t test distinguishes prisoners who are depressed and not depressed. The test variable is the proportion of food eaten by each inmate.

Understanding the Independent-Samples T Test

We next discuss the assumptions and associated effect size statistics for the independent-samples *t* test.

Assumptions Underlying the Independent-Samples T Test

Assumption 1: The Test Variable Is Normally Distributed in Each of the Two Populations (as Defined by the Grouping Variable)

With a moderate to large sample, this assumption may be violated, and the test will still yield reasonably accurate results In most circumstances, a sample size of 15 cases per group should be sufficiently large to yield fairly accurate *p*-values. If the population distributions are substantially nonnormal, larger samples may be necessary.

Assumption 2: The Variances of the Normally Distributed Test Variable for the Populations Are Equal

To the extent that this assumption is violated and the sample sizes differ for the two populations, the *p*-value from the independent-samples *t* test should not be trusted. The independent-samples *t* test procedure, however, computes an approximate *t* test that does not assume that the population variances are equal, in addition to the traditional *t* test that assumes equal population variances.

Assumption 3: The Cases Represent a Random Sample from the Population, and the Scores on the Test Variable Are Independent of Each Other

If the independence assumption is violated, the *p*-value should not be trusted.

Computing the Effect Size Statistic for an Independent-Samples T Test

SPSS supplies all the information necessary to compute two effect size indices, d and η^2 (eta square).

The d statistic may be computed using the following equation

$$d = \frac{Mean\ Difference}{SD_{pooled}}$$

where the mean difference is reported in the SPSS output, but the pooled standard deviation (SD_{pooled}) is not. SD_{pooled} can be calculated from the reported standard deviations for the two groups using the equation

$$SD_{pooled} = \sqrt{\frac{(N_1-1)\ SD_1^2+(N_2-1)\ SD_2^2}{N_1+N_2-2}}$$

However, it is easier to compute d using the following equation:

$$d=t\sqrt{\frac{N_1+N_2}{N_1 N_2}}$$

A d can range in value from negative infinity to positive infinity. The value of 0 for d indicates that there are no differences in the means. As d diverges from 0, the effect size becomes larger. Regardless of sign, d values of .2, .5, and .8 traditionally represent small, medium, and large effect sizes, respectively.

Eta square (η^2) may be computed as an alternative to d. An η^2 ranges in value from 0 to 1. It is interpreted as the proportion of variance of the test variable that is a function of the group variable. A value of 0 indicates that the difference in the mean scores is equal to 0, while a value of 1 indicates that the sample means differ, but the test scores do not differ within each group (i.e., perfect replication). You can compute η^2 using the following equation:

$$\eta^2 = \frac{\frac{N_1 N_2}{N_1+N_2}(Mean\ Difference)^2}{\frac{N_1 N_2}{N_1+N_2}(Mean\ Difference)^2+(N_1+N_2-2)SD_{pooled}^2}$$

or, alternatively, as

$$\eta^2 = \frac{t^2}{t^2+(N_1+N_2-2)}$$

Traditionally, η^2 values of .01, .06, and .14 represent small, medium, and large effect sizes, respectively.

The Data Set

The data set used to illustrate the independent-samples t test is named *Lesson 23 Data File 1* on the Student Disk. The file presents data from the example about anxiety and talking that we gave earlier. The variables in the data set are described in Table 17 (at the top of page 152).

The Research Question

The research question can be asked two ways.

1. With respect to mean differences: Does the average amount of talking differ under low-stress versus high-stress conditions?
2. With respect to the relationship between variables: Is percent of time that students talk related to level of stress?

Table 17

Variables in Lesson 23 Data File 1

Variables	Definition
stress	Stress is the grouping or independent variable. The stress variable distinguishes between two treatment conditions. If stress = 1, then a student was in the low-stress condition and anticipated completing a personality measure. If stress = 2, then a student was in the high-stress condition and anticipated questions from a panel of measurement specialists
talk	Talk is the test or dependent variable. It is defined as the percent of time that each student talked during the 10-minute test period.

Conducting an Independent-Samples T Test

To conduct an independent-samples *t* test, follow these steps:

1. Click **Analyze**, click **Compare Means**, then click **Independent-Samples T Test**. You will see the Independent-Samples T Test dialog box shown in Figure 143.

Figure 143. The Independent-Samples T Test dialog box.

2. Click **talk**, then click ► to move it to the Test Variables(s) area.
3. Click **stress**, then click ► to move it to the Grouping Variable area.
4. Click **Define Groups**. You will see the Define Groups dialog box shown in Figure 144.

Figure 144. The Define Groups dialog box.

5. In the Group 1 box, type **1**.
6. In the Group 2 box, type **2**.
7. Click **Continue**.
8. Click **OK**.

Selected SPSS Output for the Independent-Samples T Test

You can see the results of the analysis in Figure 145.

Group Statistics

	STRESS	N	Mean	Std. Deviation	Std. Error Mean
TALK	Low Stress	15	45.20	24.97	6.45
	High Stress	15	22.07	27.14	7.01

Independent Samples Test

		Levene's Test for Equality of Variances		t-test for Equality of Means					95% Confidence Interval of the Difference	
		F	Sig.	t	df	Sig. (2-tailed)	Mean Difference	Std. Error Difference	Lower	Upper
TALK	Equal variances assumed	.023	.881	2.430	28	.022	23.13	9.52	3.63	42.64
	Equal variances not assumed			2.430	27.808	.022	23.13	9.52	3.62	42.64

Figure 145. Partial results of the independent-samples t test.

The mean difference is obtained by subtracting the mean for Group 2 from the mean for Group 1, as Groups 1 and 2 were defined in the Define Groups dialog box. The sign of the mean difference dictates the sign of the t value. The results should be interpreted accordingly. For our example, students in the low-stress group were defined as a 1 on the grouping variable, and students in the high-stress group were defined as a 2. The mean difference on the test variable talk, 23.13, was obtained by subtracting the mean (22.07) for Group 2 (high stress) students from the mean (45.20) for Group 1 (low stress) students. The positive t value indicates that the mean amount of talking for the students in the low-stress group is significantly greater than the mean for the students in the high-stress group.

The results of the Levene's test evaluate the second assumption, whether the population variances for the two groups are equal. If the variances for the two groups are substantially different and the sample sizes are unequal, you should not report the standard t value, but rather the t value where equal variances are not assumed.

An argument can be made for always reporting the t value for unequal variances, regardless of the outcome of the Levene's test. In our example, the variances are very similar and, consequently, the standard t test, $t(28) = 2.43$, $p = .022$, and the t test for unequal variances, $t(27.81) = 2.43$, $p = .022$, yield identical results. As shown in this example, the degrees of freedom for the t test for unequal variances may not be an integer.

Defining Cut Points

The independent-samples t test procedure also allows you to define a grouping variable using a cut point on a quantitative variable in the Define Groups dialog box. In this way all individuals at or above that cut point are in one group, and all those below the cut point are in the second group. You should be selective about using this option. An independent-samples t test using a grouping variable (dichotomized variable) and the test variable is likely to have less power than correlational analyses between a quantitative variable that is not dichotomized and the test variable. However, an independent-samples t test using a dichotomized quantitative variable might be conducted for nonstatistical reasons if the groups that are defined by the cut point have substantive meaning beyond that of the quantitative scores themselves. For example, 70 has traditionally been used as the cut point between normality and abnormality on the MMPI, a measure of psychopathology. It would be appropriate to use the cut point of 70 to define a grouping variable on an MMPI scale to assess the validity of the labels of normal and abnormal when relating the MMPI scale to a test variable (e.g., a behavioral criterion).

Using SPSS Graphs to Display the Results

A variety of graphical displays can help the reader understand the results of the independent-samples *t* test analysis. Common examples of graphs used to display mean differences and distributions of variables across multiple groups are error bar graphs, which display the means and standard deviations for each group, and boxplots (see Lesson 20 for a discussion of the boxplot). Figure 146 is an error bar graph that shows the means and standard deviations of the percent of time spent talking in each of the stress groups.

An APA Results Section

An independent-samples $\underline{t}$ test was conducted to evaluate the hypothesis that students talk more under a high-stress condition (anticipating questions from a panel of measurement specialists) as opposed to a low-stress condition (anticipating taking a personality measure). The test was significant, $\underline{t}$ (28) = 2.43, $\underline{p}$ = .022, but the results were counter to the research hypothesis. Students in the high-stress condition ($\underline{M}$ = 22.07, $\underline{SD}$ = 27.14) on the average talked less than those in the low-stress condition ($\underline{M}$ = 45.20, $\underline{SD}$ = 24.97). The eta square index indicated that 17% of the variance of the talk variable was accounted for by whether a student was assigned to a low-stress or a high-stress condition. Figure 146 shows the distributions of the two groups.

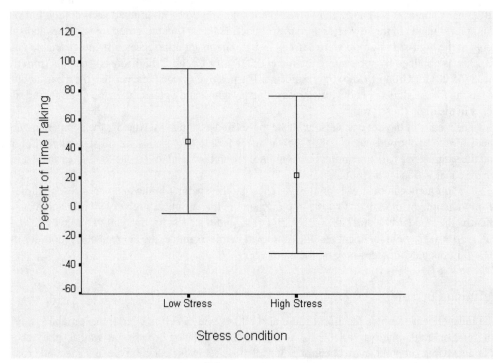

**Figure 146. Error bars (two standard deviations above and below the mean)
for the percent of time talking scores for each stress group.**

Alternative Analyses

The type of data described in this lesson can also be analyzed using one-way analysis of variance (see One-Way ANOVA, lesson 24). The independent-samples *t* test assuming equal variances and the one-way ANOVA yield identical results in that the *p*-values are the same. The advantage of the independent-samples *t* test procedure over the one-way ANOVA procedure is that the *t* test procedure calculates a *t* test that does not require the population variances to be equal. However, an effect size statistic, labeled eta square, is computed if a one-way ANOVA is calculated using the General Linear Model—Univariate procedure. Eta square is not available in the independent-samples *t* test.

Data for an independent-samples *t* test can also be analyzed using nonparametric procedures (see Lesson 41). If the assumptions of the independent-samples *t* test are met, however, the parametric test is a more powerful analysis than the nonparametric alternatives. If the normality assumption for an independent-samples *t* test is not met, the nonparametric alternative may be more powerful in some circumstances.

Exercises

The data for Exercises 1 through 5 are in the data set named *Lesson 23 Exercise File 1* on the Student Data Disk. The data are from the following research problem.

Billie wishes to test the hypothesis that overweight individuals tend to eat faster than normal weight individuals. To test this hypothesis, she has two assistants sit in a McDonald's restaurant and identify individuals who order the Big Mac special (Big Mac, large fries, and large Coke) for lunch. The Big Mackers, as they are affectionately called by the assistants, are classified as overweight, normal weight, or neither overweight nor normal weight. The assistants identify 10 overweight and 30 normal weight Big Mackers. The assistants record the amount of time it takes for the individuals to complete their Big Mac special meals. The SPSS data file contains two variables, a grouping variable with two levels, overweight (= 1) and normal weight (= 2), and time in seconds to eat the meal.

1. Compute an independent-samples *t* test on these data. Report the *t* and the *p*-values assuming equal population variances and not assuming equal population variances.
2. On the output, identify the following:
   a. mean eating time for overweight individuals
   b. standard deviation for normal weight individuals
   c. results for the test evaluating homogeneity of variances
3. Compute an effect size that describes the magnitude of the relationship between weight and the speed of eating Big Mac meals.
4. Write a results section based on your analyses.
5. If you did not include a graph in your results section, create a graph in APA format that shows the differences between the two groups.

The data for Exercises 6 through 10 are in the data set named *Lesson 23 Exercise File 2* on the Student Data Disk. The data are from the following research problem.

Fred wishes to determine whether children in regular education are hurt or helped academically by the inclusion of special education students in their classes. He has gained the cooperation of the seventh grade teachers in two similar junior high schools to participate in his study. One school recently integrated special education students into their regular classroom, while the other one has not. The teachers in both schools supply Fred the students' raw scores on a standardized achievement test at the beginning of the year and at the end of the year. The SPSS data file contains 40 cases and three variables: (1) a factor called integrat with two levels, regular education students who are not in integrated classrooms (integrat = 1) and regular education students who are in the integrated classrooms (integrat = 2), (2) a pretest, raw scores on the standardized achievement test obtained at the beginning of the year, and (3) a posttest, raw scores on the achievement measure obtained at the end of the year.

6. Create a dependent variable by computing a difference score between the pretest and posttest achievement scores.
7. Conduct an independent-samples *t* test to evaluate the effectiveness of integration on academic achievement.
8. What did the Levene's test evaluate?
9. Which *t* ratio is the appropriate result? Why?
10. Write a results section based on your analyses. What would you conclude?

Univariate and Multivariate Analysis-of-Variance Techniques

Unit 7 covers univariate and multivariate analysis-of-variance (ANOVA) techniques. These procedures assess the relationship of one or more factors with a dependent variable (univariate ANOVA) or with multiple dependent variables (MANOVA). The factors are either between-subjects or within-subjects factors. A between-subjects factor divides research participants into different groups such as gender or multiple treatments. A within-subjects factor has multiple levels, and each participant is observed on a dependent variable across those levels. An example of a within-subjects factor might be trials, with each subject having scores on the dependent variable for all trials.

Lesson 24 deals with one-way ANOVA, which allows us to analyze mean differences between two or more groups on a between-subjects factor. Lesson 25 describes two-way ANOVA, a procedure that relates two between-subjects factors to a dependent variable. Lesson 26 considers analysis of covariance (ANCOVA), an approach that evaluates differences between two or more groups on a dependent variable, statistically controlling for differences on one or more covariates. Lesson 27 presents one-way MANOVA, which evaluates the relationship between a single between-subjects factor and two or more dependent variables. Lesson 28 deals with one-way repeated-measures ANOVA. This technique allows us to analyze mean differences between two or more levels of a within-subjects factor. Lesson 29 describes two-way repeated-measures ANOVA, which relates two within-subjects factors to a dependent variable.

SPSS also can be used to analyze data from other analysis-of-variance designs. For example, analyses can be conducted that have three between-subjects factors or one between-subjects factor and one within-subjects factor. These analyses use the same procedures but require specifying slightly different choices in the dialog boxes. We briefly discuss methods used to conduct ANOVAs for designs with more than two between-subjects factors in Lesson 25.

One-Way Analysis of Variance

For a one-way analysis of variance (one-way ANOVA), each individual or case must have scores on two variables: a factor and a dependent variable. The factor divides individuals into two or more groups or levels, while the dependent variable differentiates individuals on some quantitative dimension. The ANOVA F test evaluates whether the group means on the dependent variable differ significantly from each other. Each case in a SPSS data file used to conduct a one-way ANOVA contains a factor dividing participants into groups and one quantitative dependent variable.

Applying One-Way ANOVA

A one-way ANOVA can be used to analyze data from different types of studies.

- Experimental studies
- Quasi-experimental studies
- Field studies.

We will illustrate two types of studies.

Experimental Study

Dana wishes to assess whether vitamin C is effective in the treatment of colds. To evaluate her hypothesis, she decides to conduct a 2-year experimental study. She obtains 30 volunteers from undergraduate classes to participate. She randomly assigns an equal number of students to three groups: placebo (group 1), low doses of vitamin C (group 2), and high doses of vitamin C (group 3). In the first and second years of the study, students in all three groups are monitored to assess the number of days that they have cold symptoms. During the first year, students do not take any pills. In the second year of the study, students take pills that contain one of the following: no active ingredients (group 1), low doses of vitamin C (group 2), or high doses of vitamin C (group 3). Dana's SPSS data file includes 30 cases and two variables: a factor distinguishing among the three treatment groups and a dependent variable, the difference in the number of days with cold symptoms in the first year versus the number of days with cold symptoms in the second year.

Quasi-Experimental Study

Karin believes that students with behavior problems react best to teachers who have a humanistic philosophy and have firm control of their classrooms. In a large city school system, she classifies 40 high school teachers of students with behavior problems into three categories: humanists with firm control (group 1, n = 9); strict disciplinarians (group 2, n = 21), and keepers of the behavior problems (group 3, n = 10). Karin is interested in assessing whether students who are taught by one type of teacher as opposed to another type of teacher are more likely to stay out of difficulty in school. By reviewing the records of all students in these 40 teachers' classes, she determines the number of times the students of each teacher were sent to the main office for disciplinary action during the second half of the academic year. All classes had 30 students in them. Karin's SPSS data file has 40 cases with a factor distinguishing among the three types of teachers and a dependent variable, the number of disciplinary actions for students in a class.

Understanding One-Way ANOVA

An overall analysis-of-variance test is conducted to assess whether means on a dependent variable are significantly different among groups. If the overall ANOVA is significant and a factor has more than two levels, follow-up tests are usually conducted. These follow-up tests frequently involve comparisons between pairs of group means. For example, if a factor has three levels, three pairwise comparisons might be conducted to compare the means of groups 1 and 2, the means of groups 1 and 3, and the means of groups 2 and 3. SPSS calls these follow-up tests post hoc multiple comparisons.

Assumptions Underlying One-Way ANOVA

Assumption 1: The Dependent Variable Is Normally Distributed for Each of the Populations as Defined by the Different Levels of the Factor

With moderate to large sample sizes, the assumption may be violated, and the test will still yield reasonably accurate results. In most circumstances, a sample size of 15 cases per group is large enough to yield fairly accurate p-values. Larger sample sizes may be required to produce relatively valid results if the population distributions are substantially nonnormal.

Assumption 2: The Variances of the Dependent Variable Are the Same for All Populations

To the extent that this assumption is violated and the sample sizes differ among the populations, the resulting p-value for the overall F test is not trustworthy. For post hoc tests that require equal variances, the validity of the results are questionable if the population variances differ regardless of whether the sample sizes are equal or unequal. If the variances are different, it is appropriate to choose one of the four methods available in SPSS for conducting post hoc multiple comparison tests that do not assume that the population variances are equal. Of the four methods, no one method is superior in all circumstances (Hotchberg & Tamhane, 1987). We have chosen to use the Dunnett's C procedure in instances where the variances are unequal.

Assumption 3: The Cases Represent Random Samples from the Populations and the Scores on the Test Variable Are Independent of Each Other

The ANOVA F yields inaccurate p-values if the independence assumption is violated.

Computing an Effect Size Statistic

The General Linear Model procedure computes an effect size index, η^2 (eta square). Eta square ranges in value from 0 to 1. An η^2 value of 0 indicates that there are no differences in the mean scores among groups. A value of 1 indicates that there are differences between at least two of the means on the dependent variable and that there are no differences on the dependent variable scores within each of the groups (i.e., perfect replication). In general, η^2 is interpreted as the proportion of variance of the dependent variable that is related to the factor. Traditionally, η^2 values of .01, .06, and .14 represent small, medium, and large effect sizes, respectively.

The Data Set

The data set used to illustrate a one-way ANOVA is named *Lesson 24 Data File 1* on the Student Disk. It represents data from the vitamin C example described earlier. The variables in the data set are presented in Table 18.

Table 18
Variables in Lesson 24 Data File 1

Variables	Definition
group	1 = Placebo
	2 = Low doses of vitamin C
	3 = High doses of vitamin C
diff	Number of days with cold symptoms in the second year minus the number of days with cold symptoms in the first year

The Research Question

The research question can be stated to reflect mean differences or relationships between variables.

1. Mean differences. Does the mean change in the number of days of cold symptoms differ among the three experimental populations: those who take placebo, those who take low doses of vitamin C, and those who take high doses of vitamin C?
2. Relationship between variables. Is there a relationship in the population between the amount of vitamin C taken and the change in the number of days that individuals show cold symptoms?

Conducting a One-Way ANOVA

To conduct an overall one-way ANOVA and pairwise comparisons among the three vitamin C treatment means, follow these steps:

1. Click **Analyze**, click **General Linear Model**, then click **Univariate**. You'll see the Univariate dialog box in Figure 147.

Figure 147. The Univariate dialog box.

2. Click **diff**, then click ► to move it to the Dependent Variable box.
3. Click **group**, then click ► to move it to the Fixed Factor(s) box.
4. Click **Options**. You'll see the Univariate: Options dialog box in Figure 148.

Figure 148. The Univariate: Options dialog box.

5. Click **group** in the Factor(s) and Factor Interactions box, then click ► to make it appear to the Display Means for box.
6. Click **Homogeneity tests, Estimates of effect size**, and **Descriptive statistics** in the Display box.
7. Click **Continue**.
8. Click **Post Hoc**. You'll see the Univariate: Post Hoc Multiple Comparisons for Observed Means dialog box in Figure 149.

Figure 149. The Univariate: Post Hoc Multiple Comparisons dialog box.

9. Under the Factors box, click **group**, and click ► to make it appear in the Post Hoc Tests for box.

10. In the Equal Variances Assumed box, click **Tukey** and **R-E-G-W Q**. Other post hoc tests assuming equal variances are equally valid.
11. In the Equal Variances Not Assumed box, click **Dunnett's C**. Other post hoc tests not assuming equal variances are equally valid.
12. Click **Continue**.
13. Click **OK**.

Selected SPSS Output for One-Way ANOVA

The results of analyses are shown in Figure 150, including the means and standard deviations, the one-way ANOVA F test, and the homogeneity test.

Descriptive Statistics

Dependent Variable: DIFF

Vitamin C Treatment	Mean	Std. Deviation	N
1	3.50	4.14	10
2	-2.10	4.07	10
3	-2.00	5.48	10
Total	-.20	5.18	30

Levene's Test of Equality of Error Variances[a]

Dependent Variable: DIFF

F	df1	df2	Sig.
1.343	2	27	.278

Tests the null hypothesis that the error variance of the dependent variable is equal across groups.

a. Design: Intercept+GROUP

Tests of Between-Subjects Effects

Dependent Variable: DIFF

Source	Type III Sum of Squares	df	Mean Square	F	Sig.	Eta Squared
Corrected Model	205.400[a]	2	102.700	4.836	.016	.264
Intercept	1.200	1	1.200	.057	.814	.002
GROUP	205.400	2	102.700	4.836	.016	.264
Error	573.400	27	21.237			
Total	780.000	30				
Corrected Total	778.800	29				

a. R Squared = .264 (Adjusted R Squared = .209)

Figure 150. The results of a one-way analysis of variance.

To determine whether the overall ANOVA was significant, examine the table labeled Tests of Between-Subjects Effects. The test is significant, $F(2,27) = 4.84$, $p = .016$. The p-value is located in the column labeled Sig. Because the p-value is less than .05, we reject the null hypothesis that there are no differences among the groups. The η^2 of .26 indicates a strong relationship between the vitamin C factor and the change in the number of days with cold symptoms.

Because the overall F test was significant, follow-up tests were conducted to evaluate pairwise differences among the means. A decision has to be made whether to use a post hoc procedure that assumes equal variances (Tukey or R-E-G-W Q) or one that does not assume equal variances (Dunnett's C) to control for Type I error across the multiple pairwise comparisons. In our example, the standard deviations range from 4.07 to 5.48 and the variances (the standard deviations squared) range from 16.54 to 30.00, indicating that the variances are somewhat, but not drastically, different from each other. The test of homogeneity of variance was nonsignificant, $p = .278$. Because there may be a lack of power associated with the test due to the small sample size, the result of the homogeneity test does not necessarily imply that there are no differences in the population variances. Therefore, the prudent choice for these data would be to ignore the results of the Tukey and R-E-G-W Q tests and to use the results of the Dunnett's C test, a multiple comparison procedure that does not require the population variances to be equal.

Selected SPSS Output for Post Hoc Comparisons

The results of the post hoc comparisons are shown in Figure 151.

Multiple Comparisons

Dependent Variable: DIFF

	(I) Vitamin C Treatment	(J) Vitamin C Treatment	Mean Difference (I-J)	Std. Error	Sig.	95% Confidence Interval Lower Bound	95% Confidence Interval Upper Bound
Tukey HSD	1	2	5.60*	2.06	.030	.49	10.71
		3	5.50*	2.06	.033	.39	10.61
	2	1	-5.60*	2.06	.030	-10.71	-.49
		3	-.10	2.06	.999	-5.21	5.01
	3	1	-5.50*	2.06	.033	-10.61	-.39
		2	.10	2.06	.999	-5.01	5.21
Dunnett C	1	2	5.60*	2.06		.47	10.73
		3	5.50	2.06		-.56	11.56
	2	1	-5.60*	2.06		-10.73	-.47
		3	-.10	2.06		-6.12	5.92
	3	1	-5.50	2.06		-11.56	.56
		2	.10	2.06		-5.92	6.12

Based on observed means.

*. The mean difference is significant at the .05 level.

Homogeneous Subsets

DIFF

	Vitamin C Treatment	N	Subset 1	Subset 2
Tukey HSD[a,b]	2	10	-2.10	
	3	10	-2.00	
	1	10		3.50
	Sig.		.999	1.000
Ryan-Einot-Gabriel-Welsch Range[b]	2	10	-2.10	
	3	10	-2.00	
	1	10		3.50
	Sig.		.962	1.000

Means for groups in homogeneous subsets are displayed.
Based on Type III Sum of Squares
The error term is Mean Square(Error) = 21.237.

a. Uses Harmonic Mean Sample Size = 10.000.

b. Alpha = .05.

Figure 151. The results of post hoc pairwise comparisons.

Using the Dunnett's C test, groups 1 and 2 differed significantly from one another. In the table labeled Multiple Comparisons the stars (*) in the Mean Difference column indicate which pairwise comparisons are significant.

Using SPSS Graphs to Display the Results

The same graphical methods that were presented for the independent-samples t test (Lesson 23) can be used for one-way ANOVA as well. ANOVA results may be depicted using boxplots to show the distributions of the dependent variable across the groups.

We created a boxplot to show the distributions of the changes in number of days with cold symptoms for the three vitamin C treatment groups. Figure 152 shows the distributions of the three groups.

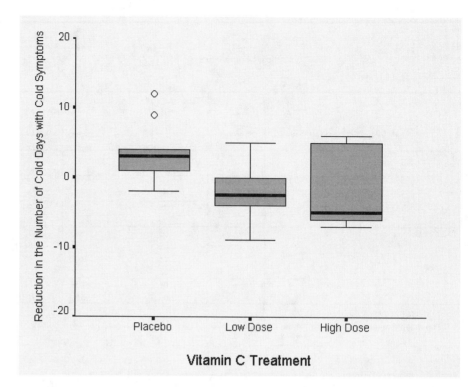

Figure 152. Changes in number of days with cold symptoms for placebo, low dose, and high dose vitamin C treatment groups.

An APA Results Section

A one-way analysis of variance was conducted to evaluate the relationship between vitamin C and the change in the number of days with cold symptoms from the first year to the second year of the study. The independent variable, the vitamin C factor, included three levels: placebo, low doses of vitamin C, and high doses of vitamin C. The dependent variable was the change in the number of days when cold symptoms were exhibited from the first year to the second year. The ANOVA was significant, $\underline{F}$ (2, 27) = 4.84, $\underline{p}$ = .016. The strength of relationship between the vitamin C treatment and the change in the number of days with cold symptoms, as assessed by η^2, was strong, with the vitamin C factor accounting for 26% of the variance of the dependent variable.

Follow-up tests were conducted to evaluate pairwise differences among the means. Because the variances among the three groups ranged from 16.54 to 30.00, we chose not to assume that the variances were homogeneous and conducted post hoc comparisons using the Dunnett's C test, a test that does not assume equal variances among the three groups. The results of these tests, as well as the means and standard deviations for the three vitamin C groups, are reported in Table 19 (at the top of page 165). There were significant differences in the means between the group that received a low dose of vitamin C and the placebo group, but no significant differences between the two vitamin C groups and the high dose and placebo groups. The group that received a low dose of vitamin C showed a greater decrease in number of days with cold symptoms in comparison to the placebo group.

Table 19

Differences among Groups on Changes in Number of Days of Cold Symptoms

Vitamin C group	M	SD	Placebo	Low dose
Placebo	3.50	4.14		
Low dose	-2.10	4.07	*	
High dose	-2.00	5.48	NS	NS

Note: NS = nonsignificant differences between pairs of means, while an asterisk (*) = significance using the Dunnett's C procedure.

Writing an APA Results Section

We present some guidelines for writing a results section for statistical procedures that may require follow-up tests, such as one-way ANOVA and MANOVA in Unit 7, or the Friedman test in Unit 10. Consequently, it may be necessary to reread this material after you have read the other lessons in Unit 7 and the lessons in Unit 10.

Some researchers initially provide a description of the general overall analytic strategy that includes the omnibus tests and the follow-up tests. This general description is necessary to the degree that the analyses are unconventional and/or complex.

Below we present steps required to write a results section.

1. Describe the statistical test(s), the variables, and the purpose of the statistical test(s). For example: "A one-way analysis of variance was conducted to evaluate the relationship between vitamin C and the change in the number of days with cold symptoms from the first year to the second year of the study."
   - Describe the factor or factors. If a factor is a within-subjects factor, be sure to label it as such. Otherwise the reader may assume that it is a between-subjects factor. If a multifactorial design has one or more within-subjects factors, describe each factor as a between-subjects or a within-subjects factor.
   - Indicate the number of levels for each factor. It may be also be informative to the reader to have a description of each level if the levels are different treatments. However, it is not necessary to report the number of levels and what the levels are for factors with obvious levels such as gender.
   - Describe what the dependent variable(s) are.
2. Report the results of the overall test(s).
   - Describe any decisions about which test was chosen based on assumptions. For example, for a one-way within-subjects ANOVA, justify the choice of using a traditional univariate test instead of a multivariate test.
   - Report the test value and significance level (for the one-way ANOVA, $\underline{F}$ (2, 27) = 4.84, $\underline{p}$ = .016). For $\underline{p}$-values of .000, report them as $\underline{p}$ < .001. For multifactor designs, report the statistic for each of the main and interaction effects. Tell the reader whether the test(s) are significant or not.
   - Report statistics that allow the reader to make a judgment about the magnitude of the effect for each overall test (e.g., for the one-way ANOVA, η^2 = .45).
   - Underline all non-Greek statistical symbols.
3. Report the descriptive statistics. Refer the reader to a table or figure that presents the relevant descriptive statistics (e.g., means and standard deviations for ANOVA designs). A table or figure may not be necessary for simpler designs, such as for a three-group ANOVA. For these simple designs, the descriptive statistics may be presented in the text when reporting the follow-up tests.
4. Describe and summarize the general conclusions of the analysis. For example: "The results of the one-way ANOVA supported the hypothesis that different types of vitamin C treatment had a differential effect on the reduction of cold symptoms in individuals."

5. Report the results of the follow-up tests.
   - Describe the procedures used to conduct the follow-up tests. Explain any decisions you made about tests based on their assumptions.
   - Report the method used to control for Type I error across the multiple tests.
   - Summarize the results of the follow-up procedures. It may be useful to present the results of the significance tests among pairwise comparisons with a table of means and standard deviations.
   - Describe and summarize the general conclusions of the follow-up analyses. Make sure to include in your description the directionality of the test. For example, the mean for one treatment group is higher or lower than the mean for another group.
6. Report the distributions of the dependent variable for levels of the factor(s) in a graph if space is available. The graph should be inserted in the text where appropriate. For example, if the graph pertains to assumptions, you would insert it in the section where assumptions are discussed. Likewise, if the graph reflects the means and standard deviations, it should be presented with the discussion of the descriptive statistics.

Alternative Analyses

Data for a one-way ANOVA can also be analyzed using the Kruskal-Wallis nonparametric procedure (see *K*-independent samples in Lesson 42). If the assumptions of a one-way ANOVA are met, ANOVA is more powerful than the nonparametric alternatives. However, if the assumptions are not met, the nonparametric alternatives may be more powerful.

Exercises

The data for Exercises 1 through 3 are in the data set named *Lesson 24 Exercise File 1* on the Student Data Disk. The data are from the following research problem.

Marvin is interested in whether blonds, brunets, and redheads differ with respect to their extrovertedness. He randomly samples 18 men from his local college campus: six blonds, six brunets, and six redheads. He then administers a measure of social extroversion to each individual.

1. Conduct a one-way ANOVA to investigate the relationship between hair color and social extroversion. Be sure to conduct appropriate post hoc tests. On the output, identify the following:
   a. *F* ratio for the group effect
   b. sums of squares for the hair color effect
   c. mean for redheads
   d. *p*-value for the hair color effect
2. What is the effect size for the overall effect of hair color on extroversion?
3. Create a boxplot to display the differences among the distributions for the three hair color groups.

The data for Exercises 4 through 6 are in the data set named *Lesson 24 Exercise File 2* on the Student Data Disk. The data are from Karin's research problem, described earlier in this lesson, involving students with behavior problems and different teaching styles. Karin's SPSS data file has 40 cases with a factor distinguishing among the three types of teachers and a dependent variable, the number of disciplinary actions for students in a class. Conduct a one-way ANOVA to answer Karin's question.

4. What does the Levene's test tell us about our data?
5. Which follow-up tests would you choose and why?
6. Write a results section based on the analyses you have conducted. What should Karin conclude?

Two-Way Analysis of Variance with Comments about Higher-Way Analysis of Variance

With a two-way analysis of variance (two-way ANOVA), each participant must have scores on three variables: two factors and a dependent variable. Each factor divides cases into two or more levels, while the dependent variable defines cases on a quantitative dimension. F tests are performed on the main effects for the two factors and on the interaction between the two factors. Follow-up tests may be conducted to assess specific hypotheses if main effect tests, interaction tests, or both are significant.

With higher-way analysis of variance, there are more than two factors in a design. Therefore, each participant must have scores on at least four variables: the three or more factors and a dependent variable. F tests are performed on multiple effects. For example, with a three-way ANOVA, tests are conducted on the three main effects for the factors, the three two-way interactions between pairs of factors, and the one three-way interaction among the three factors. Depending on which main and interaction tests yield significance, a variety of follow-up tests may be performed.

Applying Two-Way Analysis of Variance

We can analyze data from different types of studies using two-way ANOVA.

- Experimental studies
- Quasi-experimental studies
- Field studies

We illustrate an experimental and a field study.

An Experimental Study

Ethel is interested in two methods for teaching note-taking strategies and the effect of these methods on the overall GPAs of college freshmen. She believes that men would benefit most from Method 1, while women would benefit most from Method 2. After obtaining 30 men and 30 women volunteers in freshmen orientation, she randomly assigns 10 women and 10 men to Method 1, 10 women and 10 men to Method 2, and 10 women and 10 men to a control condition. During the first month of the spring semester, individuals in the two note-taking method groups receive daily instruction on the particular note-taking method to which they were assigned. The control group receives no note-taking instruction. Fall and spring GPAs for all participants are recorded. One factor for this study is note-taking method with three levels, and the second factor is gender with two levels. The design for this study may be described as a 3 x 2 ANOVA (the number of levels of note-taking method by the number of levels of gender). Ethel's SPSS data file has

60 cases and three variables: a factor distinguishing among the three note-taking method groups, a second factor differentiating men from women, and a dependent variable, the students' spring semester GPA minus their fall semester GPA.

A Field Study

Ted is interested in evaluating whether the gender of a client and the gender of a therapist affects the outcome of therapy. Specifically, he is interested in testing the gender-matching hypothesis that client-therapist pairs of the same gender produce the most positive outcomes. Ted has access to a large data base and selects a sample of 40 client-therapist pairs so that there are an equal number of each type of pair: 10 pairs each of female client with female therapist, female client with male therapist, male client with female therapist, and male client with male therapist. All 40 clients are being treated for difficulty with coping with daily stresses. Each of the 40 therapists indicates that he or she has an eclectic approach to therapy. Finally, the length of therapy for any one pair is never less than five sessions.

There are two factors in this study, gender of the client with two levels and gender of the therapist with two levels. The dependent variable is the amount of client improvement over the course of therapy. The design for this study may be described as a 2 x 2 ANOVA (the number of levels of client gender by the number of levels of therapist gender). Ted's SPSS data file has 40 cases and three variables: a factor classifying the gender of the client, a second factor classifying the gender of the therapist, and a dependent variable, client improvement.

Understanding Two-Way Analysis of Variance

The first tests conducted in a two-way ANOVA are the omnibus or overall tests of the main and interaction effects. These omnibus tests evaluate the following hypotheses:

- First Main Effect: Do the population means on the dependent variable differ across levels of the first factor averaging across levels of the second factor?
- Second Main Effect: Do the population means on the dependent variable differ across levels of the second factor averaging across levels of the first factor?
- Interaction Effect: Do the differences in the population means on the dependent variable among levels of the first factor vary as a function of the levels of the second factor?

If one or more of the overall effects are significant, various follow-up tests can be conducted. The choice of which follow-up procedure to conduct depends on which effects are significant.

If the interaction effect is significant, follow-up tests can be conducted to evaluate simple main effect, interaction comparisons, or both. The choice between simple main effects and interaction comparisons depends on which tests best address the research questions.

Depending on the research questions, a number of simple main effect tests can be evaluated: differences in population means among levels of the first factor for each level of the second factor, differences in means among levels of the second factor for each level of the first factor, or both. If any of these simple main effect tests is significant and involves more than two means, additional tests are conducted typically to assess pairwise differences among the means.

Interaction contrasts may be conducted in place of or in addition to simple main effects. The simplest interaction contrasts involve four means and are referred to as tetrad contrasts. Tetrad contrasts evaluate whether differences in population means between two levels of one factor differ for two levels of a second factor.

If the interaction effect is not significant, the focus switches to the main effects. If a main effect for a factor with more than two levels is significant, then follow-up tests can be conducted. These tests evaluate whether there are differences in the means among the levels of this factor averaged across levels of the other factor. These follow-up tests most often involve comparing means for pairs of levels of the factor associated with the significant main effect.

Assumptions Underlying a Two-Way Analysis of Variance

Assumption 1: The Dependent Variable Is Normally Distributed for Each of the Populations

The cells of the design (i.e., the combinations of levels of the two factors) define the different populations. For example, for a 3 x 2 ANOVA, there are six cells (3 x 2 = 6) and, consequently, the assumption requires the population distributions on the dependent variable to be normally distributed for all six cells. If the distributions are not normally distributed, the test should still yield reasonably accurate results with moderate to large sample sizes. In most circumstances, a sample size of 15 cases per group should be sufficiently large to yield fairly accurate p-values. Larger sample sizes may be required to produce relatively valid results if the population distributions are extremely nonnormal.

Assumption 2: The Population Variances of the Dependent Variable Are the Same for All Cells

To the extent that this assumption is violated and the sample sizes differ for the cells, the p-values from the overall two-way ANOVA are not trustworthy. In addition, the results of the follow-up tests that require equal variance should be mistrusted if the population variances differ.

Assumption 3: The Cases Represent Random Samples from the Populations, and the Scores on the Dependent Variable Are Independent of Each Other

The two-way ANOVA yields inaccurate p-values if the independence assumption is violated.

Computing an Effect Size Statistic

The General Linear Model procedure computes an effect size index, labeled eta squared. It is actually a partial eta squared and may be computed for a main or interaction source using the following equation:

$$Partial\ \eta^2_{Main\ or\ Interaction\ Source} = \frac{Sum\ of\ Squares_{Main\ or\ Interaction\ Source}}{Sum\ of\ Squares_{Main\ or\ Interaction\ Source} + Sum\ of\ Squares_{Error}}$$

Partial η^2 ranges in value from 0 to 1. A partial η^2 is interpreted as the proportion of variance of the dependent variable that is related to a particular main or interaction source, excluding the other main and interaction sources. It is unclear what are small, medium, and large values for partial η^2. In all likelihood, the traditional cutoffs of .01, .06, and .14 for small, medium, and large η^2 are too large for partial η^2.

The Data Set

We will illustrate how to conduct a two-way ANOVA using our first example, a study evaluating the effects of different note-taking methods on GPA for men and women. We developed two data files: *Lesson 25 Data File 1* and *Lesson 25 Data File 2*, which can be found on the Student Disk. The two data sets were constructed to yield different results for tests of main and interaction effects so that we could illustrate the variety of follow-up tests associated with a two-way ANOVA. With the first data set, the main effects are significant, while the interaction effect is not. These data allow us to show how to conduct pairwise comparisons among the means for levels of a significant main-effect factor. With the second data set, the interaction effect is significant. These data help us illustrate how to conduct simple main effects and interaction contrasts following a significant interaction. The variables in the two data sets are the same and are described in Table 20 (at the top of page 170).

Table 20
Variables in Lesson 25 Data Files 1 and 2

Variable	Definition
gender	1 = Men
	2 = Women
method	1 = Note-Taking Method 1
	2 = Note-Taking Method 2
	3 = Control
gpaimpr	Spring GPA - Fall GPA

The Research Question

As described earlier, Ethel conducted the study to assess primarily an interaction hypothesis. The hypothesis was that men will find the Method 1 note-taking approach more helpful in learning classroom information, and women will find Method 2 more beneficial.

In addition, a method main effect was expected: The mean on the dependent variable for Method 1 and 2 should be higher than the mean for the control condition, averaging across gender.

On the other hand, we have no hypothesis associated with the gender main effect in that the description contained no statements indicating that women will do better or worse than men averaging across note-taking methods.

Of course, the data do not always turn out as expected. Consequently, it might be useful to describe what questions the main and the interaction effects address. The questions are phrased in terms of differences among means, although they could be rewritten so that they address relationships between the factors and the dependent variable.

1. Method main effect: Do the means on changes in GPA differ among Method 1, Method 2, and control conditions? The means for the three method conditions are averaged across men and women students.
2. Gender main effect: Do the means on change in GPA differ for men and women students? The means for men and women students are averaged across the three method conditions.
3. Method x Gender interaction effect: Do the differences in the means on change in GPA among the three method conditions vary as a function of gender?

Conducting a Two-Way Analysis of Variance

A number of decisions must be made about how to conduct follow-up tests when performing a two-way ANOVA. We will start with the first data set, *Lesson 25 Data File 1*, to illustrate the case of significant main effects with no significant interaction effect. Then, we will use the second data set, *Lesson 25 Data File 2*, to conduct an overall two-way ANOVA with a significant interaction effect. For both data sets, we will show how to perform pertinent follow-up tests.

Analysis with Significant Main Effects and Nonsignificant Interaction Effects

To conduct a two-way ANOVA, follow these steps:

1. Click **Analyze**, click **General Linear Model**, then click **Univariate**. You will see the Univariate dialog box, as shown in Figure 153 (at the top of page 171).
2. Click **gpaimpr**, then click ▶ to move it to the Dependent Variable box.
3. Hold down the Ctrl key and click **gender** and **method**. Click ▶ to move them to the Fixed Factor(s) box.
4. Click **Options**.
5. In the Univariate: Options dialog box, hold down the Ctrl key, and click **gender**, **method**, and **gender*method** in Factor(s) and Factor Interactions box.
6. Click ▶ to move them to the Display Means for box.

Figure 153. The GLM - Univariate dialog box.

7. In the Display box, click **Homogeneity tests**, **Descriptive statistics**, and **Estimates of effect size**.
8. Click **Continue**.
9. Click **OK**.

Selected SPSS Output for Two-Way ANOVA

Figure 154 shows the means and standard deviations for each cell and the results of the omnibus two-way ANOVA tests.

Descriptive Statistics

Dependent Variable: Change in GPA

Gender	Note-Taking methods	Mean	Std. Deviation	N
Men	Method 1	.3350	.2286	10
	Method 2	.6400	.1776	10
	Control	.1650	.1492	10
	Total	.3800	.2699	30
Women	Method 1	.1700	.1829	10
	Method 2	.3050	.1921	10
	Control	.1050	.1462	10
	Total	.1933	.1888	30
Total	Method 1	.2525	.2185	20
	Method 2	.4725	.2489	20
	Control	.1350	.1470	20
	Total	.2867	.2494	60

Tests of Between-Subjects Effects

Dependent Variable: Change in GPA

Source	Type III Sum of Squares	df	Mean Square	F	Sig.	Eta Squared
Corrected Model	1.889[a]	5	.378	11.463	.000	.515
Intercept	4.931	1	4.931	149.582	.000	.735
GENDER	.523	1	.523	15.856	.000	.227
METHOD	1.174	2	.587	17.809	.000	.397
GENDER * METHOD	.193	2	9.629E-02	2.921	.062	.098
Error	1.780	54	3.296E-02			
Total	8.600	60				
Corrected Total	3.669	59				

[a] R Squared = .515 (Adjusted R Squared = .470)

Figure 154. Partial results of the omnibus tests for the two-way ANOVA.

From these analyses, we can see that both the gender main effect and the method main effect are significant and that the interaction between gender and method is not significant. In addition, an examination of the means indicates that the ordering of the means for the three method groups is the same for both genders. Based on these results, we chose to follow up our overall tests with pairwise comparisons among the three method means averaged across gender. Because gender has only two levels, men and women, the main effect associated with gender tells us that men and women differ significantly from one another, and no further analyses are needed to evaluate the gender main effect.

Extension to Higher-Way ANOVA

How would we conduct analyses if we had more than two factors? No problem! For example, with a three-way ANOVA, include all three factors in the Fixed Factor(s) box in the GLM-Univariate dialog box. In the Univariate: Options dialog box include all three factors and their interactions in the Display Means for box.

Conducting Follow-Up Tests to a Significant Main Effect: Pairwise Comparisons

Now that we've conducted the overall ANOVA, it is time to conduct follow-up tests to our significant main effect. We will evaluate the pairwise comparisons for the method effect because it was significant and has more than two levels. In the following steps for evaluating pairwise comparisons of the marginal means, we will conduct tests that assume equality of variances and others that do not require this assumption. To conduct pairwise comparisons among the marginal means of the method factor, follow these steps:

1. Click **Analyze**, click **General Linear Model**, then click **Univariate**.
2. The appropriate options should be selected in the Univariate dialog box. If they are not, conduct Steps 2 through 8 described earlier for our overall analysis.
3. Click **Post Hoc.**
4. In the Factor(s) box, click **method**, and then click ▶ to move it to the Post Hoc Tests for box.
5. In the Equal Variances Assumed box, click **R-E-G-W-Q** and **Tukey**. Other post hoc options assuming equal variances are also valid.
6. In the Not Equal Variances Assumed box, click **Dunnett's C**. Other post hoc options not assuming equal variances are also valid.
7. Click **Continue**.
8. Click **OK**.

Selected SPSS Output for Pairwise Comparisons of Main Effect Means

Figure 155 (at the top of page 173) shows the results of the pairwise comparisons, assuming equal variances and not assuming equal variances.

With the Tukey and Dunnett's *C* tests, only the comparison between Method 1 and the control condition was not significant. For the R-E-G-W-Q test, all three comparisons were significant.

Conducting Analyses with a Significant Interaction Effect

Now we will use the data set called *Lesson 25 Data File 2* to illustrate how to conduct follow-up analyses when there is a significant interaction effect. First, you should conduct an overall test of the main and interaction effects following the same steps used in the preceding example.

Selected SPSS Output for Two-Way ANOVA

Figure 156 (at the bottom of page 173) shows the means and standard deviations for each cell and the results of the omnibus two-way ANOVA *F* test.

Multiple Comparisons

Dependent Variable: Change in GPA

	(I) Note-Taking methods	(J) Note-Taking methods	Mean Difference (I-J)	Std. Error	Sig.	95% Confidence Interval Lower Bound	95% Confidence Interval Upper Bound
Tukey HSD	Method 1	Method 2	-.2200*	5.741E-02	.001	-.3584	-8.16E-02
		Control	.1175	5.741E-02	.111	-2.09E-02	.2559
	Method 2	Method 1	.2200*	5.741E-02	.001	8.163E-02	.3584
		Control	.3375*	5.741E-02	.000	.1991	.4759
	Control	Method 1	-.1175	5.741E-02	.111	-.2559	2.087E-02
		Method 2	-.3375*	5.741E-02	.000	-.4759	-.1991
Dunnett C	Method 1	Method 2	-.2200*	5.741E-02		-.4082	-3.18E-02
		Control	.1175	5.741E-02		-3.21E-02	.2671
	Method 2	Method 1	.2200*	5.741E-02		3.183E-02	.4082
		Control	.3375*	5.741E-02		.1733	.5017
	Control	Method 1	-.1175	5.741E-02		-.2671	3.211E-02
		Method 2	-.3375*	5.741E-02		-.5017	-.1733

Based on observed means.

*. The mean difference is significant at the .05 level.

Homogeneous Subsets

Change in GPA

	Note-Taking methods	N	Subset 1	Subset 2	Subset 3
Tukey HSD[a,b]	Control	20	.1350		
	Method 1	20	.2525		
	Method 2	20		.4725	
	Sig.		.111	1.000	
Ryan-Einot-Gabriel-Welsch Range[b]	Control	20	.1350		
	Method 1	20		.2525	
	Method 2	20			.4725
	Sig.		1.000	1.000	1.000

Means for groups in homogeneous subsets are displayed.
Based on Type III Sum of Squares
The error term is Mean Square(Error) = 3.296E-02.

a. Uses Harmonic Mean Sample Size = 20.000.

b. Alpha = .05.

Figure 155. Partial results of pairwise comparisons of Method main effect means.

Descriptive Statistics

Dependent Variable: Change in GPA

Gender	Note-Taking methods	Mean	Std. Deviation	N
Men	Method 1	.3350	.2286	10
	Method 2	.3050	.1921	10
	Control	.1650	.1492	10
	Total	.2683	.2006	30
Women	Method 1	.1700	.1829	10
	Method 2	.6400	.1776	10
	Control	.1050	.1462	10
	Total	.3050	.2925	30
Total	Method 1	.2525	.2185	20
	Method 2	.4725	.2489	20
	Control	.1350	.1470	20
	Total	.2867	.2494	60

Tests of Between-Subjects Effects

Dependent Variable: Change in GPA

Source	Type III Sum of Squares	df	Mean Square	F	Sig.	Eta Squared
Corrected Model	1.889[a]	5	.378	11.463	.000	.515
Intercept	4.931	1	4.931	149.582	.000	.735
GENDER	2.017E-02	1	2.017E-02	.612	.438	.011
METHOD	1.174	2	.587	17.809	.000	.397
GENDER * METHOD	.695	2	.348	10.543	.000	.281
Error	1.780	54	3.296E-02			
Total	8.600	60				
Corrected Total	3.669	59				

a. R Squared = .515 (Adjusted R Squared = .470)

Figure 156. Results of the omnibus two-way ANOVA.

From these analyses we can see that both the method main effect and the method-by-gender interaction effect are significant. If the interaction effect is significant, we generally do not interpret main effects, but we do wish to understand why the interaction yields significance. We can follow up a significant interaction by conducting simple main effect tests, interaction comparisons, or both.

The following sections describe how to conduct simple main effect tests and interaction comparisons.

Conducting Simple Main Effect Tests Following a Significant Interaction Effect

Conducting follow-up tests to a significant interaction involves two decisions.

Which Simple Main Effects Should Be Analyzed?

We must decide whether to examine the simple main effects for one or for both factors. Which simple main effects to explore should depend on the research hypotheses. For our example, the method simple main effects (difference in means among methods for men and for women separately) are probably more interesting than the gender simple main effects (differences in means between males and females for each method separately).

What Error Term Should Be Used to Conduct the Simple Main Effects?

We must decide whether to use the same error term for each simple main effect analysis and assume homogeneity of error variance or to use different error terms for each simple main effect test and not assume homogeneity-of-error variance. If the error variances differ across simple main effects, it would be preferable to conduct the simple main effect tests using different error variances.

Because of space limitations, we describe only how to conduct simple main effects assuming homogeneity of variance. We will describe two sets of steps. The first set of steps is for conducting simple main effect analyses, while the second set of steps is for conducting pairwise comparisons of individual means if a simple main effect is significant.

Conducting Simple Main Effects Analyses

To conduct simple main effects analyses for method within gender and gender within method, we will use the /lmatrix statement. We present the /lmatrix statements for examining differences between men and women for Method 1 (step 3), for Method 2 (step 4), and for the control group (step 5) and the /lmatrix statements for evaluating differences among the methods for men (step 6) and for women (step 7):

1. Click **Analyze**, click **General Linear Model**, then click **Univariate**. The choices that we made previously when evaluating main and interaction effects should still be selected.
2. Click on **Paste**. Delete all lines except the first three lines. The first three lines in the Syntax Editor are shown:
   UNIANOVA
   gpaimpr BY gender method
   /METHOD = SSTYPE(3)
3. After the third line, type in the following statements to test the simple main effect of gender within Method 1:
   /lmatrix 'men vs women within Method 1'
   gender*method 1 0 0 -1 0 0 gender 1 -1

4. Next, type in the following statements to test the simple main effect of gender within Method 2:

> /lmatrix 'men vs women within Method 2'
> gender*method 0 1 0 0 -1 0 gender 1 -1

5. Next, type in the following statements to test the simple main effect of gender within the control group:

> /lmatrix 'men vs women within Control'
> gender*method 0 0 1 0 0 -1 gender 1 -1

6. Next, type in the following statements to test the simple main effect of method within men:

> /lmatrix 'method within men'
> gender*method 1 -1 0 0 0 0 method 1 -1 0;
> gender*method 0 1 -1 0 0 0 method 0 1 -1

7. Next, type in the following statements to test the simple main effect of method within women:

> /lmatrix 'method within women'
> gender*method 0 0 0 1 -1 0 method 1 -1 0;
> gender*method 0 0 0 0 1 -1 method 0 1 -1.

8. Click **Run**.

We discuss the /lmatrix statement in a later section in this lesson. See "Explaining the /lmatrix Command for Simple Main Effects Tests."

Selected SPSS Output for Simple Main Effects

The output for the simple main effects for method within gender is shown in Figure 157 (below, and continued at the top of page 176).

Custom Hypothesis Tests #4

Contrast Results (K Matrix)[a]

Contrast		Dependent Variable — Change in GPA
L1	Contrast Estimate	3.000E-02
	Hypothesized Value	0
	Difference (Estimate - Hypothesized)	3.000E-02
	Std. Error	.081
	Sig.	.713
	95% Confidence Interval for Difference — Lower Bound	-.133
	Upper Bound	.193
L2	Contrast Estimate	.140
	Hypothesized Value	0
	Difference (Estimate - Hypothesized)	.140
	Std. Error	.081
	Sig.	.090
	95% Confidence Interval for Difference — Lower Bound	-2.279E-02
	Upper Bound	.303

a. Based on the user-specified contrast coefficients (L') matrix: method within men

Test Results

Dependent Variable: Change in GPA

Source	Sum of Squares	df	Mean Square	F	Sig.
Contrast	.165	2	8.233E-02	2.498	.092
Error	1.780	54	3.296E-02		

Figure 157. Partial results of the simple main effects for method within males and females.

Custom Hypothesis Tests #5

Contrast Results (K Matrix)[a]

Contrast		Dependent Variable Change in GPA
L1	Contrast Estimate	-.470
	Hypothesized Value	0
	Difference (Estimate - Hypothesized)	-.470
	Std. Error	.081
	Sig.	.000
	95% Confidence Interval for Difference — Lower Bound	-.633
	— Upper Bound	-.307
L2	Contrast Estimate	.535
	Hypothesized Value	0
	Difference (Estimate - Hypothesized)	.535
	Std. Error	.081
	Sig.	.000
	95% Confidence Interval for Difference — Lower Bound	.372
	— Upper Bound	.698

a. Based on the user-specified contrast coefficients (L') matrix: method within women

Test Results

Dependent Variable: Change in GPA

Source	Sum of Squares	df	Mean Square	F	Sig.
Contrast	1.705	2	.852	25.855	.000
Error	1.780	54	3.296E-02		

Figure 157, continued.

Although we conducted all possible simple main effects, we are probably interested in evaluating only the simple main effects for method within gender. Accordingly, we restrict our output and discussion to these two simple main effect tests.

A hypothesis that is tested using an /lmatrix statement is a custom hypothesis. Accordingly, each simple main effect is labeled a custom hypothesis on your output. The simple main effect for method within men and simple main effect for method within women are labeled Custom Hypothesis Tests # 4 and Custom Hypothesis Tests # 5, respectively, on your output. Each of these simple main effects include two pairwise comparisons, based on the coefficients on the /lmatrix statement. The Contrast Estimates in the Contrast Results box reflect differences between means for these pairwise comparisons. The tests for the simple mains effect comparing methods for each gender are presented in the Test Results boxes.

The F test of 2.50 and the p-value of .092 for evaluating the differences among methods for men are given in the table labeled Test Results for Custom Hypothesis Tests #4. The F test of 25.86 and the p-value of .000 for evaluating the differences among methods for women are given in the table labeled Test Results for Custom Hypothesis Tests #5. These results indicate significant differences among methods for women only.

Conducting Pairwise Comparisons following Significant Simple Main Effects Tests

Gender has only two levels, so we would not have to conduct follow-up tests to a significant gender simple main effect. In contrast, the method factor has three levels so that it is necessary to conduct follow-up tests if a simple main effect for method within gender is significant. We show how to conduct these tests.

1. Return to the Syntax Editor. The window should contain the following syntax lines:

    UNIANOVA
    gpaimpr BY gender method
    /METHOD = SSTYPE(3)
    /lmatrix 'men vs women within Method 1'
    gender*method 1 0 0 -1 0 0 gender 1 -1
    /lmatrix 'men vs women within Method 2'
    gender*method 0 1 0 0 -1 0 gender 1 -1
    /lmatrix 'men vs women within Control'
    gender*method 0 0 1 0 0 -1 gender 1 -1
    /lmatrix 'method within men'
    gender*method 1 -1 0 0 0 0 method 1 -1 0;
    gender*method 0 1 -1 0 0 0 method 0 1 -1
    /lmatrix 'method within women'
    gender*method 0 0 0 1 -1 0 method 1 -1 0;
    gender*method 0 0 0 0 1 -1 method 0 1 -1.

2. Because we do not need to conduct pairwise comparisons for the simple main effects for gender within method, delete the following lines:

    /lmatrix 'men vs women within Method 1'
    gender*method 1 0 0 -1 0 0 gender 1 -1
    /lmatrix 'men vs women within Method 2'
    gender*method 0 1 0 0 -1 0 gender 1 -1
    /lmatrix 'men vs women within Control'
    gender*method 0 0 1 0 0 -1 gender 1 -1

3. Next, to conduct the comparisons among the method means for men (simple main effect for method within men), replace

    /lmatrix 'method within men'
    gender*method 1 -1 0 0 0 0 method 1 -1 0;
    gender*method 0 1 -1 0 0 0 method 0 1 -1

    with

    /lmatrix 'Method 1 vs. Method 2 within men'
    gender*method 1 -1 0 0 0 0 method 1 -1 0
    /lmatrix 'Method 1 vs Control within men'
    gender*method 1 0 -1 0 0 0 method 1 0 -1
    /lmatrix 'Method 2 vs Control within men'
    gender*method 0 1 -1 0 0 0 method 0 1 -1

4. To conduct the comparisons among the method means for women (simple main effect for method within women), replace

    /lmatrix 'method within women'
    gender*method 0 0 0 1 -1 0 method 1 -1 0;
    gender*method 0 0 0 0 1 -1 method 0 1 -1

    with

    /lmatrix 'Method 1 vs. Method 2 within women'
    gender*method 0 0 0 1 -1 0 method 1 -1 0
    /lmatrix 'Method 1 vs Control within women'
    gender*method 0 0 0 1 0 -1 method 1 0 -1
    /lmatrix 'Method 2 vs Control within women'
    gender*method 0 0 0 0 1 -1 method 0 1 -1.

5. Click **Run**.

Selected SPSS Output for Pairwise Comparisons Following a Significant Simple Main Effect

Figure 158 (below, and continued at the top of page 179) shows the results for the pairwise comparisons among method levels for men only. You should have comparable results for women on your output.

Custom Hypotheses 1, 2, and 3 present the results of pairwise comparisons among methods for men. The Contrast Estimate of .030 presented as 3.000E -02 in the first table represents the difference in means between Method 1 and Method 2 for men (.030 = .335 - .305). Similarly, the Contrast Estimates of .170 and .140 are listed in comparable tables for Custom Hypothesis Tests #2 and #3, respectively. These estimates represent the difference in means between Method 1 and control for men (.170 = .335 - .165) and between Method 2 and control for men (.140 = .305 - .165). The results for the F tests for these pairwise comparisons for men are reported in the tables labeled Test Results. The p-values (labeled Sig. in the table) are .713, .041, and .090 for the comparisons between Method 1 and Method 2, Method 1 and control, and Method 2 and control, respectively.

Custom Hypothesis Tests #1

Contrast Results (K Matrix)[a]

Contrast		Dependent Variable Change in GPA
L1	Contrast Estimate	3.000E-02
	Hypothesized Value	0
	Difference (Estimate - Hypothesized)	3.000E-02
	Std. Error	.081
	Sig.	.713
	95% Confidence Interval for Difference Lower Bound	-.133
	Upper Bound	.193

a. Based on the user-specified contrast coefficients (L') matrix: Method 1 vs. Method 2 within men

Test Results

Dependent Variable: Change in GPA

Source	Sum of Squares	df	Mean Square	F	Sig.
Contrast	4.500E-03	1	4.500E-03	.137	.713
Error	1.780	54	3.296E-02		

Custom Hypothesis Tests #2

Contrast Results (K Matrix)[a]

Contrast		Dependent Variable Change in GPA
L1	Contrast Estimate	.170
	Hypothesized Value	0
	Difference (Estimate - Hypothesized)	.170
	Std. Error	.081
	Sig.	.041
	95% Confidence Interval for Difference Lower Bound	7.214E-03
	Upper Bound	.333

a. Based on the user-specified contrast coefficients (L') matrix: Method 1 vs Control within men

Figure 158. Results for pairwise comparisons among method levels for men.

Test Results

Dependent Variable: Change in GPA

Source	Sum of Squares	df	Mean Square	F	Sig.
Contrast	.145	1	.145	4.384	.041
Error	1.780	54	3.296E-02		

Custom Hypothesis Tests #3

Contrast Results (K Matrix)[a]

Contrast		Dependent Variable: Change in GPA
L1	Contrast Estimate	.140
	Hypothesized Value	0
	Difference (Estimate - Hypothesized)	.140
	Std. Error	.081
	Sig.	.090
	95% Confidence Interval for Difference Lower Bound	-2.279E-02
	Upper Bound	.303

a. Based on the user-specified contrast coefficients (L') matrix: Method 2 vs Control within men

Test Results

Dependent Variable: Change in GPA

Source	Sum of Squares	df	Mean Square	F	Sig.
Contrast	9.800E-02	1	9.800E-02	2.973	.090
Error	1.780	54	3.296E-02		

Figure 158, continued.

The results for the F tests for the pairwise comparisons among Method 1, Method 2, and control for the women are reported in the tables labeled Custom Hypothesis Tests #4, #5, and #6. The F tests for these pairwise comparisons are presented in the tables labeled Test Results. The p-values are .000, .427, and .000 for the comparisons between Method 1 and Method 2, Method 1 and control, and Method 2 and control, respectively.

The F tests evaluate the pairwise mean differences without controlling for Type I error across comparisons. Some researchers may choose to control for Type I error across these tests using a Bonferroni approach, as illustrated in the example of an APA results section later in this lesson.

Explaining the /lmatrix Command for Simple Main Effects Tests

By specifying L matrices, we are able to conduct a variety of customized tests. For an in-depth discussion of L matrices with GLM analyses, see Green, Marquis, Hershberger, Thompson, and McCollam (1999). In this section we will discuss how to work with L matrices to test simple main effect tests and pairwise comparisons among means of simple main effects.

Let's use the following syntax to discuss the /lmatrix command:

```
UNIANOVA
gpaimpr BY gender method
/METHOD = SSTYPE(3)
/lmatrix 'Method 1 vs Method 2 within men'
gender*method 1 -1 0 0 0 0 method 1 -1 0.
```

The /lmatrix on the fourth line indicates that you want to conduct a customized test, and the wording inside the single quotes allows you to label the hypothesis evaluated by the test. On the fifth line, we specify the hypothesis using coefficients. The coefficients are not associated with means, but rather with main and interaction effects. The coefficients of 1 and -1 indicate what main or interaction effects are being compared, while the coefficient of 0 indicates which of these effects are being ignored. The ordering of the coefficients for the interaction effects is based on the order of the factors on the second line of the syntax statements after the BY. For our design with two levels of gender and three levels of method, the following apply:

- The first coefficient is for level 1 of the first factor and level 1 of the second factor.
- The second coefficient is for level 1 of the first factor and level 2 of the second factor.
- The third coefficient is for level 1 of the first factor and level 3 of the second
- The fourth coefficient is for level 2 of the first factor and level 1 of the second
- The fifth coefficient is for level 2 of the first factor and level 2 of the second
- The sixth coefficient is for level 2 of the first factor and level 3 of the second

The combination of the main and interaction effects defined by the L matrix yields the hypothesis of interest concerning difference in cell means. We will not discuss how to work with these effects algebraically. Instead, we show how to conduct customized tests with the L matrix by presenting a general rule and a series of examples that illustrate the use of this rule.

Rule

To evaluate difference between levels A_j and $A_{j'}$ of Factor A for level B_k of Factor B, define the coefficients for the A main effects and for the A*B interaction effects. The coefficients for the A main effects compare A_j and $A_{j'}$, while the coefficients for the interaction effects compare A_j and $A_{j'}$ of Factor A within level B_k.

Example 1

Let's evaluate the difference between Method 1 and Method 2 for men. The coefficients for Method main effects of 1 -1 0 compare Method 1 and Method 2 and ignore control. The first three coefficients for the interaction effects of 1 -1 0 compare Method 1 and Method 2 and ignore control for men, while the last three coefficient of 0 0 0 ignore all levels of Method for women.

    /lmatrix 'Method 1 vs Method 2 within men'
    gender*method 1 -1 0 0 0 0 method 1 -1 0.

Example 2

Let's evaluate the difference between men and women for Method 1. The coefficients for the Gender main effects of 1 -1 compare men and women. The coefficients for the interaction of 1 0 0 -1 0 0 compare men for Method 1 with the women for Method 1 and ignore all other effects.

    /lmatrix 'men vs women within Method 1'
    gender*method 1 0 0 -1 0 0 gender 1 -1.

Example 3

Rather than comparing means for two levels of one factor within a level of a second factor, we might be interested in comparing three or more levels of one factor within a level of a second factor. Under these circumstances, we link together the pairwise comparisons for the adjacent levels of the first factor. For example, we might wish to evaluate whether the means among the three methods are equal for men. In this instance, we need to develop coefficients for interaction and main effects for two pairwise comparisons:

    UNIANOVA
    gpaimpr BY gender method
    /METHOD = SSTYPE(3)

/matrix 'method within men'
gender*method 1 -1 0 0 0 0 method 1 -1 0;
gender*method 0 1 -1 0 0 0 method 0 1 -1.

The last two lines represent comparisons between Method 1 and Method 2 for men and between Method 2 and control for men, respectively. The semicolon at the end of the next to the last line instructs SPSS to combine the two comparisons together to yield the simple main effects for method within men.

Before running syntax containing the /lmatrix statement, include a period at the end of the last line.

Conducting Interaction Comparisons Following a Significant Interaction

As an alternative (or perhaps in addition) to simple main effect analyses, interaction comparisons can be conducted as follow-up tests to a significant interaction. The tetrad contrast, the simplest interaction comparison associated with a two-way interaction, involves four cell means. In particular, tetrad contrasts evaluate whether the differences in population means between two levels of one factor are equal across two levels of the other factor.

For example, Ethel's hypothesis that men benefit most from note-taking Method 1, while women benefit most from note-taking Method 2 can be addressed by a specific interaction comparison involving four cell means. This comparison would evaluate the null hypothesis that the difference in population means between Method 1 and Method 2 for men minus the difference in population means between Method 1 and Method 2 for women is equal to zero. Ethel's hypothesis is that this comparison yields a positive value in the population.

Follow these steps to conduct all three tetrad comparisons:

1. Return to the Syntax Editor. Delete all lines in the Syntax window.
2. Click **Analyze**, click **General Linear Model**, then click **Univariate**. The choices that we made previously should still be selected within the Univariate dialog box.
3. Click **Paste**. Delete all lines except the first three. The first three lines in the Syntax Editor are shown:
   UNIANOVA
   gpaimpr BY gender method
   /METHOD = SSTYPE(3)
4. After the third line, type in the following statements to evaluate whether the difference in means between Method 1 and Method 2 for men is the same as the difference in means between Method 1 and Method 2 for women:
   /lmatrix '(Method 1 vs Method 2) for men vs (Method 1 vs Method 2) for women'
   gender*method 1 -1 0 -1 1 0
5. Next, type in the following statements to evaluate whether the difference in means between Method 1 and control for men is the same as the difference in means between Method 1 and control for women:
   /lmatrix '(Method 1 vs Control) for men vs (Method 1 vs Control) for women'
   gender*method 1 0 -1 -1 0 1
6. Next, type in the following statements to evaluate whether the difference in means between Method 2 and control for men is the same as the difference in means between Method 2 and control for women:
   /lmatrix '(Method 2 vs Control) for men vs (Method 2 vs Control) for women'
   gender*method 0 1 -1 0 -1 1.
7. Click **Run**.

A tetrad comparison is specified on the /lmatrix by delineating the coefficients for the interactions effects. These coefficients are identical to the coefficients that would be used for defining the tetrad comparisons among the cell means. See an ANOVA textbook for a discussion about how to specify interaction comparisons.

Selected SPSS Output for Interaction Comparisons

Figure 159 shows the results of one of the three interaction comparisons. It is the contrast labeled Custom Hypothesis #1 on the output.

Custom Hypothesis Tests

Contrast Results (K Matrix)[a]

		Dependent Variable
Contrast		Change in GPA
L1	Contrast Estimate	.500
	Hypothesized Value	0
	Difference (Estimate - Hypothesized)	.500
	Std. Error	.115
	Sig.	.000
	95% Confidence Interval Lower Bound	.270
	for Difference Upper Bound	.730

a. Based on the user-specified contrast coefficients (L') matrix: (Method 1 vs Method 2) for men vs (Method 1 vs Method 2) for women

Test Results

Dependent Variable: Change in GPA

Source	Sum of Squares	df	Mean Square	F	Sig.
Contrast	.625	1	.625	18.961	.000
Error	1.780	54	3.296E-02		

Figure 159. Results of interaction comparison of Method 1 and Method 2 for men and women.

The Contrast Estimate of .500 listed in the first table for Custom Hypothesis Tests #1 represents the difference in means between Method 1 and Method 2 for men (.030 = .335 - .305) minus the difference in means between Method 1 and Method 2 for women (-.470 = .170 - .640). The F test of 18.96 and the p-value of .000 for evaluating this tetrad comparison are given in the table labeled Test Results.

We do not present the tables for the second and third interaction comparisons, but you should see the results for both of them in your output The Contrast Estimate of .105 for Custom Hypothesis Tests #2 represents the difference in means between Method 1 and control for men (.170 = .3350 - .165) minus the difference in means between Method 1 and control for women (.065 = .170 - .105). The F test of .836 and the p-value of .365 for evaluating this tetrad comparison are given in the table labeled Test Results.

The Contrast Estimate of -.395 listed in the table for Custom Hypothesis Tests #3 represents the difference in means between Method 2 and control for men (.140 = .305 - .165) minus the difference in means between Method 2 and control for women (.535 = .640 - .105). The F test of 11.83 and the p-value of .001 for evaluating this tetrad comparison are given in the table labeled Test Results.

The F tests for these tetrad comparisons evaluate mean differences without controlling for Type I error across comparisons. Some method, such as a Bonferroni approach, may be used to control for Type I error across the three interaction comparisons.

Using SPSS Graphs to Display Results

A graph displaying a boxplot for each cell of a two-way ANOVA can make a significant interaction more understandable. To create a boxplot for *Lesson 25 Data File 2*, conduct the following steps:

1. Click **Graphs**, then click **Boxplot**.
2. Click **Clustered** and **Summaries for groups of cases** in the Boxplot dialog box.

3. Click **Define**.
4. In the Define dialog box, click **gpaimpr**, and click ▸ to move it to the Variable box.
5. Click **method**, and click ▸ to move it to the Category Axis box.
6. Click **gender**, and click ▸ to move it to the Define Clusters by box.
7. Click **OK**, and edit the graph so that it is appropriately labeled. The graph is shown in Figure 160.

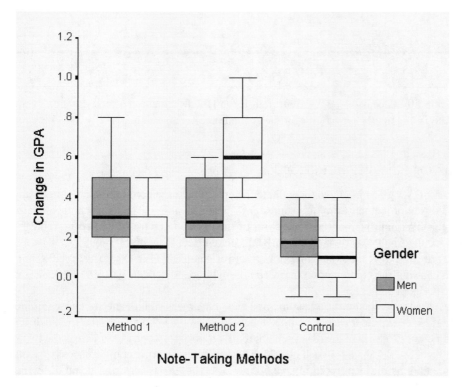

Figure 160. Boxplots of GPA improvement by note-taking method for men and women.

Two APA Results Sections

We present two results sections, one for a significant main effect and nonsignificant interaction effect and one for a significant interaction effect.

Results for Significant Main Effect and a Nonsignificant Interaction

A 3 x 2 ANOVA was conducted to evaluate the effects of three note-taking conditions and gender on GPA improvement from fall semester to spring semester. The means and standard deviations for GPA improvement as a function of the two factors are presented in Table 21 (at the top of page 184). The ANOVA indicated no significant interaction between note-taking and gender, F (2, 54) = 2.92, p = .062, partial η^2 = .10, but significant main effects for note-taking, F (2, 54) = 17.81, p < .001, partial η^2 = .40, and gender, F (1, 54) = 15.86, p < .001, partial η^2 = .23. The gender main effect indicated that men tended to have greater improvements in GPA than women, but it was not the focus of this study.

The primary purpose of the study was to determine which method of note-taking is more effective. Follow-up analyses to the main effect for note-taking examined this issue. The follow-up tests consisted of all pairwise comparisons among the three types of note-taking methods. The Tukey HSD procedure was used to control for Type I error across the pairwise comparisons. The results of this analysis indicate that the group using the second note-taking method improved GPA significantly more than either the first method group or the control group. There was no

Table 21

Means and Standard Deviations for GPA Improvement

Gender	Method	Mean	SD
Men	Method 1	.34	.23
	Method 2	.64	.18
	Control	.17	.15
Women	Method 1	.17	.18
	Method 2	.31	.19
	Control	.11	.15

significant difference between the control group and the first method of note-taking. Overall, the 3 x 2 ANOVA indicates superiority for the second note-taking method.

Results for a Significant Interaction

A 3 x 2 ANOVA was conducted to evaluate the effects of three note-taking conditions and gender on GPA improvement from fall semester to spring semester. The means and standard deviations for GPA improvement as a function of the two factors are presented in Table 22. The results for the ANOVA indicated a significant main effect for note-taking, $F (2, 54) = 17.81$, $p < .001$, partial $\eta^2 = .40$, a nonsignificant effect for gender, $F (1, 54) = .61$, $p = .438$, partial $\eta^2 = .01$, and a significant interaction between note-taking and gender, $F (2, 54) = 10.54$, $p < .001$, partial $\eta^2 = .28$.

Because the interaction between method and gender was significant, we chose to ignore the method main effect and instead examined the method simple main effects, that is, the differences among methods for men and women separately. To control for Type I error across the two simple main effects, we set alpha for each at .025. There were no significant differences between note-taking conditions for men, $F (2, 54) = 2.50$, $p = .092$, but there were significant differences for women, $F (2, 54) = 25.86$, $p < .001$.

Follow-up tests were conducted to evaluate the three pairwise differences among the means for women, with alpha set at .008 (.025 / 3 = .008) to control for Type I error over the three pairwise comparisons. The second note-taking method had significantly higher GPA improvements than either the first note-taking method or the control group for the women students. There were no significant differences between the control group and the first method of note-taking.

One final analysis was conducted to address the hypothesis that men would benefit most from note-taking Method 1 while women would benefit most from note-taking Method 2. The difference in means between Method 1 and Method 2 for men minus the difference in means between Method 1 and Method 2 for women is .50, $F (1, 54) = 18.96$, $p < .001$. The results of this comparison supported the research hypothesis.

Table 22

Means and Standard Deviations for GPA Improvement

Gender	Method	Mean	SD
Men	Method 1	.34	.23
	Method 2	.31	.19
	Control	.17	.15
Women	Method 1	.17	.18
	Method 2	.64	.15
	Control	.11	.15

A Word of Caution: Additional Complexities Occur with Unequal Sample Sizes across Cells

In our examples, the sample sizes were the same for all cells. The analyses become much more complex, however, if the number of cases differ across cells. We will discuss briefly some of the issues with ANOVAs with unequal cell frequencies. For a more extensive discussion of this topic, analysis-of-variance textbooks like Maxwell and Delaney (1990) should be consulted.

The means associated with the main effects (e.g., the mean for males and the mean for females for the gender main effect) can be calculated several ways if the number of cases are unequal (and disproportionate) across the different cells of a two-way ANOVA. For example, you might compute weighted means or unweighted means. In the SPSS output, the weighted means are presented in the Descriptive Statistics table in the row labeled Total, while the unweighted means are given in the table labeled Estimated Marginal Means. If the sample sizes for the cells are equal, the two types of means yield the same results.

To help us understand the difference between these two types of means, let's examine a new data set for our note-taking example, one that has three cases in some cells and two cases in other cells. The data for this example are shown in Table 23. For these data, we can compute unweighted means for method levels or gender levels by simply averaging cell means. Thus, the unweighted mean for Method 1 is .230 and is computed by averaging the cell mean for males in Method 1 of .300 and the cell mean for females in Method 1 of .160: .230 = (.300 + .160)/2. Alternatively, we could calculate a weighted mean for each level of method or gender by weighting each cell mean by its frequency and dividing by the sum of the cell frequencies. For Method 1, the weighted mean is .244 and is computed by weighting the cell mean for males in Method 1 of .300 by its frequency of 3 and weighting the cell mean for females in Method 1 of .160 by its frequency of 2 and dividing the result by the sum of the cell frequencies of 5: .244 = [(3).300 + (2).160]/(3 + 2).

Your choice between unweighted and weighted means (and, potentially, other means) is a complex one and deserves more space than we can give it. We will make only one comment. Unweighted means are preferable if researchers would like to interpret an ANOVA with unequal cell frequencies as if it had equal cell frequencies and if research participants who dropped out of their study did so completely at random. We'd guess that most researchers choose this option, wisely or unwisely.

Table 23

Example Data to Differentiate between Unweighted and Weighted Means

	Method 1	Method 2	Control	Gender means Unweighted means	Weighted means
Males	.200	.160	.100		
	.340	.200	.140	.200	.214
	.360				
Females	.140	.240	.150		
	.180	.260	.170	.180	.183
		.160	.160		
Method means					
Unweighted	.230	.200	.140		
Weighted	.244	.204	.144		

F tests that evaluate hypotheses concerning differences in unweighted population means yield different results from *F* tests that evaluate hypotheses about difference in weighted population means. SPSS computes *F* tests that evaluate unweighted population means if you choose Type III sum of squares in the drop-down menu in the Univariate: Model dialog box. Accordingly, if you choose Type III sum of squares (in the Univariate: Model dialog box), you must report the unweighted means (estimated marginal means), not the weighted means in your Results section. *F* tests for other types of means are calculated if you choose other types of sums of squares.

Exercises

Exercises 1 through 4 are based on the following research problem. The data are in the file labeled *Lesson 25 Exercise File 1*.

An experimenter wanted to investigate simultaneously the effects of two types of reinforcement schedules and three types of reinforcers on the arithmetic problem-solving performance of second-grade students. A sample of 66 second-graders was identified, and 11 were randomly assigned to each of the six combinations of reinforcement schedules and reinforcers. Students studied arithmetic problem solving under these six conditions for three weeks, and then took a test over the material they studied. The SPSS data file includes 66 cases and three variables: a factor distinguishing between the two types of reinforcement schedules (random or spaced), a second factor distinguishing among three types of reinforcers (token, money or food), and the dependent variable, an arithmetic problem-solving test.

Conduct a two-way ANOVA to analyze these data.

1. Identify the following information from the output.
    a.   The F value for the schedule main effect
    b.   The mean GPA dependent variable score for the cell associated with the random schedule and the money reinforcer
    c.   Effect size for the interaction effect
    d. p-value for the reinforcer type main effect
2. What follow-up tests would you conduct? Why?
3. Write a results section based on your output.
4. Create a boxplot to visually represent the interaction between schedule type and reinforcer type on test scores.

Exercises 5 through 8 are based on the following research problem. The data set for this problem is named *Lesson 25 Exercise File 2*.

Vicki was interested in how much time fathers of children with a disability play with their children who are disabled. To address this question, she found 60 fathers in six categories: (a) fathers with a male child with no physical or mental disability, (b) fathers with a female child with no physical or mental disability, (c) fathers with a male physically disabled child, (d) fathers with a female physically disabled child, (e) fathers with a male mentally retarded child, and (f) fathers with a female mentally retarded child. She asked fathers to record how many minutes per day they spent playing with their child for five days. The SPSS data file contains 60 cases and three variables, a factor indicating the disability status of the child, a factor indicating the child's gender, and a play time score averaged across the five days.

5. Conduct a two-way ANOVA to evaluate differences among the groups differentiating the gender and disability status of the child on the amount of time fathers spent playing with their children.
6. Which follow-up procedures should you use? Why?
7. Write a results section reporting the results of the analysis.
8. Create a boxplot to show the distributions for the six groups.

One-Way Analysis of Covariance

A one-way analysis of covariance (ANCOVA) evaluates whether population means on the dependent variable are the same across levels of a factor, adjusting for differences on the covariate, or more simply stated, whether the adjusted group means differ significantly from each other. With a one-way analysis of covariance, each individual or case must have scores on three variables: a factor or independent variable, a covariate, and a dependent variable. The factor divides individuals into two or more groups or levels, while the covariate and the dependent variable differentiate individuals on quantitative dimensions.

Applying One-Way ANCOVA

One-way ANCOVA is used to analyze data from several types of studies.

- Studies with a pretest and random assignment of subjects to factor levels
- Studies with a pretest and assignment to factor levels based on the pretest
- Studies with a pretest, matching based on the pretest, and random assignment to factor levels
- Studies with potential confounding

We will next illustrate each of these four types of studies and then briefly discuss them. Maxwell and Delaney (1990) discuss more extensively the use of ANCOVA with these four applications.

Studies with a Pretest and Random Assignment to Factor Levels

Dana wishes to assess whether vitamin C is effective in the treatment of colds. To evaluate her hypothesis, she decides to conduct a two-year experimental study. She obtains 30 volunteers from undergraduate classes to participate. She randomly assigns an equal number of students to three groups: placebo (group 1), low doses of vitamin C (group 2), and high doses of vitamin C (group 3). In the first and second years of the study, students in all three groups are monitored to assess the number of days that they have cold symptoms. During the first year, students do not take any pills. In the second year of the study, students take pills that contain one of the following: no active ingredient (group 1), a low dose of vitamin C (group 2), or a high dose of vitamin C (group 3). Dana's SPSS data file includes 30 cases and three variables: a factor distinguishing among the three medication groups; a covariate, the number of days with cold symptoms in the first year before any treatment; and a dependent variable, the number of days with cold symptoms in the second year when they are taking pills.

Studies with a Pretest and Assignment to Factor Levels Based on the Pretest

Jean wishes to assess whether individuals who are depressed about some event would benefit from intensively writing about their emotions. To evaluate this hypothesis, she obtains a sample of 60 runners who have had physical injuries that prevent them from running. She administers a measure of depression to these runners. The individuals who have the highest scores on the premeasure of depression (those who are most depressed) are assigned to the writing condition, while those who have lower scores are assigned to the attention placebo group. The runners in both groups meet with Jean's research assistant twice, four hours per occasion. The runners in the writing group are asked to write about how they feel about their injuries, while the runners in the attention placebo group are asked to write a short story involving adventure. Runners in both groups then retake the depression measure. Jean's SPSS data file includes 60 cases and three variables: a factor distinguishing among the two treatment groups, a covariate that assesses depression before treatment, and a dependent variable that assesses depression after treatment.

Studies with a Pretest, Matching Based on the Pretest, and Random Assignment to Factor Levels

Jim decides to conduct a study to learn how much time basketball players need to spend at the foul line preparing themselves to shoot free throws to be effective. Jim asks boys from his physical education classes to volunteer for his free-throw shooting study. Sixty boys consent to participate. These boys initially shoot 50 free throws, and their accuracy is recorded. Next, Jim rank orders the accuracy scores from lowest to highest and places the boys into 20 groups of three based on these scores. In other words, the three boys who have the lowest accuracy scores are in one group, the three boys who have the next three lowest accuracy scores are in another group, and so on. Within each of these 20 triads, one boy is randomly assigned to treatment Group 1, another boy to treatment Group 2, and the third boy to treatment Group 3. Over the next two weeks, boys are taught a specific method to shoot free throws. The boys in Group 1 are taught to shoot approximately 2 seconds after going to the free throw line; the boys in Group 2 are taught to shoot approximately 5 seconds after going to the free throw line; and the boys in Group 3 are taught to shoot approximately 8 seconds after going to the free throw line. Finally, all boys again must shoot 50 free throws, and their scores are recorded. Jim's SPSS data file has 60 cases and three variables: a factor distinguishing among the three treatment groups, a covariate that assesses their accuracy in shooting free throws before treatment, and a dependent variable that assesses their accuracy in shooting free throws after treatment.

Studies with Potential Confounding

Larry works with 60 boys who have behavior problems in the classroom. Recently, 20 of these boys participated in a special summer program. The other 40 boys did not participate because their parents did not want them to participate or failed to return the permission slip before the deadline. After the summer program, Larry had the teachers of all 60 boys complete a rating form indicating the degree that they found the boys to be behavioral problems in their classrooms. Larry wanted to compare the two groups of boys on the behavior ratings to assess the effectiveness of the summer program. Because he felt that the boys who participated in the summer program might come from families with a higher socioeconomic status (SES), he also computed a SES index for each of the 60 boys. Larry's SPSS data file includes 60 cases and three variables: a factor distinguishing between the two groups (boys who participated in the summer program and boys who did not), a covariate SES, and the behavior ratings completed by the teachers.

Understanding One-Way ANCOVA

The ANCOVA F test evaluates whether the population means on the dependent variable, adjusted for differences on the covariate, differ across levels of a factor. If a factor has more than two levels and the F is significant, follow-up tests should be conducted to determine where there are differences on the adjusted means across groups. These follow-up tests most often involve the comparison of pairs of adjusted means. For example, if a factor has three levels, three pairwise comparisons among the adjusted means can be conducted: Group 1 versus Group 2, Group 1 versus Group 3, and Group 2 versus Group 3.

The adequacy of ANCOVA to adjust the dependent variable scores for covariate differences depends on the type of study.

Studies with a Pretest and Random Assignment of Subjects to Factor Levels

ANCOVA may be applied to data in which (1) all cases are measured on a pretest, (2) cases are randomly assigned to different groups, (3) groups receive different treatments, and (4) all cases subsequently are measured on a posttest. The pretest and the posttest could be the same measure, which is administered before and after treatment. Alternatively, the pretest and posttest could be different measures and could even assess different constructs. Assuming that the ANCOVA assumptions are met, the one-way ANCOVA should adequately adjust dependent variable scores for initial covariate differences among groups for this design.

Studies with a Pretest and Assignment to Factor Levels Based on the Pretest

ANCOVA may be applied to data in which (1) all cases are measured on a pretest, (2) cases are assigned to different treatment groups based on their pretest scores, (3) groups receive different treatments, and (4) all cases are measured on a posttest. The pretest and the posttest could be the same measure, or they could be different measures that assess the same or different dimensions. If the ANCOVA assumptions are met, ANCOVA should adequately adjust the dependent variable scores for initial covariate differences among groups for this design.

Studies with a Pretest, Matching Based on the Pretest, and Random Assignment to Factor Levels

ANCOVA may be applied to data in which (1) all cases are measured on a pretest, (2) cases are assigned to different groups based on their pretest scores, (3) cases are randomly assigned to levels of the factor within each of the groups that were formed based on the pretest, (4) cases in different levels of the factor receive different treatments, and (5) all cases are measured on a posttest. Similar to the previous application, the pretest and the posttest could be the same measure or different measures assessing the same or different constructs. Assuming that the ANCOVA assumptions are met, the one-way ANCOVA should adequately adjust dependent variable scores for initial covariate differences among groups.

Studies with Potential Confounding

For studies with potential confounding, cases are in different groups, but are neither randomly assigned to groups nor assigned to groups based on their pretest scores. The difficulty with these studies is that the groups may differ due to variables other than the factor and the covariate. Because these studies are potentially confounded, conclusions about the group differences are difficult to reach. The results of an ANCOVA can be misleading for studies with this design.

Assumptions Underlying a One-Way ANCOVA

Assumption 1: The Dependent Variable Is Normally Distributed in the Population for Any Specific Value of the Covariate and for Any One Level of a Factor

This assumption describes multiple conditional distributions of the dependent variable, one for every combination of values of the covariate and levels of the factor, and requires them all to be normally distributed. With moderate to large sample sizes, the assumption may be violated and the test will probably yield reasonably accurate results. In most circumstances, a sample size of 15 cases per group may be large enough to yield fairly accurate p-values. Larger sample sizes may be required to produce relatively valid results if the population distributions are substantially nonnormal.

Assumption 2: The Variances of the Dependent Variable for the Conditional Distributions Described in Assumption 1 Are Equal

To the extent that this assumption is violated and the group sample sizes differ, the validity of the results of the one-way ANCOVA analysis should be questioned. Even with equal sample sizes, the results of the standard post hoc tests should be mistrusted if the population variances differ.

Assumption 3: The Cases Represent a Random Sample from the Population, and the Scores on the Dependent Variable Are Independent of Each Other

The test will yield inaccurate results if the independence assumption is violated.

Assumption 4: The Covariate Is Linearly Related to the Dependent Variable within All Levels of the Factor, and the Weights or Slopes Relating the Covariate to the Dependent Variable Are Equal across All Levels of the Factor

The latter part of this assumption is sometimes called the homogeneity-of-slopes assumption. To the extent that linearity or homogeneity of slopes does not hold, the results of an ANCOVA are likely to be misinterpreted. Later in this lesson, we will discuss a method for evaluating the homogeneity-of-slopes assumption.

Computing an Effect Size Statistic

The General Linear Model procedure computes an effect size index, the partial η^2. Although partial η^2s are computed for the factor and the covariate,

$$Partial\ \eta^2_{Main\ or\ Interaction\ Source} = \frac{Sum\ of\ Squares_{Main\ or\ Interaction\ Source}}{Sum\ of\ Squares_{Main\ or\ Interaction\ Source} + Sum\ of\ Squares_{Error}}$$

the partial η^2 of primary interest is the one associated with the factor.

The partial η^2 ranges in value from 0 to 1. The partial η^2 for the factor is interpreted as the proportion of variance of the dependent variable related to the factor, holding constant (partialling out) the covariate. Traditionally, an η^2 of .01, .06, and .14 represent small, medium, and large effect sizes, respectively.

The Data Set

The data set used to illustrate this procedure is named *Lesson 26 Data File 1* on the Student Disk and represents data from the vitamin C example described earlier in this lesson. The variables in the data set are shown in Table 24 (at the top of page 191).

Table 24

Variables in Lesson 26 Data File 1

Variable	Definition
group	1 = Placebo
	2 = Low doses of vitamin C
	3 = High doses of vitamin C
predays	Number of days with cold symptoms in the first year
days	Number of days with cold symptoms in the second year

The Research Question

The research question can be stated to reflect mean differences or relationships between variables.

1. Mean differences: Does the number of days of cold symptoms differ for those who take a placebo, those who take low doses of vitamin C, and those who take high doses of vitamin C assuming no prior differences among groups?
2. Relationship between variables: Is there a relationship between how much vitamin C is taken and the number of days that an individual shows cold symptoms, holding constant the number of days with cold symptoms in the year prior to treatment?

Conducting a One-Way ANCOVA

In this section we will illustrate how to conduct the following three tests: tests of the homogeneity-of-slopes assumption, tests to evaluate differences in adjusted means (the ANCOVA analysis), and post hoc tests to evaluate pairwise comparisons among the adjusted means. These tests are generally conducted in this sequence because the ANCOVA would not be carried out unless the slopes were homogeneous, and the post hoc tests would not be performed unless the ANCOVA yielded significant differences among the adjusted means. The procedures for conducting each of these three analyses are presented separately for instructional purposes. However, for efficiency, the post hoc tests are normally conducted in the same run that yields the ANCOVA results.

Evaluating the Homogeneity-of-Slopes Assumption

To conduct the test of the homogeneity-of-slopes assumption, follow these steps:

1. Click **Analyze**, click **General Linear Model**, then click **Univariate**.
2. Click **days**, then click ▶ to move it to the Dependent Variable box.
3. Click **group**, then click ▶ to move it to the Fixed Factor(s) box.
4. Click **predays**, then click ▶ to move it to the Covariate(s) box.
5. Click on **Options**.
6. In the Factor(s) and Factor Interactions box, click **group**.
7. Click ▶ to move it to the Display Means for box.
8. Select **Descriptive statistics**, **Estimates of effect size**, and **Homogeneity tests** in Display box.
9. Click **Continue**.
10. Click **Model**.
11. Click **Custom under Specify Model**.
12. Click **group(F)** under Factors & Covariates and click ▶ to make it appear in the Model box.
13. Click **predays** under Factors & Covariates and click ▶ to make it appear in the Model box.

14. Hold down the Ctrl key, and click **group(F)** and **predays(C)** in the Factors & Covariates box. Check to see that the default option Interaction is specified in the drop-down menu in the Build Terms box. If it is not, select it.
15. Click on ▸ and group*predays should now appear in the Model box.
16. Click **Continue**.
17. Click **OK**.

Selected SPSS Output for Evaluating the Homogeneity-of-Slopes Assumption

Selected results of the analysis are shown in Figure 161.

Tests of Between-Subjects Effects

Dependent Variable: DAYS

Source	Type III Sum of Squares	df	Mean Square	F	Sig.	Eta Squared
Corrected Model	351.594[a]	5	70.319	5.917	.001	.552
Intercept	186.218	1	186.218	15.670	.001	.395
GROUP	10.114	2	5.057	.426	.658	.034
PREDAYS	156.618	1	156.618	13.179	.001	.354
GROUP * PREDAYS	35.039	2	17.519	1.474	.249	.109
Error	285.206	24	11.884			
Total	2960.000	30				
Corrected Total	636.800	29				

a. R Squared = .552 (Adjusted R Squared = .459)

Figure 161. Selected results of the test of homogeneity of slopes.

Before conducting an ANCOVA, the homogeneity-of-slopes assumption should first be tested. The test evaluates the interaction between the covariate and the factor in the prediction of the dependent variable. A significant interaction between the covariate and the factor suggests that the differences on the dependent variable among groups vary as a function of the covariate. If the interaction is significant, the results from an ANCOVA are not meaningful, and ANCOVA should not be conducted. Instead, you should consider using the Potthoff adaptation of the Johnson-Neyman technique (Huitema, 1980) to follow up a significant group-by-covariate interaction. This procedure, however, is not available in SPSS.

The interaction source is labeled GROUP*PREDAYS. Our results suggest the interaction is not significant, $F (2, 24) = 1.47$, $p = .249$, partial $\eta^2 = .11$. We proceed to the ANCOVA assuming homogeneity of slopes, although we feel some hesitancy with the partial η^2 being moderate in size.

Conducting the One-Way ANCOVA

To conduct a one-way ANCOVA, follow these steps:

1. Click **Analyze**, click **General Linear Model**, then click **Univariate**.
2. If you have not exited SPSS, the appropriate options should still be selected. If not, conduct Steps 2 through 9 in the preceding homogeneity-of-slopes test.
3. Click **Model**.
4. Click **Full Factorial**.
5. Click **Continue**.
6. Click **OK**.

Selected SPSS Results for the One-Way ANCOVA

The results are shown in Figure 162.

Descriptive Statistics

Dependent Variable: DAYS

GROUP	Mean	Std. Deviation	N
1	11.60	5.36	10
2	8.40	3.84	10
3	6.40	3.47	10
Total	8.80	4.69	30

Tests of Between-Subjects Effects

Dependent Variable: DAYS

Source	Type III Sum of Squares	df	Mean Square	F	Sig.	Eta Squared
Corrected Model	316.555[a]	3	105.518	8.567	.000	.497
Intercept	172.111	1	172.111	13.973	.001	.350
PREDAYS	178.955	1	178.955	14.529	.001	.358
GROUP	158.903	2	79.452	6.450	.005	.332
Error	320.245	26	12.317			
Total	2960.000	30				
Corrected Total	636.800	29				

a. R Squared = .497 (Adjusted R Squared = .439)

Estimated Marginal Means

GROUP

Dependent Variable: DAYS

GROUP	Mean	Std. Error	95% Confidence Interval Lower Bound	Upper Bound
1	12.011[a]	1.115	9.719	14.303
2	7.715[a]	1.124	5.404	10.026
3	6.674[a]	1.112	4.388	8.960

a. Evaluated at covariates appeared in the model: PREDAYS = 9.00.

Figure 162. Results of the one-way ANCOVA.

The group source (labeled GROUP on the SPSS output) evaluates the null hypothesis that the population adjusted means are equal. The results of the analysis indicate that this hypothesis should be rejected, $F(2, 26) = 6.45$, $p = .005$, and the partial η^2 of .33 suggests a strong relationship between treatment and the number of posttreatment days with cold symptoms, controlling for pretreatment days with cold symptoms. The test assesses the differences among the adjusted means for the three groups, which are reported in the output in the Estimated Marginal Means box as 12.01, 7.71, and 6.67.

The covariate is included in the analysis to control for differences on this variable and is not the focus of the analysis. Consequently, the results for the covariate are frequently not reported in a results section. Nevertheless, the results are available as part of the output. The test of the covariate evaluates the relationship between the covariate and the dependent variable, controlling for the factor (i.e., for any particular group). In the current example, this relationship is significant, $F(1, 26) = 14.53$, $p = .001$, with the covariate accounting for about 36% (i.e., the partial η^2 of .36) of variance of the posttreatment days with cold symptoms for a treatment group.

Conducting Post Hoc Pairwise Comparisons

To conduct the pairwise comparisons among the three groups, follow these steps:

1. Click **Analyze**, click **General Linear Model**, then click **Univariate**.
2. If you have not exited SPSS, the appropriate options should already be chosen. If not, conduct Steps 2 through 5 from the preceding illustration of conducting the one-way ANCOVA.
3. Click **Paste** to exit the General Linear Model dialog box and to go to the Syntax1: SPSS Syntax Editor window. The syntax is shown in Figure 163.

Figure 163. Syntax1: SPSS Syntax Editor window for one-way ANCOVA.

4. Delete all but the first three lines:
   UNIANOVA
   days BY group WITH predays
   /method = sstype(3)
5. Type three /lmatrix commands to compare the adjusted means for Groups 1 and 2, Groups 2 and 3, and Groups 1 and 3. The completed syntax is shown in Figure 164.

Figure 164. Syntax1: SPSS Syntax Editor window for pairwise comparisons following a one-way ANCOVA.

6. Click **Run**.

Conducting Pairwise Comparisons for an ANCOVA with the /lmatrix Command

To conduct pairwise comparisons, you need to use the /lmatrix command. For example, to evaluate whether there are significant differences in adjusted means between placebo and low doses of vitamin C, you would use the following syntax:

```
UNIANOVA
days BY group WITH predays
/METHOD = SSTYPE(3)
/lmatrix 'group 1 vs group 2'
group 1 -1 0.
```

The /lmatrix indicates that you want to use an L matrix to conduct a test, and the wording inside the single quotes allows you to label the test.

To conduct pairwise comparisons among groups, you include coefficients for only the group main effects, as shown on the line after the /lmatrix line. The three coefficients after group on this line are for the first, second, and third levels of the group factor, respectively. The coefficients 1 -1 0 indicate that the effects for placebo and low doses of vitamin C are being compared, which is equivalent to comparing the adjusted means for placebo and low doses of vitamin C. You can conduct any other comparison by specifying a different set of coefficients. For example, to compare the adjusted means for the two doses of vitamin C, you would specify the following coefficients: 0 1 -1.

Selected SPSS Output for Post Hoc Pairwise Comparisons

The results of the first pairwise comparison are shown in Figure 165. This comparison evaluates the difference in adjusted means between the first and second groups.

Custom Hypothesis Tests

Contrast Results (K Matrix)[a]

Contrast		Dependent Variable DAYS
L1	Contrast Estimate	4.296
	Hypothesized Value	0
	Difference (Estimate - Hypothesized)	4.296
	Std. Error	1.596
	Sig.	.012
	95% Confidence Interval for Difference Lower Bound	1.016
	Upper Bound	7.576

a. Based on the user-specified contrast coefficients (L') matrix: group 1 vs group 2

Test Results

Dependent Variable: DAYS

Source	Sum of Squares	df	Mean Square	F	Sig.
Contrast	89.289	1	89.289	7.249	.012
Error	320.245	26	12.317		

Figure 165. The results of the pairwise comparison between the placebo and low dose vitamin C groups.

For each pairwise comparison (labeled custom hypothesis), the Contrast Estimate in the Contrast Results box reflects the difference between the two adjusted means for that contrast. The Test Results box reports the F test, degrees of freedom, and the p-value (Sig.) for a comparison.

The pairwise comparison between the first and the second groups is reported under Custom Hypothesis Tests #1. The coefficient is 4.30 (12.01 - 7.71). The pairwise comparison between the first and the third groups is reported under Custom Hypothesis Tests #2. The coefficient is 5.34 (12.01 - 6.67). The remaining pairwise comparison between the second and the third groups is reported under Custom Hypothesis Tests #3. The coefficient is 1.04 (7.71 - 6.67).

The Holm's sequential Bonferroni procedure could be used to set the level of significance for these tests. (See Appendix B for a detailed presentation of the Holm's sequential Bonferroni procedure.) In this example, two comparisons are significant: the comparison between the placebo group and the high dose vitamin C group (p of .002 is less than .0167) and the comparison between the placebo group and the low dose vitamin C group (p of .012 is less than .025). The comparison between the low dose and high dose vitamin C groups was nonsignificant ($p = .518$ is not less than .05).

Using SPSS Graphs to Display the Results

SPSS provides no way to easily create the most appropriate graphics (a representation of the mean squared residual and the adjusted group means) to illustrate the ANCOVA.

An APA Results Section

A one-way analysis of covariance (ANCOVA) was conducted. The independent variable, vitamin C, included three levels: placebo, low doses of vitamin C, and high doses of vitamin C. The dependent variable was the number of days of cold symptoms during treatment and the covariate was the number of days of cold symptoms before treatment. A preliminary analysis evaluating the homogeneity-of-slopes assumption indicated that the relationship between the covariate and the dependent variable did not differ significantly as a function of the independent variable, $\underline{F}$ (2, 24) = 1.47, MSE = 11.88, $\underline{p}$ = .249, partial η^2 = .11. The ANCOVA was significant, $\underline{F}$ (2, 26) = 6.45, MSE = 12.32, $\underline{p}$ = .005. The strength of relationship between the vitamin C factor and dependent variables was very strong, as assessed by a partial η^2, with the vitamin C factor accounting for 33% of the variance of the dependent variable, holding constant the number of days with pretreatment cold symptoms.

The means of the number days with cold symptoms adjusted for initial differences were ordered as expected across the three vitamin C groups. The placebo group had the largest adjusted mean ($\underline{M}$ = 12.01), the low dose vitamin C group had a smaller adjusted mean ($\underline{M}$ = 7.71), and the high dose vitamin C group had the smallest adjusted mean ($\underline{M}$ = 6.67). Follow-up tests were conducted to evaluate pairwise differences among these adjusted means. The Holm's sequential Bonferroni procedure was used to control for Type I error across the three pairwise comparisons. There were significant differences in the adjusted means between both groups that received vitamin C and the placebo group, but no significant difference between the two vitamin C groups.

Alternative Analyses

SPSS offers no procedures for conducting nonparametric alternatives to ANCOVA. See Huitema (1980) for a discussion of nonparametric alternatives.

As for parametric methods, researchers sometimes use alternative methods such as ANOVA on change scores. If subjects are randomly assigned to groups or assigned based on pretest scores, ANCOVA is in most cases more powerful than these alternatives. If it is unclear how subjects are assigned to groups, none of the methods including ANCOVA are likely to control adequately for prior differences. (See Maxwell and Delaney, 1990, for a discussion of this topic.)

Exercises

The data for Exercises 1 through 5 are in the data set named *Lesson 26 Exercise File 1* on the Student Data Disk. The data are from the following research problem.

Sam is interested in the relationship between college professors' academic discipline and their actual ability to fix a car, holding constant mechanical aptitude. Five professors were randomly selected from mechanical engineering, psychology, and philosophy departments at a major university. Each professor completed a mechanical aptitude scale. Scores on this measure have a mean of 100 and a standard deviation of 15. The professors were then rated on how well they performed four automotive maintenance tasks: changing oil, changing the points and plugs, adjusting the carburetor, and setting the timing on a 1985 Pontiac. Ratings were based on the degree of success in completing a task and the amount of time needed to complete it. Lower scores reflect more efficiency at completing the automotive maintenance tasks.

1. Transform the scores on the four mechanical task ratings by z-scoring them and then summing the z-scores so that Sam has a single measure of professors' mechanical performance efficiency.
2. Evaluate whether the relationship between mechanical aptitude and mechanical performance efficiency is the same for all three types of professors (homogeneity-of-slopes assumption). What should Sam conclude about the homogeneity-of-slopes assumption? Report the appropriate statistics from the output to justify your conclusion.
3. Conduct the standard ANCOVA on these data. From the output, identify the following:
    a. The *p*-value associated with the effect due to professor type
    b. The effect size associated with the effect due to professor type
    c. The *F* value associated with the covariate, mechanical aptitude
4. Conduct the appropriate post hoc tests.
5. Write a results section based on your analyses.

The data for Exercises 6 through 8 are in the data set named *Lesson 26 Exercise File 2* on the Student Data Disk. The data are from the following research problem.

Marilyn was interested in the effects of journal therapy on depression. She randomly assigned 60 individuals who had been clinically diagnosed as having severe depression to three treatment groups. The first group involved the subjects' intensively writing about their feelings in a journal for an hour each day for three weeks (journal therapy) and regular counseling. The second group received only journal therapy, and the third group received only regular counseling. All 60 participants were given a depression subscale before and after treatment.

6. Evaluate the homogeneity-of-slopes assumption. What should Marilyn conclude about this assumption? Report the appropriate statistics from the output to justify your conclusion.
7. Conduct the standard ANCOVA on these data. What conclusions should Marilyn draw?
8. Should Marilyn conduct post hoc tests? Why or why not? Report the appropriate statistics from the output to justify your conclusion.

One-Way Multivariate Analysis of Variance

Multivariate analysis of variance (MANOVA) is a multivariate extension of analysis of variance. As with ANOVA, the independent variables for a MANOVA are factors, and each factor has two or more levels. Unlike ANOVA, MANOVA includes multiple dependent variables rather than a single dependent variable. MANOVA evaluates whether the population means on a set of dependent variables vary across levels of a factor or factors. Here we will discuss only a MANOVA with a single factor, that is, a one-way MANOVA. Each case in the SPSS data file for a one-way MANOVA contains a factor distinguishing participants into groups and two or more quantitative dependent variables.

Applying One-Way MANOVA

One-way MANOVAs can analyze data from different types of studies.

- Experimental studies
- Quasi-experimental studies
- Field studies

We give examples of an experimental study and a quasi-experimental study.

An Experimental Study

Dan wished to examine the effects of various study strategies on learning. Thirty students from different sections of an introductory psychology course were randomly assigned to one of three study conditions: the think condition, the write condition, or the talk condition. Students attended one general lecture, after which they were placed into study rooms based on their assigned condition. Students in all rooms received the same set of study questions, but each room received different instructions about how to study. The write group was instructed to write responses to each question, the think group was instructed to think about answers to the questions, and the talk group was instructed to develop a talk that they could deliver centering on the answers to the questions. At the completion of the study session, all students took a quiz consisting of recall, application, analysis, and synthesis questions. Dan's SPSS data file includes 30 cases and five variables. The variables include a factor differentiating the three types of study groups (write, think, and talk groups) and the four dependent variables, scores on the recall, application, analysis, and synthesis questions.

A Quasi-Experimental Study

Wanda wanted to determine whether assurances of confidentiality or anonymity have an effect on how students respond to personality and psychopathology questionnaires. She had previously administered the same three questionnaires—the Beck Depression Inventory (BDI), the 10 clinical scales of the Minnesota Multiphasic Personality Inventory (MMPI), and the Eating Disorders Scale (EDS)—to 479 students at the beginning of three different studies. In one study, she told the students that they would complete the questionnaires anonymously. In a second study, she told the students that the results would be confidential, but she requested that they put their names on their questionnaires. In the third study, she told the students that the results would be confidential, but that she would contact them for possible referral to mental health counselors if their results warranted it. Wanda's SPSS data file has 479 cases and 13 variables, a factor differentiating among the instructional sets for the three studies (anonymity, confidentiality, and confidentiality with referral) and the 12 dependent variables (the BDI, the 10 MMPI scales, and the EDS).

Understanding One-Way MANOVA

A one-way MANOVA tests the hypothesis that the population means for the dependent variables are the same for all levels of a factor, that is, across all groups. If the population means of the dependent variables are equal for all groups, the population means for any linear combination of these dependent variables are also equal for all groups. Consequently, a one-way MANOVA evaluates a hypothesis that includes not only equality among groups on the dependent variables but also equality among groups on linear combinations of these dependent variables.

SPSS reports a number of statistics to evaluate the MANOVA hypothesis, labeled Wilks' Lambda, Pillai's Trace, Hotelling's Trace, and Roy's Largest Root. Each statistic evaluates a multivariate hypothesis that the population means are equal. We will use Wilks' lambda because it is frequently reported in the social science literature. Pillai's trace is a reasonable alternative to Wilks' lambda.

If the one-way MANOVA is significant, follow-up analyses can assess whether there are differences among groups on the population means for certain dependent variables and for particular linear combinations of dependent variables. A popular follow-up approach is to conduct multiple ANOVAs, one for each dependent variable, and to control for Type I error across these multiple tests using one of the Bonferroni approaches. If any of these ANOVAs yield significance and the factor contains more than two levels, additional follow-up tests are performed. These tests typically involve post hoc pairwise comparisons among levels of the factor, although they may involve more complex comparisons. We will illustrate follow-up tests using this strategy in this lesson.

Some people have criticized the strategy of conducting follow-up ANOVAs after obtaining a significant MANOVA because the individual ANOVAs do not take into account the multivariate nature of MANOVA. Conducting follow-up ANOVAs ignores the fact that the MANOVA hypothesis includes subhypotheses about linear combinations of dependent variables. Of course, if we have particular linear combinations of variables of interest, we can evaluate these linear combinations using ANOVA in addition to, or in place of, the ANOVAs conducted on the individual dependent variables. For example, if two of the dependent variables for a MANOVA measure the same construct of introversion, then we may wish to represent them by transforming the variables to z-scores, adding them together, and evaluating the resulting combined scores using ANOVA. This ANOVA could be performed in addition to the ANOVAs on the remaining dependent variables.

If we have no clue as to what linear combinations of dependent variables to evaluate, we may choose to conduct follow-up analyses to a significant MANOVA using discriminant analysis. Discriminant analysis (see Lesson 34) yields one or more uncorrelated linear combinations of dependent variables that maximize differences among the groups. These linear combinations are empirically determined and may not be interpretable.

Assumptions Underlying a One-Way MANOVA

Assumption 1: The Dependent Variables Are Multivariately Normally Distributed for each Population, with the Different Populations Being Defined by the Levels of the Factor

If the dependent variables are multivariately normally distributed, each variable is normally distributed ignoring the other variables and each variable is normally distributed at every combination of values of the other variables. It is difficult to imagine that this assumption could be met, so it is reassuring that a one-way MANOVA yields relatively valid results in terms of Type I errors with moderate to large sample sizes.

Assumption 2: The Population Variances and Covariances among the Dependent Variables Are the Same across All Levels of the Factor

To the extent that the sample sizes are disparate and the variances and covariances are unequal, MANOVA yields invalid results. SPSS allows us to test the assumption of homogeneity of the variance-covariance matrices with Box's M statistic. The F test from Box's M statistics should be interpreted cautiously in that a significant result may be due to violation of the multivariate normality assumption for the Box's M test, and a nonsignificant result may be due to a lack of power.

Assumption 3: The Participants Are Randomly Sampled, and the Score on a Variable for Any One Participant Is Independent from the Scores on this Variable for All Other Participants

MANOVA should not be conducted if the independence assumption is violated.

Computing an Effect Size Statistic

The multivariate General Linear Model procedure computes a multivariate effect size index. The multivariate effect size associated with Wilks' lambda (Λ) is the multivariate eta square:

$$Multivariate\ \eta^2 = 1 - \Lambda^{\frac{1}{s}}$$

Here, s is equal to the number of levels of the factor minus 1 or the number of dependent variables, whichever is smaller. This statistic should be interpreted similar to a univariate eta square and ranges in value from 0 to 1. A 0 indicates no relationship between the factor and the dependent variable, while a 1 indicates the strongest possible relationship. It is unclear what should be considered a small, medium, and large effect size for this statistic.

The Data Set

The data set used to illustrate a one-way MANOVA is named *Lesson 27 Data File 1* on the Student Disk. It represents data from the experimental study described earlier. That research evaluates which of three study strategies produces the best learning. Here, though, the data provide only two dependent variables instead of four. The variables in the data set are shown in Table 25 (at the top of page 201).

Table 25
Variables in Lesson 27 Data File 1

Variable	Definition
group	The factor in this study is group. There are three levels to the factor: think (= 1), write (= 2), and talk (= 3).
recall	Recall is the total correct score on recall questions and ranges from 0 to 8.
applicat	Applicat is the total correct score on application questions and ranges from 0 to 8.

The Research Question

We could ask the research question to reflect mean differences or relationships between variables.

1. Mean differences: Are the population means for the scores on recall and application tests (or linear combinations of these test scores) the same or different for students in the three study groups?
2. Relationships between variables: Is there a relationship between type of study strategy used and performance on recall and application test items?

Conducting a One-Way MANOVA

Here, we will outline steps to conduct a one-way MANOVA, the univariate ANOVAs following a significant overall test and the post hoc pairwise comparisons. Although these tests are typically sequential, we will illustrate how to conduct all three tests in a single step.

To conduct a one-way MANOVA, follow-up univariate tests, and post hoc comparisons, follow these steps:

1. Click **Analyze**, click **General Linear Model**, then click **Multivariate**. You'll see the Multivariate dialog box shown in Figure 166.

Figure 166. The Multivariate dialog box.

2. Click **recall**, hold down the Ctrl key and click **applicat**, and then click ▶ to move the two variables to the Dependent Variables box.
3. Click **group**, and then click ▶ to move the variable to the Fixed Factor(s) box.
4. Click **Options**. You'll see the Multivariate: Options dialog box shown in Figure 167.

Figure 167. The Multivariate: Options dialog box.

5. Click **group** in the Factor(s) and Factor Interactions box, then click ▶ to make it appear in the Display Means for box.
6. Click **Descriptive Statistics**, **Estimates of effect size**, and **Homogeneity tests** in the Display box.
7. Change the **Significance Level** from .05 to .025. (.025 was chosen by dividing .05 by the number of dependent variables. We will talk about choosing the significance level when we discuss output for pairwise comparisons.)
8. Click **Post Hoc**.
9. Under the Factors box, click **group**, and click ▶ to make it appear in the Post Hoc Tests for box.
10. In the Equal Variances Assumed box, click **Bonferroni**. Other post hoc tests assuming equal variances are equally valid. (LSD would be appropriate for our example because there are three levels of the factor, but would be inappropriate if there were more than three levels.)
11. In the Equal Variances Not Assumed box, click **Dunnett's C**. Other post hoc tests not assuming equal variances are equally valid.
12. Click **Continue**.
13. Click **OK**.

Selected SPSS Output for MANOVA

The results of the overall MANOVA are shown in Figure 168 (at the top of page 203). The multivariate test for homogeneity of dispersion matrices, Box's Test, evaluates whether the variances and covariance among the dependent variables are the same for all levels of a factor. If the F test for Box's test is significant, the homogeneity hypothesis is rejected, and we may conclude that there are differences in the matrices. The results of Box's test should be interpreted cautiously, however, in that a significant result may be due to violation of the multivariate normality assumption for

Descriptive Statistics

	GROUP	Mean	Std. Deviation	N
RECALL	1	3.30	.67	10
	2	5.80	1.03	10
	3	4.20	1.14	10
	Total	4.43	1.41	30
APPLICAT	1	3.20	1.23	10
	2	5.00	1.76	10
	3	4.40	1.17	10
	Total	4.20	1.56	30

Box's Test of Equality of Covariance Matrices[a]

Box's M	6.980
F	1.039
df1	6
df2	18169
Sig.	.398

Tests the null hypothesis that the observed covariance matrices of the dependent variables are equal across groups.

a. Design: Intercept+GROUP

Multivariate Tests[c]

Effect		Value	F	Hypothesis df	Error df	Sig.	Eta Squared
Intercept	Pillai's Trace	.962	326.035[a]	2.000	26.000	.000	.962
	Wilks' Lambda	.038	326.035[a]	2.000	26.000	.000	.962
	Hotelling's Trace	25.080	326.035[a]	2.000	26.000	.000	.962
	Roy's Largest Root	25.080	326.035[a]	2.000	26.000	.000	.962
GROUP	Pillai's Trace	.602	5.811	4.000	54.000	.001	.301
	Wilks' Lambda	.421	7.028[a]	4.000	52.000	.000	.351
	Hotelling's Trace	1.318	8.240	4.000	50.000	.000	.397
	Roy's Largest Root	1.275	17.215[b]	2.000	27.000	.000	.560

a. Exact statistic

b. The statistic is an upper bound on F that yields a lower bound on the significance level.

c. Design: Intercept+GROUP

Figure 168. The results of the one-way MANOVA.

this test and a nonsignificant result may be due to small sample size and a lack of power. In this example, the test for homogeneity of dispersion matrices is nonsignificant, $F (6, 18169) = 1.04$, $p = .398$.

Also reported on the output and of primary concern are the results of the MANOVA test. In this example, the Wilks' Λ of .42 is significant, $F (4, 52) = 7.03$, $p < .001$, indicating that we can reject the hypothesis that the population means on the dependent variables are the same for the three teaching strategies. The multivariate $\eta^2 = .35$ indicates 35% of multivariate variance of the dependent variables is associated with the group factor.

Selected SPSS Output for the Univariate ANOVAs

The results of the univariate ANOVAs are shown in Figure 169 (at the top of page 204). If there are no missing data, the ANOVAs that are printed as part of the MANOVA output are identical to those obtained by running the one-way ANOVA procedure. However, if data are missing, the univariate ANOVAs on the MANOVA output could differ from the univariate ANOVAs obtained by analyzing each dependent variable separately. The MANOVA procedure excludes an individual's data if a score is missing on any dependent variable. An individual's data are excluded when running the one-way ANOVA procedure only if a score is missing on a dependent variable for the ANOVA of interest. To be consistent with the MANOVA results, follow-up analyses of variance

Tests of Between-Subjects Effects

Source	Dependent Variable	Type III Sum of Squares	df	Mean Square	F	Sig.	Eta Squared
Corrected Model	RECALL	32.067[a]	2	16.033	17.111	.000	.559
	APPLICAT	16.800[b]	2	8.400	4.200	.026	.237
Intercept	RECALL	589.633	1	589.633	629.253	.000	.959
	APPLICAT	529.200	1	529.200	264.600	.000	.907
GROUP	RECALL	32.067	2	16.033	17.111	.000	.559
	APPLICAT	16.800	2	8.400	4.200	.026	.237
Error	RECALL	25.300	27	.937			
	APPLICAT	54.000	27	2.000			
Total	RECALL	647.000	30				
	APPLICAT	600.000	30				
Corrected Total	RECALL	57.367	29				
	APPLICAT	70.800	29				

a. R Squared = .559 (Adjusted R Squared = .526)

b. R Squared = .237 (Adjusted R Squared = .181)

Figure 169. The results of the univariate ANOVAs.

should be reported for individuals who have scores on all of the dependent variables. These are the ANOVAs that are produced in the Multivariate General Linear Model procedure.

The reported *p*-values on the MANOVA output do not take into account that multiple ANOVAs have been conducted. Methods may be used to control for Type I error across the multiple ANOVAs. For our application, we chose to control for Type I error using a traditional Bonferroni procedure and test each ANOVA at the .025 level (.05 divided by the number of ANOVAs conducted). Consequently, the univariate ANOVA for the recall scores was significant, $F(2, 27) = 17.11$, $p < .001$, while the univariate ANOVA for the application scores was nonsignificant, $F(2, 27) = 4.20$, $p = .026$. The ANOVA for the application scores was nonsignificant because .026 exceeded the required level of .025.

Selected SPSS Output for Follow-Up Pairwise Comparisons

The results of the pairwise comparisons are shown in Figure 170 (at the top of page 205). We had previously controlled for Type I error across the two univariate ANOVAs by testing each at the .025 level. To be consistent with this decision, we also need to control the probability of committing one or more Type I errors across the multiple pairwise comparisons for a dependent variable at the .025 level. We are able to maintain this familywise error rate across comparisons for a dependent variable by selecting .025 for the Significance Level in the Multivariate: Options dialog box.

Because the ANOVA for the application scores was nonsignificant, we examined only the pairwise comparisons for the recall scores. Although more powerful methods are available, the Bonferroni approach was used to control for Type I error across the pairwise comparisons for recall. With the Bonferroni method, each comparison is tested at the alpha level for the ANOVA divided by the number of comparisons; for our example, .025/3 = .008. Two of the three comparisons were significant, the comparisons associated with the thinking and writing groups and with the writing and talking groups. It should be noted that the same two comparisons were significant with Dunnett's *C* method.

A More Powerful Method for Conducting Follow-Up Tests for the Three-Group, Two-Dependent Variable MANOVA

The Bonferroni method is a general approach used to control for Type I error in a variety of MANOVA situations. However, there are more powerful procedures for specific cases of MANOVA. Levin, Serlin, and Seaman (1994) described such a method for our three-group,

Multiple Comparisons

Dependent Variable		(I) GROUP	(J) GROUP	Mean Difference (I-J)	Std. Error	Sig.	97.5% Confidence Interval	
							Lower Bound	Upper Bound
RECALL	Bonferroni	1	2	-2.50*	.43	.000	-3.73	-1.27
			3	-.90	.43	.142	-2.13	.33
		2	1	2.50*	.43	.000	1.27	3.73
			3	1.60*	.43	.003	.37	2.83
		3	1	.90	.43	.142	-.33	2.13
			2	-1.60*	.43	.003	-2.83	-.37
	Dunnett C	1	2	-2.50*	.43		-3.76	-1.24
			3	-.90	.43		-2.25	.45
		2	1	2.50*	.43		1.24	3.76
			3	1.60*	.43		2.88E-02	3.17
		3	1	.90	.43		-.45	2.25
			2	-1.60*	.43		-3.17	-2.88E-02
APPLICAT	Bonferroni	1	2	-1.80	.63	.025	-3.60	5.36E-04
			3	-1.20	.63	.206	-3.00	.60
		2	1	1.80	.63	.025	-5.36E-04	3.60
			3	.60	.63	1.000	-1.20	2.40
		3	1	1.20	.63	.206	-.60	3.00
			2	-.60	.63	1.000	-2.40	1.20
	Dunnett C	1	2	-1.80	.63		-4.00	.40
			3	-1.20	.63		-2.94	.54
		2	1	1.80	.63		-.40	4.00
			3	.60	.63		-1.57	2.77
		3	1	1.20	.63		-.54	2.94
			2	-.60	.63		-2.77	1.57

Based on observed means.

*. The mean difference is significant at the .025 level.

Figure 170. The results of the post hoc comparison procedures.

two-dependent variable case. Individual ANOVAs are conducted only if the MANOVA is significant. If the MANOVA is significant, then each ANOVA is evaluated at the .05 level. If one of the ANOVAs is significant, the follow-up pairwise comparisons for this ANOVA are evaluated at the .05 level. On the other hand, if both ANOVAs are significant, then the pairwise comparisons across both dependent variables are tested at the .05/2, or .025, level. In our example, the MANOVA was significant at the .05 level, both univariate ANOVAs were significant at the .05 level, and three of the six pairwise comparisons were significant at the .025 level. These results illustrate the greater power of this technique, since the traditional Bonferroni procedure yielded only one significant ANOVA and only two significant pairwise comparisons.

Using SPSS Graphs to Display the Results

Graphical methods, such as boxplots, can be used in the results section to allow the reader to evaluate the differences among groups. The boxplots that display the distributions for the multiple dependent variables of a MANOVA are created using a method that is slightly different from the ones used for an independent-samples *t* test or one-way ANOVA. To create the boxplot shown in Figure 171, conduct the following steps:

1. Click **Graphs**, then click **Boxplot**.
2. Click **Clustered** and **Summaries for Separate Variables** in the Boxplot dialog box.
3. Click **Define**.

4. Click **group**, then click ▶ to move it to the Category Axis box.
5. Hold down the Ctrl key, click **recall** and **applicat**, then click ▶ to move them to the Boxes Represent box.
6. Click **OK**.

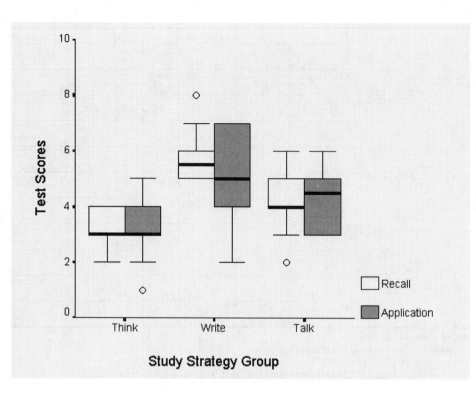

Figure 171. Distributions of application and recall scores for the three study strategy groups.

An APA Results Section for One-Way MANOVA

A one-way multivariate analysis of variance (MANOVA) was conducted to determine the effect of the three types of study strategies (thinking, writing, and talking) on the two dependent variables, the recall and the application test scores. Significant differences were found among the three study strategies on the dependent measures, Wilks' $\Lambda = .42$, $\underline{F}(4, 52) = 7.03$, $\underline{p} < .001$. The multivariate η^2 based on Wilks' Λ was quite strong, .35. Table 26 (at the top of page 207) contains the means and the standard deviations on the dependent variables for the three groups.

Analyses of variances (ANOVA) on each dependent variable were conducted as follow-up tests to the MANOVA. Using the Bonferroni method, each ANOVA was tested at the .025 level. The ANOVA on the recall scores was significant, $\underline{F}(2, 27) = 17.11$, $\underline{p} < .001$, $\eta^2 = .56$, while the ANOVA on the application scores was nonsignificant, $\underline{F}(2,27) = 4.20$, $\underline{p} = .026$, $\eta^2 = .24$.

Post hoc analyses to the univariate ANOVA for the recall scores consisted of conducting pairwise comparisons to find which study strategy affected performance most strongly. Each pairwise comparison was tested at the .025 divided by 3 or .008 level. The writing group produced significantly superior performance on the recall questions in comparison with either of the other two groups (see Table 26). The thinking and talking groups were not significantly different from each other.

Exercises

The data for Exercises 1 through 4 are in the data set named *Lesson 27 Exercise File 1* on the Student Data Disk. The data are from the following research problem.

Dana wished to evaluate the effects of conflict-resolution training on the social skills of

Table 26
Means and Standard Deviations on the Dependent Variable for the Three Groups

Study strategy	Recall		Application	
	M	*SD*	*M*	*SD*
Thinking	3.30	0.67	3.20	1.23
Writing	5.80	1.03	5.00	1.76
Talk	4.20	1.14	4.40	1.17

elementary school children. Fourth-grade students in a school district were randomly assigned to one of three groups. Two groups received training in conflict resolution from either a cognitive-based approach (group = 1) or a behavior-based approach (group = 2). The third group did not receive formal instruction in conflict resolution (group = 3). To measure the effects of the treatment, a social problem-solving inventory (SPSI) was administered to the children, and rating scales were completed by the teachers (rate_t) and by the parents (rate_p).

1. Conduct a MANOVA to evaluate the effects of the training programs. Identify the following values on the output:
   a. Wilks' lambda
   b. *F* statistic associated with Wilks' lambda
   c. multivariate η^2 associated with Wilks' lambda
   d. univariate *F* test for the teacher rating
   e. mean parent rating for group 2
2. Conduct the appropriate follow-up tests.
3. What should Dana conclude? Write a results section reporting the results of her analysis.
4. Create a boxplot to display graphically Dana's results.

The data for Exercises 5 and 6 are in the data set named *Lesson 27 Exercise File 2* on the Student Data Disk. The data are from the following research problem.

Vicki was interested in whether fathers of children with a disability feel competent to parent their children who are disabled. To address this question, she found 60 fathers with a child in one of three categories: (1) fathers with a child with no disabilities, (2) fathers with a physically disabled child, and (3) fathers with a mentally retarded child. She administered the Perceived Parenting Competence Scale (PPCS), a self-report measure. It has three subscales: (1) instrumental competence, which assesses caretaking responsibilities (instrum); (2) emotional parenting competence, which evaluates the quality of emotional support provided to the child (emot); and (3) play competence, which measures the quality of the recreational time spent with the child (play). Vicki's SPSS data file contains 60 cases and four variables, a factor indicating the disability status of the child and scores on the three PPCS subscales.

5. Conduct a one-way MANOVA to evaluate differences among the disability status groups on the three perceived competence variables. Is the multivariate test significant?
6. Write a results section.

One-Way Repeated-Measures Analysis of Variance

With one-way repeated-measures designs, each subject or case in a study is exposed to all levels of a qualitative variable and measured on a quantitative variable during each exposure. The qualitative variable is referred to as a repeated-measures factor or a within-subjects factor. The quantitative variable is called the dependent variable.

To conduct a repeated-measures ANOVA in SPSS, we do not specify the repeated-measures factor and the dependent variable in the SPSS data file. Instead, the SPSS data file contains several quantitative variables. The number of quantitative variables is equal to the number of levels of the within-subjects factor. The scores on any one of these quantitative variables are the scores on the dependent variable for a single level of the within-subjects factor.

Although we do not define the within-subjects factor in the SPSS data file, we specify it in the dialog box for the General Linear Model Repeated-Measures procedure. To define the factor, we give a name to the within-subjects factor, specify the number of levels of this factor, and indicate the quantitative variables in the data set associated with the levels of the within-subjects factor.

Applying One-Way Repeated Measures ANOVA

One-way within-subjects ANOVAs can analyze data from different types of studies.

- Experimental studies
- Quasi-experimental studies
- Field studies
- Longitudinal studies

We illustrate a longitudinal study and an experimental study.

Longitudinal Study

Janice is interested in determining whether the average man wants to express his worries to his wife more (or less) the longer they are married. Janice develops the Desire to Express Worry scale (DEW). She has men take the DEW when they initially get married and then at their 5th, 10th, and 15th wedding anniversaries. She decides to conduct a one-way within-subjects ANOVA that involves only those 30 men who made it to their 15th wedding anniversary. The within-subjects factor is time with four levels (0, 5, 10, and 15 years of marriage), and the dependent variable is the DEW scores at the four times. Janice's SPSS data file has 30 cases and four variables. The four variables are the initial DEW score and the DEW scores after 5, 10, and 15 years of marriage.

Experimental Study

Shep is interested in determining if teachers feel greater stress when coping with problems associated with students, parents, or administrators. To make this comparison, he develops nine scenarios representing problems that high school teachers are likely to encounter when they teach. Three scenarios represent problems with students, three represent problems with parents, and three represent problems with administrators. The scenarios are randomly ordered and presented to 100 teachers. The teachers are to read each scenario, think of a similar problem they have had, and indicate on a stress measure how stressed they felt as they coped with their problem. Three scores are computed by summing the stress scores for the scenarios of the same type (i.e., scenarios describing problems with students, parents, or administrators). An ANOVA is conducted with type of stressor as the within-subjects factor with three levels (students, parents, or administrators) and the stress measure as the dependent variable. For the analysis, Shep's SPSS data file includes 100 cases and three variables. The three variables are the student stress scores, the parent stress scores, and the administrator stress scores.

Understanding One-Way Repeated-Measures ANOVA

In many studies using a one-way repeated-measures design, the levels of a within-subject factor represent multiple observations on a scale over time or under different conditions. However, for some studies, levels of a within-subject factor may represent scores from different scales, and the focus may be on evaluating differences in means among these scales. In such a setting the scales must be commensurable for the ANOVA significance tests to be meaningful. That is, the scales must measure individuals on the same metric, and the difference scores between scales must be interpretable.

In some studies, individuals are matched on one or more variables so that individuals within a set are similar on a matching variable(s), while individuals not in the same set are dissimilar. The number of individuals within a set is equal to the number of levels of a factor. The individuals within a set are then observed under the various levels of this factor. The matching process for these designs is likely to produce correlated responses on the dependent variable like those of repeated-measures designs. Consequently, the data from these studies can be analyzed as if the factor is a within-subjects factor. For further discussion of these designs, consult textbooks on experimental design and analysis of variance.

Let's look at how to conduct the analyses for one-way repeated-measures designs. We address tests to evaluate the overall hypothesis as well as post hoc tests.

SPSS conducts a standard univariate F test if the within-subjects factor has only two levels. Three types of tests are conducted if the within-subjects factor has more than two levels: the standard univariate F test, alternative univariate tests, and multivariate tests. All three types of tests evaluate the same hypothesis—the population means are equal for all levels of the factor. The choice of what test to report should be made prior to viewing the results.

The standard univariate ANOVA F test is not recommended when the within-subjects factor has more than two levels because one of its assumptions, the sphericity assumption, is commonly violated, and the ANOVA F test yields inaccurate p-values to the extent that this assumption is violated. (We'll talk later about assumptions underlying one-way repeated-measures ANOVA.) The alternative univariate tests take into account violations of the sphericity assumption. These tests employ the same calculated F statistic as the standard univariate test, but its associated p-value potentially differs. In determining the p-value, an epsilon statistic is calculated based on the sample data to assess the degree that the sphericity assumption is violated. The numerator and denominator degrees of freedom of the standard test are multiplied by epsilon to obtain a corrected set of degrees of freedom for the tabled F value and to determine its p-value.

The multivariate test does not require the assumption of sphericity. Difference scores are computed by comparing scores from different levels of the within-subjects factor. For example, for a within-subjects factor with three levels, difference scores might be computed between the first and second level and between the second and third level. The multivariate test then would evaluate whether the population means for these two sets of difference scores are simultaneously equal to zero. This test evaluates not only the means associated with these two sets of difference scores, but also evaluates whether the mean of the difference scores between the first and third levels of the factor is equal to zero as well as linear combinations of these difference scores.

It should be noted that the SPSS Repeated Measures procedure computes the difference scores used in the analysis for us. However, these difference scores do not become a part of our data file and, therefore, we may or may not be aware that the multivariate test is conducted on these difference scores.

Applied statisticians tend to prefer the multivariate test to the standard or the alternative univariate test because the multivariate test and follow-up tests have a close conceptual link to each other. If the initial hypothesis that the means are equal is rejected and there are more than two means, then follow-up tests are conducted to determine which of the means differs significantly from each other. Although more complex comparisons can be performed, most researchers choose to conduct pairwise comparisons. These comparisons may be evaluated with SPSS using the paired-samples t test procedure, and a Bonferroni approach, such as the Holm's sequential procedure, can be used to control for Type I error across the multiple pairwise tests.

Standard Univariate Assumptions Underlying a One-Way Repeated-Measures Analysis of Variance

Assumption 1: The Dependent Variable Is Normally Distributed in the Population for Each Level of the Within-Subjects Factor

With moderate to large sample sizes, the assumption may be violated and the test will probably yield reasonably accurate results. In most circumstances, a sample size of 15 observations per level of the within-subjects factor may be large enough to yield fairly accurate p-values. Larger sample sizes may be required to produce relatively valid results if the population distributions are substantially non-normal.

Assumption 2: The Population Variance of the Difference Scores Computed between Any Two Levels of a Within-Subjects Factor Are the Same Value Regardless of Which Two Levels Are Chosen

This assumption is sometimes referred to as the sphericity assumption or as the homogeneity-of-variance-of-differences assumption. The sphericity assumption is meaningful only if there are more than two levels of a within-subjects factor.

If this assumption is violated, the p-value associated with the standard within-subjects ANOVA cannot be trusted. However, other methods do not require the sphericity assumption. Two approaches include an alternative univariate approach that corrects the degrees of freedom to take into account violations of this assumption as well as the multivariate approach that does not require the sphericity assumption.

Assumption 3: The Cases Represent a Random Sample from the Population, and There Is No Dependency in the Scores between Participants

The only type of dependency that should exist among dependent variable scores is the dependency introduced by having the same individuals produce multiple scores. Even this type of dependency introduced by the within-subjects factor is limited and must conform to the sphericity assumption. The results for a one-way, within-subjects ANOVA should not be trusted if the scores between individuals are related.

Multivariate Assumptions Underlying a One-Way Repeated-Measures Analysis of Variance

The multivariate test is conducted on difference scores, and, therefore, the assumptions underlying the multivariate test concern these difference scores. The number of variables with difference scores is equal to the number of levels of the within-subjects factor minus 1. Although the difference-score variables may be computed in a number of ways, we will compute them by subtracting the scores associated with one level of the within-subject factor from the scores for an adjacent level of the within-subjects factor. In our first example involving changes in desire to express worry, our within-subjects factor has four levels and, therefore, we would compute three difference scores. These three variables would be obtained by subtracting (1) the DEW scores at 5 years of marriage from the DEW scores at 0 years of marriage, (2) the DEW scores at 10 years of marriage from the DEW scores at 5 years of marriage, and (3) the DEW scores at 15 years of marriage from the DEW scores at 10 years of marriage.

Assumption 1: The Difference Scores Are Multivariately Normally Distributed in the Population

If the difference scores are multivariately normally distributed, each difference score is normally distributed, ignoring the other difference scores. Also, each difference score is normally distributed at every combination of values of the other difference scores. With moderate to large sample sizes, the multivariate normality assumption may be violated, and the test will still yield reasonably accurate results.

Assumption 2: The Individual Cases Represent a Random Sample from the Population, and the Difference Scores for Any One Subject Are Independent from the Scores for Any Other Subject

The test should not be used if the independence assumption is violated.

Computing an Effect Size Statistic

The effect size reported for the standard univariate approach is a partial eta square and may be calculated using the following equation:

$$Partial \ \eta^2_{factor} = \frac{Sum \ of \ Squares_{factor}}{Sum \ of \ Squares_{factor} + Sum \ of \ Squares_{Error}}$$

The effect size for the multivariate test associated with Wilks' lambda (Λ) is the multivariate eta square:

$$Multivariate \ \eta^2 = 1 - \Lambda$$

Both of these statistics range from 0 to 1. A 0 indicates no relation between the repeated-measures factor and the dependent variable, while a 1 indicates the strongest possible relationship.

The Data Set

The data set used to illustrate a one-way repeated-measures ANOVA is named *Lesson 28 Data File 1* on the Student Disk and represents data coming from the DEW example. The definitions for the variables in the data set are given in Table 27 (at the top of page 212).

The Research Question

The research question can be stated to reflect mean differences or relationships between variables.

1. Mean differences: Do population means on the Desire to Express Worry scale vary with how long men are married?
2. Relationship between two variables: Is there a relationship between length of marriage and how much men want to express their worries?

Table 27

Variables in Lesson 28 Data File 1

Variable	Definition
time1	DEW scores after 0 years of marriage
time2	DEW scores after 5 years of marriage
time3	DEW scores after 10 years of marriage
time4	DEW scores after 15 years of marriage

Conducting a One-Way Repeated-Measures ANOVA

We illustrate three steps in conducting a one-way repeated-measures ANOVA: conducting the overall test, conducting pairwise comparisons, and conducting polynomial contrasts. Polynomial contrasts should be conducted only if the levels of the within-subjects factor represent values along a quantitative dimension, as we will soon discuss.

Conducting the Overall Test

The following steps evaluate differences in means among levels of the within-subjects factor (univariate and multivariate) and obtain the means, standard deviations, and correlations among the quantitative scores for all levels of the within-subjects factor.

1. Click **Analyze**, click **General Linear Model**, then click **Repeated Measures**. You will see the Repeated Measures Define Variable(s) dialog box as shown in Figure 172.

Figure 172. The Repeated Measures Define Factor(s) dialog box.

2. In the Within-Subject Factor Name text box type **time** in place of factor1.
3. Type **4** in the Number of Levels box.
4. Click **Add**.
5. Click **Define**. You will see the Repeated Measures dialog box as shown in Figure 173 (at the top of page 213).
6. Hold down the Ctrl key and click on **time1**, **time2**, **time3**, and **time4** and click ▶ to move them to the Within-Subjects Variables box.
7. Click **Options**.
8. Highlight **time** in the Factor(s) and Factor Interactions box. Click ▶ to make it appear in the Display Means for box.
9. Click **Estimates of effect size** and **Descriptive statistics** in the Display box.
10. Click **Continue**.
11. Click **OK**.

Figure 173. The GLM - Repeated Measures dialog box.

Selected SPSS Output for One-Way Repeated-Measures ANOVA

The results of the analysis are shown in Figure 174 (at the top of page 214). SPSS for a one-way within-subjects ANOVA produces a lot of output: descriptive statistics, statistics for evaluating the sphericity assumption, univariate ANOVA results, and ANOVA results using multivariate tests.

The standard univariate ANOVA (labeled Sphericity Assumed) indicates a significant time effect, F (3, 87) = 7.66, p = .000. The alternative univariate tests (i.e., Greenhouse-Geisser and Huynh-Feldt) yield the same F value, but correct the degrees of freedom of the F as a function of the degree to which the data indicate that the sphericity assumption is violated. The p-value is greater for these alternative tests, but all three tests are significant at the traditional .05 level.

We will concentrate our attention on interpreting the ANOVA results using the multivariate tests and, therefore, avoid the controversy surrounding the sphericity assumption. As we have previously discussed, sphericity is not an assumption for the multivariate tests. For a one-way within-subjects ANOVA, all multivariate tests (Pillai's trace, Wilks' Lambda, as so on) must yield the same result. We recommend reporting Wilks' Λ because researchers are most likely to be familiar with it. For our example, the multivariate tests indicate a significant time effect, Wilks' Λ = .62, F (3, 27) = 5.57, p = .004.

Performing Pairwise Comparisons

If the ANOVA yields a significant result, as in this example, pairwise comparisons should be conducted to assess which means differ from each other. To conduct the pairwise comparisons among the time levels, follow these steps:

1. Click **Analyze**, click **Compare Means**, then click **Paired-Samples T-Test**.
2. Click **time1**. Time1 now appears as Variable 1 in Current Selections.
3. Click **time2**. Time2 appears as Variable 2 in Current Selections.
4. Now click ▸ , and time1-time2 appears in the Paired Variables box.
5. Repeat steps 2 through 4 for each pairwise comparison (time1-time3, time1-time4, time2-time3, time2-time4, time3-time4)
6. Click **OK**.

Descriptive Statistics

	Mean	Std. Deviation	N
TIME1	65.80	9.23	30
TIME2	65.43	10.69	30
TIME3	63.10	10.68	30
TIME4	61.93	12.57	30

Multivariate Tests[b]

Effect		Value	F	Hypothesis df	Error df	Sig.	Eta Squared
TIME	Pillai's Trace	.382	5.567[a]	3.000	27.000	.004	.382
	Wilks' Lambda	.618	5.567[a]	3.000	27.000	.004	.382
	Hotelling's Trace	.619	5.567[a]	3.000	27.000	.004	.382
	Roy's Largest Root	.619	5.567[a]	3.000	27.000	.004	.382

a. Exact statistic

b.

Design: Intercept
Within Subjects Design: TIME

Tests of Within-Subjects Effects

Measure: MEASURE_1

Source		Type III Sum of Squares	df	Mean Square	F	Sig.	Eta Squared
TIME	Sphericity Assumed	310.733	3	103.578	7.664	.000	.209
	Greenhouse-Geisser	310.733	2.094	148.410	7.664	.001	.209
	Huynh-Feldt	310.733	2.260	137.483	7.664	.001	.209
	Lower-bound	310.733	1.000	310.733	7.664	.010	.209
Error(TIME)	Sphericity Assumed	1175.767	87	13.515			
	Greenhouse-Geisser	1175.767	60.719	19.364			
	Huynh-Feldt	1175.767	65.545	17.938			
	Lower-bound	1175.767	29.000	40.544			

Figure 174. The results of the one-way repeated-measures analysis.

Selected SPSS Output for Pairwise Comparisons

The results of the analysis are shown in Figure 175.

Paired Samples Test

		Paired Differences							
					95% Confidence Interval of the Difference				
		Mean	Std. Deviation	Std. Error Mean	Lower	Upper	t	df	Sig. (2-tailed)
Pair 1	TIME1 - TIME2	.37	4.92	.90	-1.47	2.20	.408	29	.686
Pair 2	TIME1 - TIME3	2.70	5.10	.93	.80	4.60	2.900	29	.007
Pair 3	TIME1 - TIME4	3.87	7.06	1.29	1.23	6.50	3.002	29	.005
Pair 4	TIME2 - TIME3	2.33	3.40	.62	1.06	3.60	3.762	29	.001
Pair 5	TIME2 - TIME4	3.50	5.64	1.03	1.40	5.60	3.401	29	.002
Pair 6	TIME3 - TIME4	1.17	4.35	.79	-.46	2.79	1.470	29	.152

Figure 175. The results of the pairwise comparisons.

We conducted six pairwise comparisons among the means for Time 1, Time 2, Time 3, and Time 4. Four of the six pairwise comparisons are significant controlling for familywise error rate across the six tests at the .05 level, using the Holm's sequential Bonferroni procedure.

The smallest p-value is for the comparison of Time 2 and Time 3, and its p-value of .001 is less than $\alpha = .05 / 6 = .0083$ and, therefore, difference between the means for these two times is significant. The next smallest p-value is for the comparison of Time 2 and Time 4, and its p-value of .002 is less than $\alpha = .05 / 5 = .01$ and, therefore, this comparison is also significant. The next smallest p-value is for the comparison of Time 1 and Time 4 and its p-value of .005 is less than $\alpha = .05 / 4 = .0125$ and, therefore, this comparison is significant. The p-value of .007 for the comparison of Time 1 and Time 3 is smaller than $\alpha = .05 / 3 = .0167$ and, therefore, this comparison is also significant. The next comparison is not significant at the .025, and therefore none of the remaining comparisons are significant.

Conducting Polynomial Contrasts

If levels of a within-subjects factor represent quantitative scores that are equally spaced, in most cases it is more appropriate to conduct polynomial contrasts than paired-samples t tests. For our example, the levels of the within-subjects factor are 0, 5, 10, and 15 years. These levels are equally spaced with five years between adjacent levels. Consequently, polynomial contrasts are the more appropriate follow-up analysis. To conduct polynomial contrast tests, follow these steps:

1. Click **Analyze**, click **General Linear Model**, then click **Repeated Measures**, then click **Define**. If you have not exited SPSS, the appropriate options should be selected. If not, conduct Steps 2 through 10 for conducting the overall test.
2. Click **Contrasts**. You will see the Repeated Measures: Contrasts dialog box shown in Figure 176.

Figure 176. The Repeated Measures: Contrasts dialog box.

3. In the drop-down menu, click **Polynomial**.
4. Click **Change**.
5. Click **Continue**.
6. Click **OK**.

Selected SPSS Output for Polynomial Contrasts

The results of the analysis are shown in Figure 177 (at the top of page 216). There is a significant linear effect, $F(1, 29) = 11.56$, $p = .002$. Higher-order polynomial contrasts (quadratic and cubic) were nonsignificant. By inspecting the means in Figure 174, it is evident that the linear effect is due to the DEW means decreasing over time. It should be noted that there was little change in means from 0 to 5 years and, therefore, the significant linear trend was due to changes after 5 years of marriage.

Tests of Within-Subjects Contrasts

Measure: MEASURE_1

Source	TIME	Type III Sum of Squares	df	Mean Square	F	Sig.	Eta Squared
TIME	Linear	291.207	1	291.207	11.564	.002	.285
	Quadratic	4.800	1	4.800	.486	.491	.016
	Cubic	14.727	1	14.727	2.690	.112	.085
Error(TIME)	Linear	730.293	29	25.183			
	Quadratic	286.700	29	9.886			
	Cubic	158.773	29	5.475			

Figure 177. The results of the polynomial contrasts.

Using SPSS Graphs to Display the Results

Boxplots are often used to display the results of a one-way repeated measures ANOVA. For our example, we created a boxplot to show the distributions of the DEW scores at each time period. We created the boxplot shown in Figure 178 using the steps described in Lesson 20.

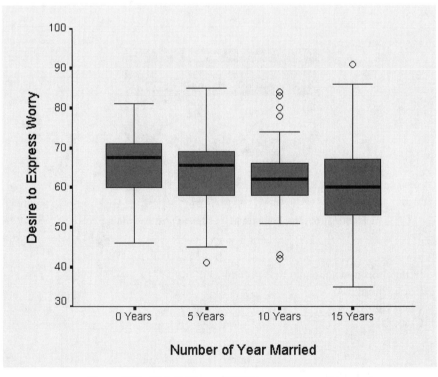

Figure 178. Distributions of DEW scores across time.

An APA Results Section

A one-way within-subjects ANOVA was conducted with the factor being number of years married and the dependent variable being the DEW scores. The means and standard deviations for DEW scores are presented in Table 28. The results for the ANOVA indicated a significant time effect, Wilks' $\Lambda = .62$, $\underline{F}(3, 27) = 5.57$, $\underline{p} = .004$, multivariate $\eta^2 = .38$.

Follow-up polynomial contrasts indicated a significant linear effect with means decreasing over time, F (1, 29) = 11.56, p = .002, partial η^2 = .29. Higher-order polynomial contrasts were nonsignificant. It should be noted that there was little change in means from 0 to 5 years and, therefore, the significant trend was due to changes after 5 years of marriage. These results suggest that men are more eager to express worry to their wives early in their marriage, and this desire decreases after five years of marriage.

Table 28

Means and Standard Deviations for DEW Scores

Number of years married	M	SD
0 years	65.80	9.23
5 years	65.43	10.69
10 years	63.10	10.68
15 years	61.93	12.57

Exercises

Exercises 1 through 4 are based on Shep's study, described earlier, about whether teachers feel greater stress when coping with problems associated with students, parents, or administrators. The data for these exercises are named *Lesson 28 Exercise File 1*. The data file contains the stress scores for the three types of problems.

1. Conduct a one-way repeated-measures ANOVA on these data. Identify the following information from the output.
   a. Multivariate *F* value based on the Wilks' lambda
   b. The *p*-value for Wilks' lambda
   c. Mean of stress scores when coping with problems associated with students
2. Conduct the appropriate follow-up tests.
3. Write a results section.
4. Create an error bar chart to show the distributions of the stress scores.

Exercises 5 through 7 are based on the following research problem. The data for these examples are in the data file named *Lesson 28 Exercise File 2* on the Student Disk.

Mary, a developmental psychologist, is interested in how children's self-esteem develops over time. She measures 25 children at ages 5, 7, 9, 11, and 13 using the Self-Esteem Descriptor (SED). The data file contains 25 cases and five variables, the self-esteem scores for each child at each age period (sed1 through sed5).

5. Conduct a repeated-measures ANOVA to see if self-esteem changes significantly over time.
6. What follow-up tests should you conduct? How would you control for Type I error across your follow-up tests?
7. Write a results section based on your analyses. What should Mary conclude? Be sure to include a graph in your results.

Lesson 29

Two-Way Repeated-Measures Analysis of Variance

With two-way repeated-measures analysis of variance (ANOVA), each subject or case in a study is exposed to all combinations of levels of two qualitative variables and measured on a quantitative variable for each combination. The qualitative variables are referred to as repeated-measures factors or within-subjects factors. The quantitative variable is called the dependent variable.

Similar to one-way repeated-measures ANOVA (Lesson 28), we do not create an SPSS data file that includes two within-subject (repeated-measures) factors and a dependent variable to conduct a two-way repeated-measures ANOVA. Instead, the data file contains a number of quantitative variables. The number of variables equals the number of levels of one within-subjects factor times the number of levels of the other within-subjects factor. The scores on any one of these quantitative variables in the SPSS data file are the scores on the dependent variable for a level of one within-subjects factor in combination with a level of the other within-subjects factor.

Although we do not define the within-subjects factors in the SPSS data set, we specify them in the dialog boxes for the General Linear Model Repeated-Measures procedure. In these boxes, we name the within-subjects factors, specify the number of levels for these factors, and indicate the quantitative variables in the data set that are associated with all combinations of levels of the two within-subjects factors.

Applying Two-Way Repeated-Measures ANOVA

We can analyze data from different types of studies using a two-way within-subjects ANOVA.

- Experimental studies
- Quasi-experimental studies
- Field studies
- Longitudinal studies

Let's look at examples of two types of studies—an experimental study with a single scale and a field study with multiple scales—that can be analyzed using two-way repeated-measures analyses.

Experimental Study with a Single Scale

Dan wishes to evaluate various coping strategies for pain. He obtains eight student volunteers to come to the lab on two consecutive days for his pain research. On both days, the students plunge their hands into freezing cold water for 90 seconds. They rate how painful the experience is on a scale from 1 (= Not painful at all) to 50 (= Excruciatingly painful) at the end of 30 seconds, 60 seconds, and 90 seconds. The eight students receive avoidance instructions one day and concentration-on-pain instructions the other day. The avoidance instructions tell the students to think about a pleasant time that they have had and to try not to think about what was occurring in the lab. The concentration-on-pain instructions tell the students to focus on the sensations in their hands. Four students are given the avoidance instructions on the first day and the concentration-on-pain instructions on the second day. The other four students are given the instructions in the opposite order. A preliminary analysis indicates that the ordering of instructions had no effect. The within-subjects factors are the following: coping treatment with two levels (avoidance and concentration) and time with three levels (30, 60, and 90 seconds). The dependent variable is rating of pain on a 50-point scale. Dan's SPSS data file includes eight cases and six variables. Three of the variables are the scores at the end of 30, 60, and 90 seconds for the avoidance instructions, and the other three variables are the scores at the end of 30, 60, and 90 seconds for the concentration-on-pain instructions.

Field Study with Multiple Scales

Jean wants to know whether students tend to emphasize one type of study strategy over others, regardless of how information is presented in class. To examine this question, she has three guest instructors come to make presentations to her class of 30 students. One instructor stresses general principles, a second emphasizes applications, and a third facts. Jean tells the class that each guest lecturer has submitted questions to be included on the exam. The day of the exam, the students complete a study questionnaire three times, once for how they prepared for the exam for the principle-oriented instructor, once for the applications-oriented instructor, and once for the facts-oriented instructor. The questionnaire yielded three scale scores for each administration: principle-level studying, application-level studying, and surface-level studying. The scales were normed previously to have a mean of 50 and a standard deviation of 10. For this study, one of the within-subjects factors is type of presentation with three levels (principles-oriented, application-oriented, and facts-oriented), while the other within-subjects factor is study strategy with three levels (principle-level studying, application-level studying, and surface-level studying). The dependent variable is study strategy. The second factor can be treated as a within-subjects factor because the three scales have a common mean and standard deviation, and differences between scales are meaningful (i.e., a person who scores higher on principle-level studying versus application-level studying puts a greater emphasis on studying principles than applications in comparison with others). Jean's SPSS data file has 30 cases and nine variables. The nine variables represent the student scores on the three types of scales for each of the three types of presentations.

Understanding Two-Way Repeated-Measures ANOVA

Two-way within-subjects ANOVAs are conducted to analyze data from a variety of studies. In many of these studies, the levels of a within-subject factor represent multiple observations on a scale over time or under different conditions. However, for some studies, levels of a within-subject factor may represent scores associated with different scales, and the focus may be on evaluating differences in means among these scales. For the significance tests in the ANOVA to be meaningful for these studies, the scales must be commensurable; that is, the scales must measure individuals on the same metric, and the difference scores between scales must be interpretable.

The factors may also be treated as within-subjects factor for a study if individuals are matched on one or more variables to create matched sets of individuals and if the number of combinations of levels for the two factors is equal to the number of individuals within each matched set. Each individual within a set is then observed under one combination of levels for the two factors. Because of the matching process, the scores on the dependent variable are likely to be correlated and, therefore, the factors are treated as within-subjects factors.

Now let's look at how to conduct the analyses for a two-way repeated-measures design. We address tests to evaluate the overall hypotheses for the main and interaction effects as well as post hoc tests.

The output for a two-way repeated-measures ANOVA includes tests of main effects for the two factors as well as their interaction. If a main effect or interaction effect has a single degree of freedom (in the numerator), SPSS produces only a standard univariate test. If a main or interaction effect has more than a single degree of freedom, SPSS can evaluate the same hypothesis with multiple methods. These tests include a traditional univariate test, an alternative (degrees-of-freedom corrected) univariate test, and a multivariate test. The first method is not recommended except in the single degree of freedom case. The choice between the last two methods should be made prior to examining the SPSS output.

The standard univariate ANOVA F test is not recommended for tests with more than a single degree of freedom because one of its assumptions, the sphericity assumption, is commonly violated. This F test yields inaccurate p-values to the extent that this assumption is violated. Alternative univariate tests take into account violations of the sphericity assumption. These tests employ the same calculated F statistic as the standard univariate test, but their associated p-values potentially differ. In determining these p-values, epsilon statistics are computed that assess the degree that the sphericity assumption is violated based on the sample data. The numerator and denominator degrees of freedom of the standard test can then be multiplied by an epsilon to obtain a corrected set of degrees of freedom for the tabled F value and to determine its p-value.

The multivariate test employs an entirely different approach and does not require sphericity. Difference scores are computed by comparing scores from different levels of within-subjects factor or factors. It should be noted that the SPSS Repeated Measures procedure computes the difference scores used in conducting this multivariate test. However, these difference scores do not become a part of our data file and, therefore, we may or may not be aware that the multivariate test is conducted on these difference scores. As discussed in Lesson 28, applied statisticians tend to prefer the multivariate test to the standard or the alternative univariate test. When we conduct a two-way repeated-measures procedure later in this lesson, we do not assume sphericity, and we conduct the multivariate tests.

Regardless of which method is used to initially evaluate the main effects and interaction effect, follow-up tests may be required if one or more of the overall tests is significant. If the interaction hypothesis is rejected, simple main effects or interaction comparison tests frequently are conducted as follow-up tests. If the interaction is not significant, then follow-up tests are conducted for a significant main effect if the factor associated with the main effect has more than two levels.

Several types of difference scores could potentially be evaluated in conducting follow-up tests for the main and interaction effects with the paired-samples t tests. We will discuss briefly three types of difference scores to help understand the methods, the sphericity assumption, and the hypotheses evaluated by the multivariate tests.

One type of difference score is computed for each of the main effects and for the interaction. We will use the first example, the pain research, and its data as shown in Table 29, to illustrate the three types of difference scores.

Table 29

Data for Pain Example

Students	Concentration on pain			Avoidance		
	Time 1	Time 2	Time 3	Time 1	Time 2	Time 3
Mary	14	14	25	4	10	30
Jane	16	17	25	1	14	28
Jill	18	17	19	6	13	23
Jean	4	6	22	3	12	24
Corey	16	14	15	8	13	20
Pam	5	11	20	1	10	24
Jennifer	2	6	10	1	12	17
Jersey	21	27	40	8	12	42

Difference Scores Associated with the Coping Main Effect

The coping main effect evaluates differences between the two coping methods averaging across the levels of the time factor. The following steps yield the relevant difference scores for this main effect:

1. Compute a mean score across Times 1, 2, and 3 for the avoidance condition for each case.
2. Compute a mean score across Times 1, 2, and 3 for the concentration-on-pain condition for each case.
3. Subtract the mean score for Step 1 from the mean score for Step 2 for each case.

The computational results of these steps are shown in Table 30.

Table 30

Data for Pain Example

Students	Mean for concentration on pain	Mean for avoidance	Difference
Mary	17.67	14.67	3.00
Jane	19.33	14.33	5.00
Jill	18.00	14.00	4.00
Jean	10.67	13.00	-2.33
Corey	15.00	13.67	1.33
Pam	12.00	11.67	.33
Jennifer	6.00	10.00	-4.00
Jersey	29.33	20.67	8.67

The single set of difference scores implies a single hypothesis is evaluated by the coping main effect: the mean of these difference scores is equal to zero. Identical *p*-values are produced by the coping main effect for our two-way ANOVA and a paired-samples *t* test on the scores produced in Steps 1 and 2. Because there is only one difference variable associated with the coping main effect, it is not necessary to conduct a multivariate test and follow-up tests.

Difference Scores Associated with the Time Main Effect

The time main effect assesses differences on the scale scores among the three time levels averaging across coping methods. Three pairwise differences for this main effect are relevant and may be computed using the following steps:

1. Compute a mean score across the two coping methods for each of the three levels of time.
2. Compute difference scores between Time 1 and Time 2, between Time 1 and Time 3, and between Time 2 and Time 3.

The computational results of these steps are shown in Table 31.

The multivariate test computed by SPSS for the time main effect assesses whether the population means for these difference scores (as well as more complex difference scores) are simultaneously equal to zero. If the test for this main effect is significant and the interaction is not significant, three follow-up paired samples *t* tests are conducted to evaluate which means of the three pairwise difference variables (last three columns of Table 31) are significantly different from zero.

Table 31

Difference Scores for Time Main Effect

Students	Mean for time 1 (T_1)	Mean for time 2 (T_2)	Mean for time 3 (T_3)	$T_2 - T_1$	$T_3 - T_1$	$T_3 - T_2$
Mary	9.0	12.0	27.5	3.0	18.5	15.5
Jane	8.5	15.5	26.5	7.0	18.0	11.0
Jill	12.0	15.0	21.0	3.0	9.0	6.0
Jean	3.5	9.0	23.0	5.5	19.5	14.0
Corey	12.0	13.5	17.5	1.5	5.5	4.0
Pam	3.0	10.5	22.0	7.5	19.0	11.5
Jennifer	1.5	9.0	13.5	7.5	12.0	4.5
Jersey	14.5	19.5	41.0	5.0	26.5	21.5

Difference Scores for the Interaction Effect

The interaction effect assesses whether differences on the scale scores between coping methods differ for the three time levels. Three difference variables for this interaction effect are relevant, and they may be computed using the following steps:

1. Compute a difference score between the two coping methods for Time 1 ($A_1 - C_1$), Time 2 ($A_2 - C_2$) and Time 3 ($A_3 - C_3$).
2. Compute the three pairwise differences among the difference variables created in Step 1.

The computational results of these steps are shown in Table 32.

Table 32

Difference Scores for Interaction Effects

Students	$A_1 - C_1$	$A_2 - C_2$	$A_3 - C_3$	$(A_1 - C_1) - (A_2 - C_2)$	$(A_1 - C_1) - (A_3 - C_3)$	$(A_2 - C_2) - (A_3 - C_3)$
Mary	-10	-4	5	-6	-15	-9
Jane	-15	-3	3	-12	-18	-6
Jill	-12	-4	4	-8	-16	-8
Jean	-1	6	2	-7	-3	4
Corey	-8	-1	5	-7	-13	-6
Pam	-4	-1	4	-3	-8	-5
Jennifer	-1	6	7	-7	-8	-1
Jersey	-13	-15	2	2	-15	-17

The multivariate test computed by SPSS for the interaction effect assesses whether the population means for the difference-of-differences variables created in Step 2 (and more complex difference-of-differences variables) are equal to zero. If the test for this interaction effect is significant, follow-up interaction comparison tests, simple main effects tests, or both may be conducted. The interaction comparisons evaluate whether the means of the three difference-of-differences variables are significantly different from zero and are conducted using a paired-samples *t* test. On the other hand, simple main effect tests can be conducted to evaluate the simple main effects for time within coping or the simple main effect for coping within time. The simple main effects for time within coping evaluates whether mean differences in scores between times within each level of coping strategy are equal to zero. Alternatively, the simple main effects for coping within time evaluates the mean differences in scores between coping methods for each level of time.

Assumptions Underlying a Two-Way Repeated-Measures Analysis of Variance

The assumptions differ for the univariate and multivariate tests.

Univariate Assumptions

Assumption 1: The Dependent Variable Is Normally Distributed in the Population for Each Combination of Levels of the Within-Subjects Factors

With moderate to large sample sizes, the assumption may be violated and the test will probably yield reasonably accurate results. In most circumstances, a sample size of 15 observations per each combination of levels of the within-subjects factors may be large enough to yield fairly accurate p-values. Larger sample sizes may be required to produce relatively valid results if the population distributions are substantially nonnormal.

Assumption 2: The Population Variances of the Difference Variables Are Equal

For each main and interaction effect, there is a separate set of difference score variances. The relevant variances for a main effect are associated with the pairwise differences among the levels of the main-effects factor. (See the last three columns of Table 31 to see sample quantities of these variables for the time main effect.) The relevant variances for an interaction effect are associated with the difference-of-differences variables. (See the last three columns of Table 32 to see sample quantities of these variables for the interaction effect.)

This assumption is sometimes referred to as the sphericity assumption or as the homogeneity-of-variance-of-differences assumption. The sphericity assumption is meaningful only if the main effect or interaction effect has more than one degree of freedom. If the assumption is violated, the p-value associated with the standard univariate tests cannot be trusted. The alternative univariate and multivariate approaches do not require the assumption of sphericity.

Assumption 3: The Individuals Represent a Random Sample from the Population, and Scores Associated with Different Individuals Are Not Related

The only type of dependency that should exist among dependent variable scores is the dependency introduced by having the same individuals produce multiple scores. Even this type of dependency introduced by the within-subjects factor is limited and must conform to the sphericity assumption for the standard univariate tests. The results of the two-way within-subjects ANOVA should not be trusted if this assumption is violated.

Multivariate Assumptions

The multivariate test is conducted on difference scores, and therefore, the assumptions underlying the multivariate test concern the difference scores for this test.

Assumption 1: The Difference Scores Are Multivariately Normally Distributed in the Population

If the difference scores are multivariately normally distributed, each difference score is normally distributed ignoring the other difference scores, and each difference score is normally distributed at every combination of values of the other difference scores. With moderate to large sample sizes the multivariate normality assumption may be violated, and the test will still yield reasonably accurate results.

Assumption 2: The Individuals Represent a Random Sample from the Population, and the Difference Scores for Any One Individual Are Independent from the Scores for Any Other Individual

If this assumption is violated, the test should not be used.

Computing an Effect Size Statistic

The effect size reported for the standard or the alternative univariate approach is a partial eta square and may be calculated using the following equation:

$$Partial\ \eta^2_{Main\ or\ Interaction} = \frac{Sum\ of\ Squares_{Main\ or\ Interaction}}{Sum\ of\ Squares_{Main\ or\ Interaction} + Sum\ of\ Squares_{Error}}$$

The effect size reported for the multivariate approach is the multivariate eta square:

$$Multivariate\ \eta^2_{Main\ or\ Interaction} = 1 - \Lambda_{Main\ or\ Interaction}$$

where the Wilks' lambda (Λ) is the multivariate statistic for a main or interaction source. Both of these statistics range from 0 to 1. A 0 indicates no relation between a repeated-measures source and the dependent variable, while a 1 indicates the strongest possible relationship.

The Data Set

The data set used to illustrate a two-way repeated-measures analysis of variance is named *Lesson 29 Data File 1* on the Student Disk. The data are based on our first example, the coping-with-pain study. Table 33 presents the definitions of the variables in the data set.

Table 33
Variables in the Lesson 29 Data File 1

Variable	Definition
conc1	Rating of pain on a 50-point scale at Time 1 using the concentration-on-pain method
conc2	Rating of pain on a 50-point scale at Time 2 using the concentration-on-pain method
conc3	Rating of pain on a 50-point scale at Time 3 using the concentration-on-pain method
avoid1	Rating of pain on a 50-point scale at Time 1 using the avoidance method
avoid2	Rating of pain on a 50-point scale at Time 2 using the avoidance method
avoid3	Rating of pain on a 50-point scale at Time 3 using the avoidance method

The Research Question

The research questions for the coping main effect, the time main effect, and the interaction between coping and time are as follows:

1. Coping main effect: Do students, on average, report different degrees of pain using the concentration-on-pain and the avoidance approaches?

2. Time main effect: Do students, on average, report different degrees of pain if their hands are in frigid water for 30 seconds, 60 seconds, and 90 seconds?

3. Interaction between coping and time: Do the differences in means for self-reported pain between the concentration-on-pain and avoidance conditions vary depending upon whether the report was made at 30 seconds, 60 seconds, or 90 seconds?

Conducting a Two-Way Repeated-Measures ANOVA

We will now conduct four analyses involving our two-way repeated-measures ANOVA. We will first illustrate how to conduct the overall ANOVA for the 3 x 2 within-subjects design. In addition, we will present methods for conducting follow-up tests associated with the time main effect. We will then demonstrate how to conduct both simple main effect tests and interaction comparison tests as follow-up tests to a significant interaction. (Lesson 25 discusses selecting follow-up tests for a two-way ANOVA.)

Conducting the Overall Analysis

The following steps evaluate the main and interaction effects for the two within-subjects factors (univariate and multivariate). The steps also let us obtain the means and standard deviations of the quantitative variables for all combinations of levels of the two within-subjects factors. To conduct an overall two-way within-subjects ANOVA, follow these steps:

1. Click **Analyze**, click **General Linear Model**, then click **Repeated Measures**.
2. In the Within-Subject Factor Name text box, type **coping** in place of factor1.
3. Type **2** in the Number of Levels text box.
4. Click **Add**.
5. In the Within-Subject Factor Name text box, type **time**.
6. Type **3** in the Number of Levels text box.
7. Click **Add**.
8. Click **Define**.
9. Hold down the Ctrl key, and click on **avoid1**, **avoid2**, **avoid 3**, **conc1**, **conc2**, and **conc3**. Click ▶ to move them to the Within-Subjects Variables box.
10. Click **Options**.
11. Click **coping** in the Factor(s) and Factor Interactions box, and click ▶ to have it appear in the Display Means for box.
12. Click **time** in the Factor(s) and Factor Interactions box, and click ▶ to have it appear in the Display Means for box.
13. Click **coping*time** in the Factor(s) and Factor Interactions box, and click ▶ to have it appear in the Display Means for box.
14. Click **Descriptives** and **Estimates of effect size**.
15. Click **Continue**.
16. Click **OK**.

Selected SPSS Output for Two-Way Repeated-Measures ANOVA

SPSS produces a lot of output for a two-way within-subjects ANOVA: descriptive statistics, statistics for evaluating the sphericity assumption, traditional and alternative univariate ANOVA results, and ANOVA results using multivariate tests. Only the multivariate tests for the main and interaction sources and the cell means are shown in Figure 179 (at the top of page 226).

We will concentrate our attention on interpreting the ANOVA results using the multivariate tests and, therefore, avoid the controversy surrounding the sphericity assumption. The multivariate tests indicate a nonsignificant coping main effect, Wilks' $\Lambda = .78$, $F(1, 7) = 1.92$, $p = .208$, a significant time main effect, Wilks' $\Lambda = .11$, $F(2, 6) = 24.59$, $p = .001$, and a significant coping-by-time interaction effect, Wilks' $\Lambda = .11$, $F(2, 6) = 23.43$, p = .001. Note that the multivariate result for the coping main effect is identical to the univariate result because the coping main effect has only two levels.

Descriptive Statistics

	Mean	Std. Deviation	N
AVOID1	4.00	3.02	8
AVOID2	12.00	1.41	8
AVOID3	26.00	7.65	8
CONC1	12.00	7.23	8
CONC2	14.00	6.80	8
CONC3	22.00	8.85	8

Multivariate Tests[b]

Effect		Value	F	Hypothesis df	Error df	Sig.	Eta Squared
COPE	Pillai's Trace	.216	1.924[a]	1.000	7.000	.208	.216
	Wilks' Lambda	.784	1.924[a]	1.000	7.000	.208	.216
	Hotelling's Trace	.275	1.924[a]	1.000	7.000	.208	.216
	Roy's Largest Root	.275	1.924[a]	1.000	7.000	.208	.216
TIME	Pillai's Trace	.891	24.589[a]	2.000	6.000	.001	.891
	Wilks' Lambda	.109	24.589[a]	2.000	6.000	.001	.891
	Hotelling's Trace	8.196	24.589[a]	2.000	6.000	.001	.891
	Roy's Largest Root	8.196	24.589[a]	2.000	6.000	.001	.891
COPE * TIME	Pillai's Trace	.886	23.432[a]	2.000	6.000	.001	.886
	Wilks' Lambda	.114	23.432[a]	2.000	6.000	.001	.886
	Hotelling's Trace	7.811	23.432[a]	2.000	6.000	.001	.886
	Roy's Largest Root	7.811	23.432[a]	2.000	6.000	.001	.886

a. Exact statistic

b.

Design: Intercept
Within Subjects Design: COPE+TIME+COPE*TIME

Figure 179. The cell means and multivariate results of the two-way repeated-measures analysis.

Because the interaction is significant, we would normally conduct follow-up simple main effect tests, interaction comparisons, or both. We will discuss how to conduct these comparisons shortly. The time main effect was also significant, but normally we would not conduct follow-up tests to this main effect in the presence of a significant interaction effect. However, if there were no significant interaction effect, we would want to conduct follow-up tests to understand why the main effect test was significant. Next, we will describe how to conduct pairwise comparison tests for the time main effect just to demonstrate how these tests would be done.

Pairwise Comparisons for Significant Time Main Effect

Conducting follow-up tests for a significant time main effect requires creating three time variables averaging across the coping factor then conducting paired-samples *t* tests. To conduct pairwise comparisons among the time main effect means, follow these steps:

1. Compute time1, time2 and time3 variables. To do so, use the Transform—Compute option and calculate the mean across the two pain ratings at each time (see Lesson 18 for complete instructions on computing mean scores). Time1 would be the mean of conc1 and avoid1, time2 would be the mean of conc2 and avoid2, and time3 would be the mean of conc3 and avoid3.
2. Click **Analyze**, click **Compare Means**, then click **Paired-Samples T Test**.
3. Click **time1**. Time1 now appears as Variable 1 in Current Selections.
4. Click **time2**. Time2 appears as Variable 2 in Current Selections.
5. Now click ▶, and time1—time2 appears in the Paired Variables box.
6. Repeat steps 3 through 5 for each pairwise comparison (time1—time3 and time2—time3)
7. Click **OK**.

Selected SPSS Output for Pairwise Comparisons for Time Main Effect

The results of the analysis are shown in Figure 180.

Paired Samples Test

		Paired Differences							
					95% Confidence Interval of the Difference				
		Mean	Std. Deviation	Std. Error Mean	Lower	Upper	t	df	Sig. (2-tailed)
Pair 1	TIME1 - TIME2	-5.0000	2.2991	.8128	-6.9221	-3.0779	-6.151	7	.000
Pair 2	TIME1 - TIME3	-16.0000	6.7295	2.3792	-21.6260	-10.3740	-6.725	7	.000
Pair 3	TIME2 - TIME3	-11.0000	6.0474	2.1381	-16.0558	-5.9442	-5.145	7	.001

Figure 180. The results of the time main effect pairwise comparisons.

All three pairwise comparisons among the means for Time 1, Time 2, and Time 3 are significant controlling for Type I error across the three tests at the .05 level, by using the Holm's sequential Bonferroni procedure.

The smallest p-value is for the comparison of Time 1 and Time 3, and its p-value of .000 is less than the α of .05 / 3 = .0167 and, therefore, difference between the means for these two times is significant, t (7) = -6.73, $p < .001$. The next smallest p-value is for the comparison of Time 1 and Time 2, and its p-value of .000 is less than the α of .05 / 2 = .025 and, therefore, this comparison is also significant, t (7) = -6.15, $p < .001$. Finally, the largest p-value of .001 for the comparison of Time 2 and Time 3 is smaller than an α of .05 / 1 = .05 and, therefore, this comparison is significant, too, t (7) = -5.15, $p = .001$.

Using the LSD Approach to Control for Type I Error with Three Groups

With pairwise comparisons among three means, a somewhat more powerful procedure is the LSD procedure. With the LSD procedure, we can test each pairwise comparison p-value against an α of .05 if the test for main effect is significant and control adequately for familywise error rate at the .05 level.

Conducting Simple Main Effect Analyses

To conduct simple main effect analyses for a two-way within-subjects design following a significant interaction, we will again use paired-samples t tests. To conduct pairwise comparison analyses for the simple main effects for coping within time, follow these steps:

1. Click **Analyze**, click **Compare Means**, then click **Paired-Samples T Test**.
2. Click **Reset** to clear the dialog box.
3. Click **avoid1**. Avoid1 now appears as Variable 1 in Current Selections.
4. Click **conc1**. Conc1 appears as Variable 2 in Current Selections.
5. Now click on ▸, and **avoid1—conc1** appears in the Paired Variables box.
6. Repeat steps 3 through 5 for avoid2—conc2 and avoid3—conc3.
7. Click **OK**.

Selected SPSS Output for Simple Main Effects

We conducted paired-samples t tests to evaluate the differences between the two coping methods for each time period. The results of these analyses are shown in Figure 181 (at the top of page 228).

We could have also conducted the time simple main effects for each coping method. Because there are three levels of time, we would have performed a separate one-way within-subjects ANOVA to evaluate the time factor for each coping method (concentration on pain and avoidance). If a one-way ANOVA yielded significance, we would have conducted pairwise comparisons among

Paired Samples Test

		Paired Differences							
					95% Confidence Interval of the Difference				
		Mean	Std. Deviation	Std. Error Mean	Lower	Upper	t	df	Sig. (2-tailed)
Pair 1	AVOID1 - CONC1	-8.00	5.45	1.93	-12.56	-3.44	-4.151	7	.004
Pair 2	AVOID2 - CONC2	-2.00	6.63	2.35	-7.55	3.55	-.853	7	.422
Pair 3	AVOID3 - CONC3	4.00	1.69	.60	2.59	5.41	6.693	7	.000

Figure 181. The results of the simple main effects analyses of coping within time.

the three times. However, we chose to ignore differences among time levels for each coping method because they were of less interest.

Two of the three pairwise comparisons are significant controlling for familywise error rate across the three tests at the .05 level, by using the Holm's sequential Bonferroni procedure. The comparison with the smallest p-value evaluates the mean difference between coping methods for Time 3, $t(7) = 6.69$, $p = .000$, which is less than an $\alpha = .05 / 3 = .0167$ and significant. The comparison with the next smallest p-value evaluates the mean difference between coping methods for Time 1, $t(7) = -4.15$, $p = .004$, which also is less than an $\alpha = .05 / 2 = .025$ and significant. Finally, the last comparison evaluates the mean difference between coping methods for Time 2, $t(7) = -.85$, $p = .422$, which is not less than an $\alpha = .05 / 1 = .05$ and, therefore, not significant.

Conducting Interaction Comparisons

An alternative way to follow up a significant interaction is to conduct interaction comparisons. Conducting interaction comparisons for a two-way within-subjects design requires computing difference scores and conducting paired-samples t tests. To conduct interaction comparisons for our example, follow these steps:

1. Compute differences. Use the Transform—Compute option to compute three difference (a_c) variables by subtracting the concentration (conc) variables from the avoidance (avoid) variables for each of the three time periods. For example, **a1_c1** would be **avoid1 - conc1**, **a2_c2** would be **avoid2 - conc2**, and **a3_c3** would be **avoid3 - conc3**.
2. Click **Analyze**, click **Compare Means**, then click **Paired-Samples T Test**.
3. Click **Reset** to clear the dialog box.
4. Click **a1_c1**. a1_c1 now appears as Variable 1 in Current Selections.
5. Click **a2_c2**. a2_c2 appears as Variable 2 in Current Selections.
6. Now click on ► and a1_c1 - a2_c2 appears in the Paired Variables: box.
7. Repeat steps 4 through 6 for a1_c1 - a3_c3 and a2_c2 - a3_c3
8. Click **OK**.

Selected SPSS Output for Interaction Comparisons

The results of the analysis are shown in Figure 182.

Paired Samples Test

		Paired Differences							
					95% Confidence Interval of the Difference				
		Mean	Std. Deviation	Std. Error Mean	Lower	Upper	t	df	Sig. (2-tailed)
Pair 1	A1_C1 - A2_C2	-6.0000	4.0708	1.4392	-9.4033	-2.5967	-4.169	7	.004
Pair 2	A1_C1 - A3_C3	-12.0000	5.1270	1.8127	-16.2862	-7.7138	-6.620	7	.000
Pair 3	A2_C2 - A3_C3	-6.0000	6.0945	2.1547	-11.0951	-.9049	-2.785	7	.027

Figure 182. The results of the interaction comparison analyses.

Tetrad comparisons involving four means evaluate whether the mean differences between the two coping methods are the same between any two time periods. All three tetrad comparisons are significant controlling for familywise error rate across the three tests at the .05 level, using the Holm's sequential Bonferroni procedure. The comparison with the smallest p-value evaluates whether the mean difference between coping methods is the same for Time 1 and Time 3, $t(7) = -6.62$, $p = .000$, which is less than an $\alpha = .05 / 3 = .0167$. The comparison with the next smallest p-value evaluates whether the mean difference between coping methods is the same for Time 1 and Time 2, $t(7) = -4.17$, $p = .004$, which is less than an $\alpha = .05 / 2 = .025$. Finally, the last comparison evaluates whether the mean difference between coping methods is the same for Time 2 and Time 3, $t(7) = -2.78$, $p = .027$, which is less than an $\alpha = .05 / 1 = .05$.

Using SPSS Graphs to Display the Results

The General Linear Model-Repeated Measures procedure allows you to create line graphs of the factor means to visually represent the interactions and main effects associated with the factors. However, these graphs are limited in that they do not display the variability of the scores around the means. To create a profile plot depicting the interaction between coping and time, follow these steps:

1. Click **Analyze**, click **General Linear Model**, then click **Repeated Measures.** If you have not exited SPSS, the appropriate options should be selected; then go to Step 2. If they are not, conduct Steps 2 through 9 of "Conducting the Overall Analysis" earlier in this lesson; then skip to Step 3.
2. In the Repeated Measures: Define Factor(s) dialog box, click **Define**.
3. Click **Plots**. You will see the Repeated Measures: Profile Plots dialog box in Figure 183.

Figure 183. The Repeated Measures: Profile Plots dialog box.

4. In the Repeated Measures: Profile Plots dialog box, click **coping**, and click ▶ to have it appear in the Horizontal Axis box.
5. Click **time**, and click ▶ to have it appear in the Separate Lines box.
6. Click **Add**.
7. Click **Continue**.
8. Click **OK**.

The edited profile plot is shown in Figure 184 (at the top of page 230).

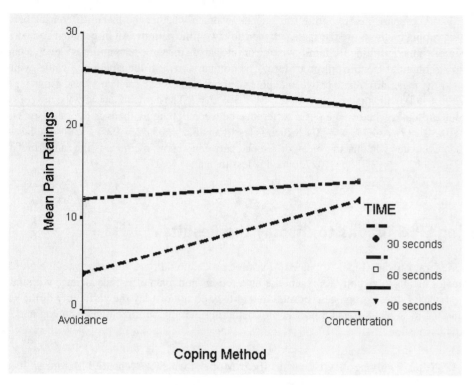

Figure 184. Profile plot of stress by time interaction.

An APA Results Section

A two-way within-subjects analysis of variance was conducted to evaluate the effect of coping strategies and length of time under stress on pain ratings. The dependent variable was a pain rating of 1 to 50. The within-subjects factors were coping methods with two levels (concentration-on-pain and avoidance) and time with three levels (30, 60, and 90 seconds). The Time main and Coping x Time interaction effects were tested using the multivariate criterion of Wilks' lambda (Λ). The Time main effect was significant, $\Lambda = .11$, $\underline{F}$ (2, 6) = 24.59, $\underline{p} = .001$, as well as the Coping x Time interaction effect, $\Lambda = .11$, $\underline{F}$ (2, 6) = 23.43, $\underline{p} = .001$. The univariate test associated with the Coping main effect was nonsignificant, $\Lambda = .78$, $\underline{F}$ (1, 7) = 1.92, $\underline{p} = .208$.

Three paired-samples $\underline{t}$ tests were conducted to follow up the significant interaction. We controlled for familywise error rate across these tests using Holm's sequential Bonferroni approach. Differences in mean ratings of pain between the two coping methods were significantly different between Times 1 and 2, $\underline{t}$ (7) = -4.17, $\underline{p} = .004$, between Times 2 and 3, $\underline{t}$ (7) = -2.78, $\underline{p} = .027$, and between Times 1 and 3, $\underline{t}$ (7) = -6.62, $\underline{p} < .001$. Table 34 (at the top of page 231) shows that although the difference in mean pain ratings was lower for the avoidance method at Time 1, the difference decreased at Time 2, and reversed itself at Time 3. These results support the hypothesis that concentration-on-pain methods are more effective than avoidance methods the longer individuals are exposed to a stressor.

Finally, three paired-samples $\underline{t}$ tests were computed to assess differences between methods at each time period, controlling for familywise error rate using Holm's sequential Bonferroni approach. At Time 1, the avoidance condition yielded a significantly lower mean rating, $\underline{t}$ (7) = -4.15, $\underline{p} = .004$. At Time 2, the two methods were not significantly different from each other, $\underline{t}$ (7) = -.85, $\underline{p} = .422$, while at Time 3, the concentration-on-pain condition yielded a significantly lower mean rating, $\underline{t}$ (7) = 6.69, $\underline{p} < .001$.

Table 34
Means (Standard Deviations) for Ratings of Pain

	Time in frigid water		
Method of coping	Time 1	Time 2	Time 3
Concentration on pain	12.00	14.00	22.00
	(7.23)	(6.80)	(8.85)
Avoidance	4.00	12.00	26.00
	(3.02)	(1.41)	(7.65)

Exercises

The data for Exercises 1 through 5 are in the data file named *Lesson 29 Exercise File 1* on the Student Disk. The data are from the following research problem.

John is interested in the development of visual attention in infants and whether it differs for novel and familiar stimuli. He collects measures of visual attention for novel and familiar stimuli from 60 infants at four time periods, 3 months, 4 months, 6 months, and 8 months. John's SPSS data file contains eight variables, including novel and familiar visual attention scores in seconds for each of the time periods. There are two within-subjects factors: time with four levels (3, 4, 6, and 8 months) and stimulus type with two levels (novel and familiar).

1. Conduct a two-way within-subjects ANOVA to evaluate these data. From the output, identify the following:
   a. The *p*-value associated with the Wilks' lambda for the time effect
   b. The *F* value associated with the Wilks' lambda for the interaction effect
   c. The effect size associated with the Wilks' lambda for the stimulus effect
   d. The mean visual attention score on the novel stimuli for 6-month-old infants
2. What should John conclude about the interaction between time and stimulus type? Report the appropriate information from the output to justify your conclusion.
3. What follow-up tests should be conducted?
4. Write a results section reporting your conclusions.
5. Create a profile plot to show the interaction between stimuli types and time.

The data for Exercises 6 through 8 are in the data file named *Lesson 29 Exercise File 2* on the Student Disk. The data are from the following research problem.

Peter, a child psychologist, is interested in the relationship between physical characteristics and popularity. Specifically, he believes that girls are more likely to find better-dressed boys and girls more likeable, although to a lesser extent if the better-dressed children are males. He conducts the following study using a group of 25 girls in the first grade. He obtains 100 pictures of first-graders whom the children in this study do not know. Twenty-five of the pictures are of well-dressed boys, 25 are of well-dressed girls, 25 are of poorly dressed boys, and 25 are of poorly dressed girls. Before having each girl come into the testing room, the experimenter shuffles the 100 cards 15 times. The child is told that she will see a series of pictures. If the child likes the person in the photographs, she is to cheer. If she dislikes the child, she is to boo. A score of 1 is assigned to a cheer and a score of -1 is assigned to a boo. Peter computes an overall scale for each child by summing the scores for the 25 cards in each of the four conditions (e.g., well-dressed boys).

6. Conduct a two-way within-subjects ANOVA to evaluate these data. One factor represents gender of the child in the picture, and the second factor represents his

or her dress. What should Peter conclude about the interaction between gender and dress type? Report the appropriate information from the output to justify your conclusion.

7. Should Peter conduct any follow-up tests? Why or why not?
8. Write a results section for these data.

Correlation, Regression, and Discriminant Analysis Procedures

Unit 8 includes lessons on the Pearson product-moment correlation coefficient, partial correlation coefficient, bivariate linear regression, multiple linear regression, and discriminant analysis. We describe how to use these statistical techniques to analyze a wide range of research problems. In some applications, the analyses may appear very simple, such as computing a Pearson product-moment correlation coefficient to assess the linear relationship between two quantitative variables. In other applications, the analyses may seem complex, such as computing partial and multiple correlations to evaluate the relative importance of various predictors in a multiple regression equation. For all techniques, it is important to have an in-depth understanding of them. If you are unfamiliar with these analytic methods, please read one or more of the following sources on these methods: Cohen and Cohen (1983), Darlington (1990), and Pehazur (1997).

The lessons in Unit 8 address the following topics:

- Lesson 30 deals with bivariate correlational analysis. We will restrict our discussion to linear relationships between two quantitative variables.
- Lesson 31 describes partial correlational analysis. We describe how to assess the relationship between two quantitative variables, statistically controlling for or partialling out differences on one or more potential confounding variables.
- Lesson 32 presents bivariate linear regression. We will focus our discussion on applications with a quantitative predictor variable and a quantitative criterion variable.
- Lesson 33 describes multiple linear regression. We'll talk about applications with two or more quantitative predictors and a quantitative criterion variable.
- Lesson 34 discusses discriminant analysis and includes applications for a qualitative criterion variable and one or more quantitative predictor variables.

The Pearson Product-Moment Correlation Coefficient

The Pearson product-moment correlation coefficient (r) indicates the degree that quantitative variables are linearly related in a sample. Each individual or case must have scores on two quantitative variables. The significance test for r evaluates whether there is a linear relationship between the two variables in the population. In this lesson we will work on understanding Pearson correlations between quantitative variables. We will not discuss correlations in which one or both variables are categorical or ordinal.

Applying the Pearson Product-Moment Correlation Coefficient

We will illustrate three types of research studies in which the Pearson correlations are computed.

- Studies with a correlation between two variables
- Studies with correlations among three or more variables
- Studies with correlations within and between sets of variables

Study with a Correlation between Two Variables

Annette is interested in the relationship between leg strength and running agility for male college students. She obtains 40 male students from undergraduate physical education classes. Each student must complete a series of leg strength exercises on a weight machine. Annette computes a total leg strength index that takes into account a student's performance across all of the exercises. In addition, each student must run 200 meters along a straight line and 200 meters along a curving, twisting line. Running clumsiness (the opposite of running agility) is the number of seconds to complete the curving, twisting course minus the number of seconds to complete the straight course. Annette's SPSS data file for this analysis includes scores on both the leg strength and running clumsiness variables for the 40 cases.

Study with Correlations among Three or More Variables

John is interested in whether people who have a positive view of themselves in one aspect of their lives also tend to have a positive view of themselves in other aspects of their lives. To address this question, he has 80 men complete a self-concept inventory that contains five scales. Four scales involve questions about how competent respondents feel in the areas of intimate relationships, relationships with friends, common sense reasoning and everyday knowledge, and academic reasoning and scholarly knowledge. The fifth scale includes items about how competent a person feels in general. John's SPSS data file includes the five self-concept variables for the 80 cases. John is interested in determining the correlations between all possible pairs of variables, that is, 10 correlations.

Study with Correlations within and between Sets of Variables

Cindy, director of personnel at an insurance company, wants to know whether a personality measure predicts on-the-job performance. She has the records of 50 life insurance sales people who took a personality measure when they were hired. The personality measure has three scales: extroversion, conscientiousness, and openness. Their on-the-job performance was assessed using two measures: amount of insurance sold in first year and ratings by supervisors. Cindy's SPSS data file has two sets of variables for the 50 cases: one set containing the three personality scales and the second set having the two on-the-job performance measures. Cindy thinks of the personality scales as predictor variables and the on-the-job performance measures as criteria. Although Cindy would undoubtedly compute the correlations within sets, she is primarily interested in correlations between the three predictors and the two criteria. There are six of these correlations, the correlations of the three personality measures with the two criteria.

Understanding the Pearson Product-Moment Correlation Coefficient

We will first consider the two assumptions underlying the significance test for the Pearson correlation. We will then examine the meaning of the Pearson correlation as an effect size statistic.

Assumptions Underlying the Significance Test

There are two assumptions underlying the significance test associated with a Pearson correlation coefficient between two variables.

Assumption 1: The Variables Are Bivariately Normally Distributed

If the variables are bivariately normally distributed, each variable is normally distributed ignoring the other variable and each variable is normally distributed at all levels of the other variable. If the bivariate normality assumption is met, the only type of statistical relationship that can exist between two variables is a linear relationship. However, if the assumption is violated, a nonlinear relationship may exist. It is important to determine if a nonlinear relationship exists between two variables before describing the results using the Pearson correlation coefficient. Nonlinearity can be assessed visually by examining a scatterplot of the data points as we illustrate later in this lesson.

Assumption 2: The Cases Represent a Random Sample from the Population and the Scores on Variables for One Case Are Independent of Scores on These Variables for Other Cases

The significance test for a Pearson correlation coefficient is not robust to violations of the independence assumption. If this assumption is violated, the correlation significance test should not be computed.

Computing an Effect Size Statistic

SPSS computes the Pearson correlation coefficient, an index of effect size. The index ranges in value from -1 to +1. This coefficient indicates the degree that low or high scores on one variable tend to go with low or high scores on another variable. A score on a variable is a low (or high) score to the extent that it falls below (or above) the mean score on that variable.

To understand how the correlation coefficient is interpreted, let's use our example involving leg strength and running clumsiness. A correlation of +1 indicates that as scores on strength increase across cases, the scores on clumsiness increase precisely at a constant rate. If r is positive, low scores on strength tend to be associated with low scores on clumsiness, and high scores on strength tend to be associated with high scores on clumsiness. If r is zero, low scores on strength tend to be associated equally with low and high scores on clumsiness, and high scores on strength tend to be associated equally with low and high scores on clumsiness. In other words, as the scores on strength increase across cases, the scores on clumsiness tend neither to increase nor to decrease. If r is negative, low scores on strength tend to be associated with high scores on clumsiness, and high scores on strength tend to be associated with low scores on clumsiness. A correlation of -1 indicates that as scores on strength increase across cases, the scores on clumsiness decrease precisely at a constant rate.

As with all effect size indices, there is no good answer to the question, "What value indicates a strong relationship between two variables?" What is large or small depends on the discipline within which the research question is being asked. However, for the behavioral sciences, correlation coefficients of .10, .30, and .50, irrespective of sign, are typically interpreted as small, medium, and large coefficients, respectively.

If one variable is thought of as the predictor and another variable as the criterion, we can square the correlation coefficient to interpret the strength of the relationship. The square of the correlation gives the proportion of criterion variance that is accounted for by its linear relationship with the predictor. For our example, if strength is the predictor and clumsiness is the criterion and the correlation between these variables is .40, we would conclude that 16% of the variance ($.40^2$) of the clumsiness variable is accounted for by its linear relationship with strength.

The Data Set

The data set used to illustrate the Pearson correlation coefficient is named *Lesson 30 Data File 1* on the Student Disk. It has data coming from the self-concept example we presented earlier in this lesson. The variables in the data set are in Table 35.

Table 35
Variables in Lesson 30 Data File

Variables	Definition
intimate	High scores on this variable indicate that respondents are self-confident in intimate relationships.
friend	High scores on this variable indicate that respondents are self-confident in relationships among friends.
common	High scores on this variable indicate that respondents are self-confident in their knowledge of everyday events and their use of common sense reasoning.
academic	High scores on this variable indicate that respondents are self-confident in their scholarly knowledge and their ability to reason in a rigorous, formal manner.
general	High scores on this variable indicate that respondents are self-confident in the way they conduct their lives. This variable is not a sum of the other four variables, but is based on items specific to this variable. The items ask how competent a person feels in general, and they do not specify a particular life domain.

The Research Question

The research question concerns the relationship between the five self-concept variables: Do men who feel confident in one life domain tend to feel confident in other domains, and conversely, do men who feel insecure in one life domain also tend to feel insecure in other domains?

Conducting a Pearson Correlation Coefficient

To compute a Pearson correlation coefficient, follow these steps:

1. Click **Analyze**, click **Correlate**, then click **Bivariate**. You will see the Bivariate Correlations dialog box as shown in Figure 185.

Figure 185. The Bivariate Correlations dialog box.

2. Holding down the Ctrl key, click **intimate**, **friend**, **common**, **academic**, and **general**, and click ▸ to move them to the Variables box.
3. Make sure **Pearson** is selected in the Correlation Coefficients area.
4. Make sure the **Two-tailed** option in the Test of Significance box (unless you have some a priori reason to select one-tailed).
5. Make sure **Flag significant correlations** is selected.
6. Click **Options**. You'll see the Bivariate Correlations: Options dialog box as shown in Figure 186.

Figure 186. The Bivariate Correlations: Options dialog box.

7. Click **Means and standard deviations** in the Statistics box.
8. Click **Continue**
9. Click **OK**.

Selected SPSS Output for Pearson Correlations

The results of the correlational analyses are shown in Figure 187 (at the top of page 238). The Correlations table in Figure 187 presents the correlations, asterisks (*) indicating whether a particular correlation is significant at the .05 level (*) or the .01 level (**), p-values associated with the

Correlations

		self concept: intimate relationships	self concept: friends	self concept: common sense intelligence	self-concept: academic intelligence	self-concept: general
self concept: intimate relationships	Pearson Correlation	1.000	.552**	.351**	.218	.393**
	Sig. (2-tailed)		.000	.001	.052	.000
	N	80	80	80	80	80
self concept: friends	Pearson Correlation	.552**	1.000	.462**	.244*	.546**
	Sig. (2-tailed)	.000		.000	.029	.000
	N	80	80	80	80	80
self concept: common sense intelligence	Pearson Correlation	.351**	.462**	1.000	.400**	.525**
	Sig. (2-tailed)	.001	.000		.000	.000
	N	80	80	80	80	80
self-concept: academic intelligence	Pearson Correlation	.218	.244*	.400**	1.000	.261*
	Sig. (2-tailed)	.052	.029	.000		.019
	N	80	80	80	80	80
self-concept: general	Pearson Correlation	.393**	.546**	.525**	.261*	1.000
	Sig. (2-tailed)	.000	.000	.000	.019	
	N	80	80	80	80	80

**. Correlation is significant at the 0.01 level (2-tailed).

*. Correlation is significant at the 0.05 level (2-tailed).

Figure 187. The bivariate correlations among the five self-concept measures.

significance tests for these correlations, and sample size (N). Note that the information in upper-right triangle of the matrix is redundant with the information in the lower-left triangle of the matrix and can be ignored.

If several correlations are computed, you may wish to consider a corrected significance level to minimize the chances of making a Type I error. One possible method is the Bonferroni approach, where .05 is divided by the number of correlations computed. A correlation coefficient would not be significant unless its p-value is less than the corrected significance level. In this example, a p-value would have to be less than .05 divided by 10 or .005 to be declared significant.

SPSS presents the correlations in tabular form. However, correlations are often presented within the text of a manuscript. For example, "The correlation between the friendships and general self-concept scales was significant, r (78) = .55, p < .001." The number in parentheses represents the degrees of freedom associated with the significance test, which is equal to the number of cases minus 2 (or N - 2). As shown on the output, the number of cases for this correlation is 80 and, therefore, the degrees of freedom are 80 - 2 = 78.

Computing Correlations between Sets of Variables

If you are interested in computing correlations between variables from two different sets but not within each set, the method changes slightly. Let's say that we were interested in the correlations of the four self-concept scales with the general self-concept scale. To conduct this analysis, follow the steps listed on page 239.

1. Follow the same instructions as those specified earlier for computing a Pearson correlation coefficient, but at Step 9, click **Paste** rather than OK. The syntax window shows the syntax for the bivariate correlation program. One of syntax lines looks similar to this:

   /VARIABLES=academic common friend intimate general

2. Depending on how you selected variables in the Bivariate Correlation dialog box, the variable general may or may not be listed last. If it is not last, retype the statement so that **general** is last, and put the word **with** before the word general. Your syntax should look like this:

   /VARIABLES=academic common friend intimate with general

3. Now click the **Run** button. The output will give the correlations of the first four self-concept variables with general self-concept.

Using SPSS Graphs to Display the Results

Scatterplots are rarely included in results sections of manuscripts, but they should be included more often since they visually represent the relationship between variables. While a correlation coefficient tries to summarize the relationship between two variables with a single value, a scatterplot gives a rich descriptive picture of this relationship. In addition, the scatterplot can show whether a few extreme scores (outliers) overly influenced the value of the correlation coefficient or whether nonlinear relationships exist between variables.

To create scatterplots among multiple variables, follow these steps:

1. Click **Graphs**, then click **Scatter**. You'll see the Scatterplot dialog box as shown in Figure 188.

Figure 188. The Scatterplot dialog box.

2. Click **Matrix**, then click **Define**. You'll see the Scatterplot Matrix dialog box as shown in Figure 189 (at the top of page 240).
3. Hold the Ctrl key down and click **intimate**, **friends**, **common**, **academic**, and **general**.
4. Click ▶ to move them to the Matrix Variables box.
5. Click **OK**. The resulting graph is shown in Figure 190 (on page 240).

An APA Results Section

Correlation coefficients were computed among the five self-concept scales. Using the Bonferroni approach to control for Type I error across the 10 correlations, a p-value of less than .005 (05 / 10 = .005) was required for significance. The results of the correlational analyses presented in

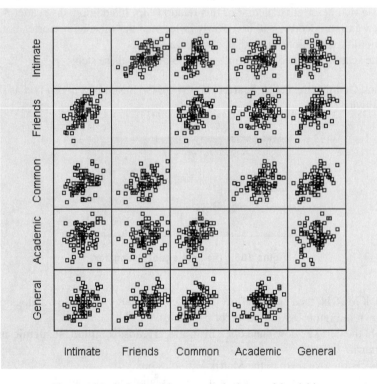

Figure 189. The Scatterplot Matrix dialog box.

Figure 190. Relationships among intimate, friendship, common-sense, academic, and general self-concepts.

Table 36 (at the top of page 241) show that 7 out of the 10 correlations were statistically significant and were greater than or equal to .35. The correlations of scholarly knowledge self-concept with the other self-concept measures tended to be lower and not significant. In general, the results suggest that if men say that they are self-confident in one area, they tend to state that they are self-confident in other areas except for scholarly knowledge.

Table 36

Correlations among the Five Self-Concept Scales (N = 80)

	Scholarly knowledge	Everyday knowledge	Friendships	Intimate relationships
Everyday knowledge	.40*			
Friendships	.24	.46*		
Intimate relationships	.22	.35*	.55*	
General	.26	.52*	.55*	.39*

* $p < .005$

Alternative Analyses

We can compute Pearson correlations by other procedures than the Bivariate Correlation procedure, such as the Bivariate Linear Regression procedure. The Bivariate Correlation procedure can also compute a Kendall's tau-b or Spearman if the measurement scales underlying the variables are ordinal (i.e., the values for the variable indicate their position in relation to each other, but the intervals between scores lack quantitative meaning).

Exercises

The data for Exercises 1 through 4 are in the data file named *Lesson 30 Exercise File 1* and are based on the following research problem.

Betsy is interested in relating quality of teaching to quality of research by college professors. She has access to a sample of 50 social science professors who were teaching at the same university for a 10-year period. Over this 10-year period, the professors were evaluated on a 5-point scale on quality as instructors and on quality of their courses. Betsy has averaged these ratings to obtain an overall quality rating as an instructor (rating_1) and the overall quality of the course (rating_2) for each professor. In addition, Betsy also has the number of articles that each professor published during this time period (num_pubs) and the number of times these articles were cited by other authors (cites).

1. Conduct a correlational analysis to investigate the relationships among these variables. Identify the following on the output:
   a. The *p*-value for the correlation between rating_1 and rating_2
   b. The correlation between cites and num_pubs
   c. The correlation between cites and rating_1
2. What is the relationship between the number of articles published and the overall quality of the instructor?
3. Write a results section based on your analysis of these data.
4. Create a scatterplot matrix to show the relationships among the four variables.

The data for Exercises 5 through 8 are in the data file named *Lesson 30 Exercise File 2* and are based on the following research problem.

Fred believes that there are excellent students, good students, mediocre students, bad students, and extremely bad students. Excellent students tend to do exceptionally well in all subjects; good students tend to do well in all subjects; mediocre students tend to do mediocre on all subjects; and so on. To test this hypothesis, he examines the records of 120 students who have recently graduated from high school. For each student, he determines their high school GPAs in five types of courses: math (mathgpa), English (enggpa), history (histgpa), science (sciengpa), and social sciences (socgpa).

5. Conduct a correlational analysis to investigate the relationships of students' GPA in math and science with students' GPA in social sciences and humanities (English and history).

6. What should Fred conclude about the correlations between the two sets of variables?
7. Create two new variables: (1) an average GPA in math and science and (2) an average GPA in social science and humanities. Conduct a correlational analysis on the two averaged scores. What is the resulting correlation?
8. What conclusions would you draw from the correlation between the two averaged scores? Would they be different from the conclusion you would draw from Exercise 6?

Partial Correlations

The partial correlation (r_p), an effect size index, indicates the degree that two variables are linearly related in a sample, partialling out the effects of one or more control variables. The partial correlation attempts to estimate the correlation between two variables given all cases had exactly the same scores on the control variables, that is, holding constant the values of the control variables. The significance test for a partial correlation evaluates whether in the population the partial correlation is equal to zero.

It makes little sense to interpret a partial correlation between two variables controlling for a third variable without considering the zero-order or bivariate correlation between the two variables. In other words, to interpret properly a partial correlation between two variables, we must also know the magnitude of the bivariate correlation between these two variables. Because there is a strong link between partial and bivariate correlations, it may be useful to reread Lesson 30 on bivariate correlations before proceeding with this lesson.

The SPSS data file associated with a partial correlation coefficient contains scores on at least three variables for each individual or case. For our purposes in this lesson, all the variables are quantitative.

Applying Partial Correlations

Partial correlations can be used in several ways, such as the following:

- Partial correlation between two variables
- Partial correlations among multiple variables within a set
- Partial correlations between sets of variables.

We illustrate these three applications using the studies described in Lesson 30, except we will add a control variable to each study.

Partial Correlation between Two Variables

Annette is conducting research in physical education and believes that there is a relationship between leg strength and running clumsiness for male college students. She believes that this relationship is a function of the amount of physical activity in which students engage. In other words, those students who tend to exercise regularly also tend to have greater leg strength and to demonstrate less running clumsiness. To evaluate her hypothesis, she obtains scores for leg strength and running clumsiness on 40 male students from undergraduate physical education classes. In addition, she records the number of hours that each student is physically active per week. Annette is interested in the correlation between leg strength and running clumsiness partialling out the effects of physical activity, the control variable. Annette's SPSS data file includes leg strength, running clumsiness, and physical activity variables for the 40 cases.

Partial Correlations among Multiple Variables within a Set

John thinks that people who have a positive view of themselves in one specific area of their life tend to have a positive view of themselves in other specific areas of their life. He believes further that the tendency of people to evaluate themselves consistently across specific life domains is a function of their general self concept. To address these issues, he has 80 male adults complete a self-concept inventory that contains the five scales described in Lesson 30. John is interested in the correlations among the first four scales that assess self-concept in specific life domains, partialling out the effects of the fifth scale, general self-concept. John's. SPSS data file includes the five self-concept variables for the 80 cases

Partial Correlations between Sets of Variables

Cindy, the director of personnel at an insurance company, theorizes that sales people with particular types of personalities are more likely to develop a positive perspective toward the product that they sell, and this positive perspective is likely to spill over to their on-the-job performance. To address this issue, Cindy obtains scores on six variables from 50 life insurance sales people. Three personality measures—extroversion, conscientiousness, and openness—are collected at the time of hiring. An attitudinal measure that assesses positive perspective toward the company's life insurance is obtained in the middle of their first year. Finally, two performance measures, amount of insurance sold in the first year and ratings by supervisors, are obtained at the end of their first year of selling insurance. Cindy is interested in the correlations between the personality variables and the on-the-job performance variables, partialling out the effects of perspective toward the company's life insurance, the control variable. Cindy's SPSS data file has scores on the three personality scales, the attitudinal measure, and the two on-the-job measures.

Understanding Partial Correlations

The partial correlation is calculated to understand why two variables are correlated. Two possible explanations are the common cause and the mediator variable hypotheses.

Common Cause Hypothesis

The common cause hypothesis says that variables *A* and *B* are correlated because they share the same causal variable or variables. The common cause hypothesis is illustrated in Figure 191.

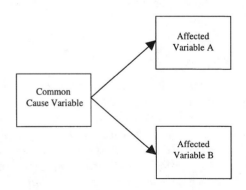

Figure 191. Common cause hypothesis.

If this hypothesis is correct, then the correlation between A and B should be non-zero in value ($r \neq 0$), but the correlation between A and B partialling out the effects of the common causal variable or variables should be equal to zero ($r_p = 0$).

In the first two applications described earlier, Annette and John are interested in evaluating the common cause hypothesis. Annette believes that the reason leg strength and running clumsiness are correlated is that they share a common cause, physical activity. If she is correct, the correlation between leg strength and running clumsiness should be negative, but the correlation between these variables partialling out the effects of physical activity should approach zero. In the second application, John believes that self-concept in specific life domains are correlated because they share a common cause, general self-concept. Accordingly, the self-concept measures across specific domains should be positively correlated, but their partial correlations, controlling for general self-concept, should be equal to zero.

Mediator Variable Hypothesis

The mediator variable hypothesis says that variables A and B are correlated because A causes B through one or more mediator variables. Figure 192 illustrates the mediator variable hypothesis.

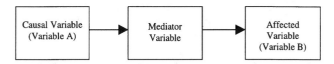

Figure 192. Mediator variable hypothesis.

If this hypothesis is correct, then the correlation between A and B should be nonzero in value ($r \neq 0$), but the correlation between A and B partialling out the effects of the mediator variable or variables should be equal to zero ($r_p = 0$).

In the third application, Cindy appears to be interested in evaluating the mediator variable hypothesis. She believes that the reason the personality and the on-the-job performance variables are correlated is that a salesperson's personality affects his/her perspective toward the company's insurance and that attitude subsequently affects how effective a salesperson he or she is. If Cindy is correct, the correlation between the personality and the on-the-job performance variables should be positive, but the correlation between these variables partialling out the effects of attitude toward the company's insurance should approach zero.

Assumptions Underlying the Significance Test for a Partial Correlation Coefficient

Assumption 1: The Variables Are Multivariately Normally Distributed

If the variables are multivariately normally distributed, each variable is normally distributed ignoring the other variables, and each variable is normally distributed at every combination of values of the other variables. If the multivariate normality assumption is met, the only type of statistical relationship that can exist between variables is linear. If this assumption is violated, however, a nonlinear relationship may be present. It is important to determine if a nonlinear relationship exists between variables before describing the results using the partial correlation coefficient. Nonlinearity between any two variables can be evaluated by visually inspecting a scatterplot, as we will show you later in this lesson.

Assumption 2: The Cases Represent a Random Sample from the Population, and Scores for One Case Are Independent of Scores on Variables for Other Cases

The significance test for a partial correlation coefficient should not be used if the independence assumption is violated.

Computing an Effect Size Statistic

The partial correlation is a type of Pearson correlation coefficient and can be interpreted in a similar manner. Like a bivariate correlation, a partial correlation can range in value from -1 to +1. If a partial correlation is positive, one can conclude that as one variable increases in value, the second variable also tends to increase in value, holding constant the control variable or variables. If a partial correlation is zero, one can conclude, that as one variable increases in value, the second variable tends neither to increase nor decrease in value, holding constant the control variable or variables. Finally, if a partial correlation is negative, one can conclude that as one variable increases in value, the second variable tends to decrease in value, holding constant the control variable or variables.

The Data Set

The data set used to illustrate the partial correlation coefficient is named *Lesson 31 Data File 1* on the Student Disk and represents data coming from the self-concept example discussed earlier in this lesson. Table 37 shows the variables in the data file.

Table 37
Variables in Lesson 31 Data File 1

Variables	Definition
intimate	High scores on this variable indicate that respondents are self-confident in intimate relationships.
friend	High scores on this variable indicate that respondents are self-confident in relationships among friends.
common	High scores on this variable indicate that respondents are self-confident in their knowledge of everyday events and their use of common sense reasoning.
academic	High scores on this variable indicate that respondents are self-confident in their scholarly knowledge and their ability to reason in a rigorous, formal manner.
general	High scores on this variable indicate that respondents are self-confident in the way they conduct their lives. This variable is not a sum of the other four variables, but is based on items specific to this variable. The items ask how competent a person feels in general, and they do not specify a particular life domain.

The Research Question

The research questions for a partial correlation are asked in two steps: (1) concerning the bivariate correlations among the variables and (2) concerning the relationship between two variables partialling out the effects of a third (control) variable. Here are the research questions for our example.

1. Bivariate relationships among variables: Do men who feel confident in one specific life domain tend to feel confident in other specific domains, and do men who feel insecure in one life domain also tend to feel insecure in other domains?
2. Relationships between two variables partialling out the effects of a control variable: If men have the same level of general self-confidence, do they tend to feel more confident in one specific life domain when they feel more confident in another domain, and do they tend to feel insecure in one specific life domain when they feel insecure in another domain?

Conducting a Partial Correlation

To evaluate fully the results of the questions, we must compute both bivariate and partial correlations. Both sets of statistics can be computed using the Partial Correlation procedure. To compute these bivariate and partial correlations, follow these steps:

1. Click **Analyze**, click **Correlate**, and then click **Partial**. You will see the Partial Correlations dialog box as shown in Figure 193.

Figure 193. The Partial Correlations dialog box.

2. Press the Ctrl key, and click **intimate**, **friend**, **common**, and **academic**.
3. Click ► to move them to the Variables box.
4. Click **general**, then click ► to move it to the Controlling for box.
5. Make sure the **Two-tailed** option is selected in the Test of Significance box (unless you have some a priori reason to select one-tailed).
6. Make sure **Display actual significance level** is selected.
7. Click **Options**, then click **Means and standard deviations**, and **Zero-order correlations** in the Statistics box.
8. Click **Continue**.
9. Click **OK**.

Selected SPSS Output for Partial Correlations

The partial correlations from the output are shown in Figure 194 (at the top of page 248). The output from the Partial Correlations procedure gives the means and standard deviations, the bivariate correlations among all the self-concept variables, and the partial correlations.

Each cell in the partial correlation table presents the partial correlation coefficient, the degrees of freedom for the significance test (in parentheses), and the p-value. If the significance level is set at .05 for each partial correlation coefficient and a p-value is less than .05, the null hypothesis that the population partial correlation coefficient is equal to zero is rejected, and the partial correlation coefficient is significant. The values in the lower-left triangle of the matrix are the same as the values in the upper-right triangle.

When you conduct several partial correlations, as we just did, you may want to consider a corrected significance level to minimize the chances of incorrectly rejecting the null hypotheses (Type I errors) across the multiple tests. One method that might be used is the Bonferroni approach where .05 is divided by the number of partial correlations that are computed. A partial correlation coefficient is not significant unless its p-value is less than the corrected significance level. In our example, a p-value must be less than .05 divided by 6, or .008, to be declared significant. Using this criterion, two of the six partial correlations are significant.

```
--- PARTIAL  CORRELATION  COEFFICIENTS -

Controlling for..    GENERAL

              INTIMATE      FRIEND      COMMON     ACADEMIC

INTIMATE      1.0000        .4385       .1856       .1302
             (    0)       (   77)     (   77)     (   77)
             P= .          P= .000     P= .102     P= .253


FRIEND         .4385       1.0000       .2458       .1260
             (   77)       (    0)     (   77)     (   77)
             P= .000       P= .        P= .029     P= .268


COMMON         .1856        .2458      1.0000       .3208
             (   77)       (   77)     (    0)     (   77)
             P= .102       P= .029     P= .        P= .004


ACADEMIC       .1302        .1260       .3208      1.0000
             (   77)       (   77)     (   77)     (    0)
             P= .253       P= .268     P= .004     P= .


(Coefficient / (D.F.) / 2-tailed Significance)

" . " is printed if a coefficient cannot be computed
```

Figure 194. The results of the Partial Correlations procedure.

Using SPSS Graphs to Display the Results

The simplest partial correlation involves three variables including the control variable. A graph associated with such a partial correlation should display the results for all three variables. SPSS offers several possibilities. Let's look at steps for creating two types of scatterplots—a three-dimensional scatterplot and a simple scatterplot with markers.

Creating 3-D Scatterplots

You could create a three-dimensional scatterplot for three of the self-concept scales, but, as with many three-dimensional graphs, it might be difficult to interpret. One solution is to dichotomize scores on the control variable and use the dichotomized score in the three-dimensional scatterplot.

We will illustrate this strategy by creating a three-dimensional scatterplot of the relationship between intimate relationship and friendship self-concepts for two levels of general self-concept, high and low. To create this graph, you will need to create a new variable (rgeneral) with one category for values that fall at or below the median (e.g., rgeneral = 0) and a second category for values that fall above the median (rgeneral = 1). Lesson 18 explains how to create a qualitative variable from a quantitative variable.

To produce the three-dimensional scatterplot, follow these steps:

1. Create the variable **rgeneral** using the steps described in Lesson 18 for creating a qualitative variable from a quantitative variable.
2. Click **Graphs**, then click **Scatter**.
3. Click **3-D**, then click **Define**. You'll see the 3-D Scatterplot dialog box as shown in Figure 195 (at the top of page 249).
4. Click **intimate**, then click ▸ to move it to the Y-Axis box.
5. Click **friend**, then click ▸ to move it to the X-Axis box.
6. Click **rgeneral**, then click ▸ to move it to the Z-Axis box.
7. Click **OK**. You'll see the graph shown in Figure 196 (on page 249).

A moderate linear relationship appears to exist between the Friendship and the Intimate

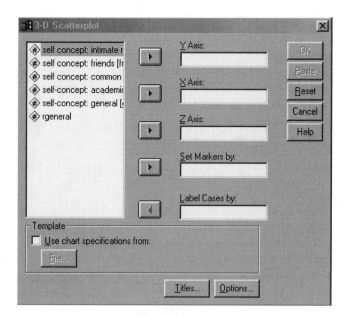

Figure 195. The 3-D Scatterplot dialog box.

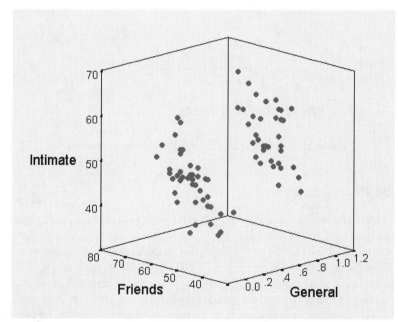

Figure 196. A three-dimensional scatterplot of the relationship between intimate and friendship self-concept for two levels of general self-concept.

Relationships scales for both low and high scorers on the General scale. This interpretation is consistent with the partial correlation of .44 between Friendships and Intimate Relationships scales holding constant the General scale.

Creating a Simple Scatterplot with Markers

Another way to illustrate the relationship between these variables is to construct a simple bivariate scatterplot using separate markers for low and high scorers on the general self-concept variable. To create a simple scatterplot with markers, follow the steps listed at the top of page 250.

1. Click **Graphs**, then click **Scatter**.
2. Click **Simple**, then click **Define**.
3. Click **intimate**, then click ▶ to move it to the Y-Axis box.
4. Click **friend**, then click ▶ to move it to the X-Axis box.
5. Click **rgeneral**, then click ▶ to move it to the Set Markers by box.
6. Click **OK**. You'll see the scatterplot, as shown in Figure 197.

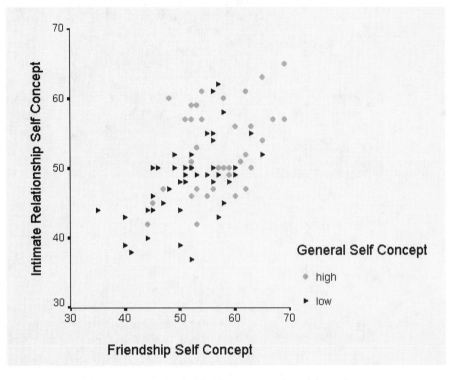

Figure 197. A simple bivariate scatterplot with markers.

An APA Results Section

Correlation coefficients were computed among the five self-concept scales. Using the Bonferroni approach to control for Type I error across the 10 correlations, a p-value of less than .005 (.05 / 10 = .005) was required for significance. The results of the correlational analyses are presented in the top half of Table 38 (at the top of page 251). Seven of the 10 correlations were statistically significant and were greater than or equal to .35. However, the correlations with self-concept in academic knowledge tended to be lower, and many were nonsignificant. In general, the results suggest that if men say they are self-confident in one area they tend to state they are self-confident in other areas except for academic knowledge.

Partial correlation coefficients were then computed among the self-concept scales for specific life domains holding constant the general self-concept scale. A p-value of less than .008 (.05 / 6 = .008) was required for significance using the Bonferroni approach to control for Type I error across the six partial correlations. The partial correlations are reported in the second half of Table 38. Two of the six partial correlations were significant and moderately large in magnitude. One of the significant partial correlations assessed the correlation between the two knowledge self-concept measures, while the other evaluated the correlation between the two relationship-oriented self-concept measures. If general self-concept is the sole determinant of self-concept in specific areas, all the partial correlations would be equal to zero. The results do not support this hypothesis.

Alternative Analyses

Partial correlations may also be computed using the Multiple Regression procedure (Lesson 33).

Table 38

Bivariate and Partial Correlations among the Self-Concept Scales (N = 80)

	Scholarly knowledge	Everyday knowledge	Friendships	Intimate relationships
	Bivariate correlations			
Everyday knowledge	.40*			
Friendships	.24	.46*		
Intimate relationships	.22	.35*	.55*	
General	.26	.52*	.55*	.39*
	Partial correlations controlling for general self concept			
Everyday knowledge	.32*			
Friendships	.13	.25		
Intimate relationships	.13	.19	.44*	

* p < .005 for bivariate correlations and p < .008 for partial correlations

Exercises

Exercises 1 through 4 are based on data in the data file named *Lesson 31 Exercise File 1* on the Student Data Disk. The data are from the following research study.

Betsy does not believe that quality of research by college professors leads to quality of teaching. She believes that any relationship between these two variables is due to work ethic. In other words, professors who are dedicated to their work will be better researchers and better teachers. Betsy has access to a sample of 50 social science professors who were teaching at the same university for a 10-year period. Over this 10-year period, the professors were evaluated on a 5-point scale on their quality as instructors and the quality of their courses. She has averaged these ratings to obtain an overall quality rating as an instructor (rating_1) and the overall quality of the course (rating_2) for each professor. Betsy also has the number of articles that each published during this time period (num_pubs) and the number of times these articles were cited by other authors (cites). Finally, Betsy has scores that reflect professors' work ethic (work_eth). These scores range from 1 to 50, with 50 indicating a very strong work ethic.

1. Evaluate Betsy's hypothesis by computing correlations between the two teaching variables and the two research variables controlling for the work ethic variable. From the output, identify the following:
   a. The bivariate correlation between the number of publications and number of citations
   b. The *p*-value associated with the bivariate relationship between number of publications and quality rating as an instructor
   c. The correlation between quality of the course and number of citations partialling out the effect of work ethic.
2. What effect does partialling out the effects of work ethic have on the relationship between quality rating as an instructor and number of publications?
3. Write a results section based on your analyses.
4. Create a 3-D scatterplot to display the relationship between quality rating as an instructor and number of publications.

Exercises 5 through 8 are based on data in the data file named *Lesson 31 Exercise File 2* on the Student Data Disk. The data are from the following research study.

A local newspaper reports that the number of violent crimes committed in a region is strongly related to the amount of beer drank in the region. Susan, a sociologist interested in crime prevention, elects to investigate this relationship. She decides that the relationship between beer drinking and violent crimes is spurious and that a third variable, air temperature, could explain this relationship. She collects data for the month of July on the amount of beer purchased (in hundreds of gallons), the number of violent crimes committed, and the average daily high temperatures in 30 U.S. cities.

5. What is the bivariate correlation between amount of beer purchased and violent crimes?
6. What is the partial correlation between amount of beer purchased and violent crimes, holding temperature constant?
7. What should Susan conclude about the relationship between amount of beer purchased and the number of violent crimes committed?
8. Write a results section based on your analyses. Be sure to include a graphical display of your data.

Bivariate Linear Regression

For a bivariate linear regression problem, data are collected on an independent or predictor variable (X) and a dependent or criterion variable (Y) for each individual. Bivariate linear regression computes an equation that relates predicted Y scores ($\hat{Y}$) to X scores. The regression equation includes a slope weight for the independent variable, B_{slope}, and an additive constant, $B_{constant}$:

$$\hat{Y} = B_{slope} \, X + B_{constant}$$

Indices are computed to assess how accurately the Y scores are predicted by the linear equation.

This lesson focuses on applications in which both the predictor and criterion are quantitative variables. However, bivariate regression analysis may be used in other applications. For example, a predictor could have two levels like gender and be scored 0 for male and 1 for female. A criterion may also have two levels like pass-fail performance, scored 0 for fail and 1 for pass.

Linear regression can be used to analyze data from experimental or nonexperimental designs. If the data are collected using experimental methods (e.g., a tightly controlled study in which participants have been randomly assigned to different treatment groups), the X and Y variables may be referred to appropriately as the independent and the dependent variables, respectively. SPSS uses these terms. However, if the data are collected using nonexperimental methods (e.g., a study in which subjects are measured on a variety of variables), the X and the Y variables are more appropriately referred to as the predictor and the criterion, respectively.

Applying Bivariate Linear Regression

We will illustrate two types of studies that can be analyzed using bivariate linear regression—nonexperimental studies and experimental studies

A Nonexperimental Study

Mary conducts a nonexperimental study to evaluate what she refers to as the strength-injury hypothesis. It states that overall body strength in elderly women determines the number and severity of accidents that cause bodily injury. If the results of her prediction study support her strength-injury hypothesis, she plans to conduct an experimental study to assess whether weight training reduces injuries in elderly women. In the prediction study, Mary collects data from 100 women who range in age from 60 to 75 years old at the time the study begins. The women initially undergo a number of measures that assess lower and upper body strength, and these measures are summarized using an overall index of body strength. Over the next five years, the women record each time they have an accident that results in a bodily injury and describe fully the extent of the injury. On the basis of these data, Mary calculates an overall injury index for each woman. Mary is interested in conducting a regression analysis with the overall index of body strength as the predictor (independent) variable and the overall injury index as the criterion (dependent) variable. Mary's SPSS data file has 100 cases and scores on six variables, five individual strength measures (quads, gluts, abdoms, grip, and arms) that are to be combined to yield an overall index of body strength and the criterion variable, the overall injury index.

An Experimental Study

Jack is interested in the effect of coffee drinking on cigarette smoking. He gains the cooperation of 40 men and women who smoke 20 or more cigarettes and drink 2 or more cups of coffee a day. He randomly assigns 10 participants to each of the four treatment conditions: 0 cups of coffee, 1 cup of coffee, 2 cups of coffee, and 3 cups of coffee. Each participant is asked to sit in a small room and watch TV for 45 minutes. Those in the coffee drinking conditions are asked to drink their coffee at a uniform pace over the first 35 minutes of the 45-minute period. All subjects are told they may not smoke their own cigarettes, but they may smoke the cigarettes that are on the desk in the room. On the basis of a videotape of each session and the cigarette butts left in the ashtray on the desk, Jack estimates the number of millimeters of cigarettes smoked by each research subject. Jack is interested in conducting a regression analysis with the amount of coffee drunk as the independent variable and the number of millimeters of cigarettes smoked as the dependent variable. Jack's SPSS data file has scores on these two variables for the 40 cases.

Understanding Bivariate Linear Regression

A significance test can be conducted to evaluate whether X is useful in predicting Y. This test can be conceptualized as evaluating either of the following null hypotheses: the population slope weight is equal to zero or the population correlation coefficient is equal to zero.

The significance test can be derived under two alternative sets of assumptions, assumptions for a fixed-effects model and those for a random-effects model. The fixed-effects model is probably more appropriate for experimental studies, while the random-effects model seems more appropriate for nonexperimental studies. If the fixed-effects assumptions hold, linear or nonlinear relationships can exist between the predictor and criterion. On the other hand, if the random-effects assumptions hold, the only type of statistical relationship that can exist between two variables is a linear one.

Regardless of choice of assumptions, it is important to examine a bivariate scatterplot of the predictor and the criterion variables prior to conducting a regression analysis to assess if a non-linear relationship exists between X and Y and to detect outliers. If the relationship appears to be nonlinear based on the scatterplot, you should not conduct a simple bivariate regression analysis, but should evaluate the inclusion of higher-order terms (variables that are squared, cubed, and so on) in your regression equation (see a regression textbook, e.g., Pedhazur, 1997). Outliers should be checked to ensure that they were not incorrectly entered in the data set and, if correctly entered, to determine their effect on the results of the regression analysis.

Fixed-Effects Model Assumptions Underlying the Significance Test for Bivariate Linear Regression

As discussed earlier, there are two potential sets of assumptions to be considered—those for a fixed-effects model and those for a random-effects model. The following are assumptions for a fixed-effects model.

*Assumption 1: The Dependent Variable Is Normally Distributed in the Population
for Each Level of the Independent Variable*

With moderate to large sample sizes, the assumption may be violated to some degree, and the test will still yield reasonably accurate results. Larger sample sizes may be required to produce relatively valid results if the population distributions are substantially nonnormal.

*Assumption 2: The Population Variances of the Dependent Variable Are the Same
for All Levels of the Independent Variable*

To the extent that this assumption is violated and the sample sizes differ among the levels of the independent variable, the resulting p-value for the overall F test is not trustworthy.

*Assumption 3: The Cases Represent a Random Sample from the Population,
and the Scores Are Independent of Each Other from One Individual to the Next*

The significance test for regression analysis will yield inaccurate p-values if the independence assumption is violated.

Random-Effects Model Assumptions Underlying the Significance Test for Bivariate Linear Regression

*Assumption 1: The X and Y Variables Are Bivariately Normally Distributed
in the Population*

If the variables are bivariately normally distributed, each variable is normally distributed ignoring the other variable and each variable is normally distributed at every level of the other variable. The significance test for bivariate regression yields relatively valid results in terms of Type I errors when the sample is moderate to large in size. If X and Y are bivariately normally distributed, the only type of relationship that exists between these variables is linear.

*Assumption 2: The Cases Represent a Random Sample from the Population,
and the Scores on Each Variable Are Independent of Other Scores
on the Same Variable*

The significance test for regression analysis will yield inaccurate p-values if the independence assumption is violated.

Computing an Effect Size

This lesson focuses on using linear regression to evaluate how well a single independent variable predicts a dependent variable. However, linear regression is a more general procedure that assesses how well one or more independent variables predict a dependent variable. Consequently, SPSS reports strength-of-relationship statistics that are useful for regression analyses with multiple predictors. Four correlational indices are presented in the output for the Linear Regression procedure: the Pearson product-moment correlation coefficient (r), the multiple correlation coefficient (R), its squared value (R^2), and the adjusted R^2. However, there is considerable redundancy among these statistics for the single-predictor case: $R = |r|$, $R^2 = r^2$, and the adjusted R^2 is approximately equal to R^2. Accordingly, the only correlational indices you need to report in your manuscript for a bivariate regression model are r and r^2.

The Pearson product-moment correlation coefficient ranges in value from -1 to +1. A positive value suggests that as the independent variable X increases, the dependent variable Y increases. A zero value indicates that as X increases, Y neither increases nor decreases. A negative value indicates that as X increases, Y decreases. Values closer to -1 or +1 indicate stronger linear relationships. Correlation coefficients of .10, .30, and .50, irrespective of sign, may be interpreted as small, medium, and large coefficients, respectively.

By squaring r, we obtain an index that directly tells us how well we can predict Y from X. r^2 indicates the proportion of Y variance that is accounted for by its linear relationship with X. Alternatively, r^2 can be conceptualized as the proportion reduction in error that we achieve by including X in the regression equation in comparison with not including X in the regression equation.

Other strength-of-relationship indices may be reported for bivariate regression problems. For example, SPSS gives Std. Error of the Estimate on the output. The standard error of estimate is an index indicating how large the typical error is in predicting Y from X. It is a useful index over and above correlational indices because it indicates how badly we predict the dependent variable scores in the metric of these scores. In comparison, correlational statistics are unitless indices and, therefore, are abstract and difficult to interpret.

The Data Set

The data set used to illustrate bivariate linear regression is named *Lesson 32 Data File 1* on the Student Disk. It presents data from our strength-injury example. The variables in the data set are in Table 39.

Table 39

Variables in Lesson 32 Data File 1

Variable	Definition
quads	A measure of strength primarily associated with the quadriceps
gluts	A measure of strength of the muscles in the upper part of the back of the leg and the buttocks
abdoms	A measure of strength of the muscles of the abdomen and the lower back
arms	A measure of strength of the muscles of the arms and the shoulders
grip	An assessment of the hand-grip strength
injury	Overall injury index based on the records kept by the participants

The Research Question

The research question addresses the relationship between two variables: What is the linear equation that predicts the extent of physical injury from body strength for elderly women, and how accurate does this equation predict the extent of physical injuries?

Conducting a Bivariate Linear Regression Analysis

The data set includes the dependent variable for the regression analysis (injury) but does not include the independent variable, an overall index of body strength. It can be calculated by creating z-scores for the five strength measures and adding them together. See Lesson 18 for a more detailed explanation for creating an overall variable from standardized variables. To conduct a bivariate linear regression analysis, follow these steps:

1. Create the total strength variable named **ztotstr** by z-scoring the five individual strength measures and summing them.
2. Click **Analyze**, click **Regression**, then click **Linear**. You will see the Linear Regression dialog box shown in Figure 198 (at the top of page 257).
3. Click **injury**, then click ▶ to move it to the Dependent box.
4. Click **ztotstr**, then click ▶ to have it appear in the Independent(s) box.
5. Click **Statistics**. You will see the Linear Regression: Statistics dialog box shown in Figure 199 (on page 257).

Figure 198. The Linear Regression dialog box.

Figure 199. The Linear Regression: Statistics dialog box.

6. Click **Descriptives**. Make sure that **Estimates** and **Model Fit** are also selected.
7. Click **Continue**.
8. Click **OK**.

Selected SPSS Output for Bivariate Linear Regression

The results of the bivariate linear regression analysis are shown in Figure 200 (at the top of page 258).

The *B*s, as labeled on the output in the Coefficients box, are the additive constant (145.80) and the slope weight (-4.89) of the regression equation used to predict the dependent variable from the independent variable. Accordingly, the regression or prediction equation is as follows:

Predicted Overall Injury = -4.89 *Overall Strength* + 145.80

The slope weight indicates that greater overall strength predicts lower scores on the overall injury index.

A standardized regression equation can be computed if the independent and dependent variables are transformed to *z* scores with a mean of 0 and a standard deviation of 1:

$$\text{Predicted } Z_{\text{Injury}} = -.32 \, Z_{\text{Overall Strength}}$$

Correlations

		INJURY	ZTOTSTR
Pearson Correlation	INJURY	1.000	-.325
	ZTOTSTR	-.325	1.000
Sig. (1-tailed)	INJURY	.	.000
	ZTOTSTR	.000	.
N	INJURY	100	100
	ZTOTSTR	100	100

Model Summary

Model	R	R Square	Adjusted R Square	Std. Error of the Estimate
1	.325[a]	.106	.097	49.61

a. Predictors: (Constant), ZTOTSTR

ANOVA[b]

Model		Sum of Squares	df	Mean Square	F	Sig.
1	Regression	28520.191	1	28520.191	11.588	.001[a]
	Residual	241193.8	98	2461.161		
	Total	269714.0	99			

a. Predictors: (Constant), ZTOTSTR

b. Dependent Variable: INJURY

Coefficients[a]

Model		Unstandardized Coefficients		Standardized Coefficients	t	Sig.
		B	Std. Error	Beta		
1	(Constant)	145.800	4.961		29.389	.000
	ZTOTSTR	-4.891	1.437	-.325	-3.404	.001

a. Dependent Variable: INJURY

Figure 200. The results of the bivariate linear regression analysis.

For bivariate regression analysis based on standardized scores, the slope is always equal to the correlation coefficient and the additive constant must be equal to zero. The standardized slope is labeled beta on the SPSS output. Based on the magnitude of the correlation coefficient, we can conclude that overall strength is moderately related to injury level in this elderly sample. Eleven percent ($r^2 = .106$) of the variance of the injury index is associated with overall strength.

The hypothesis test of interest evaluates whether the independent variable significantly predicts the dependent variable. More specifically, it assesses whether the population correlation coefficient is equal to zero or, alternatively, whether the population slope is equal to zero. This significance test appears in two places for a bivariate regression analysis: the F test reported as part of the ANOVA table and the t test associated with the independent variable in the Coefficients table. They yield the same p-value because they are identical tests: $F(1, 98) = 11.59$, $p = .001$ and $t(98) = -3.40$, $p = .001$.

Using SPSS Graphs to Display the Results

A variety of graphs have been suggested for interpreting linear regression results. Below, we discuss two types of graphs, the bivariate scatterplot and the plot of predicted and residual values.

Bivariate Scatterplot

The results of the bivariate regression analysis can be summarized using a bivariate scatterplot. Conduct the following steps to create a simple bivariate scatterplot:

1. Click **Graphs** then click **Scatter**.
2. Click **Simple** then click **Define**.
3. Click **injury** and click ▶ to move it to the Y axis box.
4. Click **ztotstr** and click ▶ to move it to the X axis box.
5. Click **OK**.

Once you have created a scatterplot showing the relationship between the number of injuries and the total strength index, you can add a regression line by following these steps:

1. Double-click on the chart to select it for editing and maximize the chart editor.
2. Click **Chart** from the menu at the top of window in the chart editor, then click **Options**.
3. Click **Total** in the Fit Line box.
4. Click **OK**. You will see the scatterplot in Figure 201 (with additional edits to conform to APA guidelines).

Figure 201. Relationship between number of injuries and total body strength.

An examination of the plot allows us to assess how accurately the regression equation predicts the dependent variable scores. In this case, the equation offers some predictability, but many points fall far off the line, indicating poor prediction for those points.

Plot of Predicted and Residual Values

The plot of predicted and residual values may form a pattern that indicates that an assumption has been violated. For example, a U-shaped plot would suggest that the two variables are nonlinearly related. Or, if the residuals are tightly clustered for some values of the predicted scores and widely varying for other values, one might suspect that the homogeneity-of-variance assumption has been violated. A plot of predicted and residual values can be created by following these steps:

1. Click **Analyze**, click **Regression**, then click **Linear**.
2. The appropriate options should already be selected. If not, conduct steps 3 through 7 as described in the section labeled Conducting a Bivariate Linear Regression Analysis.
3. Click **Plots** in the Linear Regression dialog box. You will see the Linear Regression: Plots dialog box shown in Figure 202.

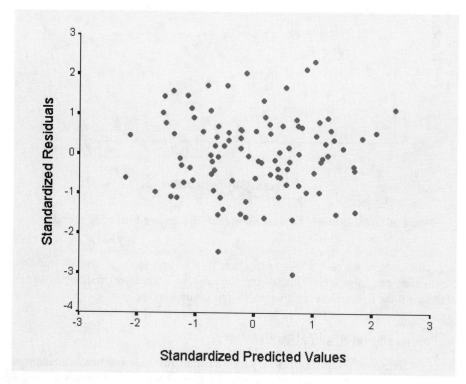

Figure 202. The Linear Regression: Plots dialog box.

4. Click **ZRESID** then click ▶ to move it to the Y box.
5. Click **ZPRED**, then click ▶ to move it to the X box.
6. Click **Continue**.
7. Click **OK**. The graph is shown in Figure 203.

Figure 203. Scatterplot depicting the relationship between predicted and residual injury scores.

There is no apparent pattern to the scatterplot that would make us conclude that the assumptions have been violated.

An APA Results Section

A linear regression analysis was conducted to evaluate the prediction of the physical injury index from the overall strength index for elderly women. The scatterplot for the two variables, as shown in Figure 201, indicates that the two variables are linearly related such that as overall strength increases the overall injury index decreases. The regression equation for predicting the overall injury index is

$$\text{Predicted Overall Injury} = -4.89 \text{ Overall Strength} + 145.80$$

As hypothesized, elderly women who are stronger tended to have lower overall injury scores. Accuracy in predicting the overall injury index was moderate. The correlation between the strength index and the injury index was -.32, $\underline{t}$ (98) = -3.40, $\underline{p}$ = .001. Approximately 11% of the variance of the injury index was accounted for by its linear relationship with the strength index.

Exercises

The data for Exercises 1 through 4 is in the data file named *Lesson 32 Exercise File 1* on the Student Disk. The data are based on the following research problem.

Peter was interested in determining if children who hit a bobo doll more frequently would display more or less aggressive behavior in the playground. He was given permission to observe 10 boys in a nursery school classroom. Each boy was encouraged to hit a bobo doll for 5 minutes. The number of times each boy struck the bobo doll was recorded (bobo). Next, Peter observed the boys on the playground for an hour and recorded the number of times each boy struck a classmate (peer).

1. Conduct a linear regression to predict the number of times a boy would strike a classmate from the number of times the boy hit a bobo doll. From the output, identify the following:
   a. The slope associated with the predictor
   b. The additive constant for the regression equation
   c. The mean number of times they struck a classmate
   d. The correlation between the number of times they hit the bobo doll and the number of times they struck a classmate
   e. The standard error of estimate
2. What is the relationship between the multiple R and the bivariate correlation between the predictor and the criterion?
3. Create a scatterplot of the relationship between the two variables. Plot the regression line on the graph. What can you tell from this graph about the predictability of the dependent variable?
4. Write a results section based on your analyses. What should Peter conclude?

The data for Exercises 5 through 7 are found in the data file named *Lesson 32 Exercise File 2* on the Student Disk. The data are based on the following research problem.

Betsy is interested in determining whether the number of publications by a professor can be predicted from work ethic. She has access to a sample of 50 social science professors who were teaching at the same university for a 10-year period. Betsy has collected data on the number of publications each professor has (num_pubs). She also has scores that reflect professors' work ethic (work_eth). These scores range from 1 to 50, with 50 indicating a very strong work ethic.

5. Conduct a bivariate linear regression to evaluate Betsy's research question. From the output, identify the following:
   a. The significance test to assess the predictability of number of publications from work ethic
   b. The regression equation
   c. The correlation between number of publications and work ethic
6. Create a scatterplot between the number of publications and work ethic. What does this graph tell you about your analyses?
7. Write a results section based on your analyses.

Multiple Linear Regression

In Lesson 32, you learned about conducting a bivariate linear regression where one variable can be used to predict another. With multiple regression analysis, each individual or case has scores on multiple independent variables (e.g., X_1, X_2, and X_3 if there are three independent variables) and on a dependent variable (Y). A predicted dependent variable ($\hat{Y}$) is formed that is a linear combination of the multiple independent variables. With three predictors, the linear combination or regression equation is

$$\hat{Y} = B_1 X_1 + B_2 X_2 + B_3 X_3 + B_0$$

Here B_1 through B_3 are slope weights for the three independent variables X_1 through X_3 and B_0 is an additive constant. The values for B_0 through B_3 are calculated so that the actual dependent variable scores (Y) and the predicted dependent variable scores ($\hat{Y}$) are as similar as possible for the sample data.

The multiple correlation (R) is a strength-of-relationship index that indicates the degree that the predicted scores are correlated with the Y scores (observed scores) for a sample. The significance test for R evaluates whether the population multiple correlation coefficient is equal to zero (i.e., $\hat{Y}$ and Y are uncorrelated in the population).

Multiple regression/correlation analyses are extensions of bivariate regression/correlation analyses and are related to partial correlation analysis. In many applications, when researchers present multiple regression results, they also introduce bivariate and partial correlation results. Consequently, it is important to have read Lessons 30 through 32 on bivariate correlation coefficients, partial correlations, and bivariate linear regression before reading Lesson 33.

Multiple regression is used to analyze data from studies with experimental or nonexperimental designs. If data are collected using experimental methods (e.g., a tightly controlled study in which subjects have been randomly assigned to different treatment groups), the variables in a regression analysis may be called independent and dependent variables. SPSS uses these terms. However, if data are collected using nonexperimental methods (e.g., a study in which subjects are measured on a variety of variables), the variables in the regression analysis may be called the predictors and the criterion rather than the independent variables and the dependent variable, respectively.

Our presentation of multiple regression analysis focuses on applications in which both the independent and dependent variables are quantitative. However, the regression procedure may also be used if one or more of the independent variables or the dependent variable has only two values or levels. For example, a variable could be gender or pass-fail performance on a task. Also, a multiple regression analysis could be conducted with qualitative independent variables that have multiple categories by using coded variables (see Pedhazur, 1997).

Applying Multiple Regression

We can differentiate multiple regression analyses based on whether data are from studies with experimental or nonexperimental designs. This distinction is useful because the design of the study suggests which set of assumptions is most applicable. We'll talk more about those issues in a moment.

We'll present three applications that require different analytical strategy. We differentiate the applications based on whether the predictors can be divided into sets and, if so, whether the sets can be ordered.

- One set of predictors
- Unordered sets of predictors
- Ordered sets of predictors

In studies with one set of predictors, the research questions do not differentiate among predictors and, therefore, the predictors are treated as a single set. In studies with unordered sets of predictors, the research question divides predictors into two or more sets, but there is no particular ordering of these sets. The multiple regression analysis for it examines the validity of each set of predictors, the incremental validity of each set of predictors over other sets of predictors, and the validity of all sets in combination. In studies with ordered sets of predictors, the research question indicates not only sets of predictors, but also suggests an order to the sets. The multiple regression analysis for the third application examines the validity of the first set of predictors, the incremental validity of the second set of predictors over and above the first set, and so on. In addition, the analysis yields results that assess the validity of all predictors.

One Set of Predictors

Mary conducts a study to evaluate her strength-injury hypothesis. Her hypothesis states that overall body strength in elderly women determines the number and severity of accidents these women have. In her field study to evaluate this hypothesis, she collects data on a group of 100 elderly women. The women initially undergo a number of measures that assess lower and upper body strength. Over the next five years, the women record each time they have an accident that results in a bodily injury and a full description of the injury. On the basis of these data, Mary calculates for these women scores on an overall injury index. In Lesson 32 Mary conducted analyses that related an overall index of body strength (the independent variable) to the overall injury index (the dependent variable).

Laurie, Mary's research colleague, feels that Mary should not use the overall strength index as the predictor variable but that she should use the individual strength measures as separate predictors. Laurie argues that some of the strength variables are bound to be better predictors than others; however, she makes no a priori hypotheses about what predictors will be better predictors. Based on Laurie's suggestion, Mary decides to conduct a multiple regression analysis with five predictor variables, assessing strength in quadriceps, gluteus/hamstrings, abdominals/lower back, arms/shoulders, and grip strength. The dependent variable remains the same, the overall injury index. Mary's SPSS data file has 100 cases and six variables containing scores on the five strength variables and the overall injury index.

Unordered Sets of Predictors

Once Mary begins to consider the usefulness of the individual strength measures rather than the overall strength index, she formulates a corollary to her main hypothesis: lower-body strength in comparison with upper-body strength is a better determinant of the number and severity of accidents that older women have that cause bodily injury. Therefore, Mary decides to divide her predictors into two sets: lower-body and upper-body strength predictors. The lower-body predictors include the quadriceps, the gluteus/hamstrings, and the abdominals/lower back. The upper-body predictors include the arms/shoulders and grip strength. Her SPSS data file contains the same six variables described in the first example. The regression analyses evaluate the contribution of upper body and lower body strength sets of predictors, each by itself and over and above the other set.

Ordered Sets of Predictors

Laurie reminds Mary that they collected not only strength measures at the beginning of the study but also age and measures of general medical history. Laurie believes that age and general medical history should be included in the regression analyses. She thinks that women who are having medical problems, partially as a function of their age, may be weaker. They also may be less agile, more likely to have serious accidents, and less likely to recover quickly from these accidents. If this disease-oriented hypothesis is true, then it is not the lack of strength that is causing the serious accidents. Instead, the medical difficulties generate both the lack of strength and the injuries from the accidents. In addition, strength training with women who have medical problems may not be an appropriate or effective intervention strategy. To investigate this alternative, disease-oriented hypothesis, Laurie suggests that Mary determine first if age and medical difficulties predict the overall injury index. If it does, then Mary needs to assess whether the strength indices predict the overall injury index over and above age and medical difficulties. Mary's SPSS data file contains not only the five strength variables and the overall injury index, but also variables containing age and scores from the medical history measure for all 100 women.

Understanding Multiple Regression

Although linear regression analysis can be conducted with a single independent variable, it becomes a more complex and delicate tool with multiple independent variables. How a multiple regression analysis is carried out depends on whether the independent variables can be divided into sets. For example, if we are interested in predicting on-the-job performance, we may be unable to differentiate our independent variables into different sets of variables. On the other hand, if we are interested in predicting adolescent behavior, we may be able to differentiate the independent variables into different sets of variables, one set of family variables and a second set of peer-group variables. By dividing the predictors into sets, we can attempt to answer questions like "Are family or peer-group variables more useful in predicting adolescent behavior?" or "Do the family variables help in the prediction of adolescent behavior over and above the peer-group variables and vice versa?"

The specific analytical steps taken in conducting multiple regression analyses also depend on whether the sets are unordered or ordered. If the sets are unordered, we might be interested in many types of relationships. With our adolescent behavior example, we could handle the family and peer-group variable sets as unordered. Under these conditions, we might conduct analyses to assess how well we predict adolescent behavior (1) from family variables, (2) from peer-group variables, (3) from family variables over and above peer-group variables, (4) from peer-group variables over and above family variables, and (5) from family and peer-group variables.

If the sets are ordered, we could focus our interests on a more limited number of relationships. For example, we may have a second data set in which we are interested in predicting late adolescent behavior from two sets of variables—childhood variables and early adolescent variables. Because of the longitudinal nature of the data, we could restrict our analyses to assess how well we predict late adolescent behavior (1) from childhood variables, (2) from early adolescent variables over and above childhood variables, and (3) from childhood and early adolescent variables.

Assumptions Underlying the Significance Test for the Multiple Correlation Coefficient

The significance test for a multiple correlation is based on two alternative sets of assumptions: assumptions for the fixed-effects model and assumptions for the random-effects model. The fixed-effects model is probably more appropriate for experimental studies, while the random-effects model seems more appropriate for nonexperimental studies.

Assumptions Underlying the Fixed-Effects Model

Assumption 1: The Dependent Variable Is Normally Distributed in the Population for Each Combination of Levels of the Independent Variable or Variables

With moderate to large sample sizes, the assumption may be violated to some degree, and the test will still yield reasonably accurate results. Larger sample sizes may be required to produce relatively valid results if the population distributions are substantially nonnormal.

Assumption 2: The Population Variances of the Dependent Variable Are the Same for All Combinations of Levels of the Independent Variable(s)

To the extent that this assumption is violated and the sample sizes differ among the levels of the independent variable, the resulting p-value for the overall F test is not trustworthy.

Assumption 3: The Cases Represent a Random Sample from the Population, and the Scores Are Independent of Each Other from One Individual to the Next

The F test for regression analyses yields inaccurate p-values if the independence assumption is violated.

Assumptions Underlying the Random-Effects Model

Assumption 1: The Variables Are Multivariately Normally Distributed in the Population

If the variables are multivariately normally distributed, each variable is normally distributed ignoring the other variables and each variable is normally distributed at every combination of values of the other variables. If the multivariate normality assumption is met, the only type of statistical relationship that can exist between variables is a linear one.

Assumption 2: The Cases Represent a Random Sample from the Population, and the Scores on Variables Are Independent of Other Scores on the Same Variables

The F test for regression analyses yields inaccurate p-values if the independence assumption is violated.

It is important to evaluate whether nonlinear relationships exist between the predictors and the criterion, regardless of choice of models. With the fixed-effects model, either linear or nonlinear relationships may exist between the predictors and the criterion. With the random-effects model, nonlinear relationships may be present if the assumption of multivariate normality is violated. Accordingly, for all data sets, we should assess whether nonlinear relationships exist. At an absolute minimum, scatterplots between each predictor and the criterion should be scrutinized for nonlinearity.

Computing an Effect Size

We limit our discussion to two types of effect sizes for multiple regression analysis: multiple correlation indices to assess the overall effect of the predictors on the dependent variable, and part and partial correlations to assess the relative effects of individual predictors.

Multiple Correlation Indices

SPSS computes a multiple correlation (R), a squared multiple correlation (R^2), and an adjusted squared multiple correlation (R^2_{adj}). All three indices assess how well the linear combination of predictor variables in the regression analysis predicts the criterion variable. In addition, SPSS calculates changes in R^2 if there are multiple sets of predictors (blocks).

The multiple correlation is a Pearson product-moment correlation coefficient between the predicted criterion scores ($\hat{Y}$) and the actual criterion scores (Y). The multiple correlation could be symbolized as $r_{y\hat{y}}$. Because $\hat{Y}$ is based on results of multiple regression analysis, $r_{y\hat{y}}$ has some special properties and is denoted as R.

R ranges in value from 0 to 1. A value of 0 means there is no linear relationship between the predicted scores and the criterion scores. A value of 1 implies that the linear combination of the predictor variables perfectly predicts the criterion variable; that is, $\hat{Y}$ is equal to Y for all individuals in the sample. Values between 0 and 1 indicate a less than perfect linear relationship between the predicted and criterion scores, but that one or more of the Xs are useful to some extent in predicting Y.

To interpret the values of R between 0 and 1, R may be squared and multiplied by 100 to make "a percent of variance accounted for" interpretation. For example, if an R is .5, R^2 is .25, and we can make the following interpretation: The R^2 of .25 indicates that 25% of the criterion variance can be accounted for by its linear relationship with the predictor variables.

The sample multiple correlation and the squared multiple correlation are biased estimates of their corresponding population values. The sample R^2 typically overestimates the population R^2 and needs to be adjusted downward. The adjusted R^2 reported by SPSS makes the adjustment assuming a fixed-effects model using the following equation:

$$\text{Adjusted } R^2 = 1-(1-R^2)\frac{N\text{-}1}{N\text{-}k\text{-}1}$$

where N = sample size and k = number of predictors. Based on this equation, it is apparent that the sample R^2 shows greater bias when the sample size is small and the number of predictors is large. When comparing regression equations with different numbers of predictors and a small sample size, it is particularly important to report the adjusted R^2 as well as the R^2 because of the effect of the number of predictors on R^2.

A change in R^2 is the difference between an R^2 for one set of predictors and an R^2 for a subset of these predictors. An example of this change would be an R^2 based on a combination of two sets of predictors (e.g., lower-body and upper-body strength variables) minus an R^2 based on only one of the two sets of predictors (e.g., upper-body strength variables). The value of the change in R^2 ranges from 0 to 1 and is interpreted as an increment in the percent of criterion variance accounted for by including two sets of predictors in the regression equation versus only a single set of predictors. For example, if an R^2 change is .25, you can interpret this finding to mean that an additional 25% of the variance in the criterion (e.g., overall injury index) is contributed by having both sets of variables in the regression equation predictors (e.g., lower-body and upper-body strength variables) versus having only a single set of predictor variables in the equation (e.g., upper-body strength variables). Sometimes more abbreviated, less accurate language is used to describe this R^2 change: "An additional 25% of the criterion (e.g., overall injury index) variance is contributed by one set of predictors (e.g., lower-body strength variables) over and above a second set of predictors (e.g., upper-body strength variables)."

The Relative Importance of Predictors: Using Part and Partial Correlations

On the basis of correlation-regression analyses, we may attempt to reach conclusions about the relative importance of variables in predicting a criterion. These judgments may be made based on the size of the bivariate correlation between each predictor and the criterion, the standardized regression weight for each predictor within a regression equation, the part or partial correlations between each predictor and the criterion (partialling out the effect of all other predictors in the regression equation), or any combinations of these indices. None of these indices, alone or together, however, yields an unequivocal answer to the question of relative importance.

Now we will discuss the interpretation of part and partial correlations, two indices used in reaching a decision about the importance of any one predictor. We'll discuss the interpretation of standardized regression weights in the section labeled Selected SPSS Output for a Single Set of Predictors.

As explained in Lesson 31, a partial correlation is the correlation between two variables while partialling out the effects of one or more control variables. Within the regression procedure, a partial correlation is computed between a predictor and criterion variable partialling out the effects of all other predictor variables. In contrast, the part correlation gives the correlation between a predictor and a criterion variable, partialling out the effects of all other predictors in the regression equation from the predictor but not the criterion.

A part correlation or a partial correlation between a predictor and a criterion variable may range in value from -1 to +1. A positive sign indicates that the predictor and criterion are directly related after partialling out the effects of the other predictors, while a negative sign indicates that they are inversely related after the partialling process.

The same decision about the relative importance of predictors is made using either partial or part correlation. The relative magnitudes of the partial correlations between each predictor and the criterion (partialling out the effects of the other predictors) are identical to the relative magnitudes of the part correlations.

The Data Set

The data we will use to illustrate multiple regression comes from the strength and injury study described earlier in this lesson. They are in the data file named *Lesson 33 Data File 1*. Table 40 shows the variables in the data set.

Table 40

Variables in Lesson 33 Data File 1

Variable	Definition
quads	A measure of strength primarily associated with the quadriceps
gluts	A measure of strength of the muscles in the upper part of the back of the leg and the buttocks
abdoms	A measure of strength of the muscles of the abdomen and the lower back
arms	A measure of strength of the muscles of the arms and the shoulders
grip	An assessment of the hand-grip strength
injury	Overall injury index based on the records kept by the participants
age	The age of the woman when the study began
medindex	A general medical history index based on information obtained from an interview about the health of the women at the beginning of the study

The Research Question

Research questions are asked for the three different applications we described earlier.

1. One set of predictors: How accurately can a physical injury index be predicted from a linear combination of strength measures for elderly women?
2. Two unordered sets of predictors: How well do the lower-body strength measures predict the total injury index for elderly women? How well do the upper-body strength measures predict the total injury index for elderly women? For elderly women, how well does the lower-body strength measures predict the total injury index over and above the upper-body strength measures? For elderly women, how well does the upper-body strength measures predict the total injury index over and above the lower-body strength measures?

3. Two ordered sets of predictors: How well do previous medical difficulties and age predict total injuries for elderly women? For elderly women, how well do the strength measures predict total injuries controlling for previous medical difficulties and age?

Conducting Multiple Regression

We will demonstrate how to conduct analyses for a single set of predictors, two unordered sets of predictors, and two ordered sets of predictors.

Using a Single Set of Predictors

To conduct the multiple regression analysis with one set of predictors follow these steps:

1. Click **Analyze**, click **Regression**, and click **Linear**.
2. Click **injury**, and click ▶ to move it to the Dependent box.
3. Hold down the Ctrl key, and click **quads**, **gluts**, **abdoms**, **arms**, and **grip**, and click ▶ to have them appear in the Independent(s) box.
4. Click **Statistics**. The Linear Regression: Statistics dialog box is shown in Figure 204. The default options of **Estimates** and **Model Fit** should already be selected.

Figure 204. The Linear Regression: Statistics dialog box.

5. Click **Descriptives** and **Part and partial correlations**.
6. Click **Continue**.
7. Click **OK**.

Selected SPSS Output for a Single Set of Predictors

The results of the multiple regression analysis are shown in Figure 205 (at the top of page 270). The descriptive statistics and the bivariate correlations are not presented.

The regression equation with all five strength predictors was significantly related to the injury index, $R^2 = .18$, adjusted $R^2 = .14$, $F(5, 94) = 4.18$, $p = .002$. The Bs, as labeled on the output, are the weights associated with the regression equation. According to these B weights, the regression equation is as follows:

$$Predicted\ Injury = .63_{Quads} - 3.24_{Gluts} - .56_{Abdoms} - 1.13_{Arms} + .79_{Grip} + 260.39$$

Although this equation yields predicted dependent variable scores, the weights are not useful for

Model Summary

Model	R	R Square	Adjusted R Square	Std. Error of the Estimate
1	.426[a]	.182	.138	48.45

a. Predictors: (Constant), GRIP, QUADS, GLUTS, ARMS, ABDOMS

ANOVA[b]

Model		Sum of Squares	df	Mean Square	F	Sig.
1	Regression	49058.061	5	9811.612	4.180	.002[a]
	Residual	220655.94	94	2347.404		
	Total	269714.00	99			

a. Predictors: (Constant), GRIP, QUADS, GLUTS, ARMS, ABDOMS

b. Dependent Variable: INJURY

Coefficients[a]

Model		Unstandardized Coefficients		Standardized Coefficients			Correlations		
		B	Std. Error	Beta	t	Sig.	Zero-order	Partial	Part
1	(Constant)	260.393	30.170		8.631	.000			
	QUADS	.628	.645	.116	.973	.333	-.162	.100	.091
	GLUTS	-3.245	1.038	-.360	-3.125	.002	-.393	-.307	-.292
	ABDOMS	-.563	.674	-.097	-.836	.406	-.232	-.086	-.078
	ARMS	-1.130	.702	-.185	-1.609	.111	-.243	-.164	-.150
	GRIP	.794	1.083	.079	.733	.465	-.099	.075	.068

a. Dependent Variable: INJURY

Figure 205. The results of the multiple linear regression analysis for a single set of predictors.

understanding the relative importance of the predictors. Weights are more interpretable if the independent and dependent variables are standardized to have a mean of 0 and a standard deviation of 1 (z scores). These standardized weights are labeled Beta on the output. The prediction equation for the standardized variables is as follows:

$$Z_{Predicted\ Injury} = .12\ Z_{Quads} - .36\ Z_{Gluts} - .10\ Z_{Abdoms} - .18\ Z_{Arms} + .08\ Z_{Grip}$$

It should be noted that the next set of statistics—the t and the Sig—are t values and p-values to evaluate the significance of the B weights. These t and p-values can also be used to assess the significance of the beta weights, the part correlations, and the partial correlations. The other three indices—the bivariate correlations (labeled Zero-order), the part correlations (labeled Part), the partial correlations (labeled Partial)—are presented in the Coefficients box next to the Sig. and the t-value.

Multiple Linear Regression Using Two Unordered Sets of Predictors

We must determine how well the criterion is predicted by each set of predictors, which in this example are the lower-body and upper-body measures of strength. In addition, we want to determine how well each set of variables predicts the criterion over and above the other set. We will do this by examining the change in R^2.

To evaluate how well the criterion is predicted by the lower-body strength measures (called Set 1), and by the upper-body strength measures (Set 2) over and above the lower-body strength measures, follow these steps:

1. Click **Analyze**, click **Regression**, and click **Linear**.
2. Click **Reset** to clear the dialog box.
3. Hold down the Ctrl key, click **quads**, **gluts**, and **abdoms**, and click ▶ to have them appear in the Independent(s) box. This is the first set of predictors.
4. Click **Next**.

5. Hold down the Ctrl key, click **arms** and **grips**, and click ► to have them appear in the Independent(s) box. This is the second set of predictors.
6. Click **injury** and click ► to move it to the Dependent box.
7. Click **Statistics**. The default options of **Estimates** and **Model Fit** should already be selected.
8. Click **R Squared Change**, **Descriptives**, and **Part and partial correlations**.
9. Click **Continue**.
10. Click **OK**.

Because the sets are unordered, you will also want to evaluate how well the criterion is predicted by the upper-body strength measures (Set 2) and how well the criterion is predicted by the lower-body strength measures (Set 1) over and above the upper-body strength measures. To conduct these analyses, follow the same steps as before, except in steps 3 and 5 reverse the sets of predictors.

Selected SPSS Output for Two Unordered Sets of Predictors

The results of the first run are shown in Figure 206.

Model Summary

Model	R	R Square	Adjusted R Square	Std. Error of the Estimate	Change Statistics				
					R Square Change	F Change	df1	df2	Sig. F Change
1	.399[a]	.159	.133	48.60	.159	6.066	3	96	.001
2	.426[b]	.182	.138	48.45	.023	1.294	2	94	.279

a. Predictors: (Constant), ABDOMS, GLUTS, QUADS
b. Predictors: (Constant), ABDOMS, GLUTS, QUADS, GRIP, ARMS

ANOVA[c]

Model		Sum of Squares	df	Mean Square	F	Sig.
1	Regression	42981.028	3	14327.009	6.066	.001[a]
	Residual	226732.97	96	2361.802		
	Total	269714.00	99			
2	Regression	49058.061	5	9811.612	4.180	.002[b]
	Residual	220655.94	94	2347.404		
	Total	269714.00	99			

a. Predictors: (Constant), ABDOMS, GLUTS, QUADS
b. Predictors: (Constant), ABDOMS, GLUTS, QUADS, GRIP, ARMS
c. Dependent Variable: INJURY

Coefficients[a]

Model		Unstandardized Coefficients		Standardized Coefficients			Correlations		
		B	Std. Error	Beta	t	Sig.	Zero-order	Partial	Part
1	(Constant)	250.546	29.615		8.460	.000			
	QUADS	.355	.624	.066	.570	.570	-.162	.058	.053
	GLUTS	-3.489	1.016	-.387	-3.433	.001	-.393	-.331	-.321
	ABDOMS	-.454	.672	-.078	-.676	.501	-.232	-.069	-.063
2	(Constant)	260.393	30.170		8.631	.000			
	QUADS	.628	.645	.116	.973	.333	-.162	.100	.091
	GLUTS	-3.245	1.038	-.360	-3.125	.002	-.393	-.307	-.292
	ABDOMS	-.563	.674	-.097	-.836	.406	-.232	-.086	-.078
	ARMS	-1.130	.702	-.185	-1.609	.111	-.243	-.164	-.150
	GRIP	.794	1.083	.079	.733	.465	-.099	.075	.068

a. Dependent Variable: INJURY

Figure 206. Selected results of the multiple linear regression analysis for two unordered sets of predictors.

The analysis evaluates how well the criterion is predicted by the lower-body strength measures (Set 1) and how well the criterion is predicted by the upper-body strength measures (Set 2) over and above the lower-body strength measures. The relationship between the lower-body measures and the injury index was significant, $R^2 = .16$, adjusted $R^2 = .13$, $F(3, 96) = 6.07$, $p = .001$. The upper-body strength measures did not predict significantly over and above the lower-body measures, R^2 change = .02, $F(2, 94) = 1.29$, $p = .279$. The numerator degrees of freedom is the number of predictors in a set, while the denominator degrees of freedom is the degrees of freedom associated with the residual source.

The results of the second run are not shown. If you conducted these analyses, you would discover that the regression equation with the upper-body measures as predictors was not significant, $R^2 = .06$, adjusted $R^2 = .04$, $F(2, 97) = 3.06$, $p = .051$. The lower-body strength measures predicted significantly over and above the upper-body measures, R^2 change = .12, $F(3, 94) = 4.69$, $p = .004$.

Two Ordered Sets of Predictors

To answer the research questions posed in the third application, we must evaluate whether the total number of injuries is predicted by previous medical difficulties and age as well as whether the strength measures predict overall injuries after controlling for the effects of previous medical difficulties and age. To conduct the analyses, follow these steps:

1. Click **Analyze**, click **Regression**, and click **Linear**.
2. Click **Reset** to clear the dialog box.
3. Hold down the Ctrl key, and click **medindex** and **age**, and click ▸ to have them appear in the Independent(s) box. This is the first set of predictors.
4. Click **Next**.
5. Hold down the Ctrl key, click **quads**, **gluts**, **abdoms**, **arms**, and **grips**, and click ▸ to have them appear in the Independent(s) box. This is the second set of predictors.
6. Click **injury**, and click ▸ to move it to the Dependent box.
7. Click **Statistics**. The default options of **Estimates** and **Model Fit** should already be selected.
8. Click **R Squared Change**, **Descriptives**, and **Part and partial correlations**.
9. Click **Continue**.
10. Click **OK**.

Selected SPSS Output for Two Ordered Sets of Predictors

The results of the analysis are shown in Figure 207 (at the top of page 273). The results present an evaluation of how well the number of injuries is predicted by previous medical difficulties and age (Set 1), and how well the set of strength measures (Set 2) predicts injuries over and above medical difficulties and age. The first set of predictors, previous medical difficulties and age, accounted for a significant amount of the injury variability, $R^2 = .16$, $F(2,97) = 9.35$, $p < .001$. The five strength measures accounted for a significant proportion of the injury variance after controlling for the effects of medical history and age, R^2 change = .15, $F(5,92) = 3.97$, $p = .003$.

The research question for this example was "How well do the strength measures predict total injuries, controlling for previous medical difficulties and age?" This question indicates that the sets of predictors should be ordered such that medical difficulties and age are entered first in the equation and then the strength predictors are added to these initial two predictors. The research question is addressed by the R^2 change for the two equations. Because these analyses answer the research question, it is unnecessary to reverse the order of the two sets of variables and to reanalyze the data.

Model Summary

Model	R	R Square	Adjusted R Square	Std. Error of the Estimate	Change Statistics				
					R Square Change	F Change	df1	df2	Sig. F Change
1	.402[a]	.162	.144	48.28	.162	9.349	2	97	.000
2	.557[b]	.310	.258	44.97	.149	3.966	5	92	.003

a. Predictors: (Constant), MEDINDEX, AGE

b. Predictors: (Constant), MEDINDEX, AGE, GRIP, QUADS, ABDOMS, ARMS, GLUTS

ANOVA[c]

Model		Sum of Squares	df	Mean Square	F	Sig.
1	Regression	43589.135	2	21794.568	9.349	.000[a]
	Residual	226124.86	97	2331.184		
	Total	269714.00	99			
2	Regression	83683.975	7	11954.854	5.912	.000[b]
	Residual	186030.03	92	2022.065		
	Total	269714.00	99			

a. Predictors: (Constant), MEDINDEX, AGE

b. Predictors: (Constant), MEDINDEX, AGE, GRIP, QUADS, ABDOMS, ARMS, GLUTS

c. Dependent Variable: INJURY

Coefficients[a]

Model		Unstandardized Coefficients		Standardized Coefficients	t	Sig.	Correlations		
		B	Std. Error	Beta			Zero-order	Partial	Part
1	(Constant)	-244.230	104.14		-2.345	.021			
	AGE	3.628	1.541	.225	2.353	.021	.290	.232	.219
	MEDINDEX	284.142	95.017	.286	2.990	.004	.337	.291	.278
2	(Constant)	-141.553	101.65		-1.393	.167			
	AGE	5.331	1.501	.330	3.553	.001	.290	.347	.308
	MEDINDEX	89.909	99.132	.090	.907	.367	.337	.094	.079
	QUADS	.540	.600	.100	.900	.371	-.162	.093	.078
	GLUTS	-3.386	1.042	-.375	-3.250	.002	-.393	-.321	-.281
	ABDOMS	-.682	.627	-.117	-1.087	.280	-.232	-.113	-.094
	ARMS	-.842	.657	-.138	-1.281	.203	-.243	-.132	-.111
	GRIP	.805	1.005	.081	.801	.425	-.099	.083	.069

a. Dependent Variable: INJURY

Figure 207. The results of the multiple linear regression analysis for two ordered sets of predictors.

Using SPSS Graphs to Display the Results

Scatterplots can be used to display the relationships between two variables or among three variables. To look at the relationship between two variables, the bivariate scatterplots demonstrated in Lesson 32 can be created for each pair of variables or the matrix scatterplot described in Lesson 30 can be used to look at all pairs of variables. To look at relationships among three variables, the 3-D scatterplots described in Lesson 31 can be created.

Several graphs are often used to evaluate the assumptions of multiple linear regression. They are quite complex and beyond the scope of this book.

Three APA Results Sections

Results sections were written for each of the three applications.

Results for One Set of Predictors

A multiple regression analysis was conducted to evaluate how well the strength measures predicted physical injury level. The predictors were the five strength indices, while the criterion variable was the overall injury index. The linear combination of strength measures was significantly related to the injury index, $F(5, 94) = 4.18$, $p = .002$. The sample multiple correlation coefficient was .43, indicating that approximately 18% of the variance of the injury index in the sample can be accounted for by the linear combination of strength measures.

In Table 41, we present indices to indicate the relative strength of the individual predictors. All the bivariate correlations between the strength measures and the injury index were negative, as expected, and three of the five indices were statistically significant ($p < .05$). Only the partial correlation between the strength measure for the gluteus/hamstring muscles and the injury index was significant. On the basis of these correlational analyses, it is tempting to conclude that the only useful predictor is the strength measure for the gluteus/hamstring muscles. It alone accounted for 15% ($-.39^2 = .15$) of the variance of the injury index, while the other variables contribute only an additional 3% (18% - 15% = 3%). However, judgments about the relative importance of these predictors are difficult because they are correlated. The correlations among the strength measures, except grip, ranged from .37 to .52.

Table 41

The Bivariate and Partial Correlations of the Predictors with Injury Index

Predictors	Correlation between each predictor and the injury index	Correlation between each predictor and the injury index controlling for all other predictors
Quadriceps	-.16	.10
Gluteus/Hamstrings	-.39***	-.31**
Abdominals/Lower back	-.23*	-.09
Arms/Shoulder	-.24*	-.16
Grip	-.10	.08

* $p < .05$, ** $p < .01$, *** $p < .001$

Results for Two Unordered Sets of Predictors

Two multiple regression analyses were conducted to predict the overall injury index. One analysis included the three lower-body strength measures as predictors (quadriceps, gluteus/hamstrings, and the abdominal/lower back), while the second analysis included the two upper-body strength measures (arms/shoulders and grip strength). The regression equation with the lower-body measures was significant, $R^2 = .16$, adjusted $R^2 = .13$, $F(3, 96) = 6.07$, $p = .001$. However, the regression equation with the upper-body measures was not significant, $R^2 = .06$, adjusted $R^2 = .04$, $F(2, 97) = 3.06$, $p = .051$. Based on these results, the lower-body measures appear to be better predictors of the injury index.

Next, a multiple regression analysis was conducted with all five strength measures as predictors. The linear combination of the five strength measures was significantly related to the injury index, $R^2 = .18$, adjusted $R^2 = .14$, $F(5, 94) = 4.18$, $p = .002$. The lower-body strength measures predicted significantly over and above the upper-body measures, R^2 change = .12, $F(3, 94) = 4.69$, $p = .004$, but the upper-body strength measures did not predict significantly over and above the lower-body measures, R^2 change = .02, $F(2, 94) = 1.29$, $p = .279$. Based on these results, the upper-body measures appear to offer little additional predictive power beyond that contributed by a knowledge of lower-body measures.

Of the lower-body strength measures, the strength measure for the gluteus/hamstring muscles was most strongly related to the injury index. Supporting this conclusion is the strength of the bivariate correlation between the gluteus/hamstring measure and the injury index, which was -.39, $p < .001$, as well as the comparable correlation partialling out the effects of the other two lower-body measures, which was -.33, $p = .001$.

Results for Two Ordered Sets of Predictors

A multiple regression analysis was conducted to predict the overall injury index from previous medical difficulties and age. The results of this analysis indicated that medical difficulties and age accounted for a significant amount of the injury variability, $R^2 = .16$, $F (2,97) = 9.35$, $p < .001$, indicating that older women who had more medical problems tended to have higher scores on the overall injury index.

A second analysis was conducted to evaluate whether the strength measures predicted injury over and above previous medical difficulties and age. The five strength measures accounted for a significant proportion of the injury variance after controlling for the effects of medical history and age, R^2 change = .15, $F (5,92) = 3.97$, $p = .003$. These results suggest that women who have similar medical histories and are the same age are less likely to have injuries if they are stronger.

Tips for Writing an APA Results Section for Multiple Regression

Here are some guidelines for writing a results section for multiple regression analyses. Some researchers initially provide a description of the general overall analytic strategy that includes different regression analyses conducted to answer the research questions. This general description is necessary to the degree that the analyses are unconventional, complex or both.

The steps required to write a results section:

1. Describe the test or tests, the variables, and the purpose of the test or tests. For example: "A multiple regression analysis was conducted to predict the overall injury index from previous medical difficulties and age."
   - Describe the independent or predictor variables. If the variables can be divided into conceptually distinct sets, describe the predictors in each set. In addition, indicate whether the sets are ordered or nonordered.
   - Describe what the criterion variable is.
2. Report the descriptive statistics (e.g., means, standard deviations, and bivariate correlations). These statistics may be reported prior to the presentation of the multiple regression analyses or in conjunction with them (e.g., along with the standardized beta weights).
   - If you are reporting only a few correlations, report them in the text (e.g., "r (98) = .39, $p < .001$").
   - For regression analyses, there are often many bivariate correlations. These statistics can be summarized in tabular form. Typically, you would present the lower diagonal of a correlation matrix. Means and standard deviations for the variables also can be reported in the table.
3. Report the results of the overall regression analyses. If several analyses have been conducted, report the results for each one separately.
   - Report the effect size (e.g., "$R^2 = .43$") for each overall test and the significance test associated with it. Also consider reporting the adjusted R^2. If sets of predictors are evaluated, report the changes in R^2 and the significance tests associated with those changes in R^2.
   - Report the standard error of estimate if the dependent variable has a meaningful metric.
4. Describe and summarize the general conclusions of the overall analysis. For example: "The multiple regression results suggest that women who have similar medical histories and are the same age are less likely to have injuries if they are stronger."
5. Report the contributions of the individual predictors.
   - Consider relevant statistics to evaluate the relative importance of each predictor. Typically, the standardized regression coefficients, the partial correlations, or both are presented in a table.
   - Report whether the individual variables make a significant contribution to the prediction equation (e.g., "t (98) = -3.13, $p < .001$").

6. Present the results graphically, if possible. You may present graphs to show relationships among variables. The graph should be inserted in the text where appropriate. For example, if the graph pertains to assumptions, you would insert it in the section where you discuss assumptions.

Exercises

Exercises 1 through 5 are based on the data set named *Lesson 33 Exercise File 1* on the Student Data Disk. The data are from the following research study.

Jenna is interested in understanding who does well and who does poorly in statistics courses. Jenna collects data from the 100 students in her statistics course. Besides their performance on her exams in the course, she obtains students' scores on math and English aptitude tests that students took in their senior year of high school and their high school grade point averages in math, English, and all other courses. The variables in the data set are shown in Table 42.

Table 42
Variables in Lesson 33 Exercise File 1

Variable	Definition
mathtest	Score on a math aptitude test taken senior year of high school
engtest	Score on a English aptitude test taken senior year of high school
eng_gpa	High school GPA in English courses
math_gpa	High school GPA in math courses
othr_gpa	High school GPA in courses other than English and math
statexam	Average percentage correct on exams in a college statistics course

The research questions for these data: (a) How well do high school test scores and grade point averages predict test performance in statistics course? (b) Is it necessary to have both high school test scores and grade point averages as predictors of exams scores in statistics? Conduct the appropriate regression analysis to answer these questions.

1. Should the predictor variables be divided into sets and, if so, what variables should be included in each set? What is the criterion variable? If you divided the predictors into sets, do you think that they should be ordered?
2. What is the regression equation for all predictors?
3. What is the contribution of high school test scores over and above high school grade point averages? Report the appropriate statistic from the output.
4. What is the contribution of high school grade point averages over and above high school test scores? Report the appropriate statistic from the output.
5. Write a results section based on your analyses that address the two research questions.

Exercises 6 through 10 are based on the data set named *Lesson 33 Exercise File 2* on the Student Data Disk. The data are from the following research study.

Sally is interested in predicting the number of relapses that occur after participation in an intensive inpatient substance abuse program. She has data from 120 women who are at least five years beyond their initial admission to the program. Upon entry into the treatment program, the women were evaluated with respect to their psychological state and, in particular, on depression, propensity for substance abuse, and daily life stress. In addition, they completed two measures of social support—amount of social support available to them (number of close relationships) and perceptions of the quality of their social support. She also has records that indicate the number of relapses that each woman has had in the first five years after entry into the treatment program. The SPSS file contains six variables: three psychological state variables (named depress for depression, subst for substance abuse, and stress for daily life stress), two social support predictors (named amt_ss for amount of social support and per_ss for perception of social support), and the number of relapses (named relapses).

6. Conduct a regression analysis to evaluate the relative importance of the psychological state predictors and the social support predictors in predicting the number of substance abuse relapses.
7. What is the contribution of the set of social support predictors? Report the appropriate statistics.
8. What is the contribution of the psychological state predictors? Report the appropriate statistics.
9. Which variables in each set are the best predictors of the number of relapses? How did you arrive at your answer?
10. Write a results section reporting the analyses you conducted.

Lesson 34

Discriminant Analysis

Discriminant analysis can be used to classify individuals into groups on the basis of one or more measures or to distinguish groups based on linear combinations of measures after obtaining a significant F test with a MANOVA. (See Lesson 27 for a discussion of MANOVA.) For discriminant analysis, each case must have a score or scores on one or more quantitative variables and a value on a classification variable that indicates group membership.

The quantitative variables for discriminant analysis are frequently called independent variables or predictors, and the group membership variable is referred to as a dependent variable or a criterion variable. This terminology may be confusing when discriminant analysis is used as a follow-up procedure to a significant MANOVA. In contrast to discriminant analysis, the quantitative variables for a MANOVA are typically referred to as dependent or criterion variables, while the classification variable is called an independent variable or a factor.

Applying Discriminant Analysis

We'll discuss only two types of applications of discriminant analysis:

- Studies that have as their purpose the classification of individuals into groups on the basis of quantitative predictor variables
- Studies that have a one-way MANOVA as their focal analysis and discriminant analysis as a follow-up procedure

Predicting Group Membership

Mike has applicants for engineering positions in a large company complete three measures: a job history, a job test that assesses knowledge in engineering, and a personality measure that assesses friendliness. He also asks the applicants for college transcripts. Four scores are derived from these measures: a quality rating of job history, a test score of engineering knowledge, a friendliness score, and a grade point average. Mike is interested in determining whether these four scores are useful in predicting job performance. One-hundred-and-twenty-four applicants are hired and work for the company for at least one year. At the end of the year, a panel evaluates the employees and classifies them into one of three categories: a poor performer (=1), a good individual achiever (=2), or a good team player (=3). Mike's SPSS data file contains 124 cases and five variables, the four predictor variables and the grouping variable distinguishing among the three job-performance groups.

Discriminant Analysis as a Follow-Up Procedure to MANOVA

Diane wants to determine which of several therapeutic approaches is most effective in remediating articulation disorders. She randomly assigns 20 children to each of the following intervention programs: (1) individual therapy, (2) classroom-based intervention, and (3) parent training procedures. At the end of the semester, she tests the children using three different articulation measures. Diane conducts a one-way MANOVA. The factor reflects the three types of therapy, and the dependent variables are the three articulation measures. She conducts a discriminant analysis as a follow-up procedure to the significant MANOVA. For the discriminant analysis, the grouping variable is type of therapy and the independent variables are the three articulation measures. Diane's SPSS data file contains four variables: one variable indicating type of intervention program and the three articulation measures.

Understanding Discriminant Analysis

With discriminant analysis, one or more linear combinations of quantitative predictors are created that are called discriminant functions. The number of possible discriminant functions for an analysis with N_g groups and p quantitative variables is either $(N_g - 1)$ or p, whichever is smaller. For example, our first application has three groups and four quantitative variables. Consequently, the number of functions is 2 because 2 is the smaller of the two values, $(N_g - 1) = (3 - 1) = 2$ and $p = 4$.

The first discriminant function is extracted such that it maximizes the differences on this function among groups. A second discriminant function may then be extracted that maximizes the differences on this function among groups but with the added constraint that it is uncorrelated with the first discriminant function. Additional discriminant functions may be extracted that maximize the differences among groups but always with the constraint that they are uncorrelated with all previously extracted functions.

Eigenvalues associated with discriminant functions indicate how well the functions differentiate the groups; the larger the eigenvalue, the better the groups are discriminated. An eigenvalue for a discriminant function is the ratio of the between-groups sums of squares to the within-group sums of squares for an ANOVA that has the discriminant function as the dependent variable and groups as levels of a factor. Because eigenvalues reflect how well the functions discriminate the groups, the largest eigenvalue is associated with the first discriminant function, the second largest eigenvalue is associated with the second discriminant function, and so on.

A frequently used option within the SPSS discriminant analysis procedure is the classification of cases into groups. With classification, the predictors are linearly combined together to predict group membership, as defined by the grouping variable. These linear combinations of predictor variables are called Fisher's linear discriminant functions (or classification functions) by SPSS, and their coefficients are referred to as Fisher's function coefficients. Accuracy in classification is appraised by computing the percent of cases correctly classified into groups based on the classification functions. An alternative statistic, kappa, also evaluates the percent of cases correctly classified except that it corrects for chance agreements.

Assumptions Underlying Discriminant Analysis

There are three assumptions associated with the significance tests for the discriminant analysis.

Assumption 1: The Quantitative Variables Are Multivariately Normally Distributed for Each of the Populations, with the Different Populations Being Defined by the Levels of the Grouping Variable

If the dependent variables are multivariately normally distributed, each variable is normally distributed ignoring the other variables, and each variable is normally distributed at every combination of values of the other variables. Given that it is hard to imagine that we would ever meet this assumption, it is reassuring that discriminant analysis yields relatively valid results in terms of Type I errors with moderate to large sample sizes.

Assumption 2: The Population Variances and Covariances among the Dependent Variables Are the Same across All Levels of the Factor

To the extent that the sample sizes are disparate and the variances and covariances are unequal, the *p*-values yield invalid results. SPSS allows us to test the assumption of homogeneity of the variance-covariance matrices with Box's *M* statistic. The *F* test from Box's *M* statistics should be interpreted cautiously in that a significant result may be due to violation of the multivariate normality assumption associated with Box's test and a nonsignificant result may be due to small sample size and a lack of power.

Assumption 3: The Participants Are Randomly Sampled, and the Score on a Variable for Any One Participant Is Independent from the Scores on This Variable for All Other Participants

The significance test for the discriminant analyses should not be trusted if the independence assumption is violated.

Computing an Effect Size Index

SPSS prints out a number of indices to help assess the effect size for each discriminant function. An eigenvalue (λ) is listed for each discriminant function. An eigenvalue is the ratio of the between-groups sums of squares to the within-group sums of squares for an ANOVA that has groups as levels of a factor and the discriminant function as the dependent variable. Accordingly, an eigenvalue can assume any value that is greater than or equal to zero.

A difficulty with interpreting an eigenvalue is that it has no upper limit. Most researchers would prefer to have an index like R^2 that ranges in value from 0 to 1. A more interpretable index than an eigenvalue may be a ratio of the between-groups sums of square to the total sums of squares. It is a function of the eigenvalue: $\lambda / (1 + \lambda)$. The square root of this index is labeled on the SPSS output as the canonical corr. (canonical correlation).

SPSS also reports for each discriminant function a percent of variance. It is computed by dividing the eigenvalue for the discriminant function by the sum of the eigenvalues, and multiplying the resulting value by 100. This index tells how strong the relationship is for a discriminant function relative to all discriminant functions.

The Data Set

The data set used to illustrate discriminant analysis is based on our example about predicting job performance of engineers and is in *Lesson 34 Data File 1* on your Data Disk. The variables in the data set are presented in Table 43.

The Research Question

The research question can be asked for group differences or classification into appropriate groups.

1. Group differences: Are there differences among the three job-performance groups in the population on linear combinations of the four predictor variables?
2. Classification into groups: Can the individuals in the three job-performance groups be correctly classified into these three categories based on their scores on the four predictor variables?

Table 43

Variables in Lesson 34 Data File 1

Variable	Definition
friendly	Friendliness scale
gpa	College GPA
job_cat	Employees classified into one of three categories based on their job performance: 1 = Poor performer 2 = Individual achiever 3 = Team player
job_hist	Rating of job history on a scale from 1 = unimpressive to 10 = Extremely impressive
job_test	Percent correct on a job test

Conducting a Discriminant Analysis

Now we will illustrate how to conduct a discriminant analysis.

How to Conduct a Discriminant Analysis

To conduct a discriminant analysis, follow these steps:

1. Click **Analyze**, click **Classify**, and click **Discriminant**. You will see the Discriminant Analysis dialog box in Figure 208.

Figure 208. The Discriminant Analysis dialog box.

2. Click **job_cat** and click ▶ to move it to the Grouping Variable text box.
3. Click **Define Range**. In the Define Range dialog box, type in **1** for Minimum and **3** for Maximum.
4. Click **Continue**.
5. Hold down the Ctrl key to highlight **friendly**, **gpa**, **job_hist**, and **job_test** and click ▶ to move them to the Independents box.
6. Click **Statistics**. You will see the Discriminant Analysis: Statistics dialog box in Figure 209 (at the top of page 282).
7. Click **Means**, **Univariate ANOVAs**, and **Box's M** in the Descriptives box.
8. Click **Fisher's** and **Unstandardized** in the Function Coefficients box.
9. Click all four options in the Matrices box.

Figure 209. The Discriminant Analysis: Statistics dialog box.

10. Click **Continue**.
11. Click **Classify**. You will see the Discriminant Analysis: Classification dialog box before any choices are made in Figure 210.

Figure 210. The Discriminant Analysis: Classification dialog box.

12. Click **Compute from group sizes** in the Prior Probabilities box if the relative sample sizes for the groups are estimates of population proportions. If the population proportions for the groups are equal, choose All groups equal.
13. Click **Combined-groups** and **Separate-groups** in the Plots box.
14. Click **Within-groups** in the Use Covariance Matrix box. However, the option Separate groups should be chosen if you cannot assume that the covariance matrices for all groups are equal.
15. Click **Summary table** and **Leave-one-out classification** in the Display box.
16. Click **Continue**.
17. Click **Save**. You will see the Discriminant Analysis: Save New Variables dialog box before any choices are made in Figure 211.
18. Click **Predicted Group Membership**.
19. Click **Continue**.
20. Click **OK**.

Figure 211. The Discriminant Analysis: Save New Variables dialog box.

Selected SPSS Output for Preliminary Statistics of Discriminant Analysis

As shown in Figure 212, a number of preliminary statistics are reported in the output: the means and standard deviations of the predictors within job-performance groups, ANOVAs assessing differences among the four predictors for the three job-performance groups, covariance

Group Statistics

JOB_CAT		Mean	Std. Deviation	Valid N (listwise) Unweighted	Valid N (listwise) Weighted
1	FRIENDLY	44.2963	9.8793	27	27.000
	GPA	2.9517	.6483	27	27.000
	JOB_HIST	5.5556	1.7831	27	27.000
	JOB_TEST	68.2593	9.0239	27	27.000
2	FRIENDLY	51.8372	12.1576	43	43.000
	GPA	3.1318	.5576	43	43.000
	JOB_HIST	6.4419	1.6374	43	43.000
	JOB_TEST	79.8605	9.9704	43	43.000
3	FRIENDLY	55.1111	8.6432	54	54.000
	GPA	2.7612	.4782	54	54.000
	JOB_HIST	5.5741	1.6552	54	54.000
	JOB_TEST	69.2037	9.2377	54	54.000
Total	FRIENDLY	51.6210	10.9742	124	124.000
	GPA	2.9312	.5660	124	124.000
	JOB_HIST	5.8710	1.7154	124	124.000
	JOB_TEST	72.6935	10.7493	124	124.000

Tests of Equality of Group Means

	Wilks' Lambda	F	df1	df2	Sig.
FRIENDLY	.858	10.040	2	121	.000
GPA	.916	5.533	2	121	.005
JOB_HIST	.941	3.813	2	121	.025
JOB_TEST	.761	19.004	2	121	.000

Covariance Matrices[a]

JOB_CAT		FRIENDLY	GPA	JOB_HIST	JOB_TEST
1	FRIENDLY	97.601	2.221	-1.479	19.036
	GPA	2.221	.420	.384	.584
	JOB_HIST	-1.479	.384	3.179	-3.496
	JOB_TEST	19.036	.584	-3.496	81.430
2	FRIENDLY	147.806	1.822	3.978	7.905
	GPA	1.822	.311	.312	3.000
	JOB_HIST	3.978	.312	2.681	6.849
	JOB_TEST	7.905	3.000	6.849	99.409
3	FRIENDLY	74.704	5.173E-02	2.671	-4.231
	GPA	5.173E-02	.229	.242	1.429
	JOB_HIST	2.671	.242	2.740	1.843
	JOB_TEST	-4.231	1.429	1.843	85.335
Total	FRIENDLY	120.432	.836	2.292	7.224
	GPA	.836	.320	.353	2.507
	JOB_HIST	2.292	.353	2.943	4.586
	JOB_TEST	7.224	2.507	4.586	115.548

a. The total covariance matrix has 123 degrees of freedom.

Test Results

Box's M		26.716
F	Approx.	1.265
	df1	20
	df2	28453.612
	Sig.	.190

Tests null hypothesis of equal population covariance matrices.

Figure 212. Preliminary statistics of the discriminant analysis.

matrices for the three job-performance groups, and a test of equality of the within-group covariance matrices.

These statistics indicate significant differences in means on the predictors among the three job-performance groups (p-values range from .00 to .025). There were not significant differences in the covariance matrices among the three groups (p-value of .190 for the Box's M test). However, some of the covariances do appear to differ across groups. For example, the covariance between friendly and job_test varies from -4.231 to 19.036.

Selected SPSS Output for Significance Tests and Strength-of-Relationship Statistics

The output for significance tests and strength-of-relationship statistics for the discriminant analysis is shown in Figure 213.

Eigenvalues

Function	Eigenvalue	% of Variance	Cumulative %	Canonical Correlation
1	.343[a]	60.4	60.4	.506
2	.225[a]	39.6	100.0	.429

a. First 2 canonical discriminant functions were used in the analysis.

Wilks' Lambda

Test of Function(s)	Wilks' Lambda	Chi-square	df	Sig.
1 through 2	.608	59.527	8	.000
2	.816	24.243	3	.000

Figure 213. Significance tests and strength-of-relationship statistics for discriminant analysis.

In the box labeled Wilks' Lambda, a series of chi-square significance tests are reported. These tests assess whether there are significant differences among groups across the predictor variables, after removing the effects of any previous discriminant functions. In our example in the first row, SPSS reports the overall Wilks' lambda, $\Lambda = .61$, $\chi^2 (8, N = 124) = 59.53$, $p < .001$. This test is significant at the .05 level and indicates that there are differences among groups across the four predictor variables in the population. In the second row, SPSS reports $\Lambda = .82$, $\chi^2 (3, N = 124) = 24.24$, $p < .001$. This test is significant at the .05 level and indicates that there is a significant difference among groups across all predictor variables in the population, after removing the effects associated with the first discriminant function.

Significance tests can help determine how many discriminant functions should be interpreted. For example, if the overall Wilks' lambda is significant but none of the remaining functions is significant, only the first discriminant function is interpreted. If the first two Wilks' lambdas are significant but none of the remaining ones is significant, then only the first two discriminant functions are interpreted. For our example, because the overall lambda and the lambda after removing the first discriminant function are significant, both discriminant functions could be interpreted according to the chi-square tests.

A series of statistics associated with each discriminant function are reported in the box labeled Eigenvalues. The first discriminant function has an eigenvalue of .34 and a canonical correlation of .51. By squaring the canonical correlation for the first discriminant function ($.506^2 = .256$), you obtain the eta square that would result from conducting a one-way ANOVA on the first discriminant function. Accordingly 26% of the variability of the scores for the first discriminant function is accounted for by differences among the three job-performance groups. In comparison, the second discriminant function has an eigenvalue of .22 and a canonical correlation of .43. Therefore, 18% ($.429^2 = .184$) of the variability of the scores for the second discriminant function is accounted for by the job-performance factor.

Selected SPSS Output of Coefficients for the Discriminant Functions

The coefficients for the discriminant functions are shown in Figure 214.

Standardized Canonical Discriminant Function Coefficients

	Function	
	1	2
FRIENDLY	-.087	.955
GPA	.088	-.563
JOB_HIST	.275	.040
JOB_TEST	.884	.245

Structure Matrix

	Function	
	1	2
JOB_TEST	.953*	.105
GPA	.467*	-.272
JOB_HIST	.428*	.020
FRIENDLY	.012	.859*

Pooled within-groups correlations between discriminating variables and standardized canonical discriminant functions
Variables ordered by absolute size of correlation within function.

*. Largest absolute correlation between each variable and any discriminant function

Figure 214. Standardized coefficients and the pooled within-groups correlations for discriminant analysis.

Each discriminant function may be given a name by determining which variables are most strongly related to it. A discriminant function is named by examining the magnitudes of the standardized coefficients for the predictor variables in the function and the correlation coefficients between the predictor variables and the function within a group (coefficients in the structure matrix). For the first discriminant function in our application, job_test has a relatively large positive coefficient (standardized function and structure coefficients), while gpa and job_hist have weaker coefficients. For the second discriminant function, the largest positive coefficient is for friendly, while a negative relationship exists for gpa. On the basis of these standardized function and structure coefficients, we will name the first and second discriminant functions engineering knowledge and gregariousness, respectively.

Selected SPSS Output for Group Centroids

The output for the group centroids is shown in Figure 215.

Functions at Group Centroids

JOB_CAT	Function	
	1	2
1	-.401	-.826
2	.794	1.304E-02
3	-.432	.403

Unstandardized canonical discriminant functions evaluated at group means

Figure 215. Group centroids for discriminant functions.

The values labeled group centroids are the mean values on the discriminant functions for the three groups. In our illustration, based on our interpretation of the discriminant function, it appears that the individual achiever group (Group 2) tended to score highest on the engineering knowledge dimension (Function 1). On the other hand, the team player group (Group 3) tended to have the highest mean scores on the gregariousness dimension (Function 2). The pattern of the means for the discriminant functions appears consistent with our interpretation of the two functions.

Selected SPSS Output for Group Classification

The output for group classification is shown in Figure 216. The classification results allow us to determine how well we can predict group membership using a classification function.

Classification Results[b,c]

			Predicted Group Membership			
	JOB_CAT		1	2	3	Total
Original	Count	1	12	5	10	27
		2	4	27	12	43
		3	4	7	43	54
	%	1	44.4	18.5	37.0	100.0
		2	9.3	62.8	27.9	100.0
		3	7.4	13.0	79.6	100.0
Cross-validated[a]	Count	1	10	5	12	27
		2	5	25	13	43
		3	5	7	42	54
	%	1	37.0	18.5	44.4	100.0
		2	11.6	58.1	30.2	100.0
		3	9.3	13.0	77.8	100.0

a. Cross validation is done only for those cases in the analysis. In cross validation, each case is classified by the functions derived from all cases other than that case.

b. 66.1% of original grouped cases correctly classified.

c. 62.1% of cross-validated grouped cases correctly classified.

Figure 216. Group classification for discriminant analysis.

The top part of the table (labeled Original) indicates how well the classification function predicts in the sample. Correctly classified cases appear on the diagonal of the classification table. For example, of the 27 cases in the poor performer group, 12 (44%) were predicted correctly. In the individual achiever group, 27 of 43 cases (63%) were classified correctly. In the team player group, 43 of 54 (80%) were classified correctly. Of the total sample of 124 cases, the overall number of cases classified correctly was 82 or 66% of the sample.

The bottom part of the table (labeled Cross-validated) is generated by choosing the leave-one-out option within the classification dialog box. With the leave-one-out option, classification functions are derived based all cases except one and then the left out case is classified. This is repeated N times, until all cases have been left out once and classified based on classification functions for the $N - 1$ cases. The results for how well the classification functions predicted the N left out cases are reported in the cross-validated table. These results can be used to estimate how well the classification functions derived on all N cases should predict with a new sample. As shown in the cross-validated table, 10 of the poor performers, 25 of the individual achievers, and 42 of the team players were correctly classified. Overall 62% of the cases were correctly classified.

Computing Kappa

The overall percent of cases correctly classified is 66% in the sample. This value is affected by chance agreement. Kappa (κ), an index that corrects for chance agreements, could be reported in your results section along with the proportion of individuals who are correctly classified.

We will compute kappa to assess the accuracy in prediction of group membership. To compute kappa, we use the variable, dis_1, which was created by choosing Predicted Group Membership in the Discriminant Analysis: Save New Variables dialog box. To calculate kappa, conduct these steps:

1. Click **Analyze**, click **Descriptive Statistics**, and click **Crosstabs**.
2. Click **job_cat**, then click ▶ to move it to the box labeled Row(s).
3. Click **dis_1**, then click ▶ to move it to the box labeled Column(s).
4. Click **Statistics**.
5. Click **Kappa**.
6. Click **Continue**.
7. Click **Cells**.
8. Click **Expected** in the Counts box. Be sure Observed is selected.
9. Click **Row** in the Percentages box.
10. Click **Continue**.
11. Click **OK**.

Selected SPSS Output for Kappa

The output presenting the kappa coefficient is shown in Figure 217.

Symmetric Measures

	Value	Asymp. Std. Error[a]	Approx. T[b]	Approx. Sig.
Measure of Agreement Kappa	.460	.066	7.074	.000
N of Valid Cases	124			

a. Not assuming the null hypothesis.

b. Using the asymptotic standard error assuming the null hypothesis.

Figure 217. Results of kappa analysis.

As shown in Figure 217, the kappa is .46. Kappa values of .46 indicate moderately accurate prediction. Kappa ranges in value from -1 to +1. A value of 1 for kappa indicates perfect prediction, while a value of 0 indicates chance-level prediction. Values that are less than 0 indicate poorer than chance-level prediction, and those that are greater than 0 indicate better than chance-level prediction.

Using SPSS Graphs to Display the Results

We requested a combined groups plot to illustrate the classification of the three groups. Figure 218 (at the top of page 288) shows the edited combined groups plot for our example.

An APA Results Section

A discriminant analysis was conducted to determine whether four predictors—friendliness scale scores, college grade point average, ratings of job history, and job test scores—could predict on-the-job performance. The overall Wilks' lambda was significant, $\Lambda = .61$, $\chi^2 (8, \underline{N} = 124) = 59.53$, $\underline{p} < .001$, indicating that overall the predictors differentiated among the three on-the-job performance groups. In addition, the residual Wilks' lambda was significant, $\Lambda = .82$, $\chi^2 (3, \underline{N} = 124) = 24.24$, $\underline{p} < .001$. This test indicated that the predictors differentiated significantly among the three on-the-job performance groups after partialling out the effects of the first discriminant function. Because these tests were significant, we chose to interpret both discriminant functions.

In Table 44 (on page 288), we present the within-groups correlations between the predictors

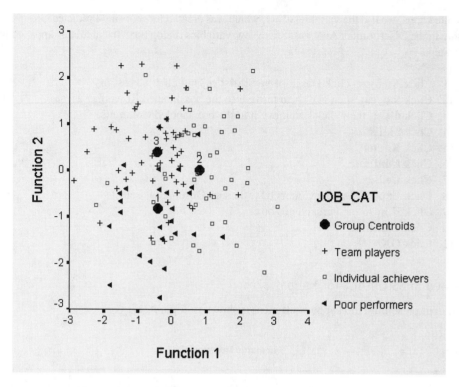

Figure 218. Separation of groups on discriminant functions.

and the discriminant functions as well as the standardized weights. Based on these coefficients, the job test scores demonstrate the strongest relationship with the first discriminant function, while college grade point average and job-history ratings show a weaker relationship. On the other hand, the friendliness scale shows the strongest relationship with the second discriminant function, while college GPA demonstrates a negative relationship with this function. On the basis of the results presented in Table 44, we labeled the first and second discriminant functions engineering knowledge and gregariousness, respectively.

Table 44

Standardized Coefficients and Correlations of Predictor Variables with the Two Discriminant Functions

	Correlation coefficients with discriminant functions		Standardized coefficients for discriminant functions	
	Function 1	Function 2	Function 1	Function 2
Friendliness scale	.01	.86	-.09	.96
College GPA	.47	-.27	.09	-.56
Rating of job history	.43	.02	.28	.04
Job test	.95	.10	.88	.24

The means on the discriminant functions are consistent with this interpretation. The individual achievers ($\underline{M}$ = .79) had the highest mean scores on the engineering knowledge dimension (the first discriminant function), while the poor performers ($\underline{M}$ = -.40) and the team players ($\underline{M}$ = -.43) had lower mean scores. On the other hand, the team players ($\underline{M}$ = .40) had the highest mean scores on the gregariousness dimension, the individual performers ($\underline{M}$ = .01) the next highest mean score, and the poor performers ($\underline{M}$ = -.83) the lowest mean scores.

When we tried to predict on-the-job group membership, we were able to classify correctly 66% of the individuals in our sample. In order to take into account chance agreement, we computed a kappa coefficient and obtained a value of .46, a moderate value. Finally to assess how well the classification procedure would predict in a new sample, we estimated the percent of employees accurately classified using the leave-one-out technique and correctly classified 62% of the cases.

Alternative Analyses

Logistic regression can be used as an alternative to discriminant analysis to classify individuals into groups on the basis of multiple measures. Logistic regression is available in SPSS under Analyze—Regression.

Exercises

Exercises 1 through 5 are based on data found in the data file named *Lesson 34 Exercise File 1* on the Student Disk. The data are from the following study.

Dave wants to classify college professors into two groups—research scientists and teaching moguls. He obtains scores on four variables from 50 college professors: number of publications in last two years, amount of grant funding generated in last five years, mean teaching evaluation score for the last three semesters, and number of student committees served on during last five years. Dave then has three university administrators evaluate all 50 professors as one of two types, research scientists and teaching moguls. The SPSS data file has 50 cases and five variables. The five variables are the four predictors and a grouping variable distinguishing research scientists and teaching moguls based on the judgments of the university administrators.

1. Conduct a discriminant analysis to distinguish professors who are research scientists from professors who are teaching moguls. From the output, identify the following:
   a. The research scientist group mean for number of publications
   b. The univariate ANOVA *F* value for grant money
   c. χ^2 associated with the discriminant function
2. What percentage of research scientists are correctly classified? What is the overall percentage of professors correctly classified as teaching moguls and research scientists?
3. Which predictor variables contribute the most to discriminating between research scientists and teaching moguls?
4. Create a combined groups plot to show the classification of the two groups.
5. Write a results section based on your analyses.

Exercises 6 through 8 are based on data found in the data file named *Lesson 34 Exercise File 2* on the Student Disk. The data are from the following study.

Jacki is interested in differentiating successful women basketball coaches into three categories: successful coaches as character builders, successful winning coaches, and successful winning coaches and character builders. Based on interview data, she is able to differentiate reliably 100 successful women coaches into these three categories. She collects a series of measures for each coach: average number of points per game over last five years, number of ranked players recruited from high schools for the last five years, a measure of problem-focused coping, a rating of likability by the team, a measure of social support offered by the coach, a measure of coach persistence, and a measure reflecting the continuum of authoritative-authoritarian discipline styles. The SPSS file contains 100 cases, seven predictors, and the grouping variable.

6. Conduct a discriminant. Determine whether both discriminant functions should be interpreted.
7. Interpret the discriminant function or functions.
8. Write a results section based on your analysis.

Scaling Procedures

Unit 9 discusses methods involved in evaluating the psychometric quality of measures. These techniques focus on relationships among scales, items and/or other evaluation instruments to assess their psychometric properties.

- Lesson 35 introduces exploratory factor analysis. Factor analysis is an exploratory multivariate technique used to assess the dimensionality of a set of variables. For example, a common application of factor analysis would be to assess whether a number of scales have a single dimension underlying them. The Factor Analysis program in SPSS is relatively flexible and allows for a variety of factor extraction and rotation options.
- Lesson 36 discusses internal consistency estimates of reliability. Internal consistency coefficients obtained through the Reliability Analysis program are estimates of a scale's reliability. Reliability is computed for these estimates based on the relationships among items on a measure. In this topic, we focus on split-half and coefficient alpha estimates.
- Lesson 37 addresses item analysis procedures. Item analysis procedures evaluate whether items should be maintained on a scale or whether revisions to a scale are necessary. Revisions to a unidimensional scale are based on the relationships between the items and their total scale (e.g., corrected item total correlations) as well as the researcher's understanding of what he or she is trying to measure. Revisions to multidimensional scales are based on similar information. In addition, for multidimensional scales item scores assessing a particular dimension are correlated with total scale scores assessing different dimensions to evaluate discriminant validity.

Lesson 35

Factor Analysis

Factor analysis is a technique used to identify factors that statistically explain the variation and covariation among measures. Generally, the number of factors is considerably smaller than the number of measures and, consequently, the factors succinctly represent a set of measures. From this perspective, factor analysis can be viewed as a data-reduction technique since it reduces a large number of overlapping measured variables to a much smaller set of factors. If a study is well designed so that different sets of measures reflect different dimensions of a broader conceptual system, factor analyses can yield factors that represent these dimensions. More specifically, the factors can correspond to constructs (i.e., unobservable latent variables) of a theory that helps us understand behavior. Examples of constructs that might emerge as factors from factor analyses include altruism, test anxiety, mechanical aptitude, attention span, and academic self-esteem.

Ideally variables to be factor analyzed should be quantitative, have a wide range of scores, and be unimodally, symmetrically distributed. However, researchers, for better or for worse, do sometimes analyze variables with a very limited range of scores (e.g., 3-point Likert scales and right-wrong items). You should consult textbooks on factor analysis to understand the difficulties with analyzing such variables.

Factor analysis can be conducted directly on the correlations among the variables. In this lesson, we will learn how to create a data file containing a correlation matrix for factor analysis.

Applying Factor Analysis

We will examine three applications of factor analysis. Each application illustrates a different objective for factor analysis:

- Defining indicators of constructs
- Defining dimensions for an existing measure
- Selecting items or scales to be included on a measure

Defining Indicators of Constructs

Dave believes that our verbal and nonverbal reactions to art are a function of two underlying dimensions, emotional reactions and intellectual reactions. Dave conducts a study to examine nonverbal behavior displayed when viewing art. He has 300 students view 10 different pieces of art while being videotaped. Two judges evaluate the tapes by rating the degree to which students engaged in 30 specific behaviors across the 10 art pieces. For example, judges rate the degree to which students sit and stare at an art piece, the degree that students inspect specific portions of an art piece, the degree that they read about an art piece, the degree they change their facial expressions when they first view an art piece, and how frequently they return to an art piece after viewing it. Dave selected 15 of the behaviors because he thought they represented intellectual reactions, while the other 15 behaviors represented emotional reactions. For each student, 30 scale scores are obtained by totaling across the 10 art pieces and two judges for each type of behavior. Dave is interested in determining if these 30 variables are indicators of the two constructs, emotional and intellectual reactions. Dave's SPSS data file has the scores on these 30 variables for the 300 students.

Defining Dimensions for an Existing Measure

George had developed a 10-item questionnaire concerning how teachers cope with difficult students. When completing the questionnaire, teachers indicate the degree to which they use 10 different approaches to deal with problems between themselves and their most recalcitrant students. Teachers respond to the items on a 4-point scale, with 1 = Did not try this approach to 4 = Used this approach extensively. A single score for this measure is computed by simply summing the 10 items. By recommending a single scale score, George implicitly assumed that a single dimension underlies the coping measure. Kandace decides to conduct a study to gain some insights into the dimensionality of George's coping measure. She administers the coping measure to 91 teachers. Kandace's SPSS data file has the scores on these 10 variables for the 91 teachers.

Selecting Items or Scales to be Included in a Measure

Kandace decides to revise the coping measure on the basis of her factor analysis. Based on her factor analysis, she may decide to delete some items and add others. Kandace's SPSS data file is the same as in the previous application and includes the scores on the 10 items for the 91 teachers.

Understanding Factor Analysis

The results of factor analyses are controlled through our choice of measures and subjects. Ideally, four or more measures should be chosen to represent each construct of interest. Accordingly, if the focus is on identifying measures to assess two constructs (as in Dave's art study), at least 8 measures should be included in the factor analysis, 4 measures for each of the 2 constructs that might emerge as factors from the analysis. Because the dimensionality of the measures may vary as a function of the participants sampled in the study, it is important to consider not only the measures but also the respondents when designing factor analytic studies.

A common use of factor analysis is to define dimensions underlying existing measurement instruments (as in Kandace's initial problem). In this case, we have not chosen the variables to be analyzed, but rather are stuck with analyzing a predetermined set of items or scales. The subsequent results of the factor analysis may be difficult to interpret for several reasons. The items or scales may not have been created to reflect a construct or constructs, and, therefore, they may be poor indicators of the construct or constructs. There may be too few items or scales to represent each underlying dimension. Finally, the items or scales may be complexly determined in that they may be a function of multiple factors.

Factor analysis also may be used to determine what items or scales should be included on and excluded from a measure (as in Kandace's second use). The results of the factor analysis should not be used alone in making these decisions, but in conjunction with what is known about the construct or constructs that the items or scales assess. (See Lesson 36 for a discussion of why item analysis decisions should not be made based on empirical results alone.)

Factor analysis requires two stages, factor extraction and factor rotation. The primary objective of the first stage is to make an initial decision about the number of factors underlying a set of measured variables. The goal of the second stage is twofold: (1) to statistically manipulate (i.e., to rotate factors) the results to make the factors more interpretable and (2) to make final decisions about the number of underlying factors.

The first stage involves extracting factors from a correlation matrix to make initial decisions about the number of factors underlying a set of measures. Principal components analysis (a type of factor analysis) is used to make these decisions. The first extracted factor of a principal components analysis (unrotated solution) accounts for the largest amount of the variability among the measured variables, the second factor the next most variability, and so on. The variability of a factor is called an eigenvalue. In Stage 1, two statistical criteria are used to determine the number of factors to extract: (1) the absolute magnitude of the eigenvalues of factors (e.g., eigenvalue-greater-than-one criterion) and (2) the relative magnitudes of the eigenvalues (e.g., scree test). In addition to these two statistical criteria, one should make initial decisions about the number of factors based on a priori conceptual beliefs about the number of underlying dimensions. Because the decision about the number of factors is not a final one, we do not have to choose a single value for the number of factors (e.g., 6 factors), but instead may choose a range of values (e.g., 4 to 6 factors).

In Stage 2, we rotate the factors. Unrotated factors are typically not very interpretable. Factors are rotated to make them more meaningful. The rotated factors may be uncorrelated (orthogonal) or correlated (oblique). The most popular rotational method, VARIMAX, yields orthogonal factors. Oblique rotations are less frequently applied, perhaps because their results are more difficult to summarize. A factor is interpreted or named by examining the largest values linking the factor to the measured variables in the rotated factor matrix.

In Stage 2, we rotate factor solutions with different numbers of factors if the decision in Stage 1 was to consider a range of values for the number of factors. The final decision about the number of factors to choose is the number of factors for the rotated solution that is most interpretable.

Across Stages 1 and 2, four criteria determine the number of factors to include in a factor analysis: (1) a priori conceptual beliefs about the number of factors based on past research or theory, (2) the absolute values of the eigenvalues computed in Stage 1, (3) the relative values of the eigenvalues computed in Stage 1, and (4) the relative interpretability of rotated solutions computed in Stage 2.

Assumptions Underlying Factor Analysis

A single assumption underlies factor analysis extraction for a variety of methods: The measured variables are linearly related to the factors. This assumption is likely to be violated if items are factor-analyzed, particularly if the items have very limited response scales (e.g., a two-point response scale like those associated with right-wrong or true-false items), and the item distributions vary in skewness. Violation of this assumption may lead to the identification of spurious factors. If the assumption is met, the relationships among the measured variables are also linear. To determine whether the variables are linearly related, you can evaluate scatterplots for pairs of items. (See Lesson 30.)

The statistical tests associated with some of the factor extraction options in SPSS have additional assumptions. For example, the χ^2 test for the maximum likelihood solution assumes that the measured variables are multivariately normally distributed.

The Data Set

The data set for illustrating factor analysis is named *Lesson 35 Data File 1* on the Student Disk. The data set contains the results of a survey of 91 teachers who were asked to indicate the degree to which they used 10 different approaches to deal with problems between themselves and their most difficult students. They made their responses to each of these items on a 4-point scale, with 1 = Did not try this approach to 4 = Used this approach extensively. The 10 items on the coping questionnaire are shown in the Table 45 (at the top of page 295).

Table 45

Variables in Lesson 35 Data File 1

Variables	Definition
Item_a	I discussed my frustrations and feelings with person(s) at school.
Item_b	I tried to develop a step-by-step plan of action to remedy the problems.
Item_c	I expressed my emotions to my family and close friends.
Item_d	I read, attended workshops, or sought some other educational approach to correct them.
Item_e	I tried to be emotionally honest with myself about the problems.
Item_f	I sought advice from others on how I should solve the problems.
Item_g	I explored the emotions caused by the problems.
Item_h	I took direct action to try to correct the problems.
Item_I	I told someone I could trust about how I felt about the problems.
Item_j	I put aside other activities so that I could work to solve the problems.

The Research Question

Research questions in factor analysis are framed to reflect the purpose underlying the application. The purpose of our factor analysis is to define dimensions for an existing measure:

1. Is there a single dimension or are multiple dimensions underlying the 10 coping items?
2. Are there items not associated with the identified factors that might be eliminated from the measure because they are irrelevant?

Conducting Factor Analysis

Factor analysis is conducted in two stages: factor extraction and factor rotation.

Factor Extraction

As part of the first decision to determine the number of extracted factors, we want to obtain the eigenvalues based on the principal components solution to assess their absolute and relative magnitudes.

To conduct the initial analysis, follow these steps:

1. Click **Analyze**, click **Data Reduction**, and click **Factor**. You will see the Factor Analysis dialog box shown in Figure 219.

Figure 219. The Factor Analysis dialog box.

2. Hold down the Ctrl key, and click the 10 coping variables (items a through j). Then click ► to move them to the Variables box in the Factor Analysis dialog box.
3. Click **Extraction**. You will see the Factor Analysis: Extraction dialog box shown in Figure 220.

Figure 220. The Factor Analysis: Extraction dialog box.

4. Click **Scree Plot**.
5. Click **Continue**.
6. Click **OK**.

Selected SPSS Output for the Initial Factor Extraction

The output showing the initial statistics and the scree plot from the principal components analysis is shown in Figure 221 (below) and Figure 222 (at the top of page 297).

Total Variance Explained

Component	Initial Eigenvalues			Extraction Sums of Squared Loadings		
	Total	% of Variance	Cumulative %	Total	% of Variance	Cumulative %
1	3.046	30.465	30.465	3.046	30.465	30.465
2	1.801	18.011	48.476	1.801	18.011	48.476
3	1.009	10.091	58.566	1.009	10.091	58.566
4	.934	9.336	67.902			
5	.840	8.404	76.307			
6	.711	7.107	83.414			
7	.574	5.737	89.151			
8	.440	4.396	93.547			
9	.337	3.368	96.915			
10	.308	3.085	100.000			

Extraction Method: Principal Component Analysis.

Figure 221. Initial statistics from factor extraction procedure.

In Figure 221, the eigenvalues are listed for components 1 through 10. These are important quantities. The total amount of variance of the variables in an analysis is equal to the number of variables (in our example, 10). The extracted factors (or components because principal components was used as the extraction method) account for the variance among these variables. An eigenvalue is the amount of variance of the variables accounted for by a factor. An eigenvalue for a factor should be greater than or equal to zero and cannot exceed the total variance (in our example, 10). The percent of variance of the variables accounted for by the factor, as shown in the

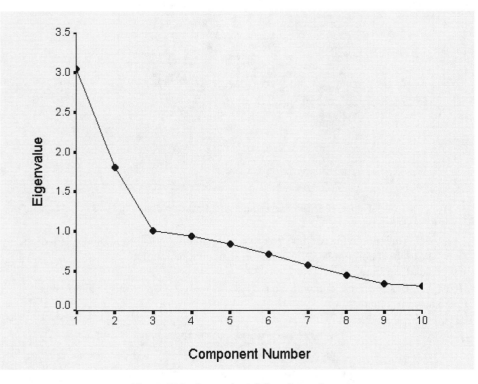

Figure 222. Scree plot of the eigenvalues.

output, is equal to the eigenvalue divided by the total amount of variance of the variables times 100. For example, the eigenvalue associated with the first factor is 3.046 and the percent of total variance accounted for by the first factor is (3.046 / 10) 100 = 30.46 (as shown in the first row in Figure 221).

Eigenvalues are helpful in deciding how many factors should be used in the analysis. Many criteria have been proposed in the literature for deciding how many factors to extract based on the magnitudes of the eigenvalues. One criterion is to retain all factors that have eigenvalues greater than 1. This criterion is the default option in SPSS. It may not always yield accurate results. Another criterion is to examine the plot of the eigenvalues, also known as the scree test, and to retain all factors with eigenvalues in the sharp descent part of the plot before the eigenvalues start to level off. This criterion more frequently yields accurate results than the eigenvalue-greater-than-1 criterion. Based on the scree plot in Figure 222, we concluded that two factors should be rotated.

Factor Rotation

Our next stage is to rotate a two-factor solution. To conduct a factor analysis with two rotated factors, follow these steps:

1. Click **Analyze**, click **Data Reduction**, and click **Factor.** The 10 coping items should already be visible in the Variables box.
2. Click **Extraction**.
3. Click next to **Number of factors**. Type **2** in the box next to the number of factors that you wish to extract and rotate. We chose two factors based on the scree plot.
4. Choose **Maximum likelihood** in the Method drop-down menu. Other extraction methods may be reasonable alternatives.
5. Click next to **Scree plot** so that it contains no check.
6. Click **Continue**.
7. Click **Rotation**. You will see the Factor Analysis: Rotation dialog box shown in Figure 223 (at the top of page 298).

Figure 223. The Factor Analysis: Rotation dialog box.

8. Click **Varimax** in the Method box to choose an orthogonal rotation of the factors. Click Direct oblimin if you would prefer an oblique rotation.
9. Click **Continue**.
10. Click **Descriptives**. You will see the Factor Analysis: Descriptives dialog box shown in Figure 224.

Figure 224. The Factor Analysis: Descriptives dialog box.

11. Click **Univariate descriptives** in the Statistics box.
12. Click **Continue**.
13. Click **OK**.

Selected SPSS Output for Two Rotated Factors

The rotated factor matrix is shown in Figure 225 (at the top of page 299). This matrix shows factor loadings, which are the correlations between each of the variables and the factors for a Varimax rotation. The factors are interpreted by naming them based on the size of the loadings. In our example, items a, c, f, and i are associated with the first factor, and items b, d, e, h, and j are related strongest to the second factor. On the basis of looking of the content of these two sets of items, we named the two factors, other-directed coping and self-directed coping.

The proportion of variance accounted for by each of the rotated factors is frequently reported in articles to indicate the relative importance of each factor. SPSS reports these statistics in the right side of the table labeled Total Variance Explained. As reported, the first and second factors accounted for 22.62% and 14.07% of the variance of the ten variables. In total, the two factors accounted for 36.69% of the variable variance. Note that this percentage must be identical to percent of variance accounted for by the unrotated factors (labeled Extraction Sums of Squared Loadings). Also note that this percentage does not match the percentage based on the initial eigenvalues. It does not match because the initial extraction is based on principal components and not maximum likelihood extraction methods.

If an oblique rotation such as Direct Oblimin is chosen in Step 8 rather than Varimax, be sure to refer to a factor analysis book to see how to interpret the results.

	Initial Eigenvalues			Extraction Sums of Squared Loadings			Rotation Sums of Squared Loadings		
Factor	Total	% of Variance	Cumulative %	Total	% of Variance	Cumulative %	Total	% of Variance	Cumulative %
1	3.046	30.465	30.465	2.495	24.954	24.954	2.262	22.616	22.616
2	1.801	18.011	48.476	1.173	11.734	36.688	1.407	14.072	36.688
3	1.009	10.091	58.566						
4	.934	9.336	67.902						
5	.840	8.404	76.307						
6	.711	7.107	83.414						
7	.574	5.737	89.151						
8	.440	4.396	93.547						
9	.337	3.368	96.915						
10	.308	3.085	100.000						

Extraction Method: Maximum Likelihood.

Rotated Factor Matrix[a]

	Factor	
	1	2
ITEM_A	.773	.147
ITEM_B	.218	.708
ITEM_C	.535	4.230E-02
ITEM_D	.166	.354
ITEM_E	.155	.437
ITEM_F	.747	5.894E-02
ITEM_G	.341	.341
ITEM_H	-.171	.475
ITEM_I	.759	5.604E-02
ITEM_J	-2.919E-02	.467

Extraction Method: Maximum Likelihood.
Rotation Method: Varimax with Kaiser Normalization.

a. Rotation converged in 3 iterations.

Figure 225. The rotated factor matrix from the factor analysis.

Using Correlation Matrices as Data

In some instances, you may not have the raw data available to conduct a factor analysis, but you may have the correlation matrix among variables. Under these circumstances, the correlation matrix can be read into SPSS using the Matrix Data command in the Syntax Editor.

To illustrate how a correlation is read by SPSS, let's show how we would read in the correlation matrix for our coping example using SPSS syntax.

1. Click **File**, then click **New**, and then click **SPSS Syntax**.
2. Type in the syntax statements. The values in the correlation matrix embedded in the syntax statements have been rounded to three decimal places.

   MATRIX DATA VARIABLES = ROWTYPE_ item_a item_b item_c item_d item_e item_f
       item_g item_h item_i item_j.
   BEGIN DATA
   N 91 91 91 91 91 91 91 91 91 91
   CORR   1.000
   CORR   .284   1.000
   CORR   .384   .144   1.000
   CORR   .161   .257   .008   1.000
   CORR   .161   .307   .060   .173   1.000
   CORR   .631   .251   .327   .223   .053   1.000
   CORR   .292   .284   .256   .313   .384   .209   1.000
   CORR   -.128   .356 -.021   .138   .156 -.085   .001   1.000
   CORR   .566   .173   .526   .107   .232   .555   .300 -.052   1.000
   CORR   .138   .332   .033   .159   .210 -.073   .097   .202 -.031   1.000
   END DATA.

The variable ROWTYPE_ is required to tell SPSS the meaning of the information in each row of the data (the lines between BEGIN DATA and END DATA). The N in the row immediately after Begin Data indicates that what follows in this row are the sample sizes, while CORR at the beginning of the next 10 rows indicates that correlations are in these rows.

3. Highlight all of the syntax commands by holding down the Ctrl key and typing an **a**.

4. Click **Run**. The Data Editor contains your correlation matrix so now you can factor analysis this matrix.

Warning! Because the data in the data editor are different from standard data, SPSS must be told that it is analyzing a correlation matrix each time you conduct an analysis on the correlation matrix. You must follow the steps under Conducting Factor Analysis with a Correlation Matrix each time you conduct a factor analysis. For example, you may run two separate analyses on the same data, one to make initial factor decisions and one to rotate the extracted factors. For both analyses, you must follow the steps to tell SPSS that it is analyzing a correlation matrix.

Conducting Factor Analysis with a Correlation Matrix

To conduct a factor analysis on a correlation matrix, follow these steps:

1. Conduct all steps up to clicking OK in the Factor Analysis dialog box. For example for factor extraction, follow Steps 1 through 5 presented earlier in this lesson.

2. Instead of **OK**, click **Paste**. The first four lines of the Syntax Editor should look more or less like this:

FACTOR
/VARIABLES item_a item_b item_c item_d item_e item_f item_g item_h item_i item_j
/MISSING LISTWISE
/ANALYSIS item_a item_b item_c item_d item_e item_f item_g item_h item_i item_j

3. Delete the /VARIABLES and the /MISSING statements and substitute for these two statements a single statement, /MATRIX IN(COR=*). The initial lines should now read as follows:

FACTOR
/MATRIX IN(COR=*)
/ANALYSIS item_a item_b item_c item_d item_e item_f item_g item_h item_i item_j

4. You should not have to make any changes to any later statements in the syntax window.

5. Click **Run**.

An APA Results Section

The dimensionality of the 10 items from the teacher coping measure was analyzed using maximum likelihood factor analysis. Three criteria were used to determine the number of factors to rotate: the a priori hypothesis that the measure was unidimensional, the scree test, and the interpretability of the factor solution. The scree plot indicated that our initial hypothesis of unidimensionality was incorrect. Consequently, two factors were rotated using a Varimax rotation procedure. The rotated solution, as shown in Table 46 (at the top of page 301), yielded two interpretable factors, other-directed and self-directed coping. The other-directed coping factor accounted for 22.6% of the item variance, and the self-directed coping factor accounted for 14.1% of the item variance. Only one item loaded on both factors.

Alternative Analyses

Multidimensional scaling can be used as an alternative to factor analysis to assess the dimensionality among measures. Multidimensional scaling is available in SPSS under the Statistics—Scale—Multidimensional Scaling option, but the topic is beyond the scope of this book. Item

Table 46

Correlations between the Coping Items and the Coping Factors

	Factors	
Items	Self-Directed	Other-Directed
Self-Directed (SD) items		
I tried to develop a step-by-step plan of action to remedy the problems.	**.71**	.22
I read, attended workshops, or sought some other educational approach to correct them.	**.35**	.17
I tried to be emotionally honest with myself about the problems.	**.44**	.16
I took direct action to try to correct he problems.	**.48**	-.17
I put aside other activities so that I could work to solve the problems.	**.47**	-.03
Other-Directed (OD) items		
I discussed my frustrations and feelings with person(s) at school.	.15	**.77**
I expressed my emotions to my family and close friends.	.04	**.54**
I sought advice from others on how I should solve the problems.	.06	**.75**
I told someone I could trust about how I felt about the problems.	.06	**.76**
Complexly Determined Item		
I explored the emotions caused by the problems.	.34	.34

analysis procedures can be used when making decisions about what items to delete from an existing measure See Lesson 37 for a discussion of item analysis.

Exercises

The data for Exercises 1 through 4 are in the data file named *Lesson 35 Exercise File 1* on the Student Disk. The data are based on the following research problem:

Terrill is interested in assessing how much women value their careers. He develops a 12-item scale, the Saxon Career Values Scale (SCVS). He has 100 college women take the SCVS. All of the items reflect the value women place on having a career versus having a family. Students are asked to respond to each on a 4-point scale with 0 indicating "disagree" and 3 indicating "agree" The items are shown in Table 47.

Table 47

Items on the Saxon Career Values Scale

Variables	Definition
q01	I consider marriage and having a family to be more important than a career.
q02	To me, marriage and family are as important as having a career.
q03	I prefer to pursue my career without the distractions of marriage, children, or a household.
q04	I would rather have a career than a family.
q05	I often think about what type of job I'll have 10 years from now.
q06	I could be happy without a career.
q07	I would feel unfulfilled without a career.
q08	I don't need to have a career to be fulfilled.
q09	I would leave my career to raise my children.
q10	Having a career would interfere with my family responsibilities.
q11	Planning for and succeeding in a career is one of my primary goals.
q12	I consider myself to be very career-minded.

1. Conduct a factor analysis. How many factors underlie the measure based on the scree plot?
2. On the basis of your factor analysis, identify the following:
   a. Mean of q03
   b. Eigenvalue associated with the first factor from the factor extraction.
   c. The number of eigenvalues greater than 1 from the factor extraction.
   d. Factor loading or loadings for q10 for the rotated solution.
3. What judgment should Terrill make about the number of factors to extract? Justify your decision based on your results.
4. Write a results section reporting your analyses.

The data for Exercises 5 through 7 are the correlations in the correlation matrix. The data are based on the following research problem:

Jessica is interested in assessing humor. She develops a 10-item measure in which some items represent humor demeaning to others (Don Rickles items), while other items reflect self-deprecating humor (Woody Allen items). She administers her measure to 100 college students. Students are asked to respond to each on a 5-point scale with 1 indicating "disagree" and 5 indicating "agree." The variables in the data set are shown in Table 48.

Table 48

Items from a Humor Measure

Variables	Definition
Item01	I like to make fun of others. (Don Rickles)
Item02	I make people laugh by making fun of myself. (Woody Allen)
Item03	People find me funny when I make jokes about others. (Don Rickles)
Item04	I talk about my problems to make people laugh. (Woody Allen)
Item05	I frequently make others the target of my jokes. (Don Rickles)
Item06	People find me funny when I tell them about my failings. (Woody Allen)
Item07	I love to get people to laugh by using sarcasm. (Don Rickles)
Item08	I am funniest when I talk about my own weaknesses. (Woody Allen)
Item09	I make people laugh by exposing other people's stupidities. (Don Rickles)
Item10	I am funny when I tell others about the dumb things I have done. (Woody Allen)

5. Create an SPSS data file containing the following correlations among items using the syntax window:

	Item01	Item02	Item03	Item04	Item05	Item06	Item07	Item08	Item09	Item10
Item01	1.000									
Item02	-.218	1.000								
Item03	.268	-.100	1.000							
Item04	-.116	.575	.116	1.000						
Item05	.221	-.024	.591	.163	1.000					
Item06	-.089	.294	.174	.261	.071	1.000				
Item07	.233	-.165	.420	-.058	.297	.056	1.000			
Item08	-.024	.245	.041	.434	.038	.381	-.146	1.000		
Item09	.071	-.130	.338	-.010	.345	.057	.274	-.070	1.000	
Item10	-.136	.284	-.056	.182	-.042	.554	-.010	.369	.098	1.000

6. Conduct a factor analysis on the correlation matrix to assess whether a single factor underlies the scores. How many factors should you extract?
7. Write a results section based on your analyses.

Internal Consistency Estimates of Reliability

Multiple-item or multiple-observation scales are often developed to assess characteristics about individuals. One important element in deciding the merit of such a scale is its reliability and validity. A number of methods can establish a scale's reliability including test-retest, equivalent-forms, and internal consistency estimates of reliability.

With test-retest reliability, individuals are administered a measure on two occasions with some time interval between them. Equivalent-forms estimates are based on a similar methodology, except an equivalent form is administered on the second occasion rather than the same measure. For either of these methods, the easiest way to compute a reliability coefficient is through the use of the Bivariate Correlation procedure discussed in Lesson 30. In these cases, the reliability estimate is the correlation between the scores obtained on the two occasions.

With an internal consistency estimate of reliability, individuals are measured on a single occasion using a scale with multiple parts. The parts may be items on a paper-and-pencil measure, responses to questions from structured interview, multiple observations on an observational measure, or some other units of a measure that are summed to yield scale scores. For ease of discussion, we will frequently refer to items rather than describing the analyses in terms of all types of parts. The reliability procedure computes estimates of reliability based on the consistency among the items (parts). In this lesson, we'll discuss two internal consistency estimates, split-half and coefficient alpha.

Split-half estimates and coefficient alpha may be used to estimate the reliability of the total score if a scale has multiple items and the multiple items are summed to obtain a total score. If a measure consists of multiple scales, separate internal consistency estimates should be computed for each scale score.

In some instances, you may need to transform one or more items (or whatever the parts are) on a measure prior to conducting the analyses so that the total score computed by the Reliability procedure is meaningful. We'll look at three types of applications, which vary depending on whether or how items are transformed:

- No transformation of items. If the responses to these items are in the same metric, and if high scores on them represent high scores on the underlying construct, no transformations are required. The reliability analysis can be conducted on the untransformed scores.
- Reverse scoring of some item scores. For this case, all items on a measure have the same response scale, but high scores on some items represent high scores on the underlying construct, while high scores on other items represent low scores on the underlying construct. The scores on these latter items need to be reverse scaled. Such items are commonly found on attitude scales. Lesson 18 explains how to reverse scale items.
- Z-score transformation of item scores. Z-scores must be created when items on a scale lack the same response scale. Before summing the items to obtain a total

score, you must transform the item scores to standard scores so that these items share a common metric. In some instances, some of the z-transformed items may need to be reverse-scored by multiplying the z-scores by a -1. Lesson 18 demonstrates how to perform z-score transformations and how to reverse-scale z-transformed items.

Applying the Reliability Procedure

Here are examples of the three types of research problems we just described.

No Transformation of Items

Sarah is interested in whether a measure she developed has good reliability. She has 83 students complete the 20-item Emotional Expressiveness Measure (EEM). Ten of the items are summed to yield a Negative Emotions scale, and the other 10 items are summed to produce a Positive Emotions scale. Sarah's SPSS data file contains 83 cases and 20 items as variables. These 20 items are the variables analyzed using the Reliability program. She computes an internal consistency estimate of reliability (split half or coefficient alpha) for the Negative Emotions scale and another internal consistency estimate for the Positive Emotions scale.

Reverse-Scoring of Some Items

Janet has developed a 10-item measure called the Emotional Control Scale. She asks 50 individuals to respond to these items on a 0 to 4 scale, with 0 being completely disagree and 4 being completely agree. Half the items are phrased so that agreement indicates a desire to keep emotions under control (under control items), while the other half are written so that agreement indicates a desire to express emotions openly (expression items). Janet's SPSS data file contains 50 cases and 10 item scores for each. The expression items need to be reverse-scaled so that a response of 0 is transformed to a 4, a 1 becomes a 3, a 2 stays a 2, a 3 becomes a 1, and a 4 is transformed to a 0. Janet computes an internal consistency estimate based on the scores for the five under control items and the transformed scores for the five expression items.

Z-Score Transformations of Item Scores

George is interested in developing an index of perseverance. He has 83 college seniors answer 15 questions about completing tasks. Some questions ask students how many times in an hour they would be willing to dial a telephone number that is continuously busy, how many hours they would be willing to commit to solving a 10,000-piece jigsaw puzzle, how many times would they be willing to reread a 20-line poem in order to understand it, and how many different majors they have had in college. George's SPSS data file contains the 83 cases and the 15 item scores. All 15 items need to be transformed to standard scores. In addition, some items need to be reverse-scaled. For example, the number of different majors in college presumably is negatively related to the construct of perseverance (i.e., the more they switch majors, the less perseverance they have). George computes an internal consistency estimate on the transformed scores for the 15 questions.

Understanding Internal Consistency Estimates

The coefficients for split-half reliability and alpha assess reliability based on different types of consistency. The split-half coefficient is obtained by computing scores for two halves of a scale. With SPSS, scores are computed for the first and second halves of the scale. The value of the reliability coefficient is a function of the consistency between the two halves. In contrast, consistency with coefficient alpha is assessed among items. The greater the consistency in responses among items, the higher coefficient alpha will be.

Both the split-half coefficient and coefficient alpha should range in value between 0 and 1. To the extent that items on a scale are ambiguous and produce unreliable responses, there will be a lack of consistency between halves or among items, and internal consistency estimates of reliability should be smaller. It is possible for these reliability coefficients to fall outside the range of 0 to 1 if the correlation between halves is negative for a split-half coefficient or if a number of the correlations among items are negative for coefficient alpha.

You should base your choice between split-half reliability and coefficient alpha on whether the assumptions for one or the other methods can be met.

Assumptions Underlying Internal Consistency Reliability Procedures

There are three assumptions underlying the two internal consistency estimates.

Assumption 1: The Parts of the Measure Must Be Equivalent

For split-half coefficients, the parts—two halves of the measure—must be equivalent. With equivalent halves, individuals who score high on one half of the scale should score high on the other half of the scale, and individuals who score low on one half of the scale should also score low on the other half of the scale if the halves of the scale contain no measurement error. Individuals may respond differently to the first half and the second half of a measure for reasons other than measurement error and, consequently, it may not be appropriate to split the scales in this fashion (the method used by SPSS) to compute a split-half coefficient. For example, the respondents may answer differently on the first and the second halves of an achievement measure because they tire or because the second half involves more difficult problems. Alternatively, respondents may answer differently on the first and second halves of an attitude measure because they may become more bored as they answer items. Rather than divide scales into a first half and a second half, you can divide scales using other splits. For example, you can add the odd-numbered items together to create one half and add the even-numbered items to create the other half. You can then use these two halves to compute split-half coefficients.

For coefficient alpha, every item is assumed to be equivalent to every other item. All items should measure the same underlying dimension. Differences in responses should occur only as a function of measurement error. It is unlikely that this assumption is ever met completely, although with some measures it may be met approximately.

To the extent that the equivalency assumption is violated, internal consistency estimates tend to underestimate reliability.

Assumption 2: Errors in Measurement between Parts Are Unrelated

A respondent's ability to guess well on one item or one part of a test should not influence how well he or she guesses on another part. The unrelated-errors assumption can be violated a number of ways. For example, speeded measures tend to violate the unrelated-errors assumption. Internal consistency estimates (split half or coefficient alpha) should not be used if respondents' scores depend on whether they can complete the scale in an allotted time. For example, coefficient alpha should not be used to assess the reliability of a 100-item math test to be completed in 10 minutes because the scores are partially a function of completing the test. Another instance of violation of this assumption involves items that are linked together. For example, an achievement measure may have a number of sets of matching items, or a reading comprehension test may ask different sets of questions for different reading texts. Neither coefficient alpha nor split half measures should be used as a reliability estimate for these scales since items within a set are likely to have correlated errors and yield overestimates of reliability.

Assumption 3: An Item or Half Test Score Is a Sum of Its True and Its Error Scores

This assumption is necessary for an internal consistency estimate to reflect accurately a scale's reliability. It is difficult to know whether this assumption has been violated or not.

For more exact description of these assumptions, you should consult appropriate references in the psychometric literature. For example, see Green and Hershberger (in press) and Green, Lissitz, and Mulaik (1977) for discussion of assumptions underlying coefficient alpha.

The Data Set

The data set used in this lesson to illustrate how to compute reliability estimates is based on the emotional control example and is named *Lesson 36 Data File 1* on the Student Disk. The data set contains the results of a survey of 50 respondents. Half the items are phrased so that agreement indicates a desire to keep emotions under control (under control items), and the other half are written so that agreement indicates a desire to express emotions openly (expression items). Table 49 shows the items on the Emotional Control Scale.

Table 49

Items on the Emotional Control Scale in Lesson 36 Data Set 1

Variables	Definition
item1	I keep my emotions under control.
item2	Under stress I remain calm.
item3	I like to let people know how I am feeling.
item4	I express my emotions openly.
item5	It is a sign of weakness to show how one feels.
item6	Well-adjusted individuals are ones who are confident enough to express their true emotions.
item7	Emotions get in the way of clear thinking.
item8	I let people see my emotions so that they know who I am.
item9	If I am angry with people, I tell them in no uncertain terms that I am unhappy with them.
item10	I try to get along with people and not create a big fuss.

The Research Question

The research question can be phrased, "How reliable is our 10-item measure of emotional control?"

Conducting a Reliability Analysis

Before conducting any internal consistency estimates of reliability, we must determine if all items use the same metric and whether any items have to be reverse-scaled. All items share the same metric since the response scale for all items is 0 = completely disagree to 4 = completely agree. However, the five items in which high scores indicate a willingness to express emotion must be reverse-scaled so that high scores on the total scale reflect a high level of emotional control. These items are 3, 4, 6, 8, and 9. We discuss how to reverse-scale items for a Likert scale in Lesson 18.

You should reverse-scale items 3, 4, 6, 8, and 9 before going through the steps to compute coefficient alpha and split-half internal consistency estimates. Name the variables with reversed scales item3r, item4r, item6r, item8r, and item9r.

Computing Coefficient Alpha

To compute a coefficient alpha, follow these steps:

1. Click **Analyze**, click **Scale**, then click **Reliability Analysis**. You'll see the Reliability Analysis dialog box shown in Figure 226.

Figure 226. The Reliability Analysis dialog box.

2. Hold down the Ctrl key, and click **item1**, **item2**, **item5**, **item7**, **item10**, **item3r**, **item4r**, **item6r**, **item8r**, **item9r** to select the appropriate items.
3. Click ▶ to move them to the Items box.
4. Click **Statistics**. You'll see the Reliability Analysis: Statistics dialog box, as shown in Figure 227.

Figure 227. The Reliability Analysis: Statistics dialog box.

5. Click **Item**, click **Scale** in the Descriptives for area, then click **Correlations** in the Inter-Item area.
6. Click **Continue**. In the Reliability Analysis dialog box, make sure that **Alpha** is chosen in the box labeled Model.
7. Click **OK**.

Selected SPSS Output for Coefficient Alpha

The results are shown in Figure 228.

```
****** Method 2 (covariance matrix) will be used for this analysis ******
      R E L I A B I L I T Y   A N A L Y S I S   -   S C A L E   (A L P H A)

                              Mean        Std Dev      Cases

      1.    ITEM1            1.9200        1.3068        50.0
      2.    ITEM2            2.1600        1.2014        50.0
      3.    ITEM5            2.0000        1.1429        50.0
      4.    ITEM7            2.3400        1.1178        50.0
      5.    ITEM10           2.0800        1.2911        50.0
      6.    ITEM3R           2.2000         .9897        50.0
      7.    ITEM4R           1.9800        1.3013        50.0
      8.    ITEM6R           2.2000        1.2778        50.0
      9.    ITEM8R           2.1000        1.2495        50.0
     10.    ITEM9R           2.3400        1.1178        50.0


                         Correlation Matrix

                  ITEM1       ITEM2       ITEM5       ITEM7       ITEM10

     ITEM1       1.0000
     ITEM2        .4633      1.0000
     ITEM5        .4509       .5202      1.0000
     ITEM7        .4521       .4602       .1917      1.0000
     ITEM10       .4272       .4389       .4011       .3343      1.0000
     ITEM3R       .4702       .4188       .3067       .4723       .2587
     ITEM4R       .4071       .4459       .4528       .4257       .4747
     ITEM6R       .3520       .3776       .4053       .4087       .3117
     ITEM8R       .5174       .5601       .5002       .4866       .4504
     ITEM9R       .3683       .3082       .2237       .4446       .3484


                  ITEM3R      ITEM4R      ITEM6R      ITEM8R      ITEM9R

     ITEM3R      1.0000
     ITEM4R       .4627      1.0000
     ITEM6R       .4357       .4811      1.0000
     ITEM8R       .4456       .3652       .5369      1.0000
     ITEM9R       .4169       .2854       .2086       .2674      1.0000



      R E L I A B I L I T Y   A N A L Y S I S   -   S C A L E   (A L P H A)

          N of Cases =        50.0

                                                           N of
      Statistics for       Mean      Variance    Std Dev   Variables
            Scale        21.3200     67.2016      8.1977        10



      Reliability Coefficients     10 items

      Alpha =   .8715              Standardized item alpha =    .8721
```

Figure 228. Results of coefficient alpha.

As with any analysis, the descriptive statistics need to be checked to confirm that the data have no major anomalies. For example, are all the means within the range of possible values (0 to 4)? Are there any unusually large variances that might indicate that a value has been mistyped? In general, are the correlations among the variables positive? If not, should you have reversed-scaled one or more of the items associated with the negative correlations? Once it appears that data have been entered and scaled appropriately, the reliability estimate of alpha can be interpreted.

The output reports two alphas, alpha and standardized item alpha. In this example, we are interested in the alpha. The only time that we would be interested in the standardized alpha is if the scale score is computed by summing item scores that have been standardized to have a uniform mean and standard deviation (such as z-scores). The coefficient alpha of .87 suggests that the scale scores are reasonably reliable for respondents like those in the study.

Computing Split-Half Coefficient Estimates

SPSS computes a split-half coefficient by evaluating the consistency in responding between the first half and the second half of the items listed in the reliability analysis. It is important to carefully choose which items to include in each half so that the two halves are as equivalent as possible. Different item splits may produce dramatically different results. The best split of the items is the one that produces equivalent halves (see Assumption 1).

For our example, we chose to split the test into two halves for the purpose of the reliability analysis in the following fashion:

Half 1: Item 1, Item 3, Item 5, Item 8, and Item 10
Half 2: Item 2, Item 4, Item 6, Item 7, and Item 9

We chose this split to take into account the ordering of items on the measure (with one exception, no two adjacent items are included on the same half) as well as the two type of items, under control and expression items (2 items of one type and 3 of the other on a half).

To compute a split-half coefficient, follow these steps:

1. Click **Analyze**, click **Scale**, and then click **Reliability Analysis**.
2. Click **Reset** to clear the dialog box.
3. Hold down the Ctrl key, and click the variables that are in the first half for our reliability analysis: **item1**, **item3r**, **item5**, **item8r**, and **item10**.
4. Click ▸ to move them to the Items box.
5. Hold down the Ctrl key, and click the variables that are in the second half for our reliability analysis: **item2**, **item4r**, **item6r**, **item7**, and **item9r**.
6. Click ▸ to move them to the Items box in the Reliability Analysis dialog box. Figure 229 shows the Reliability Analysis dialog box.

Figure 229. The Reliability Analysis dialog box after completing step 6.

7. Click **Statistics**.
8. Click **Item** and **Scale** in the Descriptives for area.
9. Click **Correlations** in the Inter-Item area.
10. Click **Continue**.
11. Click **Split-half** in the drop-down menu labeled Model.
12. Click **OK**.

Selected SPSS Output for Split-Half Reliability

The results of the analysis are shown in Figure 230.

```
                                              N of
Statistics for     Mean    Variance   Std Dev  Variables
      Part 1      10.3000   19.4388    4.4089      5
      Part 2      11.0200   18.4282    4.2928      5
      Scale       21.3200   67.2016    8.1977     10




    R E L I A B I L I T Y    A N A L Y S I S    -    S C A L E    (S P L I T)



Reliability Coefficients     10 items

Correlation between forms =    .7750     Equal-length Spearman-Brown =    .8732

Guttman Split-half =           .8730     Unequal-length Spearman-Brown =   .8732

Alpha for part 1 =             .7856     Alpha for part 2 =               .7570

   5 items in part 1                        5 items in part 2
```

Figure 230. The results of the split-half analysis.

The descriptive statistics need to be checked to confirm that the data have no anomalies as described in our earlier discussion of coefficient alpha. The descriptive statistics associated with the split-half coefficient are identical to the descriptives for coefficient alpha discussed earlier.

The most frequently reported split-half reliability estimate is the one based on the correlation between forms. The correlation between forms is .78, but it is not the reliability estimate. At best, it is the reliability of half the measure (because it is the correlation between two half-measures). The Spearman-Brown corrected correlation, $r = .87$, is the reliability estimate.

If there were an odd number of items, a split would produce an unequal number of items in each half. Under these conditions, the value for the Unequal-length Spearman-Brown should be reported.

Using SPSS Graphs to Display the Results

Graphics procedures are not necessary to display the results of the coefficient alpha or split-half reliability coefficients.

An APA Results Section

Two internal consistency estimates of reliability were computed for the Emotional Control Scale: coefficient alpha and a split-half coefficient expressed as a Spearman-Brown corrected correlation. For the split-half coefficient, the scale was split into two halves such that the two halves would be as equivalent as possible. In splitting the items we took into account the sequencing of the items as well as whether the item indicated control of emotion or expression of emotion. The first half included items 1, 3, 5, 8, and 10, while the other half included items 2, 4, 6, 7, and 9. Both values for coefficient alpha and the split-half coefficient were the same, .87, each indicating satisfactory reliability.

Exercises

The data for Exercises 1 through 3 are in the data file named *Lesson 36 Exercise File 1* on the Student Disk. The data are based on the following research problem.

Terrill is interested in assessing how much women value their careers. He develops a 12-item scale, the Saxon Career Values Scale (SCVS). He has 100 college women take the SCVS. All of the items reflect the value women place on having a career versus having a family. Students are asked to respond to each on a 4-point scale with 0 indicating "disagree" and 3 indicating "agree" The items are shown in Table 50.

Table 50

Items on the Saxon Career Values Scale

Variables	Definition
q01	I consider marriage and having a family to be more important than a career.*
q02	To me, marriage and family are as important as having a career.*
q03	I prefer to pursue my career without the distractions of marriage, children, or a household.
q04	I would rather have a career than a family.
q05	I often think about what type of job I'll have 10 years from now.
q06	I could be happy without a career.*
q07	I would feel unfulfilled without a career.
q08	I don't need to have a career to be fulfilled.*
q09	I would leave my career to raise my children.*
q10	Having a career would interfere with my family responsibilities.*
q11	Planning for and succeeding in a career is one of my primary goals.
q12	I consider myself to be very career-minded.

*Items are reverse-scaled to create a total score.

1. Reverse-scale the appropriate items so a higher total score reflects a greater emphasis on career.
2. Conduct a reliability analysis for the SCVS scale using coefficient alpha. From the output, identify the following:
   a. Coefficient alpha
   b. The correlation between Item 3 and Item 4
   c. The mean for Item 12
3. What judgment should Terrill make about the overall scale reliability? Write a results section reporting your analyses.

The data for Exercises 4 through 7 are in the data file named *Lesson 36 Exercise File 2* on the Student Disk. The data are based on the following research problem.

Jessica is interested in assessing humor demeaning to others versus self-deprecating humor. She develops a 10-item measure in which some items represent humor demeaning to others (Don Rickles items), while other items reflect self-deprecating humor (Woody Allen items). She administers her measure to 100 college students. Students are asked to respond to each on a 5-point scale with 1 indicating "disagree" and 5 indicating "agree." Jessica computes a total score by reverse scaling the Woody Allen items and then summing all ten items. The variables in the data set are shown in Table 51 (at the top of page 312).

Table 51

Items from a Humor Measure

Variables	Definition
item01	I like to make fun of others. (Don Rickles)
item02	I make people laugh by making fun of myself. (Woody Allen)
item03	People find me funny when I make jokes about others. (Don Rickles)
item04	I talk about my problems to make people laugh. (Woody Allen)
item05	I frequently make others the target of my jokes. (Don Rickles)
item06	People find me funny when I tell them about my failings. (Woody Allen)
item07	I love to get people to laugh by using sarcasm. (Don Rickles)
item08	I am funniest when I talk about my own weaknesses. (Woody Allen)
item09	I make people laugh by exposing other people's stupidities. (Don Rickles)
item10	I am funny when I tell others about the dumb things I have done. (Woody Allen)

4. Compute a reliability analysis on the total score using coefficient alpha.
5. Conduct the analysis again, this time computing a split-half reliability coefficient. Can you justify the method you chose to split the items?
6. Which estimate of reliability is the more appropriate one? Why?
7. Write a results section based on your analyses.

Item Analysis Using the Reliability Procedure

Multiple-item scales can be developed to assess characteristics about individuals. These characteristics are called constructs (or dimensions) because they are constructed by researchers to explain behavior and are not directly observable. Examples of constructs include verbal fluency, emotionality, leg strength, and preference for Republican candidates. Constructs like leg strength may be assessed using multiple measures or items, such as maximal weight lifted using leg flexion, maximal weight lifted using leg extensions, and number of leg extensions with a 20-pound weight. However, even when we combine scores across these multiple measures, we do not obtain a perfectly accurate assessment of a construct because our measures contain measurement error.

We conduct item analyses to decide which items to include or to exclude from a scale. The objective of item analysis is to select a set of items that yields a summed score that is more strongly related to the construct of interest than any other possible set of items. Item analysis is problematic because we cannot relate our items to a direct measure of a construct to make our item selections. Instead, we use a poor representation of the construct, the sum of the items, and make decisions about items based on their relationship to this total score. Given the problems inherent in item analysis, researchers should select items to include on their scale based not only on the correlations between item scores and total scores, but also on their knowledge about the items and how they rationally and theoretically relate to the constructs.

The data required to conduct an item analysis are the item scores for a group of participants. Each participant is a case in the SPSS data file, and the items are the variables in the data set.

Applying Item Analysis Using the Reliability Analysis Procedure

The Reliability Analysis procedure can analyze items on measures that assess one or more constructs. The methods used in the Reliability Analysis procedure assume that scale scores will be computed by summing item scores. Consequently, before we conduct an item analysis, we must determine whether any items need to be transformed to create a total score. Lesson 18 explains how to perform the transformations. We'll look at three examples of item analysis for a measure assessing a single construct and one example of item analysis for a measure assessing multiple constructs.

- Measure of single construct requiring no transformations
- Measure of single construct requiring reverse-scoring of some item scores
- Measure of single construct requiring z-transformations of all item scores and reverse-scoring of some items
- Measure that assesses multiple constructs

For applications with measures that assess multiple constructs, results from the Bivariate Correlation procedure are useful above and beyond those reported by the Reliability Analysis procedure.

Measure of a Single Construct Requiring No Transformations

Bob teaches a high school history class of 60 students and would like to item-analyze a 50-item achievement test on Civil War history that he has administered. Each item on the test is scored 0 for incorrect and 1 for correct. The scale score is the sum of these scored items. Bob's SPSS data file contains 60 cases and 50 variables representing the 50 items. These 50 items are the variables analyzed using the Reliability Analysis procedure.

Measure of a Single Construct Requiring Reverse-Scoring of Some Item Scores

Mickey has developed a 14-item measure called the Bias Against Women scale. He asks 100 individuals to respond to these items on a 1 to 5 scale, with 1 being completely disagree and 5 being completely agree. Half the items are phrased so that agreement indicates a bias against women (the biased items), while the other half are written so that agreement indicates a lack of bias against women (the unbiased items). Mickey's SPSS data file contains 100 cases and 14 variables representing the 14 items. The unbiased items need to be reverse-scaled so that a response of 1 is transformed to a 5, a 2 is transformed to a 4, and so on. The scores used by the Reliability Analysis procedure includes the scores for the seven biased items and the transformed scores for the seven unbiased items.

Measure of a Single Construct Requiring Z-Transformations of All Item Scores and Reverse-Scoring of Some Items

Julie wants to develop a behavioral index of friendliness. She has the 60 participants in her study discuss for five minutes with a stranger what they like to do in their free time. The index includes 15 behavioral measures (items), such as how far in feet participants stand when talking to a stranger, percent of time smiling, number of sentences initiated by participants, and a 5-point rating of warmth of voice. Julie's SPSS data file contains 60 cases and 15 item scores. All 15 items have to be transformed to standard scores. In addition, some of the items need to be reverse-scaled. For example, distance in feet participants stand when talking to the stranger would need to be reverse-scaled since distance presumably is inversely related to the construct of friendliness; that is, the closer a person stands to the stranger the more friendly they are. The scores used by the Reliability Analysis procedure include the 15 z-transformed item scores, at least one of which has been reverse-scaled.

A Measure That Assesses Multiple Constructs

Margaret wants to develop a coping measure that evaluates the degree that teachers use problem-focused and emotion-focused coping with difficult students. She has 91 teachers take a coping measure that has five items that assess problem-focused coping and 5 items that assess emotion-focused coping. Margaret's SPSS data file contains 91 cases and 10 items as variables.

Understanding Item Analysis

After transforming items appropriately to create a meaningful total score for a scale, a correlation is computed between each item on the scale and the total score, excluding the item of interest from the total score. SPSS refers to these correlations as corrected item-total correlations. The term "corrected" is used to indicate that the item of interest is not included in the total score so that the correlation is not spuriously positive. To the extent that the item total represents the construct of interest, the items should be strongly correlated with the corrected total score. Under these circumstances, researchers should choose items to include on their scales if they have high positive correlations and delete or revise items on their scales if they have negative or low positive correlations.

You may need to conduct the item analysis procedure multiple times to evaluate the appropriateness of items. The first time the procedure is conducted, the worst item can be eliminated from the scale. Once this item is eliminated the total scores change. Thus, it is necessary to redo the item analysis with the worst item removed to evaluate whether any additional items should be deleted. This process continues until a satisfactory set of items remains. Because of the changing nature of the corrected total score, it is certainly possible to add one of the items deleted in an earlier step back to the scale to ensure that the corrected item-total correlation still indicates that it is a poor item.

There are difficulties with choosing items based on corrected item-total correlations. In practice, it is likely that items assess not only the construct of interest but also irrelevant factors and that the corrected total score is a function of the relevant construct and the irrelevant factors. Accordingly, a positive correlation between an item and the corrected total indicates that an item assesses the relevant construct, the irrelevant factors that are shared with the other items on the scale, or both. For example, let's say that 8 of 10 items on a supervisory feedback scale begin with "My supervisor tells me ..." and the other 2 items begin with "I receive feedback...." The items starting with "My supervisor" may produce higher corrected item-total correlations than the other items because they are similarly worded, not because they are better measures of supervisory feedback.

There are additional reasons for not blindly following the results of an item analysis. There may be a number of narrowly defined constructs that are a function of a more broadly defined construct of interest. For example, let's say that we are interested in the broadly defined construct of constructive play and that the items on the scale assess, in addition to the broadly defined construct, one or more narrowly defined constructs: constructive play by oneself indoors, constructive play with games indoors, constructive play with games outdoors, and so on. Let's also assume that the scale was not initially developed well and a majority of the items on the constructive play scale pertain to constructive play with games indoors. A researcher who conducts an item analysis and chooses the items with the highest correlations with the corrected total may create a scale measuring constructive play with games indoors rather than constructive play in general.

A more complex procedure is required for measures that are designed to assess multiple constructs or dimensions. You should compute correlations between item scores and corrected total scores for the items' dimension. You also should compute correlations between item scores and total scores assessing different dimensions. An item should be correlated with its own scale (convergent validity). In addition, an item should be correlated more with its own scale than with scales assessing different constructs (discriminant validity). The Reliability procedure can be used to determine the correlation of an item with its own corrected total scale. However, the Bivariate Correlation procedure has to be used to determine the correlation between item scores and total scores for other scales. Again, when making decisions about keeping or omitting items, you must consider the content of the items and not just the magnitudes of the correlation coefficients.

Assumption Underlying Item Analyses

It is assumed that all items that are supposed to assess a single factor are linearly related to that single factor plus measurement error. Measurement error for an item is assumed to be random and uncorrelated with the factor and measurement errors for other items.

As discussed in the section "Understanding Item Analysis," this assumption is problematic. Researchers can reach wrong conclusions using only the results of an item analysis. It is important for researchers not to make decisions about what items to include on a scale based solely on the results of an item analysis.

The Data Set

The data set used to illustrate two of our examples is named *Lesson 37 Data File 1* on the Student Disk. The data set contains the results of Margaret's survey of 91 teachers. The teachers were asked to indicate the degree to which they used 10 different approaches to deal with problems between themselves and their most recalcitrant students. The 10 items on the coping questionnaire are shown in the table. The teachers rated each item on a 4-point scale, with 1 = Did not try this approach to 4 = Used this approach extensively. Table 52 shows the variables in the data file.

Table 52

Variables in Lesson 37 Data File 1

Variables	Definition
item_a	I discussed my frustrations and feelings with person(s) at school.
item_b	I tried to develop a step-by-step plan of action to remedy the problems.
item_c	I expressed my emotions to my family and close friends.
item_d	I read, attended workshops, or sought some other educational approach to correct them.
item_e	I tried to be emotionally honest with myself about the problems.
item_f	I sought advice from others on how I should solve the problems.
item_g	I explored the emotions caused by the problems.
item_h	I took direct action to try to correct the problems.
item_i	I told someone I could trust about how I felt about the problems.
item_j	I put aside other activities so that I could work to solve the problems.

The Research Question

The research question to be asked depends upon whether the measure is viewed as assessing a single construct, Active Coping, or assessing two constructs, Emotion-Focused Coping and Problem-Focused Coping.

1. Single construct approach: Should one or more items on Margaret's measure be deleted or revised to obtain a better measure of Active Coping?
2. Multiple constructs approach: Should one or more items on Margaret's measure be deleted or revised to obtain better measures of Emotion-Focused Coping and Problem-Focused Coping? Items a, c, e, g, and i are hypothesized to measure Emotion-Focused Coping, while items b, d, f, h, and j are hypothesized to measure Problem-Focused Coping.

Conducting Item Analyses

We illustrate how to conduct item analyses for a single construct and for multiple constructs of Margaret's measure.

Assessing a Single Construct

To conduct an item analysis assessing a single construct, follow these steps:

1. Click **Analyze**, click **Scale**, and click **Reliability Analysis**.
2. Holding down the Ctrl key, select all 10 variables (**item_a** through **item_j**) by clicking on each one.
3. Click ▸ to move the variables to the Items box.

4. Click **Statistics**.
5. Click **Item**, **Scale**, and **Scale if Item Deleted** in the Descriptives area.
6. Click **Correlations** in the Inter-Item area.
7. Click **Continue**.
8. In the Reliability Analysis dialog box, make sure that **Alpha** is chosen in the Model drop-down menu.
9. Click **OK**.

Selected SPSS Output for Item Analyses Assessing a Single Construct

The results of the analysis are shown in Figure 231.

```
Item-total Statistics

                Scale       Scale      Corrected
                Mean        Variance    Item-        Squared      Alpha
                if Item     if Item     Total        Multiple     if Item
                Deleted     Deleted     Correlation  Correlation  Deleted

ITEM_A          25.4505     17.2503     .5462        .5303        .6711
ITEM_B          25.5055     16.8972     .4840        .3533        .6762
ITEM_C          26.0769     17.0940     .3526        .3181        .7004
ITEM_D          26.3736     17.3700     .3085        .1837        .7094
ITEM_E          25.1538     18.3094     .3566        .2515        .6980
ITEM_F          25.3956     17.3973     .4485        .5137        .6832
ITEM_G          25.9780     16.4884     .4567        .2979        .6798
ITEM_H          25.0330     20.1211     .1134        .2117        .7270
ITEM_I          25.5495     16.7170     .5104        .5156        .6716
ITEM_J          26.5275     18.9631     .2027        .2029        .7213


Reliability Coefficients     10 items

Alpha =     .7167         Standardized item alpha =    .7157
```

Figure 231. The results of the item analysis.

Item_h had the lowest corrected item-total correlation, and item_j had the next lowest correlation; therefore, they were candidates for elimination. To ensure that item_j would still have a low correlation after deleting item_h from the scale, we reran the Reliability Analyses procedure without item_h. The output is shown in Figure 232 (at the top of page 318). As expected, item_j now had the lowest corrected item-total correlation.

Examining the item content of item_h and item_j, we concluded that they differed from the other eight items in that a teacher who endorses them indicates that he or she took immediate action to correct the difficulties. We decided that it might be worthwhile to create a second scale that included these two items plus additional items that we would have to develop.

The Reliability procedure was rerun without both these items to determine whether additional revisions needed to be made. The output is shown in Figure 233 (on page 318). After examining the results in Figure 233 and the content of the items, we chose not to eliminate any other items.

Assessing Multiple Constructs

We now want to conduct an item analysis to evaluate whether items a, c, e, g, and i are associated with one scale (Emotion-Focused Coping) and items b, d, f, h, j are associated with a second scale (Problem-Focused Coping). We will conduct these analyses in four stages and discuss the output after describing these four stages.

```
Item-total Statistics

                      Scale          Scale        Corrected
                      Mean          Variance        Item-        Squared        Alpha
                    if Item        if Item         Total        Multiple      if Item
                    Deleted        Deleted       Correlation   Correlation    Deleted

ITEM_A              21.9231        16.1162         .5849         .5130         .6766
ITEM_B              21.9780        16.2662         .4386         .2648         .6964
ITEM_C              22.5495        16.0503         .3672         .3173         .7109
ITEM_D              22.8462        16.5316         .2952         .1759         .7259
ITEM_E              21.6264        17.4366         .3422         .2471         .7127
ITEM_F              21.8681        16.2935         .4766         .5127         .6907
ITEM_G              22.4505        15.4725         .4713         .2896         .6894
ITEM_I              22.0220        15.6440         .5358         .5150         .6788
ITEM_J              23.0000        18.1556         .1778         .1973         .7387


Reliability Coefficients      9 items

Alpha =    .7270        Standardized item alpha =    .7351
```

Figure 232. A rerun of the item analysis without item_h.

```
Item-total Statistics

                      Scale          Scale        Corrected
                      Mean          Variance        Item-        Squared        Alpha
                    if Item        if Item         Total        Multiple      if Item
                    Deleted        Deleted       Correlation   Correlation    Deleted

ITEM_A              19.8901        14.3211         .5899         .4920         .6879
ITEM_B              19.9451        14.7858         .3878         .2024         .7204
ITEM_C              20.5165        14.1414         .3838         .3155         .7239
ITEM_D              20.8132        14.8425         .2771         .1644         .7475
ITEM_E              19.5934        15.7328         .3160         .2362         .7318
ITEM_F              19.8352        14.2281         .5261         .4887         .6954
ITEM_G              20.4176        13.6681         .4795         .2871         .7023
ITEM_I              19.9890        13.6332         .5809         .5103         .6829


Reliability Coefficients      8 items

Alpha =    .7387        Standardized item alpha =    .7494
```

Figure 233. A rerun of the item analysis without item_h and item_j.

Stage 1: Corrected Item-Total Correlations for the Emotion-Focused Coping Items

We first compute correlations for the Emotion-Focused Coping items, which are items a, c, e, g, and i. (See Figure 234 at the top of page 319.) To do so, follow Steps 1 through 9 in our previous example, except use items a, c, e, g, and i only.

Stage 2: Corrected Item-Total Correlations for the Problem-Focused Coping Items

For the Problem-Focused Coping items, follow again Steps 1 through 9, except use items b, d, f, h, and j only. (See Figure 235 on page 319.)

```
Item-total Statistics

                    Scale        Scale      Corrected
                    Mean         Variance   Item-          Squared        Alpha
                    if Item      if Item    Total          Multiple       if Item
                    Deleted      Deleted    Correlation    Correlation    Deleted

ITEM_A              11.4835      6.2969      .5176          .3446          .6233
ITEM_C              12.1099      5.5656      .4415          .3059          .6520
ITEM_E              11.1868      7.0647      .2867          .1749          .7027
ITEM_G              12.0110      5.7443      .4283          .2282          .6562
ITEM_I              11.5824      5.4904      .6089          .4542          .5732




    R E L I A B I L I T Y    A N A L Y S I S    -    S C A L E    (A L P H A)



Reliability Coefficients        5 items

Alpha =    .6937          Standardized item alpha =    .6979
```

Figure 234. The corrected item-total correlations for the Emotion-Focused Coping items.

```
Item-total Statistics

                    Scale        Scale      Corrected
                    Mean         Variance   Item-          Squared        Alpha
                    if Item      if Item    Total          Multiple       if Item
                    Deleted      Deleted    Correlation    Correlation    Deleted

ITEM_B              10.9121      3.7033      .5051          .2969          .3095
ITEM_D              11.7802      3.7734      .3223          .1104          .4427
ITEM_F              10.8022      4.9382      .1522          .1545          .5409
ITEM_H              10.4396      5.0935      .2451          .1679          .4899
ITEM_J              11.9341      4.5956      .2430          .1498          .4895




    R E L I A B I L I T Y    A N A L Y S I S    -    S C A L E    (A L P H A)



Reliability Coefficients        5 items

Alpha =    .5187          Standardized item alpha =    .5162
```

Figure 235. The corrected item-total correlations for the Problem-Focused Coping items.

Stage 3: Computing Correlations between the Emotion-Focused Coping Items and the Problem-Focused Coping Scale

To assess the discriminant validity of the Emotion-Focused Coping items, we need to compute correlations between each item on the Emotion-Focused Coping scale and the total score for the Problem-Focused Coping scale. (See Figure 236 at the top of page 320.) To do so, follow these steps:

1. Create a new variable named **prob_tot** that is the sum of all items on the Problem-Focused Coping scale using the Compute option on the Transform menu. See Lesson 18 for information on how to do this.

Correlations

		PROB_TOT
ITEM_A	Pearson Correlation	.391**
	Sig. (2-tailed)	.000
	N	91
ITEM_C	Pearson Correlation	.168
	Sig. (2-tailed)	.112
	N	91
ITEM_E	Pearson Correlation	.308**
	Sig. (2-tailed)	.003
	N	91
ITEM_G	Pearson Correlation	.333**
	Sig. (2-tailed)	.001
	N	91
ITEM_I	Pearson Correlation	.266*
	Sig. (2-tailed)	.011
	N	91

**. Correlation is significant at the 0.01 level

*. Correlation is significant at the 0.05 level (2-tailed).

Figure 236. The correlation between the Emotion-Focused Coping items and a total Problem-Focused Coping scale.

2. Click **Analyze**, click **Correlation**, then click **Bivariate**.
3. Select **item_a**, **item_c**, **item_e**, **item_g**, and **item_i** by holding down the Ctrl key and clicking on each item.
4. Click ▸ to move the variables to the Variables box.
5. Click **prob_tot**, then click ▸ to move it to the Variables box.
6. Click **Paste**. Type **with** between item_i and prob_tot on the /VARIABLES line. It should read:

    /VARIABLES = item_a item_c item_e item_g item_i with prob_tot

7. Click **Run**.

Stage 4: Computing Correlations between the Problem-Focused Coping Items and the Emotion-Focused Coping Scale

To assess the discriminant validity of the Problem-Focused items, correlations need to be computed between each item on the Problem-Focused Coping scale and the total score for the Emotion-Focused Coping scale. (See Figure 237 at the top of page 321.) To do so, follow the process as in Stage 3 except that you will create a new variable named emo_tot instead of prob_tot. The new variable will be the sum of all items on the Emotion-Focused Coping scale, and you will correlate this new variable with each Problem-Focused Coping item, items b, d, f, h, and j.

Selected SPSS Output for Emotion-Focused and Problem-Focused Coping Items

The outputs for Stages 1 through 4 are shown in Figures 234 through 237. We created Table 53 (on page 321) from the results presented in these figures.

Based on the results in Table 53, it appears that the scales should be revised. For example, item_f is much more correlated with Emotion-Focused Coping than it is with its own scale. Also, item_e is equally strongly related to both coping scales. After considerable thought about the construct system of coping and examination of the content of the items, they were reconceptualized as measuring two related constructs. These are Other-Directed Coping, assessed by items a, c, f, and i, and Self-Directed Coping, measured by items b, d, e, h, and j. Because it is not clear whether item_g reflects a self-directed or other-directed coping strategy, and the correlations between item_g and the two scales did not clearly differentiate it, item_g was omitted from the revised scale.

Correlations

		EMO_TOT
ITEM_B	Pearson Correlation	.344**
	Sig. (2-tailed)	.001
	N	91
ITEM_D	Pearson Correlation	.223*
	Sig. (2-tailed)	.034
	N	91
ITEM_F	Pearson Correlation	.518**
	Sig. (2-tailed)	.000
	N	91
ITEM_H	Pearson Correlation	-.015
	Sig. (2-tailed)	.888
	N	91
ITEM_J	Pearson Correlation	.122
	Sig. (2-tailed)	.248
	N	91

**. Correlation is significant at the 0.01 level

*. Correlation is significant at the 0.05 level (2-tailed).

Figure 237. The correlation between Problem-Focused Coping items and a total Emotion-Focused Coping scale.

Table 53

Correlations of Each Coping Item with Its Own Scale after Removing Focal Item (Bold) and with the Other Scale

	Factors	
Items	Problem-Focused Coping	Emotion-Focused Coping
Problem-Focused Coping items		
b. I tried to develop a step-by-step plan of action to remedy the problems.	**.51**	.34
d. I read, attended workshops, or sought some other educational approach to correct them.	**.32**	.22
f. I sought advice from others on how I should solve the problems.	**.15**	.52
h. I took direct action to try to correct he problems.	**.25**	-.02
j. I put aside other activities so that I could work to solve the problems.	**.24**	.12
Emotion-Focused Coping items		
a. I discussed my frustrations and feelings with person(s) at school.	.39	**.52**
c. I expressed my emotions to my family and close friends.	.17	**.44**
e. I tried to be emotionally honest with myself about the problems.	.31	**.29**
g. I explored the emotions caused by the problems.	.33	**.43**
i. I told someone I could trust about how I felt about the problems	.27	**.61**

We then conducted item analyses on these revised scales using the stages for a measure assessing multiple constructs just outlined. The output for the revised item analysis and correlations are shown in Figure 238 (on page 322).

Based on the results presented in Figure 238, we constructed Table 54 (at the top of page 323). We chose not to make any additional changes to scales after examining Table 54.

Item-total Statistics

	Scale Mean if Item Deleted	Scale Variance if Item Deleted	Corrected Item- Total Correlation	Squared Multiple Correlation	Alpha if Item Deleted
ITEM_B	11.1538	4.0650	.4934	.2630	.4391
ITEM_D	12.0220	4.2884	.2760	.0817	.5862
ITEM_E	10.8022	4.9382	.3243	.1163	.5409
ITEM_H	10.6813	5.2640	.3222	.1372	.5470
ITEM_J	12.1758	4.6354	.3424	.1339	.5305

Reliability Coefficients   5 items

Alpha =   .5857   Standardized item alpha =   .5974

Correlations

		OTH_TOT
ITEM_B	Pearson Correlation	.262*
	Sig. (2-tailed)	.012
	N	91
ITEM_D	Pearson Correlation	.149
	Sig. (2-tailed)	.160
	N	91
ITEM_E	Pearson Correlation	.156
	Sig. (2-tailed)	.139
	N	91
ITEM_H	Pearson Correlation	-.085
	Sig. (2-tailed)	.423
	N	91
ITEM_J	Pearson Correlation	.018
	Sig. (2-tailed)	.865
	N	91

*. Correlation is significant at the 0.05 level (2-tailed).

Item-total Statistics

	Scale Mean if Item Deleted	Scale Variance if Item Deleted	Corrected Item- Total Correlation	Squared Multiple Correlation	Alpha if Item Deleted
ITEM_A	8.6593	4.7827	.6438	.4730	.7186
ITEM_C	9.2857	4.2730	.4895	.2877	.8041
ITEM_F	8.6044	4.6195	.5984	.4559	.7329
ITEM_I	8.7582	4.1631	.6919	.4789	.6827

Reliability Coefficients   4 items

Alpha =   .7866   Standardized item alpha =   .7989

Correlations

		SELF_TOT
ITEM_A	Pearson Correlation	.223*
	Sig. (2-tailed)	.034
	N	91
ITEM_C	Pearson Correlation	.075
	Sig. (2-tailed)	.478
	N	91
ITEM_F	Pearson Correlation	.147
	Sig. (2-tailed)	.163
	N	91
ITEM_I	Pearson Correlation	.148
	Sig. (2-tailed)	.163
	N	91

*. Correlation is significant at the 0.05 level (2-tailed).

Figure 238. Results of item analysis for revised Other-Directed Coping and Self-Directed Coping scales.

Table 54

Correlations of Each Coping Item with Its Own Scale after Removing Focal Item (Bold) and with the Other Scale

	Factors	
Item	Self-Directed	Other-Directed
Self-Directed (SD) items		
b. I tried to develop a step-by-step plan of action to remedy the problems.	**.49**	.26
d. I read, attended workshops, or sought some other educational approach to correct them.	**.28**	.15
e. I tried to be emotionally honest with myself about the problems.	**.32**	.16
h. I took direct action to try to correct he problems.	**.32**	-.08
j. I put aside other activities so that I could work to solve the problems.	**.34**	.02
Other-Directed (OD) items		
a. I discussed my frustrations and feelings with person(s) at school.	.22	**.64**
c. I expressed my emotions to my family and close friends.	.08	**.49**
f. I sought advice from others on how I should solve the problems.	.15	**.60**
i. I told someone I could trust about how I felt about the problems.	.15	**.69**

Using SPSS Graphs to Display the Results

No graphics procedures are necessary to display the results of the item analysis procedure.

Two APA Results Sections

We demonstrate how to write a sample results section for both a single construct application and a multiple constructs application.

Results for a Single Construct

Item analyses were conducted on the 10 items hypothesized to assess Active Coping. Initially, each of the 10 items was correlated with the total score for Active Coping (with the item removed). All the correlations were greater than .30 except for two items: "I put aside other activities so that I could work to solve the problems" (r = .20) and "I took direct action to try to correct the problems" (r = .11). These two items differed in content from the other eight items in that a teacher who endorses them indicates that he or she took immediate action to correct the difficulties.

Based on these results, the two items assessing immediate coping methods were eliminated from the scale. However, these items represent an important coping approach. Additional items should be developed to create a separate scale to assess immediate coping strategies.

Item-total correlations for the revised eight-item scale yielded only one correlation that was less than .30: "I tried to read, attend workshops, or sought some other educational approach to correct them." This item was retained in that its content did not appear to differ markedly from the content of the other seven items. The revised scale was renamed "Preliminary Coping Strategies" to reflect the content of the items.

Coefficient alpha for the Preliminary Coping Strategies scale was .74. Because the same sample was used to conduct the item analyses and to assess coefficient alpha, the reliability estimate is likely to be an overestimate of the population coefficient alpha.

Results for Multiple Constructs

Item analyses were conducted on the 10 items hypothesized to assess Emotion-Focused and Problem-Focused Coping. Initially, each item was correlated with its own scale (with the item removed) and with the other coping scale. In two cases, items were more highly correlated with the other coping scale than their own scale. The two items were "I sought advice from others on how I should solve the problems," and "I tried to be emotionally honest with myself about the problems." Based on these results and additional item analyses, the two scales were redefined based on 9 of the 10 items and renamed as Other-Directed Coping and Self-Directed Coping.

To assess the convergent and discriminant validity of these newly derived coping scales, we again correlated each item with its own scale (with the item removed) and with the other coping scale. The results of these analyses are shown in Table 54. In support of the measure's validity, items always were more highly correlated with their own scale than with the other scale.

Coefficient alphas were computed to obtain internal consistency estimates of reliability for these two coping scales. The alphas for the Self-Directed and Other-Directed Coping scales were .59 and .79, respectively. These values might be overestimates of the population alphas because the same sample was used to conduct the item analyses and to compute the reliability estimates.

Alternative Analyses

With item analyses, researchers are attempting to determine if items are associated with particular constructs. An alternative statistical approach is to use factor analysis. With factor analysis, all items associated with the same construct should have high loadings on the same factor and relatively low loadings on other factors. Factor analyses of items can be more precisely conducted using confirmatory methods rather than the exploratory factor analysis approaches available with SPSS. Problems may emerge using factor analysis if items have limited response scales and the items are differentially skewed.

Exercises

The data for Exercises 1 through 4 are in the data file named *Lesson 37 Exercise File 1* on the Student Disk. The data are based on the following research problem.

Terrill is interested in assessing how much women value their careers. He develops a 12-item scale, the Saxon Career Values Scale (SCVS). He has 100 college women take the SCVS. All of the items reflect the value women place on having a career versus having a family. Students are asked to respond to each on a 4-point scale with 0 indicating "disagree" and 3 indicating "agree" The items are shown in Table 55 (at the top of page 325).

1. Reverse-scale the appropriate items so a higher total score reflects a greater emphasis on career.
2. Conduct an item analysis for the SCVS scale. From the output, identify the following:
   a. The corrected item total correlation for Item 6
   b. The correlation between Item 5 and Item 9
   c. The mean for Item 10
3. Do the items on the current form of the scale seem appropriate? Justify your answer based on the statistical indices.
4. Write a results section reporting your analyses.

Table 55
Items on the Saxon Career Values Scale

Variables	Definition
q01	I consider marriage and having a family to be more important than a career.*
q02	To me, marriage and family are as important as having a career.*
q03	I prefer to pursue my career without the distractions of marriage, children, or a household.
q04	I would rather have a career than a family.
q05	I often think about what type of job I'll have 10 years from now.
q06	I could be happy without a career.*
q07	I would feel unfulfilled without a career.
q08	I don't need to have a career to be fulfilled.*
q09	I would leave my career to raise my children.*
q10	Having a career would interfere with my family responsibilities.*
q11	Planning for and succeeding in a career is one of my primary goals.
q12	I consider myself to be very career-minded.

*Items are reverse-scaled to create a total score.

The data for Exercises 5 through 9 are in the data file named *Lesson 37 Exercise File 2* on the Student Disk. The data are based on the following research problem.

Jessica is interested in assessing humor. She develops a 10-item measure in which some items represent humor demeaning to others (Don Rickles items), while other items reflect self-deprecating humor (Woody Allen items). She administers her measure to 100 college students. Students are asked to respond to each on a 5-point scale with 1 indicating "disagree" and 5 indicating "agree." Table 56 shows the variables in the data set.

Table 56
Items from a Humor Measure

Variables	Definition
item01	I like to make fun of others. (Don Rickles)
item02	I make people laugh by making fun of myself. (Woody Allen)
item03	People find me funny when I make jokes about others. (Don Rickles)
item04	I talk about my problems to make people laugh. (Woody Allen)
item05	I frequently make others the target of my jokes. (Don Rickles)
item06	People find me funny when I tell them about my failings. (Woody Allen)
item07	I love to get people to laugh by using sarcasm. (Don Rickles)
item08	I am funniest when I talk about my own weaknesses. (Woody Allen)
item09	I make people laugh by exposing other people's stupidities. (Don Rickles)
item10	I am funny when I tell others about the dumb things I have done. (Woody Allen)

5. Conduct an item analysis on this scale for a single dimension. (Note. You will want to reverse-scale either the Woody Allen or Don Rickles items, but not both sets of items.)
6. Conduct the analysis again, this time computing item-total correlations for separate scales: (1) the Don Rickles scale and (2) the Woody Allen scale.

7. Compute correlations between each item and the other scale to assess discriminant validity.
8. Create a table to summarize your item analysis for the Don Rickles and Woody Allen scales.
9. Write a results section based on your analyses.

Nonparametric Procedures

Unit 10 describes a set of nonparametric tests. They are useful for problems that include one or more variables measured on a nominal or ordinal scale. These procedures can apply to problems involving interval or ratio data if the distributional assumptions associated with parametric procedures are not met. Even if a parametric test is relatively robust to violation of a distributional assumption, the nonparametric alternative may be more powerful for certain types of population distributions.

Two of the nonparametric tests—the binomial test and the chi-square test—evaluate whether the proportions associated with categories on a single variable are equal to hypothesized values. The remaining techniques evaluate relationships between two variables. One of the two variables is always categorical, while the other variable will be either categorical or quantitative. The lessons that discuss techniques for evaluating relationships between variables are divided according to whether the categorical variable is based on independent or related samples and on the number of samples.

Here is a brief introduction to each lesson of Unit 10.

- Lesson 38 introduces the binomial test, which evaluates whether the proportions associated with a two-category variable are equal to hypothesized values.
- Lesson 39 presents the one-sample chi-square test. It evaluates whether the proportions associated with a variable with two or more categories are equal to hypothesized values.
- Lesson 40 deals with two-way contingency table analysis. We will use the Crosstabs procedure to evaluate the relationship between two qualitative variables. Each qualitative variable may have two or more categories.
- Lesson 41 discusses nonparametric procedures for analyzing two independent samples. We will focus on the Mann-Whitney U test, which evaluates differences on an outcome variable between the two independent samples.
- Lesson 42 summarizes nonparametric procedures used to analyze two or more independent samples. We will focus on the Kruskal-Wallis test and the median test, which evaluate the differences on an outcome variable among two or more independent samples.
- Lesson 43 examines nonparametric procedures for analyzing two related samples. Here, we will discuss the McNemar, Sign, and Wilcoxon tests. These tests evaluate differences between paired observations on an outcome variable.
- Lesson 44 describes nonparametric procedures used to analyze two or more related samples. We will describe analyses using the Cochran test, the Friedman test and Kendall's W (coefficient of concordance). These statistics assess differences among levels of a within-subjects factor on an outcome variable.

The Binomial Test

The binomial test evaluates whether the proportion of individuals who fall into the categories of a two-category variable are equal to hypothesized values. The test is more likely to yield significance if the sample proportions for the two categories differ greatly from the hypothesized proportions and if the sample size is large.

In SPSS, we make a hypothesis about only one of the two categories, the category specified for the variable's first case in the data file. SPSS calls the hypothesized proportion the test proportion. SPSS computes the hypothesized proportion for the second category by subtracting the hypothesized proportion for the first category from the value of 1.

In many applications, the test proportion is hypothesized to be .50. This value is also the SPSS default option. However, it is possible to specify values other than .50 based on previous research, theory, research methods, or speculation.

An SPSS data file for the binomial test may be structured two ways. With the standard method, the SPSS data file contains as many cases as individuals. For each case, there is a single variable that can have two values that represent the two categories for the variable of interest. With the weighted cases method, the SPSS data file contains two cases, one for each category, and two variables. The two variables are the focal variable with two values for the two categories and the weight variable containing frequencies for the two categories.

Applying the Binomial Test

We consider two applications of the binomial test:

- Binomial test with equal proportions
- Binomial test with unequal proportions

Binomial Test with Equal Proportions

Tucker is interested in assessing whether 1-year-old girls prefer boys or girls. He randomly forms triplets of children from a sample of 120 1-year-old girls and 60 1-year-old boys. Within each triplet, there are two girls and one boy. One of the two girls is randomly determined to be the focal subject, and the other girl and the boy are designated as companions. Each triplet is placed in a playroom for 10 minutes and observed behind a one-way mirror. An observer assesses whether the focal subject spends more time closer to the male companion or the female companion. The gender preference for each focal subject is recorded.

Tucker's SPSS data file can have one of two types of structure. With the standard structure, the data file consists of 60 cases to represent the 60 focal subjects. Each girl is measured on a single variable sexpref. The scores on sexpref are 1 = prefer girl and 2 = prefer boy. The values of 1 and 2 are arbitrary and could have been any other set of values such as 0 and 1. With the weighted cases structure, Tucker would have two cases, representing the two categories. Each case would have scores on two variables: sexpref, with one case having a score of 1 and the other case having a score of 2, and a weight variable. Values for the weight variable represent the number of individuals who are classified as belonging to the categories defined by sexpref. If the weighted cases method is used, you must weight the cases using the Weight Cases option under Data from the main menu before conducting a binomial test.

For Tucker's problem the test proportion is .50. If the first case in the data file is a score of 1, then the test proportion would be the hypothesized proportion for prefer girl. Of course because the proportion is .50, it does not make any difference whether the hypothesized proportion refers to prefer girl or prefer boy because they are both equal to .50.

Binomial Test with Unequal Proportions

Based on past research, Pam knows that children who are seated in a room with four doors—one in front of them, one to their left, one to their right, and one behind them—are equally likely to pick any door when asked which door they would choose when leaving the room. As part of a larger research program, she wants to demonstrate that children labeled by a psychologist as oppositional are more likely to choose the door behind them. To determine whether her conjecture is correct, she conducts a study with 80 oppositional children. On the basis of these data, Pam constructs a data file using the standard method by creating a single variable, door, for the 80 cases. The scores on door are 0 = other door and 1 = door behind. The first case in the data file has a 0 for other door. The values of 0 and 1 are arbitrary and could have been any other set of values such as 1 and 2. For this problem, the test proportion is the hypothesized proportion associated with door = 0, the first value for door in data file. Previous research showed that children pick the four doors equally often in general. Because there are four doors, the test proportion for the other door is .75 (3 out of 4 doors).

These data could also be entered using the weighted cases method. With this method, Pam would have two cases, representing the two categories. Each case would have scores on two variables: door, with the first case having a score of 0 and the second case having a score of 1, and a weight variable. Values for the weight variable represent the number of individuals who are classified as belonging to the categories defined by door. If the weighted cases method is used, you must weight the cases using the Weight Cases option under Data from the main menu before conducting a binomial test.

Understanding the Binomial Test

The binomial test procedure uses a binomial distribution if the sample size is 25 or less and a z test if the sample size is 26 or more. Let's discuss the underlying assumptions for these tests and effect size statistics.

Assumptions Underlying the Binomial Test

Both tests—the test using a binomial distribution and the z test—assume independence. In addition, the z test also requires a relatively large sample size to yield accurate results.

To meet this assumption, studies should be designed to prevent dependency in the data. Research participants should be sampled independently, participate in the study independently, and should contribute only a single score to the data. If the assumption is violated, the test is likely to yield inaccurate results.

*Assumption 2: The z Test Yields Relatively Accurate Results to the Extent That
the Sample Size Is Large and the Test Proportion Is Close to .50*

The z test is likely to yield fairly accurate results if the test proportion is .50 because the z test is performed only if sample size exceeds 25 cases. However, to the extent that the hypothesized proportion deviates from .50, you should have larger sample sizes.

One guideline for sample size would be to apply the expected-frequency-greater-than-five standard. Let P_{small} be equal to the test proportion or 1 minus the test proportion, whichever is smaller. Then the minimum sample size should be equal to $5 / P_{small}$. For example, if the test proportion is .90, then $P_{small} = 1 - .90 = .10$ because .10 is smaller than .90, and the minimum sample size is $5 / .10 = 50$.

Computing an Effect Size Index

SPSS does not report an effect size index. However, a simple and elegant effect size index for this test is the difference between the observed and the hypothesized (test) proportion.

$$Effect\ Size = P_{observed} - P_{hypothesized}$$

The Data Set

The data file is named *Lesson 38 Data File 1*, and it uses the weighted cases structure. The data are based on the oppositional children example. For this application, there are two possible outcomes, door behind and other door. The description of the variables in the file is given in Table 57.

Table 57
Variables in Lesson 38 Data File 1

Variables	Definition
door	Children can choose either the door behind them or another door.
	0 = other door
	1 = door behind
number	Number of oppositional children who picked category 0 or category 1

The Research Question

The research question can be asked in the following way: Is the proportion associated with oppositional children choosing the door behind them different from .25, as suggested based on previous research?

Conducting a Binomial Test

Before these data can be analyzed, the cases must be weighted by the values in the number variable by conducting the following steps:

1. Click **Data**, then click **Weight Cases**. You will see the Weight Cases dialog box shown in Figure 239.

Figure 239. The Weight Cases dialog box.

2. Click **Weight cases by**.
3. Click **number**, then click ▶ to move the variable into the Frequency Variable box.
4. Click **OK**.

To conduct a binomial test, follow these steps:

1. Click **Analyze**, click **Nonparametric Tests**, then click **Binomial Test**. You will see the Binomial Test dialog box as shown in Figure 240.

Figure 240. The Binomial Test dialog box.

2. Click **door**, then click ▶ to move it to the Test Variable List box.
3. Change the Test Proportion to **.75**. This value is the hypothesized proportion associated with the value of 0 (other door), which is the first case in the data file.
4. Click **OK**.

In the Binomial Test dialog box, there are two options in the Define Dichotomy area. The default option is "Get from data." The second option is "Cut point." If you are interested in creating a two-category variable from a quantitative variable, you can click on the "Cut point" option and enter a value such that any score less than the cut point is assigned to one category and any score greater than or equal to the cut point is assigned to the second category. There is no change made to the variable in your data file.

Selected SPSS Output for the Binomial Test

The results of the analysis are shown in Figure 241.

Binomial Test

		Category	N	Observed Prop.	Test Prop.	Asymp. Sig. (1-tailed)
Choice of door	Group 1	Other Door	55	.6875	.75	.123[a]
	Group 2	Door Behind	25	.31		
	Total		80	1.00		

a. Alternative hypothesis states that the proportion of cases in the first group < .75.

b. Based on Z Approximation.

Figure 241. The results of the binomial test.

If the test proportion is .50, SPSS computes a two-tailed p-value. If the test proportion is a value other than .50, such as .75 as in our example, SPSS computes a one-tailed p-value. You may want to conduct a two-tailed test since two-tailed tests are more frequently applied. A two-tailed p-value can be computed if the test is based on the z-approximation (sample size of greater than 25) by multiplying the one-tailed p-value by 2. For our example, the two-tailed p-value would be $.246 = (2)(.123)$.

In this example, the null hypothesis is not rejected using the traditional alpha level of .05 using either a one-tailed or a two-tailed test. More specifically, the results for this example indicate that the observed proportion for other door of .6875 is not significantly different from the hypothesized proportion of .75. Alternatively stated, the results suggest that the observed proportion for door behind of .3125 (1 - .6875) is not significantly different from the hypothesized value of .25 (1 - .75).

It should be noted that you could not calculate directly a two-tailed p-value from a one-tailed p-value based on the exact binomial (sample size of less than 26). Consult a nonparametric textbook to determine how to compute a two-tailed p-value based on the binomial distribution.

Using SPSS Graphs to Display the Results

Because of the simplicity of the data used in the binomial test, it is probably unnecessary to graphically represent the data. Nevertheless, a simple bar chart allows readers to see the proportions associated with each category (see Lesson 19 for steps to create a bar chart). Figure 242 (at the top of page 333) shows the frequencies associated with the door choices.

An APA Results Section

Previous research with nonoppositional children indicated that they would choose the door behind them 25% of the time. We hypothesized that oppositional children would choose the door behind them with a higher percentage than 25%. A one-tailed, $\underline{z}$-approximation test was conducted to assess whether the population proportion for oppositional children is .25. The observed proportion of .31 did not differ significantly from the hypothesized value of .25, one-tailed $\underline{p} = .123$. Although a larger sample size might have yielded significance, our results suggest that oppositional children do not differ dramatically from nonoppositional children in the percent of times that they choose the door behind them.

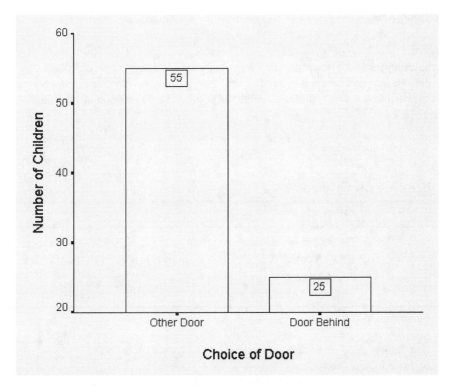

Figure 242. The frequencies of children who chose the door behind versus some other door.

Alternative Analyses

The binomial test discussed in this lesson is very similar to the one-sample chi-square test, which we will cover in Lesson 39. With both tests, the focus is on investigating whether the proportions associated with categories of a single variable are equal to a hypothesized set of values. The difference is that the variable of interest may have two or more categories for a one-sample chi-square test, while the variable of interest for the binomial test must have two categories.

For variables with two categories, analyses could be conducted with either the binomial test or the one-sample chi-square test. The binomial test procedure is preferred for two reasons. First, for sample sizes of 26 or greater, the two tests use related test statistics, the χ^2 and the z. Squaring the z-test value should produce the χ^2 value and yield comparable results (same p-value) except that in SPSS, the one-sample chi-square procedure does not apply a continuity correction, while the z for the binomial test procedure does. Because the continuity correction procedure is used with the binomial test procedure, the binomial test is preferred. Second, for sample sizes of 25 or less, the p-value for the binomial test procedure is based on the binomial distribution and is exact if the assumptions are met. The p-value for the one-sample chi-square procedure is based on the chi-square distribution and is an approximation to the p-value based on the binomial distribution. Consequently, the binomial test procedure is preferred for a study with a relatively small sample.

Exercises

Exercises 1 through 3 are based on the data in the data file named *Lesson 38 Exercise File 1* on the Student Disk. The data are based on the following study.

Tucker is interested in assessing whether 1-year-old girls prefer boys or girls. He randomly forms triplets of children from a sample of 120 1-year-old girls and 60 1-year-old boys. Within each triplet, there are two girls and one boy. One of the two girls is randomly determined to be the focal subject, while the other girl and the boy are designated as companions. Each triplet is placed in a playroom for 10 minutes and observed behind a one-way mirror. An observer assesses whether the focal subject spends more time closer to the male companion or more time closer to the female companion. The gender preference for each focal subject is recorded.

The data for the problem are on your disk in the weighted cases structure. There are two cases for the two possible outcomes, prefer girl and prefer boy. The description of the variables in the file is given in Table 58.

Table 58

Variables in Lesson 38 Exercise Data Set 1

Variables	Definition
sexpref	Sexpref has two levels:
	1 = prefer girl
	2 = prefer boy
number	number of 1-year-olds who preferred to play with a specified gender

1. Use the weighted cases method to weight the data file by the number of cases before conducting the analysis.
2. Conduct a binomial test to evaluate Tucker's hypothesis.
3. Write a results section based on your analyses.

Exercises 4 through 6 are based on the data in the data file named *Lesson 38 Exercise File 2* on the Student Disk. The data are based on the following study.

After reviewing the literature on depression and childbirth, Moe claims that half of all women become less depressed and the other half become more depressed as a function of childbirth. Emma believes that Moe is wrong, and she audiotapes interviews with 60 women before and after childbirth. The interviews include no questions pertaining to childbirth or children. After the interviews, Emma deletes any references on the tape that indicate whether the women are anticipating or have given birth to their babies. Emma then asks a group of trained clinicians to listen to the 60 pairs of interviews. For interviews with 30 of the women, the clinicians listen to the before-birth interview first and the after-birth interview second, and for interviews with the other 30 women, the clinicians listen initially to the after-birth interview and then to the before-birth interview. The trained clinicians come to a consensus judgment about whether each woman sounded less depressed or more depressed in the first interview. Emma is interested in whether the population proportion for women who become less depressed after birth (depress = -1) is equal to the population proportion for woman who become more depressed after birth (depress = 1).

4. What is the test value?
5. Conduct a binomial test to evaluate whether the population proportion for women who become less depressed is equal to the population proportion for woman who become more depressed. From the output, identify the following:
    a. The observed frequency of women who become more depressed
    b. The *p*-value
    c. Proportion of women who become more depressed
6. Write a results section based on your analyses.

One-Sample Chi-Square Test

The one-sample chi-square test evaluates whether the proportions of individuals who fall into categories of a variable are equal to hypothesized values. The variable may have two or more categories. The one-sample chi-square test is more likely to yield significance if the sample proportions for the categories differ greatly from the hypothesized proportions and if the sample size is large.

The categories for the variable either may have quantitative meaning so that one category reflects a higher value than another category or may differentiate only between qualitative groupings of individuals. For example, categories may indicate what type of explanation students prefer when they are learning algebra: 1 = graphical explanation of how a method works; 2 = equational explanation of how method works; or 3 = explanation through real-world applications. The one-sample chi-square test does not recognize any quantitative distinction among categories, but simply assesses whether the proportions associated with the categories are significantly different from hypothesized proportions.

When conducting a one-sample chi-square test using SPSS, you must specify the expected frequencies associated with the categories on the variable of interest. To know the expected frequencies, you must first be able to specify the values for the hypothesized proportions.

If we hypothesize equal proportions, then the hypothesized proportion for any category is equal to 1 divided by the number of categories. If the hypothesized proportions are not equal, they must be determined based on previous research, theory, research methods, or speculation.

The expected frequency for any category is the product of the hypothesized proportion times the total sample size for the study. If the hypothesized proportions are equal, the expected frequencies will be equal. If the hypothesized proportions are unequal, the expected frequencies will be unequal.

An SPSS data file for the one-sample chi-square test may be structured two ways. With the standard method, the SPSS data file contains as many cases as individuals. For each case, there is a single variable that can have two or more values that represent the two or more categories for the variable of interest. With the weighted cases method, the SPSS data file contains as many cases as there are categories and two variables. The two variables are the focal variable with two or more values and the weight variable containing the frequencies for the categories. We'll describe the standard and weighted cases methods in our first example.

Applying the One-Sample Chi-Square Test

Here we'll examine two applications of the one-sample chi-square tests.

- Testing an hypothesis with equal proportions
- Testing an hypothesis with unequal proportions

Testing an Hypothesis with Equal Proportions

After reviewing the literature on depression and childbirth, Moe claims that a third of women become less depressed, a third become neither less depressed nor more depressed, and a third become more depressed as a function of childbirth. Emma believes that Moe is wrong, and she audiotapes interviews with 60 women before and after childbirth. The interviews include no questions pertaining to childbirth or children. After the interviews, Emma deletes any reference on the tape that indicates whether the women are anticipating or have given birth to their babies. Emma then asks a group of trained clinicians to listen to the 60 pairs of interviews. For interviews with 30 of the women, the clinicians listen to the before-birth interview first and the after-birth interview second and for interviews with the other 30 women, the clinicians listen initially to the after-birth interview and then to the before-birth interview. The trained clinicians come to a consensus judgment about whether each woman sounded less depressed, neither less nor more depressed, or more depressed in the first interview.

For this problem, the expected frequencies for all categories are equal. Emma is attempting to present evidence that evaluates Moe's claim that a third of women after giving birth are less depressed, a third are unchanged, and a third become more depressed.

Using the standard structure, Emma creates a data file with 60 cases to represent the 60 women. Each woman is measured on a single variable, status. The scores on status are -1 = more depressed before birth, 0 = same amount of depression before and after birth, and 1 = more depressed after birth. The values of -1, 0, and 1 are arbitrary, and other values could have been chosen.

If Emma had used the weighted cases structure, she would have had three cases representing the three categories. Each case would have scores on two variables: status with categories of -1, 0, and 1 for the three cases and a weight variable. A value for the weight variable represents the number of individuals who are classified as belonging to the category represented by that case. If you use the weighted cases method, you must weight the cases using the Weight Cases option under Data from the main menu before conducting a one-sample chi-square test.

Testing an Hypothesis with Unequal Proportions

Based on past research, Pam knows that children who are seated in a room with four doors—one in front of them, one to their left, one to their right, and one behind them— are equally likely to pick any door when asked which door they would choose when leaving the room. As part of a larger research program, Pam wants to demonstrate that children labeled by a psychologist as oppositional are more likely to choose the door behind them. To test her hypothesis, she conducts a study with 80 oppositional children and creates a data file that includes a single variable, door, for the 80 cases. The categories on door are 0 = any other door and 1 = door behind. The expected frequency for the 0 cell is 60, while expected frequency for the 1 cell is 20. These expected frequencies are based on the results of previous research that showed the doors are picked equally by children in general. Because there are four doors, the hypothesized proportions for door behind is .25 (1 out of 4 doors), and the hypothesized proportion for other door is .75 (3 out of 4 doors). The expected frequency is the hypothesized proportion times the number of cases: 20 [= (.25) (80)] for door behind and 60 [= (.75) (80)] for the other door.

TIP

For variables with two categories, analyses can be conducted with either the binomial test or the one-sample chi-square test, but the binomial test procedure is preferred. To see why, read the "Alternative Analyses" section in Lesson 38.

Understanding the One-Sample Chi-Square Test

If the resulting chi-square value is significant and the variable has more than two levels, follow-up tests may be conducted. The methods employed in these follow-up tests are conceptually similar to those used to conduct post hoc tests for a one-way ANOVA to evaluate differences in means among three or more levels of a factor (see Lesson 24).

Assumptions Underlying the One-Sample Chi-Square Test

Assumption 1: The Observations Must Be from a Random Sample, and the Scores Associated with the Observation Are Independent of Each Other

To meet this assumption, experiments should be designed to prevent dependency in the data. Research participants should be sampled independently, participate in the study independently, and contribute only a single score to the data. If the assumption is violated, the test is likely to yield inaccurate results.

Assumption 2: The One-Sample Chi-Square Test Yields a Test Statistic That Is Approximately Distributed as a Chi-Square When the Sample Size Is Relatively Large

It is important to examine the expected frequencies on the SPSS output when conducting this test to assess whether the sample size is sufficiently large. In general, the test should yield relatively accurate results if the expected frequencies are greater than or equal to 5 for 80% or more of the categories.

Although many textbooks indicate that the resulting chi-square value should be corrected for lack of continuity, SPSS does not apply this correction. You should use the binomial test procedure (Lesson 38) if the variable of interest has only two categories because the binomial procedure does apply the continuity correction.

Computing an Effect Size Statistic

SPSS does not supply an effect size index. However, an effect size index can be easily computed based on the reported statistics:

$$Effect\ Size = \frac{x^2}{(Total\ Sample\ Size\ Across\ all\ Categories)\ (Number\ of\ Categories\ \text{-}1)}$$

The coefficient can range in value from 0 to 1. A value of 0 indicates that the sample proportions are exactly equal to the hypothesized proportions, while a value of 1 indicates that the sample proportions are as different as possible from the hypothesized proportions.

The Data Set

The data used to illustrate the one-sample chi-square test are based on the postpartum depression example. The results of the study, the hypothesized proportions, and the expected frequencies are shown in Table 59.

Table 59

Results of the Postpartum Depression Study

Depression after birth in comparison with before birth	Observed frequencies	Hypothesized proportions	Expected frequencies
Less depressed	14	.33	20
Neither less nor more depressed	33	.33	20
More depressed	13	.33	20

The SPSS data file is structured using the standard method. There are 60 cases in the SPSS data file, one for each woman in the study. For each case, the woman's status on change in depression is indicated on the status variable as shown in Table 60. (A second variable, statusr, is included on the file to illustrate how to conduct tests with unequal expected frequencies.) The data are on the Student Disk in *Lesson 39 Data File 1*.

Table 60

Variables in Lesson 39 Exercise Data Set 1

Variables	Definition
status	status has three categories:
	-1 = Less depressed
	0 = Same amount of depression
	1 = More depressed
statusr	statusr has two categories:
	0 = Same amount of depression
	1 = More or less depressed

A second approach, the weighted cases approach, requires fewer entries to create your data file. With this approach, there would be three cases to represent the three possible categories. There would be two variables in the file (ignoring the statusr variable). A variable named status could be defined with three categories (-1, 0, and 1) for the three depression categories. A second variable, number, would contain the frequencies (14, 33, 13) associated with the three categories.

The Research Question

The research question can be asked several different ways.

1. Are women equally likely to show an increase, no change, or a decrease in depression as a function of childbirth?
2. Are the proportions associated with a decrease, no change, and an increase in depression from before to after childbirth the same?

Conducting a One-Sample Chi-Square Test

Now, we will illustrate how to conduct an overall chi-square test, follow-up tests with equal expected frequencies, and follow-up tests with unequal expected frequencies.

Conducting the Overall Chi-Square Test

Conduct the following steps to obtain an overall chi-square test using the standard structure method. If the data file used the weighted cases method, the cases must be weighted following the procedure described in Lesson 38.

1. Click **Analyze**, click **Nonparametric Tests**, then click **Chi Square**. The Chi-Square Test dialog box is shown in Figure 243 (at the top of page 339).
2. Click **status**, then click ▶ to move to the Test Variable List box.
3. Click **OK**.

Figure 243. The Chi-Square Test dialog box.

Selected SPSS Output for One-Sample Chi-Square Test

You will see the results of the analysis in Figure 244.

Postpartum Depression

	Observed N	Expected N	Residual
less depressed	14	20.0	-6.0
same	33	20.0	13.0
more depressed	13	20.0	-7.0
Total	60		

Test Statistics

	Postpartum Depression
Chi-Square[a]	12.700
df	2
Asymp. Sig.	.002

a. 0 cells (.0%) have expected frequencies less than 5. The minimum expected cell frequency is 20.0.

Figure 244. The results of the chi-square analysis with equal frequencies.

The results indicate that the sample proportions are significantly different from the hypothesized values of 1/3, 1/3, and 1/3, χ^2 (2, $N = 60$) = 12.70, $p = .002$.

In addition an effect size statistic can be computed:

$$Effect\ Size = \frac{12.7}{(60)\ (3 - 1)} = .11$$

The observed frequencies of 14, 33, and 13 tend to support Moe's original hypothesis that women are not more or less depressed after childbirth. The effect size of .11 indicates that the observed frequencies (Observed N on the output) deviate somewhat from the expected frequencies (Expected N).

TIP

In the Chi Square Test dialog box, there are two options in the Expected Range area. The default option is "Get from data." The second option is "Use specified range." If you are interested in evaluating a more limited number of categories for a variable and these categories are within some restricted range of values, then you should click on Use specified range, and indicate the lower and upper values of the range in the appropriate boxes. For example, if you were interested in the categories of -1 and 0 on status rather than -1, 0, and 1, you would type -1 in the lower box and 0 in the upper box.

It might be useful to conduct two follow-up one-sample chi-square tests to demonstrate that the initial significant result is not due to differences in proportion between the less depressed and more depressed women, but due to the disproportional number of women in the 0 category. We'll do those tests now.

Follow-Up Tests with Equal Expected Frequencies

The first follow-up test assesses whether the proportion of women who become more depressed differs from the proportion of women who become less depressed. In other words, we want to ignore the women who do not change on depression. To conduct this analysis, we must tell SPSS to select the cases that have scores of -1 or 1 on status.

To select these cases, conduct the following steps:

1. Click **Data**, then click **Select Cases**.
2. In the Select Cases dialog box, click **If condition is satisfied**, and click **If**.
3. In the Select Cases: If dialog box, indicate what cases to select by typing **status = -1** or **status = 1**.
4. Click **Continue**.
5. Click **OK**.

Now you are ready to conduct your chi-square test as previously described. To conduct the test, perform the following steps:

1. Click **Analyze**, then click **Nonparametric Tests**, and click **Chi-Square**.
2. If **status** is not in the box labeled Test Variable List, click **status** and move it to this box.
3. Click **OK**.

Selected SPSS Output for One-Sample Chi-Square Test

You will see the results of the analysis in Figure 245.

The results indicate that the test is nonsignificant, $\chi^2 (1, N = 27) = 0.04, p = .847$, and the sample proportions are very similar to each other.

Postpartum Depression

	Observed N	Expected N	Residual
less depressed	14	13.5	.5
more depressed	13	13.5	-.5
Total	27		

Test Statistics

	Postpartum Depression
Chi-Square[a]	.037
df	1
Asymp. Sig.	.847

a. 0 cells (.0%) have expected frequencies less than 5. The minimum expected cell frequency is 13.5.

Figure 245. The results of the chi-square analysis with equal frequencies.

Follow-Up Tests with Unequal Expected Frequencies

For this second test, we want to demonstrate that there is a significant difference from Moe's expectations for the same-amount-of-depression category and for the combined categories of less depressed and more depressed.

The expected frequencies for the two cells are 20, or one-third of 60, for the same-amount-of-depression category, and 40, or two-thirds of 60, for the combined category of less depressed and more depressed. To perform this test, the variable statusr in the data set is analyzed. Statusr has a score of 0 for same amount of depression or a score of 1 for less depressed and more depressed. (We have included the variable statusr in the data file for ease of use. It would not have been very difficult to create it based on the status variable using the Transform option.)

Follow these steps to complete the analysis:

1. Click **Data**, click **Select Cases**. Click **All Cases** to select all 60 cases for analysis. Click **OK**.
2. Click **Analyze**, click **Nonparametric Test**, then click **Chi-Square**. Click the reset button if you need to clear any variables from any of the boxes.
3. Click **statusr**, then click ▸ to move it to the Test Variable List box.
4. Click **Values** in the Expected Values area.
5. Type **20** in the Values text box to indicate the expected frequency associated with the smallest value of the variable of interest.
6. Click **Add**.
7. Type **40** in the Values text box to indicate the expected frequency associated with the next smallest value of the variable of interest.
8. Click **Add**.
9. Click **OK**.

Selected SPSS Output for Testing Unequal Expected Frequencies

The results are shown in Figure 246.

Postpartum Depression--Recoded

	Observed N	Expected N	Residual
same	33	20.0	13.0
more or less depressed	27	40.0	-13.0
Total	60		

Test Statistics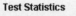

	Postpartum Depression--Recoded
Chi-Square[a]	12.675
df	1
Asymp. Sig.	.000

a. 0 cells (.0%) have expected frequencies less than 5. The minimum expected cell frequency is 20.0.

Figure 246. The results of the chi-square analysis with unequal frequencies.

This analysis shows that observed proportions do differ significantly from the hypothesized proportions, $\chi^2 (1, N = 60) = 12.68$, $p < .001$.

Using SPSS Graphs to Display the Results

The applications presented in this lesson include variables with just a few categories. The results for these variables can be easily described in the text of a results section without presenting a graph. However, if the number of categories is large, a bar chart might be provided to summarize the results for a categorical variable. In Figure 247, we illustrate a bar chart for our postpartum data for the status variable.

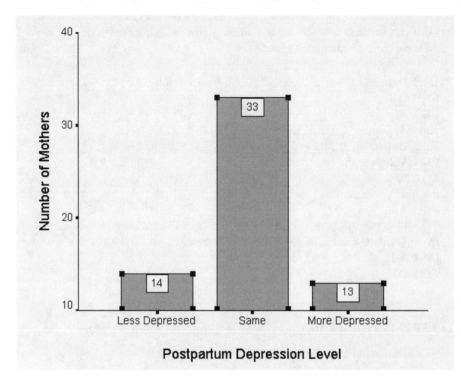

Figure 247. The frequencies of women who are less depressed, show no depression change, and are more depressed after childbirth.

An APA Results Section

A one-sample chi-square test was conducted to assess whether women become less depressed, remain unchanged, or become more depressed after giving birth to children. The results of the test were significant, χ^2 (2, $\underline{N}$ = 60) = 12.70, $\underline{p}$ = .002. The proportion of women who were unchanged ($\underline{P}$ = .55) was much greater than the hypothesized proportion of .33, while the proportion of women who became less depressed ($\underline{P}$ = .23) and the proportion who became more depressed ($\underline{P}$ = .22) were approximately the same value and less than the hypothesized proportions of .33. A follow-up test indicated that the proportion of women who became less depressed did not differ significantly from the proportion of women who became more depressed, χ^2 (1, $\underline{N}$ = 27) = 0.04, $\underline{p}$ = .847. Overall, these results suggest that women in general do not become more or less depressed as a function of childbirth.

Alternative Analyses

The one-sample chi-square test is sometimes used to compare the distribution for a quantitative variable with a particular theoretical distribution, most frequently the normal distribution. The Kolmogrov-Smirnov test is the preferred test for making the comparison with a normal distribution. See the next section for the steps for testing whether a distribution is normally distributed.

If the focal variable has two categories, the binomial test may be used instead of the one-sample chi-square test. (See Lesson 38.)

Conducting a Kolmogrov-Smirnov Test

A Kolmogrov-Smirnov test evaluates whether the data on a quantitative variable are normally distributed. We will give the steps for conducting this test using the Explore procedure under Descriptive Statistics in the Analyze menu. Note that the results using this procedure differ from those obtained using 1-Sample K-S test under Nonparametrics in the Statistics menu. The latter procedure assumes that the mean and standard deviation of the distribution are known, which is very unlikely.

The steps for conducting a Kolmogrov-Smirnov test are as follows:

1. Click **Analyze**, then click **Descriptive Statistics**, and click **Explore**.
2. Click on the variable of interest and move it to the Dependent List box.
3. Click the **Plots** button, and click in the box next to Normality plots with test.
4. Click **Continue**.
5. Click **OK**.

The results of the test are labeled K-S (Lilliefors) in the output. The test is a modified Kolmogrov-Smirnov test called the Lilliefors test. If the test is significant, it indicates that the distribution is significantly different from a normal distribution.

Exercises

The data for Exercises 1 through 4 are in the data files named *Lesson 39 Data File 1* on the Student Disk. The data are based on the following research study.

Kristen is interested in evaluating whether the method of cooking potato chips affects the taste of the chips. She has 48 individuals volunteer to participate in her potato chip study. Each participant tastes chips cooked using three different methods: fried in animal fat (chip = 1), fried in canola oil (chip = 2), and baked (chip = 3). Individuals are instructed to indicate which type of potato chips they prefer: chip type 1, chip type 2, or chip type 3. Kristen hypothesizes that individuals will prefer potato chips that are fried in canola oil over those that are fried in animal fat or baked.

1. Weight the data file by the number of cases to conduct the analysis.
2. Conduct a one-sample chi-square test to evaluate whether cooking method affects taste. From the output, identify the following:
   a. The observed frequency for potato chips fried in canola oil
   b. The *p*-value
   c. The χ^2 value
3. What are the expected frequencies for the three categories of potato chips?
4. Write a results section based on your analyses.

Two-Way Contingency Table Analysis Using Crosstabs

A two-way contingency table analysis evaluates whether a statistical relationship exists between two variables. A two-way contingency table consists of two or more rows and two or more columns. The rows represent the different levels of one variable and the columns represent different levels of a second variable. Such a table is sometime described as an r x c table, where r is the number of rows, and c is the number of columns. For example, a 3 x 4 contingency table is a table with a 3-level row variable and a 4-level column variable. The cells in the table, which are the combinations of the levels of the row and the column variables, contain frequencies. For the 3 x 4 contingency table, there would be 12 cells with frequencies. A cell frequency for a particular row and column represents the number of individuals in a study who can be cross-classified as belonging to that particular level of the row variable and that particular level of the column variable. Analyses of two-way contingency tables focus on these cell frequencies to evaluate whether the row and column variables are related.

Levels of a row or a column variable can represent quantitative distinctions among individuals, differences indicating an ordering of individuals, or simply a categorization of individuals. In this lesson we will talk only about methods for analyzing tables where the row and the column variables are qualitative or categorical in nature. These methods are not designed to take full advantage of the properties of quantitative or ordered variables.

Three types of studies can be analyzed using two-way contingency table analyses (Wickens, 1989), and they produce three different types of hypotheses:

- *Independence between variables.* Research participants are sampled and then measured on two response variables—the row and the column variables. In other words, in these studies, the total number of participants is controlled, but not the number of individuals in the columns or in the rows. The relationship between the row and the column variables in the population is being evaluated.
- *Homogeneity of proportions.* Samples are drawn to represent populations of interest, either by sampling from different populations or by randomly assigning subjects to groups and treating them differently. The individuals in these samples are measured on a response variable. The rows might represent the different populations and the columns might be the response categories on the response variable. For these studies, the total number of research participants in each row is controlled but not the total number of participants in each column. The contingency table analysis evaluates whether the proportions of individuals in the levels of the column variable are the same for all populations (i.e., for all levels of the row variable).
- *Unrelated classification.* Here, we control the total number of subjects in each row and in each column. Researchers infrequently design studies investigating unrelated classifications.

Regardless of the design of the study, an SPSS data file for a two-way contingency table analysis can be structured in one of two ways. With the standard method, the SPSS data file contains as many cases as individuals. There are two variables, each of which can have two or more values that represent the two or more categories for that variable. With the weighted cases method, the SPSS data file contains as many cases as category combinations (cells) across the two focal variables. For example, there are 12 cases for a 3 x 4 contingency table. For the weighted cases method, there are three variables. Two are the focal variables with values representing their categories, and the third variable is a weight variable containing frequencies for the category combinations (cells) across the two focal variables.

Applying Two-Way Contingency Table Analysis

Here are applications for studies that evaluate independence between variables and homogeneity of proportions.

Independence between Variables

Carrie is interested in assessing the relationship between religion and occupation for men. She samples a group of 2,000 men between the ages of 30 and 50 and asks them to complete a demographic questionnaire. On the basis of their answers, she classifies each man as practicing one of four religions (Protestant, Catholic, Jewish, and Other) and employed in one of six occupations (Professional, Business-Management, Business-Nonmanagement, Skilled Tradesman, Laborer, and Unemployed). Religion and occupation are the row and the column variables, and the frequencies are the number of men who are classified as belonging to the 24 (4 x 6) combinations of religious and occupational categories.

Using the standard structure, Carrie would have 2,000 cases to represent the 2,000 men. Each man would have scores on at least two variables, religion with four levels and occupation with six levels. With the weighted cases structure, Carrie would have 24 cases, representing the 24 combinations of the two variables. Each case would have scores on at least three variables: the two research variables of religion and occupation and a weight variable. A score on the weight variable for a case would represent the number of individuals who are classified as belonging to the cell represented by that case.

Homogeneity of Proportions

Claude wants to determine whether young men are unjustifiably more likely to treat elderly people in a condescending manner. To address this hypothesis, he recruits a young woman from his class who indicates that both her mother and her grandmother are physically, emotionally, and intellectually active. The daughter, mother, and grandmother are 20, 43, and 72 years old, respectively. Claude gains the cooperation of all three women to participate as confederates in his study. The three women take a two-hour lesson to learn a computer game called Wits. At the end of the two hours, they pass a criterion indicating total mastery of the game. In addition, they learn a script so that they can all act in the same manner as confederates in the study.

Claude recruits 90 male college students between the ages of 17 and 22 to participate in his study. All 90 males take a 20-minute lesson to learn the game of Wits and pass a test indicating minimal knowledge of the game, although on the basis of their test scores none of the males shows total mastery. Next, he tells each student that he is now going to instruct a woman who has no experience with the game. The students are then asked to switch seats from the chair in front of the computer to the one behind it. Each student is then introduced to one of the women, as determined by random assignment. A third of the men meet the daughter, a third meet the mother, and a third meet the grandmother. The men next give verbal instructions from their seats on how to win at Wits. Regardless of the instructions given by the men, all three women show exactly the same rate of improvement for all 90 participants.

All sessions are videotaped. The tapes show only the faces of the male participants and exclude all verbal comments made by the women so that observers of the tape are completely blind to which woman is being "trained." A reliable judge observes the tapes and concludes whether each male college student acts condescendingly or not.

For this study, the row variable is age of women with three levels (young, middle-aged, and elderly) and the column variable is condescension with two levels (not condescending and condescending). The frequencies are the number of participants who are classified as belonging to the six combinations of age and condescension (3 levels x 2 levels).

Understanding Two-Way Contingency Table Analysis

The same chi-square test for a two-way contingency table may be applied to studies investigating both the independence and homogeneity hypotheses. If the resulting chi-square value is significant and the table includes at least one variable with more than two levels, a follow-up test may be conducted. These follow-up tests are particularly crucial for studies assessing homogeneity of three or more proportions. The methods employed in these follow-up tests are conceptually similar to those used to conduct post hoc tests for a one-way ANOVA to evaluate differences in means among three or more levels of a factor (see Lesson 24).

Assumptions Underlying a Two-Way Contingency Table Analysis

The Crosstabs procedure applies a χ^2 test for contingency table analysis.

Assumption 1: The Observations for a Two-Way Contingency Table Analysis Are Independent of Each Other

To meet this assumption, studies should be designed to prevent dependency in the data. If this assumption is violated, the test is likely to yield inaccurate results.

Assumption 2: Two-Way Contingency Table Analyses Yield a Test Statistic That Is Approximately Distributed as a Chi-Square When the Sample Size Is Relatively Large

There is no simple answer to the question of what sample size is large enough. However, to answer this question, the size of the expected cell frequencies rather than the total sample size should be examined. For tables with 2 rows and 2 columns, there is probably little reason to worry if all the expected frequencies are greater than or equal to 5. For large tables, if more than 20% of the cells have expected frequencies that are less than 5, you should be concerned about the validity of the results.

Computing an Effect Size

SPSS provides a number of indices that assess the strength of the relationship between row and column variables. They include the contingency coefficient, phi, Cramér's *V*, lambda, and the uncertainty coefficient. We will focus our attention on two of these coefficients, phi and Cramér's *V*.

The phi coefficient for a 2 x 2 table is a special case of the Pearson product-moment correlation coefficient for a 2 x 2 contingency table. Because most behavioral researchers have a good working knowledge of the Pearson product-moment correlation coefficient, they are likely to feel comfortable using its derivative, the phi coefficient. Phi, Φ, is a function of the Pearson chi-square statistic, χ^2, and sample size, N:

$$\Phi = \sqrt{\chi^2/N}$$

Like the Pearson product-moment correlation coefficient, the phi ranges in value from -1 to +1. Values close to 0 indicate a very weak relationship, and values close to 1 indicate a very strong relationship. If the row and column variables are qualitative, the sign of phi is not meaningful and any negative phi values can be changed to positive values without affecting their meaning. Traditionally, phi's of .10, .30, and .50 represent small, medium, and large effect sizes, respectively.

If both the row and the column variables have more than two levels, phi can exceed 1 and, therefore, is hard to interpret. Cramér's V rescales phi so that it also ranges between 0 and 1:

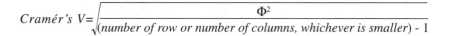

$$Cram\acute{e}r's\ V = \sqrt{\frac{\Phi^2}{(number\ of\ row\ or\ number\ of\ columns,\ whichever\ is\ smaller) - 1}}$$

For 2 x 2, 2 x 3, and 3 x 2 tables, phi and Cramér's V are identical.

The Data Set

The data for this example are on the Student Disk under the name *Lesson 40 Data File 1*. They are based on the condescension study exploring homogeneity of proportions. The variables are in Table 61.

Table 61

Variables in Lesson 40 Exercise Data Set 1

Variables	Definition
age	Age has three levels: 1 = Young, 2 = Middle-Aged, and 3 = Elderly.
condes	Condes stands for condescension and has two levels: 0 = not condescending and 1 = condescending.
number	Number is the number of individuals in the cell defined by the combination of levels for age and condes.

The data file uses the weighted cases method, so there are six cases that represent the six cells. The six cells are identified by the scores on the two variables of age and condescension. In addition, a third variable, number, is defined that contains the frequency for that case (cell).

The Research Question

The research question can be asked as follows: Are the proportions of male college students who treat young, middle-aged, and elderly women with disdain the same?

Conducting a Two-Way Contingency Table Analysis

We will illustrate how to conduct an overall two-way contingency analysis and follow-up procedures.

Before the data can be analyzed, the cases must be weighted by the values in the number variable. The cases can be weighted by conducting the following steps:

1. Click **Data**, and click **Weight Cases**.
2. Click **Weight cases by** in the Weight Cases dialog box.
3. Click **number**, then click ▶ to move it to the Frequency Variable box.
4. Click **OK**.

Conducting the Overall Analysis

To conduct the Crosstabs analysis, follow these steps:

1. Click **Analyze**, click **Descriptive Statistics**, and click **Crosstabs**. You'll see the Crosstabs dialog box, as shown in Figure 248.

Figure 248. The Crosstabs dialog box.

2. Click **age**, then click ▶ to move it to the box labeled Row(s).
3. Click **condes**, then click ▶ to move it to the box labeled Column(s).
4. Click **Statistics**. You'll see the Crosstabs: Statistics dialog box, as shown in Figure 249.

Figure 249. The Crosstabs: Statistics dialog box.

5. Click Chi-square and Phi and Cramér's V in the Nominal Data box.
6. Click Continue.
7. Click Cells. You'll see the Crosstabs: Cell Display dialog box, as shown in Figure 250.

Figure 250. The Crosstabs: Cell Display dialog box.

8. Click **Expected** in the Counts box. **Observed** should already be selected.
9. Click **Row** in the Percentages box.
10. Click **Continue**.
11. Click **OK**.

Selected SPSS Output for Crosstabs

The output is shown in Figure 251 (at the top of page 350). SPSS reports the results of a number of significance tests, including the often reported Pearson chi-square test statistic. In this example, the Pearson χ^2 is 6.32, $p = .042$. If the table has 2 rows and 2 columns, then a corrected Pearson chi-square test also is reported, but this result is not recommended since it tends to be overly conservative for many applications.

The likelihood ratio test (also reported in Figure 251 as χ^2 (2, $N = 90$) = 6.46, $p = .040$) tests the same hypothesis as the Pearson chi-square, has similar properties, and is an alternative to the Pearson. The remaining reported chi-square statistic, the chi square for a linear-by-linear association, is inappropriate for analyzing tables with qualitative variables.

If the chi-square test (Pearson or likelihood ratio) has more than 1 degree of freedom, it is an omnibus test, which evaluates the significance of an overall hypothesis containing multiple subhypotheses. These multiple subhypotheses can then be tested using follow-up tests.

In this example, the results of the chi-square test indicated significant differences among the three age levels. Follow-up tests should be conducted to examine particular subhypotheses. One possible set of subhypotheses would involve the pairwise comparisons among the three age conditions. For example, one of the pairwise comparisons poses the question, "Do the proportions of college men who are condescending vary depending upon whether the men are teaching young or elderly women?" The remaining two pairwise comparisons would evaluate differences in proportions between the young and the middle-aged conditions and between the middle-aged and the elderly conditions.

Conducting Follow-Up Tests

To compute the chi-square values for the comparison between the young and middle-aged conditions, follow these steps:

1. Click **Data** and click **Select Cases**.
2. Click **If condition is satisfied**.
3. Click **If**.
4. To the right of the ▶, type **age = 1** or **age = 2**.

AGE * CONDES Crosstabulation

			CONDES		
			Not Condescending	Condescending	Total
AGE	Young	Count	21	9	30
		Expected Count	20.7	9.3	30.0
	Middle-Aged	Count	25	5	30
		Expected Count	20.7	9.3	30.0
	Elderly	Count	16	14	30
		Expected Count	20.7	9.3	30.0
Total		Count	62	28	90
		Expected Count	62.0	28.0	90.0

Chi-Square Tests

	Value	df	Asymp. Sig. (2-sided)
Pearson Chi-Square	6.325[a]	2	.042
Likelihood Ratio	6.457	2	.040
Linear-by-Linear Association	1.923	1	.166
N of Valid Cases	90		

a. 0 cells (.0%) have expected count less than 5. The minimum expected count is 9.33.

Symmetric Measures

		Value	Approx. Sig.
Nominal by Nominal	Phi	.265	.042
	Cramer's V	.265	.042
N of Valid Cases		90	

a. Not assuming the null hypothesis.

b. Using the asymptotic standard error assuming the null hypothesis.

Figure 251. Results of the Crosstabs analysis.

5. Click **Continue**.
6. Click **OK**.
7. Click **Analyze**, click **Descriptive Statistics**, and click **Crosstabs**.
8. If you have just previously conducted the omnibus chi-square test for all three age categories, you do not have to make any changes in the Crosstabs dialog box, and you simply click **OK**. Otherwise, repeat the steps previously described for the omnibus chi-square test.

To conduct the other two comparisons between young and elderly conditions and the middle-aged and elderly conditions, follow these steps:

1. For the second comparison, repeat Steps 1 through 8, except at Step 4, type **age = 1** or **age = 3** in the Select Cases: If dialog box.
2. For the third comparison, Steps 1 through 8 are repeated, except at Step 4 type **age = 2** or **age = 3** in the Select Cases: If dialog box.

Selected SPSS Output of Follow-up Tests

The results of the pairwise comparison between the young and the middle-aged women are shown in Figure 252 (at the top of page 351).

AGE * CONDES Crosstabulation

			CONDES		Total
			Not Condescending	Condescending	
AGE	Young	Count	21	9	30
		Expected Count	23.0	7.0	30.0
	Middle-Aged	Count	25	5	30
		Expected Count	23.0	7.0	30.0
Total		Count	46	14	60
		Expected Count	46.0	14.0	60.0

Chi-Square Tests

	Value	df	Asymp. Sig. (2-sided)	Exact Sig. (2-sided)	Exact Sig. (1-sided)
Pearson Chi-Square	1.491[b]	1	.222		
Continuity Correction[a]	.839	1	.360		
Likelihood Ratio	1.507	1	.220		
Fisher's Exact Test				.360	.180
Linear-by-Linear Association	1.466	1	.226		
N of Valid Cases	60				

a. Computed only for a 2x2 table

b. 0 cells (.0%) have expected count less than 5. The minimum expected count is 7.00.

Symmetric Measures

		Value	Approx. Sig.
Nominal by Nominal	Phi	-.158	.222
	Cramer's V	.158	.222
N of Valid Cases		60	

a. Not assuming the null hypothesis.

b. Using the asymptotic standard error assuming the null hypothesis.

Figure 252. The results of the pairwise comparison between the young and middle-aged conditions.

Based on the Pearson χ^2 test, the p-value for the comparison between young women and middle-aged women is .222. The p-values for the comparisons between young and elderly women and between middle-aged and elderly women are .184 and .012, respectively. The results of these three tests using the Holm's sequential Bonferroni method (see Appendix B) for controlling Type I error are reported in Table 62 (on page 353).

Using SPSS Graphs to Display the Results

Clustered bar charts provide a visual representation of the results of two qualitative variables. With a clustered bar chart, it is easy to see whether the proportions in each category of the first variable are the same for all categories of the second variable. To create a clustered bar chart, follow these steps (and make sure that you have reset Select Cases to All Cases):

1. Click **Graphs,** and click **Bar**.
2. Click **Clustered**, and click **Summaries for groups of cases**.

3. Click **Define**.
4. Click **age** and click ▶ to move it to the Category Axis box.
5. Click **condes** and click ▶ to move it to the Define Clusters By box.
6. Click **OK**.

In Figure 253, you can see the clustered bar chart for the frequency of each level of condescension within the three age categories.

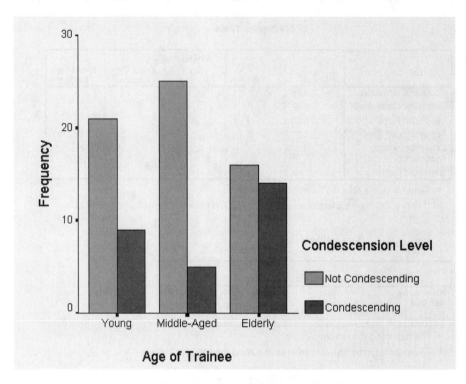

Figure 253. A clustered bar chart of condescension within the age categories.

An APA Results Section

A two-way contingency table analysis was conducted to evaluate whether male college students were more condescending to young, middle-aged, or elderly women. The two variables were age of female trainee with three levels (young, middle-aged, and elderly) and condescension of male trainer with two levels (not condescending and condescending). Age and condescension were found to be significantly related, Pearson χ^2 (2, $\underline{N}$ = 90) = 6.32, $\underline{p}$ = .042, Cramér's $\underline{V}$ = .26. The proportions of males who were condescending toward the young, the middle-aged, and the elderly female trainees were .30 .17, and .47, respectively.

Follow-up pairwise comparisons were conducted to evaluate the difference among these proportions. Table 62 (at the top of page 353) shows the results of these analyses. The Holm's sequential Bonferroni method was used to control for Type I error at the .05 across all three comparisons. The only pairwise difference that was significant was between the middle-aged and the elderly trainee. The probability of a trainee being treated in a condescending fashion was about 2.8 times (.47/.17) more likely when the trainee was elderly as opposed to middle-aged.

Table 62

Results for the Pairwise Comparisons Using the Holm's Sequential Bonferroni Method

Comparison	Pearson chi square	p-value	Required p-value for significance	Significance	Cramér's V
Middle-aged vs. elderly	6.24	.012	.0167	*	.32
Young vs. elderly	1.76	.184	.025	NS	.17
Young vs. middle-aged	1.49	.222	.05	NS	.16

*p-value (required p-value for significance)

Exercises

Exercises 1 through 3 are based on the following research problem. The data for these exercises can be found in the data file named *Lesson 40 Exercise File 1* on the Student Disk.

Lilly collects data on a sample of 130 high school students to evaluate whether the proportion of female high school students who take advanced math courses in high school varies depending upon whether they have been raised primarily by their father or by both their mother and their father. The SPSS data file contains two variables: math (0 = no advanced math and 1 = some advanced math) and parent (1 = primarily father and 2 = father and mother).

1. Conduct a crosstabs analysis to examine whether the proportion of female high school students who take advanced math course is different for different levels of the parent variable. From the output, identify the following:
   a. The percent of female students who took some advanced math classes
   b. The percent of female students who took no advanced math classes when female students were raised by their fathers
   c. The percent of female students raised by their father only
   d. The χ^2 value
   e. The strength of relationship between taking advanced math classes and level of parenting
2. Create a clustered bar graph to show differences in the number of female students taking some advanced math classes for the different categories of parenting.
3. Write a results section based on your analysis.

Exercises 4 through 6 are based on the following research problem.

Bobby is interested in knowing whether teaching method has an effect on interest in subject matter. To investigate this question, he randomly assigns 90 high school students enrolled in history to one of three teaching conditions. All 90 students are exposed to exactly the same information for the same length of time. However, 30 of the students are presented a filmed reenactment of the historical events; 30 see an MTV-type video presentation of the events; and 30 are presented the information using a traditional lecture approach. At the end of the presentation, the students in each condition are asked whether they found the information interesting. They were to check one of three alternatives: Really Like to Know More About That; Excuse Me—You Call That a Presentation?; and Boring—Please, No More of That! The data are in Table 63 (at the top of page 354).

4. Create a data file containing the data in Table 60 using the weighted cases method.
5. Conduct a two-way contingency analysis to analyze the data.
6. Write a results section based on your analysis.

Table 63

Frequencies of Interest as a Function of Type of Presentation

Type of presentation	Interest in history area		
	Like to know more	Excuse me—You call ...	Boring—Please, no more ...
Film	12	10	8
Video	4	10	16
Lecture	6	6	18

Two Independent-Samples Tests: The Mann-Whitney U Test

The Mann-Whitney U test evaluates whether the medians on a test variable differ significantly between two groups. In an SPSS data file, each case must have scores on two variables, the grouping variable and the test variable. The grouping variable divides cases into two groups or categories, and the test variable assesses individuals on a variable with at least an ordinal scale.

Although SPSS uses the terms grouping variable and test variable, the grouping variable may also be referred to as the independent or categorical variable, and the test variable may be referred to as the dependent or the quantitative variable.

Applying the Mann-Whitney *U* Test

A Mann-Whitney U test can analyze data from experimental, quasi-experimental, and field studies. We illustrate how to conduct a Mann-Whitney U test for a quasi-experimental study.

Quasi-Experimental Study

Based on a developmental theory of cognitive processing, Bob predicted that elderly individuals would have greater difficulty with a particular visual spatial memory task (VSMT) than middle-aged individuals. Fourteen elderly women (65 years and older) and 26 younger women (31 to 50 years of age), all of whom were college graduates, agreed to participate in the study. These 40 women were administered the VSMT, a measure that yields scores that range in value from 0 to 100. Bob's data file has 40 cases, one case for each woman in the sample. The file contains one variable designating whether a woman is part of the younger or older group and a second variable representing the VSMT scores for each woman.

Understanding the Mann-Whitney *U* Test

To understand how the Mann-Whitney U test evaluates differences in medians, it is useful to first describe what data are analyzed with this test. We will use the VSMT data for young and elderly women to illustrate. The data are in Table 64 (on page 356).

For a Mann-Whitney U test, the scores on the test variable are converted to ranks, ignoring group membership. For our data, the VSMT scores are converted to ranked VSMT scores, ignoring whether the VSMT scores are for younger or older women. The Mann-Whitney U test then evaluates whether the mean ranks for the two groups differ significantly from each other. In our example, the test evaluates whether the mean rank for the younger group of 23.17 differs significantly from the mean rank for the older group of 15.54.

Because analyses for the Mann-Whitney U test are conducted on ranked scores, the distributions of the test variable for the two populations do not have to be of any particular form (e.g., normal). However, these distributions should be continuous and have identical forms.

Table 64

Data for Example on Aging and Visual Spatial Memory Task (VSMT)

	Young			Elderly	
ID	VSMT	Ranked VSMT	ID	VSMT	Ranked VSMT
1	98	39.0	27	41	3.0
2	73	25.0	28	54	10.0
3	41	3.0	29	61	13.0
4	51	7.5	30	98	39.0
5	82	30.0	31	41	3.0
6	66	15.5	32	54	10.0
7	97	37.0	33	69	19.0
8	92	34.5	34	82	30.0
9	74	26.5	35	34	1.0
10	71	20.5	36	92	34.5
11	98	39.0	37	47	6.0
12	43	5.0	38	55	12.0
13	92	34.5	39	54	10.0
14	81	28.0	40	79	27.0
15	65	14.0			
16	72	23.0			
17	71	20.5			
18	72	23.0			
19	72	23.0			
20	92	34.5			
21	66	15.5			
22	82	30.0			
23	51	7.5			
24	86	32.0			
25	67	17.5			
26	67	17.5			

Assumptions Underlying a Mann-Whitney U Test

Assumption 1: The Continuous Distributions for the Test Variable Are Exactly the Same for the Two Populations

To the extent that the population distributions differ, the test does not evaluate whether the medians differ between populations, but only whether the distributions themselves differ. Difficulties can arise with the Mann-Whitney U test if there are not a number of possible scores on the dependent variable and ties are produced in the ranked scores. SPSS employs a correction for such ties.

Assumption 2: The Cases Represent Random Samples from the Two Populations, and the Scores on the Test Variable Are Independent of Each Other

The Mann-Whitney U test will yield inaccurate p-values if the independence assumption is violated.

Assumption 3: The z Approximation Test for the Mann-Whitney U Test Requires a Large Sample Size

An exact test is printed by SPSS if the number of cases is less than or equal to 42. Accordingly, the *z* approximation test does not have to be used unless the sample size exceeds 42. A sample size of greater than 42 should be sufficiently large to yield relatively accurate *p*-values. The *z*-approximation test includes a correction for ties but does not include a continuity correction. The results for the Mann-Whitney test using SPSS may differ from results in other statistical computer packages depending on whether the software uses the same correction procedures.

Computing an Effect Size Statistic

SPSS does not report an effect size index for this test, but simple indices can be computed to communicate the size of the effect. For example, the difference in mean ranks between the two groups can serve as an effect size index.

The Data Set

The data set used to illustrate this test is named *Lesson 41 Data File 1* on the Student Disk. The set represents data coming from the example on aging and performance on a visual spatial memory task. The variables are shown in Table 65.

Table 65
Variables in Lesson 41 Data File 1

Variables	Definition
age	Age is the grouping variable. The age variable distinguishes between two age conditions:
	If a younger woman, then age = 1.
	If an older woman, then age = 2.
vsmt	VSMT is the test variable. VSMT is the visual spatial memory task, which yields scores that range in value potentially from 0 to 100. Higher scores indicate better memory.

The Research Question

The research question can be asked in terms of differences in the medians between groups or for a relationship between two variables.

1. Differences between the medians: Does median performance on the visual spatial memory task differ for younger and older women?
2. Relationship between two variables: Is performance on the visual spatial memory task related to a woman's age?

Conducting a Mann-Whitney U Test

To conduct a Mann-Whitney *U* Test, follow these steps:

1. Click **Analyze**, click **Nonparametric Tests**, then click **2 Independent-Samples**. You will see the Two-Independent-Samples Tests dialog box, as shown in Figure 254 (at the top of page 358).

Figure 254. The Two-Independent-Samples Tests dialog box.

2. Click **vsmt**, then click ▸ to move it to the Test Variable List box.
3. Click **age**, then click ▸ to move it to the Grouping Variable box.
4. Click **Define Groups**.
5. Type **1** in the Group 1 box to indicate that Group 1 is the younger group.
6. Type **2** in the Group 2 box, indicating that Group 2 is the elderly group.
7. Click **Continue**.
8. Be sure **Mann-Whitney U** is checked in the Test Type area.
9. Click **OK**.

Selected SPSS Output for the Mann-Whitney U Test

The output from the analysis is shown in Figure 255.

Ranks

	AGE	N	Mean Rank	Sum of Ranks
VSMT	younger	26	23.17	602.50
	elderly	14	15.54	217.50
	Total	40		

Test Statistics[b]

	VSMT
Mann-Whitney U	112.500
Wilcoxon W	217.500
Z	-1.974
Asymp. Sig. (2-tailed)	.048
Exact Sig. [2*(1-tailed Sig.)]	.048[a]

a. Not corrected for ties.

b. Grouping Variable: AGE

Figure 255. The results of the Mann-Whitney U analysis.

Two p-values are reported, an exact two-tailed p, which is not corrected for ties, and a two-tailed p, which is based on the z-approximation test and is corrected for ties. As is typically the case, the difference between the two p-values is negligible.

Using SPSS Graphs to Display the Results

Because the computations for the Mann-Whitney U test are on ranked scores of a test variable, a reader of the results section reporting this test would have very little knowledge of what the original, raw scores would look like. Consequently, a graph presenting distributions of raw scores for the two groups would be very informative. Boxplots offer the reader more information than the other graphical options within SPSS. We present a boxplot in Figure 256 showing the distributions for the visual spatial memory scores for the two age groups.

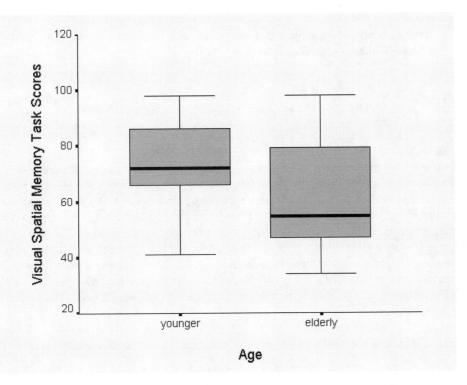

Figure 256. The distributions of VSMT scores for elderly and younger women.

An APA Results Section

A Mann-Whitney U test was conducted to evaluate the hypothesis that elderly women would score lower, on the average, than younger women on a visual spatial memory task. The results of the test were significant, z = -1.97, p = .048. As expected the elderly women had an average rank of 15.54, while the younger women had an average rank of 23.17. Figure 256 shows the distributions of the scores on the VSMT measure for the two age groups.

Alternative Analyses

If a study has two independent samples and individuals in the samples are assessed on a dependent variable measured on an interval or ratio scale, then the data from the study can be analyzed using an independent-samples t test or a Mann-Whitney U test. However, if the dependent variable is measured on an ordinal scale, it is better to conduct a Mann-Whitney U test because medians are a more meaningful measure of central tendency for ordinal data.

If the dependent variable is at least an interval variable, the decision about what test to use depends on whether the assumptions underlying the test are met. The Mann-Whitney U test assumes that the population distributions are identical, although the distributions can have any shape. The independent-samples t test assumes not only that the distributions are identical, but also that the distributions are normal. The choice between tests is complex because the independent-samples t test yields relatively accurate p-values even if the normality assumption is violated when the sample sizes are moderate or larger, and because the power of the test depends on the shape of the population distribution.

Here are some guidelines for choosing between a Mann-Whitney U test and an independent-samples t test for designs with a dependent variable that has at least an interval scale. The choices are dictated by the power of the tests.

- If the normality assumption is met, an independent-samples t test is preferred.
- If the population distributions are symmetrical and flat, either a Mann-Whitney U test or an independent-samples t test could be used to analyze the data.
- If the distributions are symmetrical but with thicker tails than a normal distribution, a Mann-Whitney U test should be used.

Exercises

The data for Exercises 1 through 4 are in the data file named *Lesson 41 Exercise File 1* on the Student Disk. The data are based on the following study.

Billie wishes to test the hypothesis that overweight individuals tend to eat faster than normal weight individuals. To test this hypothesis, she has two assistants sit in a McDonald's restaurant and identify individuals who order at lunch time the Big Mac special (Big Mac, large fries, and large coke). The Big Mackers, as the assistants affectionately called them, were classified by the assistants as overweight, normal weight, or neither overweight nor normal weight. The assistants identify 10 overweight Big Mackers and 30 normal weight Big Mackers. (Individuals who were neither overweight nor normal weight were disregarded.) The assistants record the amount of time it took for the individuals in the two groups to complete their Big Mac special meals. One variable is weight with two levels, overweight (= 1) and normal weight (= 2). The second variable is time in seconds.

1. Compute a Mann-Whitney U test on these data. On the output, identify the following:
   a. *p*-value
   b. *z*-value corrected for ties
   c. Mean rank for normal weight individuals
2. Conduct an independent-samples t test. Compare the p-value for the Mann-Whitney U test with the p-value for the independent-samples t test.
3. Write a results section based on your analyses. What should you conclude?
4. If you did not include a graph in your results section, create a graph that shows the distributions of the two groups.

K Independent-Samples Tests: The Kruskal-Wallis and the Median Tests

Both the Kruskal-Wallis and the median tests evaluate whether the population medians on a dependent variable are the same across all levels of a factor. For the Kruskal-Wallis and the median tests using the *K* independent-samples procedure, cases must have scores on an independent or grouping variable and on a dependent or test variable. The independent or grouping variable divides individuals into two or more groups, and the dependent or test variable assesses individuals on at least an ordinal scale.

If the independent variable has only two levels, no additional significance tests need to be conducted beyond the Kruskal-Wallis or median test. On the other hand, if a factor has more than two levels and the overall test is significant, follow-up tests are usually conducted. These follow-up tests most frequently involve comparisons between pairs of group medians.

Applying the Kruskal-Wallis and the Median Tests

Like the one-way ANOVA, the Kruskal-Wallis and median tests can analyze data from three types of studies:

- Experimental studies
- Quasi-experimental studies
- Field studies

Here we will apply the tests in an experimental study. We will use the Kruskal-Wallis and median tests on these data. You may wish to compare the results from these tests with those in Lessons 24 and 26, which use the one-way ANOVA and one-way ANCOVA to analyze the same data.

Experimental Study

Dana wishes to assess whether vitamin C is effective in the treatment of colds. To evaluate her hypothesis, she decides to conduct a 2-year experimental study. She obtains 30 volunteers from undergraduate classes to participate. She randomly assigns an equal number of students to three groups: placebo (group 1), low doses of vitamin C (group 2), and high doses of vitamin C (group 3). In the first and second years of the study, students in all three groups are monitored to assess the number of days with cold symptoms that they have. During the first year, students do not take any pills. In the second year of the study, students take pills that contain one of the following: no active ingredients (group 1), low doses of vitamin C (group 2), or high doses of vitamin C (group 3). Dana's SPSS data file includes 30 cases and two variables: a factor distinguishing among the three treatment groups and a dependent variable, the difference in the number of days with cold symptoms in the first year versus the number of days with cold symptoms in the second year.

Understanding the Kruskal-Wallis and Median Test

To understand how Kruskal-Wallis and the median test evaluate differences in medians among groups, we must first describe what data are analyzed for each test. Let's use our example dealing with vitamin C to understand better the characteristics of the data for each test.

As shown in Table 66, all scores on the dependent variable (difference in number of colds from one year to the next) are rank-ordered, disregarding levels of a factor (vitamin C group), from lowest to highest for the Kruskal-Wallis test. With the Kruskal-Wallis test, a chi-square statistic is used to evaluate differences in mean ranks to assess the null hypothesis that the medians are equal across groups.

The data are recast for the median test to create a two-way contingency table with frequencies in the cells (see Lesson 40 on two-way contingency table analysis). The columns of the table are defined by the levels of the factor (grouping variable), in this case the three vitamin C treatment groups. The rows of the table, of which there are always two, represent two levels of performance on the dependent variable: (1) performance at or below the median disregarding group membership and (2) performance above the median disregarding group membership. Table 66 shows how to obtain the data for the median test. For those who took pills with no active ingredients, one individual scored at or below the median (a rank of 15 or less) and nine individuals scored above the median (a rank of greater than 15). Similarly, as shown in the last row of the table, the frequencies for the other two groups are the same: seven individuals scored at or below the median, and three individuals scored above the median. These frequencies are presented in a two-way contingency format in Table 67 (at the top of page 363).

Table 66

Difference-in-Days-with-Colds Scores Transformed for a Kruskal-Wallis Test and for a Median Test

No active ingredients			Low dose of vitamin C			High dose of vitamin C		
Diff. Score	Rank of score	At or below (-) vs. above (+) median	Diff. score	Rank of score	At or below (-) vs. above (+) median	Diff. score	Rank of score	At or below (-) vs. above (+) median
12	30.0	+	-2	13.5	-	6	27.5	+
-2	13.5	-	-3	10.5	-	-7	2.0	-
9	29.0	+	3	21.5	+	-6	5.0	-
3	21.5	+	-2	13.5	-	-6	5.0	-
3	21.5	+	0	16.5	+	-6	5.0	-
0	16.5	+	-4	8.5	-	-4	8.5	-
3	21.5	+	-3	10.5	-	-2	13.5	-
2	19.0	+	5	25.5	+	-6	5.0	-
4	24.0	+	-9	1.0	-	6	27.5	+
1	18.0	+	-6	5.0	-	5	25.5	+
Mean rank =	21.45	1 minus 9 pluses	Mean rank =	12.60	7 minus 3 pluses	Mean rank =	12.45	7 minus 3 pluses

The median test is a contingency table analysis that involves assessing whether the column variable (the factor) and the row variable (the dependent variable) are related. In other words, the results of the median significance test are identical to those obtained by recasting the data as a two-way contingency table and conducting a contingency table analysis using the Crosstabs procedure.

Table 67

How Students in Each Vitamin C Group Scored Relative to the Median
Regarding Difference in Days with Colds

Difference in number days with colds with respect to the median	Vitamin C factor		
	No active ingredients	Low dose of vitamin C	High dose of vitamin C
Less than or equal to median	1	7	7
Greater than the median	9	3	3

Assumptions Underlying the Median Test

Because the median test is a two-way contingency table analysis, the assumptions are the same as those for a two-way contingency table analysis. See Lesson 40 for additional discussion about these assumptions.

- Assumption 1: The observations for a two-way contingency table analysis are independent of each other.
- Assumption 2: Two-way contingency table analysis yields a test statistic that is approximately distributed as a chi-square when the sample size is relatively large.

Assumptions for the Kruskal-Wallis Test

Because analysis for the Kruskal-Wallis test is conducted on ranked scores, the population distributions for the test variable (the scores that the ranks are based on) do not have to be of any particular form (e.g., normal). However, these distributions should be continuous and have identical form.

Assumption 1: The Continuous Distributions for the Test Variable Are Exactly the Same for the Two Populations

To the extent that the population distributions differ, the test does not evaluate whether the medians differ between populations but only whether the distributions differ from each another. Difficulties arise with the Kruskal-Wallis test if there are not a number of possible scores on the measure of interest and ties are produced in the ranked scores. However, SPSS uses methods for correction of ties.

Assumption 2: The Cases Represent Random Samples from the Populations and the Scores on the Test Variable Are Independent of Each Other

The Kruskal-Wallis test will yield inaccurate p-values if the independence assumption is violated.

Assumption 3: The Chi-Square Statistic for This Test Is Only Approximate and Becomes More Accurate with Larger Sample Sizes

The p-value for the chi-square approximation test is fairly accurate if the number of cases is greater than or equal to 30.

Computing an Effect Size Statistic

SPSS does not report an effect size index for either the Kruskal-Wallis or the median tests. However, simple indices can be computed for both.

For the Kruskal-Wallis test, the median and the mean rank for each of the groups (the three vitamin C groups for our example) can be reported. Another possibility for the Kruskal-Wallis is to compute an index that is normally associated with a one-way ANOVA, such as eta square (η^2), except η^2 in this case would be computed on the ranked data such as those in Table 66. To do so, transform the scores to ranks, conduct an ANOVA, and compute an eta square on the ranked scores. Eta square can also be computed directly from the reported chi-square value for the Kruskal-Wallis test using the following equation:

$$\eta^2 = \frac{\chi^2}{N-1}$$

where N is the total number of cases (30 for our example).

Simple effect sizes can also be reported for the median test. For example, you could report the median for each group and the proportion of individuals who scored higher than the overall median for each of the groups (e.g., .9, .3, and .3 for our data). Also, any effect size index that might be reported for a two-way contingency table analysis, such as Cramér's V, could be reported for the median test in that a median test is a two-way contingency table analysis.

The Data Set

The data set used to illustrate this procedure is named *Lesson 42 Data File 1* on the Student Disk and represents data from the vitamin C example. The variables in the data set are shown in Table 68.

Table 68

Variables in Lesson 42 Data File 1

Variables	Definition
group	1 = Placebo
	2 = Low doses of vitamin C
	3 = High doses of vitamin C
diff	The number of days in year 2 with cold symptoms minus the number of days in year 1 with cold symptoms.

The Research Question

The research question can be asked in terms of differences in the distributions or in terms of a relationship between two variables.

1. Differences between the distributions: Does the median change in the number of days of cold symptoms differ among those who take placebo, those who take low doses of vitamin C, and those who take high doses of vitamin C?
2. Relationship between two variables: Is there a relationship between the amount of vitamin C taken and the change in the number of days that individuals show cold symptoms?

Conducting a Median Test

Let's conduct the overall median test and follow-up tests using the Crosstabs procedure.

Conducting the Overall Test

To evaluate the differences among all groups with the median test, follow these steps:

1. Click **Analyze**, click **Nonparametrics**, then click **K Independent Samples**. You'll see the Tests for Several Independent Samples dialog box shown in Figure 257.

Figure 257. Tests for Several Independent Samples dialog box.

2. Click **Median** in the Test Type area. Be sure this is the only option checked.
3. Click **diff**, and then click ► to move it to the Test Variable List box.
4. Click **group**, and then click ► to move it to the Grouping Variable box.
5. Click the **Define Range**.
6. Type **1** as the Minimum value for group.
7. Type **3** as the Maximum value for group.
8. Click **Continue**.
9. Click **OK**.

Selected SPSS Output for the Median Test

The results are shown in Figure 258.

Frequencies

		Vitamin C Treatment		
		1	2	3
DIFF	> Median	9	3	3
	<= Median	1	7	7

Test Statistics[b]

	DIFF
N	30
Median	-1.00
Chi-Square	9.600[a]
df	2
Asymp. Sig.	.008

a. 0 cells (.0%) have expected frequencies less than 5. The minimum expected cell frequency is 5.0.

b. Grouping Variable: Vitamin C Treatment

Figure 258. The results of the median test.

The test evaluating differences among the three medians is significant, $p = .008$. Consequently, follow-up tests should be conducted to evaluate the three pairwise comparisons.

Computing Pairwise Comparisons after a Significant Median Test

For the pairwise comparisons with the median test, it is preferable to use the Crosstabs procedure. The median test is a two-way contingency table analysis in which the rows variable is a dichotomized dependent variable and the columns variable is an independent or grouping variable. The Crosstabs procedure will allow you to apply the same cut point (the overall median) to create the dichotomized test variable for all pairwise comparisons. In contrast, the median test would use a different cut point for each pairwise comparison making the dichotomous variable inconsistently defined across comparisons and the overall median test.

To conduct a pairwise comparison between Groups 1 and 2 with the Crosstabs procedure, follow these steps:

1. Click **Transform**, then click **Rank Cases**.
2. Click **diff**, then click ► to move it to the Variable(s) box.
3. Click **OK**. A variable named rdiff is created as part of the data file.
4. Click **Transform**, click **Recode**, then click **Into Different Variables**. In steps 4 through 18, you will create a new variable, rdiff2, which has two scores: 1 if a case or individual falls at or below the median on the test variable (diff) and 2 if a case is above the median.
5. Click **rdiff**, then click ► to move it to Numeric Variable —> Output Variable.
6. Type **rdiff2** in Name text area within the Output Variable area.
7. Click **Change**.
8. Click **Old and New Values**.
9. Click **Range** (first Range option) in the Old Value area.
10. Type **1** in the box below Range.
11. Type **15** in the box after Through. Given N is the number of cases, the midrank is N divided by 2 if N is even and $(N + 1) / 2$ if N is odd. For this example, 15 is the midranked score.
12. Type **1** in the Value text box in the New Value area.
13. Click **Add**.
14. Click **All other values** in Old Value area.
15. Type **2** in the Value box in the New Value area.
16. Click **Add**.
17. Click **Continue**.
18. Click **OK**. SPSS will return you to the Data Editor.
19. Click **Data**.
20. Click **Select Cases**.
21. Click **If condition is satisfied**.
22. Click **If**.
23. Type **group = 1 or group = 2** in the Select Cases If dialog box to compare Groups 1 and 2.
24. Click **Continue**.
25. Click **OK**.
26. Click **Analyze**, click **Descriptive Statistics**, then click **Crosstabs**.
27. Click **rdiff2**, then click ► to move it to the Row(s) box.
28. Click **group**, then click ► to move it to the Columns(s) box.
29. Click **Statistics**.
30. Click **Chi-square**, and click **Phi and Cramér's V**.
31. Click **Continue**.
32. Click **Cells**.
33. Click **Expected**.
34. Click **Continue**.
35. Click **OK**.

To compare Groups 1 and 3, repeat Steps 19 through 35 except at Step 23, type **group = 1 or group = 3** in the Select Cases If dialog box. To compare Groups 2 and 3, repeat Steps 19 through 35 except at Step 23, type **group = 2 or group = 3** in the Select Cases If dialog box.

Selected SPSS Output for Follow-up Tests

The results for the comparison between the placebo and the low dose vitamin C groups are in Figure 259.

RDIFF2 * Vitamin C Treatment Crosstabulation

			Vitamin C Treatment		Total
			1	2	
RDIFF2	1.00	Count	1	7	8
		Expected Count	4.0	4.0	8.0
	2.00	Count	9	3	12
		Expected Count	6.0	6.0	12.0
Total		Count	10	10	20
		Expected Count	10.0	10.0	20.0

Chi-Square Tests

	Value	df	Asymp. Sig. (2-sided)	Exact Sig. (2-sided)	Exact Sig. (1-sided)
Pearson Chi-Square	7.500[b]	1	.006		
Continuity Correction[a]	5.208	1	.022		
Likelihood Ratio	8.202	1	.004		
Fisher's Exact Test				.020	.010
Linear-by-Linear Association	7.125	1	.008		
N of Valid Cases	20				

a. Computed only for a 2x2 table

b. 2 cells (50.0%) have expected count less than 5. The minimum expected count is 4.00.

Symmetric Measures

		Value	Approx. Sig.
Nominal by Nominal	Phi	-.612	.006
	Cramer's V	.612	.006
N of Valid Cases		20	

a. Not assuming the null hypothesis.

b. Using the asymptotic standard error assuming the null hypothesis.

Figure 259. Follow-up results to a significant median test comparing the placebo and the low dose vitamin C groups.

The LSD procedure (see Appendix B) can be used to control for Type I error across the three pairwise comparisons. Using this procedure, there are two significant pairwise comparisons, those between Groups 1 and 2 and those between Groups 1 and 3.

Conducting a Kruskal-Wallis Test

Now, we will conduct the overall Kruskal-Wallis test and follow-up tests using the Mann-Whitney U test.

Conducting the Overall Test

To conduct a Kruskal-Wallis test for differences among all groups, follow these steps:

1. Click **Data**, click **Select Cases**, then click **All Cases**, and click **OK** to select all cases for the analysis.
2. Click **Analyze**, click **Nonparametrics**, then click **K Independent Samples**.
3. Click **Reset** to clear the dialog box.
4. In the Test Type box, be sure that only the **Kruskal-Wallis** option is selected.
5. Click **diff**, and then click ▶ to move it to the Test Variable List box.
6. Click **group**, and then click ▶ to move it to the Grouping Variable box.
7. Click **Define Range**.
8. Type **1** as the Minimum value for group.
9. Type **3** as the Maximum value for group.
10. Click **Continue**.
11. Click **OK**.

Selected SPSS Output for the Kruskal-Wallis Test

The results of the analysis are shown in Figure 260.

Ranks

	Vitamin C Treatment	N	Mean Rank
DIFF	1	10	21.45
	2	10	12.60
	3	10	12.45
	Total	30	

Test Statistics[a,b]

	DIFF
Chi-Square	6.923
df	2
Asymp. Sig.	.031

a. Kruskal Wallis Test

b. Grouping Variable: Vitamin C Treatment

Figure 260. The results of the Kruskal-Wallis analysis.

The Kruskal-Wallis test indicates that there is a significant difference in the medians, χ^2 (2, $N = 30$) = 6.92, $p = .031$. Because the overall test is significant, pairwise comparisons among the three groups should be conducted.

Evaluating Pairwise Comparisons after Obtaining a Significant Kruskal-Wallis Test

The pairwise comparisons will be conducted using the Mann-Whitney U test, which yields identical results with the Kruskal-Wallis test for two independent samples. For each pairwise comparison, the values in the Define Groups dialog box will be changed to match the comparison of interest.

To conduct a Mann-Whitney U test, follow these steps:

1. Click **Analyze**, click **Nonparametrics**, then click **2 Independent Samples**.
2. Click **diff**, then click ► to move it to the Test Variable(s) box.
3. Click **group**, then click ► to move it to the Grouping Variable box.
4. Click **Define Groups**.
5. Type **1** to indicate that 1 is Group 1.
6. Type **2** to indicate that 2 is Group 2.
7. Click **Continue**.
8. Be sure that the **Mann-Whitney U test** option is checked.
9. Click **OK**.

To perform the second and the third comparisons, repeat these steps, except in Steps 5 and 6 indicate in the Define Groups dialog box the groups of interest: groups 1 and 3 for the second comparison and groups 2 and 3 for the third comparison.

Selected SPSS Output for Follow-Up Tests

The results for the first comparison between the placebo group and low-dose vitamin C group are shown in Figure 261.

Ranks

	Vitamin C Treatment	N	Mean Rank	Sum of Ranks
DIFF	1	10	13.90	139.00
	2	10	7.10	71.00
	Total	20		

Test Statistics[b]

	DIFF
Mann-Whitney U	16.000
Wilcoxon W	71.000
Z	-2.586
Asymp. Sig. (2-tailed)	.010
Exact Sig. [2*(1-tailed Sig.)]	.009[a]

a. Not corrected for ties.

b. Grouping Variable: Vitamin C Treatment

Figure 261. The results of the pairwise comparison between the placebo group and the low dose vitamin C group.

The Holm's sequential Bonferroni procedure can be used to control for Type I error. Using this procedure, only the comparison between Groups 1 and 2 is significant.

Using SPSS Graphs to Display the Results

The data for these tests are ranked, and a reader of the results would have very little knowledge of what the distributions for the dependent variable scores look like for the three groups. A graph presenting distributions of diff scores for the three groups, such as the boxplot graph shown in Figure 262 (at the top of page 370), is very informative.

Figure 262. Distributions of the change in the number of days
with colds for vitamin C treatment groups.

Two APA Results Sections

Results for the Median Test

A two-way contingency table analysis was conducted, relating the vitamin C variable (placebo, low dose of vitamin C, and high dose of vitamin C) to the dependent variable (the number of days of cold symptoms while taking medication minus the number of days of cold symptoms before taking medication) that was dichotomized at the overall median. All individuals who fell at or below the median were classified as better responders to medication, and all individuals who fell above the median were classified as poorer responders to medication.

The two-way contingency table analysis was significant, χ^2 (2, $\underline{N}$ = 30) = 9.60, $\underline{p}$ = .008. The strength of relationship between the independent and dependent variables, as assessed by Cramér's $\underline{V}$, was .57, indicating a strong relationship between the vitamin C factor and the dichotomized response-to-medication variable.

Follow-up tests were conducted to evaluate pairwise differences among the three groups using the LSD procedure. The results of these tests indicated two of the three pairwise differences were significant: the difference between the placebo group and the low dosage vitamin C group and the difference between the placebo group and the high dosage vitamin C group. Regardless of the dosage level, taking vitamin C produced a greater proportion of participants who were better responders to medication than the placebo group.

Results for the Kruskal-Wallis Test

A Kruskal-Wallis test was conducted to evaluate differences among the three vitamin C conditions (placebo, low dose of vitamin C, and high dose of vitamin C) on median change in number of days with cold symptoms (number of days with colds during treatment minus number of days with colds prior to treatment). The test, which was corrected for tied ranks, was significant, χ^2 (2, $\underline{N}$ = 30) = 6.92, $\underline{p}$ = .031. The proportion of variability in the ranked dependent variable accounted for by the vitamin C treatment variable was .24, indicating a fairly strong relationship between vitamin C treatment and the change in the number of days with colds.

Follow-up tests were conducted to evaluate pairwise differences among the three groups, controlling for Type I error across tests using the Holm's sequential Bonferroni approach. The results of these tests indicated a significant difference between the placebo group and the low-dose vitamin C group. The typical decrease in number of days with cold symptoms after treatment was greater for the low-dose vitamin C treatment group than for the placebo group.

Alternative Analyses

If a study has a single factor and a dependent variable that is measured on an interval or ratio scale, the data from the study can be analyzed using a one-way ANOVA, a Kruskal-Wallis, or a median test. However, if the nature of the dependent variable is ordinal, it is preferable to conduct a Kruskal-Wallis or median test because medians are a more meaningful measure of central tendency than means for ordinal data.

If the dependent variable is at least an interval variable, the decision about what test to use depends upon whether the assumptions underlying the test are met. The median test makes no requirement about the population distributions. The Kruskal-Wallis test assumes that the population distributions are identical, although the distributions can have any shape. The one-way ANOVA assumes not only that the distributions are identical, but also that the distributions are normal. The choice among tests is complex in that the one-way ANOVA yields relatively accurate p-values even if the normality assumption is violated if the sample sizes are moderate or larger, and power for an ANOVA depends on the shape of the population distributions.

Here are some guidelines for choosing between a Kruskal-Wallis test, a median test, and a one-way ANOVA for designs with a dependent variable that has at least an interval scale. The choices are dictated by the power of the three tests.

- If the normality assumption is met, a one-way ANOVA is the preferred test.
- If the population distributions are symmetrical and flat (uniform), a Kruskal-Wallis or a one-way ANOVA could be used to analyze your data.
- If the distributions are symmetrical, but with thicker tails than a normal distribution, you should use the Kruskal-Wallis test in that it has greater power than the one-way ANOVA.
- In most situations, the median test should probably be avoided.

Exercises

The data for Exercises 1 through 5 are in the data set named *Lesson 42 Exercise File 1* on the Student Data Disk. The data are from the following research problem.

Marvin is interested in whether blonds, brunets, and redheads differ in their extroversion. He randomly samples 18 men from his local college campus: six blonds, six brunets, and six redheads. He then administers a measure of social extroversion to each individual.

1. Conduct a Kruskal-Wallis test to investigate the relationship between hair color and social extroversion. Should you conduct post hoc tests?
2. Compute an effect size for the overall effect of hair color on extroversion.
3. Create a boxplot to display the differences among the three groups' distributions.
4. Conduct a one-way ANOVA on these data. How do the results for the ANOVA compare to the results of the Kruskal-Wallis test?
5. Write a results section based on your analyses.

The data for Exercises 6 through 8 are in the data set named *Lesson 42 Exercise File 2* on the Student Data Disk. The data are from the following research problem.

Karin believes that students with behavior problems react best to teachers who have a humanistic philosophy but have firm control of their classrooms. In a large city school system, she classifies 40 high school teachers of students with behavior problems into three categories: humanists with control (Group 1; $n = 9$); strict disciplinarians (Group 2; $n = 21$), and keepers of the behavior problems (Group 3; $n = 10$). Karin is interested in assessing whether students who are taught by one type of teacher as opposed to another type of teacher are more likely to stay out of difficulty in school. By reviewing the records of all students in these 40 teachers' classes, Karin determines the number of times the students of each teacher are sent to the main office for disciplinary action during the second half of the academic year. All classes had 30 students in them. Karin's SPSS data file has 40 cases with a factor distinguishing among the three types of teachers and a dependent variable, the number of disciplinary actions for students in a class.

6. Conduct a median test to answer Karin's question. Is the test significant?
7. Conduct follow-up tests, if appropriate.
8. Write a results section based on the analyses you have conducted.

The McNemar, sign, and Wilcoxon tests were developed to analyze data from studies with similar designs. These three tests, as well as the paired-samples *t* test, can be applied to problems with repeated-measure designs and matched-subjects designs.

For a repeated-measures design, an individual is assessed on a measure on two occasions or under two conditions. Each individual is a case in the SPSS data file and has scores on two variables, the score obtained on the measure on one occasion (or under one condition) and the score obtained on the measure on a second occasion (or under a second condition). The goal of repeated-measures designs is to determine whether participants changed significantly across occasions (or conditions).

For a matched-subjects design, participants are paired, typically on one or more nuisance variable, and each participant in the pair is assessed once on a measure. Each pair of participants is a case in the SPSS data file and has scores on two variables, the score obtained on the measure by one participant under one condition and the score obtained on the measure by the other participant under the other condition. The purpose of matched-subjects designs is to evaluate whether the pairs of participants differ significantly under the two conditions.

For both types of studies, each case in the SPSS data file has scores on two variables (that is, paired scores). The McNemar, sign, and Wilcoxon tests evaluate differences between paired scores, either repeated or matched. For the McNemar test, the variables have two categories. The McNemar test evaluates whether the proportion of participants who fall into a category on one variable differs significantly from the proportion of participants who fall into the same category on the second variable. In contrast, the variables for the sign and the Wilcoxon have multiple possible scores. With these tests, the focus is on whether the medians of the variables differ significantly.

Applying the McNemar, Sign, and Wilcoxon Tests

The McNemar, sign, and Wilcoxon tests can be used to analyze data from a number of different designs.

- Repeated-measures designs with an intervention
- Repeated-measures designs without an intervention
- Matched-subjects designs with an intervention
- Matched-subjects designs without an intervention

For each application, we will define different dependent variables to illustrate the use of the McNemar test as well as the sign and Wilcoxon tests.

Repeated-Measures Designs with an Intervention

Bill wants to assess the effectiveness of a leadership workshop for 60 middle-management executives. The 60 executives are judged by their immediate superiors on their leadership capabilities before and after the workshop. The SPSS data file contains 60 cases, one for each executive, and two variables, leadership adequacy judgments before the workshop and leadership adequacy after the workshop. For the McNemar test, the leadership adequacy variables have two scores, 0 for just adequate or inadequate and 1 for better-than-adequate. The values of 0 and 1 are arbitrary. For the sign or Wilcoxon test, the leadership adequacy variables are ratings from Leadership Rating Form (LRF), which consists of ten 5-point rating scales (LRF total scores ranging in value from 10 to 50).

Repeated-Measures Designs with No Intervention

Michelle is interested in determining if workers are more concerned with job security or job pay. She gains the cooperation of 30 individuals who work in a variety of work settings and asks each employee to indicate how concerned they are about their salary level and about their job security. Michelle's data file contains 30 cases, one for each employee, and two variables, judgments about concern for salary level and judgments about concern for job security. For the McNemar test, the scores on these variables are 0, indicating not extremely concerned, and 1, indicating extremely concerned. The values of 0 and 1 are arbitrary. For the sign and Wilcoxon tests, the scores on the variables are based on rating scales that range in value from 1 = no concern to 10 = ultimate concern.

Matched-Subjects Designs with an Intervention

Bob is interested in determining if individuals who are exposed to depressed individuals become sad. He obtains scores on the mood measure of sadness (MMS) scale for 40 students and rank orders their scores. He then pairs adjacent students with similar MMS scores. Accordingly, the students within a matched pair have more similar MMS scores than the students from different pairs. Bob randomly assigns the students within each matched pair to one of two conditions. One student is exposed to an individual who acts depressed, and the other person is exposed to an individual who acts nondepressed. After each of the students is exposed to the individual who acted either depressed or nondepressed, the exposed person is evaluated using a measure of depression by an independent observer. The observer is blind to the treatment condition to which the student has been exposed. Bob's SPSS data file contains 20 cases, one for each matched pair of students, and two variables, the depression judgment for the student exposed to the individual who acted depressed and the depression judgment for the student exposed to the individual who acted nondepressed. For the McNemar test, the scores on the variables assessing depression are 0 for not depressed and 1 for depressed. For the sign or Wilcoxon test, the scores represent the posttest MMS scores based on judgments of the independent observer for each matched pair.

Matched-Subjects Designs with No Intervention

Terri is interested in investigating if husbands and wives who are having infertility problems feel equally anxious. She obtains the cooperation of 24 infertile couples. She then interviews both the husbands and the wives and has an independent observer listen to the 48 tapes randomly ordered. After listening to each tape, the observer evaluates the anxiety level of the taped individual. Terri's SPSS data file contains 24 cases, one for each husband-wife pair, and two variables, the anxiety judgments for the husband and for the wife. Note that in this study the subjects come as matched pairs (infertile couples) and that the conditions under which the experimenter obtains the anxiety judgments are the two levels of gender, male and female. For the McNemar test, the scores on the variables assessing infertility anxiety are 0 for not anxious and 1 for anxious. For the sign or Wilcoxon test, the scores on the variables for each matched pair of husbands and wives are from the infertility anxiety measure (IAM) that yields quantitative scores.

Understanding the McNemar, Sign, and Wilcoxon Tests

To help us understand the three tests, we will first describe what data are analyzed for each test. Let's use our example dealing with concern for job security and job pay.

The data for the McNemar test in the example are presented in Table 69. Eighteen employees have tied scores, and they are disregarded in calculations for the McNemar test. The tied scores are associated with the 11 employees who are not extremely concerned about either pay or security and the seven employees who are extremely concerned about both pay and security. Analyses for the McNemar test involve comparing the proportion of employees with nontied scores who are extremely concerned about pay, but not with security (proportion = 8 / 12) with the proportion of employees with nontied scores who are extremely concerned about security, but not with pay (proportion = 4 / 12). More specifically, the McNemar test is a binomial test that evaluates whether these proportions differ significantly from .50. Although the McNemar test directly evaluates the difference between these two proportions, it simultaneously evaluates the difference between the proportion of employees who have concern for pay versus the proportion of employees who have concern for security. If the first pair of proportions differ, the second pair of proportions must also differ.

Table 69

Frequencies of Concern for Job Pay and Job Security for 30 Employees—McNemar Test

	Job Security	
Job Pay	Not extremely concerned	Extremely concerned
Not extremely concerned	11	4
Extremely concerned	8	7

The data for the sign test are presented in Table 70 (on page 376). Four employees have tied scores on concern for job security and concern for job pay (ID numbers 8, 15, 25, and 27), and they are disregarded in calculations for the sign test. The sign test ignores the quantitative differences between scores on the two variables (security - pay) and pays attention only to the sign of these difference scores, positive or negative. Two proportions are computed.

$$Proportion\ of\ Positive\ Differences = \frac{Number\ of\ Positive\ Differences}{Number\ of\ Non\text{-}Tied\ Sources}$$

and

$$Proportion\ of\ Negative\ Differences = \frac{Number\ of\ Negative\ Differences}{Number\ of\ Non\text{-}Tied\ Sources}$$

The proportion of positive differences and the proportion of negative differences for our data are 6 / 26 = .23 and 20 / 26 = .77. The sign test is a binomial test that evaluates whether these proportions differ significantly from .50.

The data for the Wilcoxon test also are presented in Table 70 (on page 376). Tied data are defined comparably for the sign and Wilcoxon tests and, therefore, the same four difference scores (differences of 0 for IDs 8, 15, 25, and 27) that were excluded from the analyses for the sign test are also eliminated from the analyses for the Wilcoxon test. The Wilcoxon test involves ranking all nonzero difference scores disregarding sign, reattaching the sign to the ranks, and then evaluating the mean of the positive and the mean of the negative ranks. For our data the mean of the positive ranks is 12.25, and the mean of the negative ranks is 13.88. The mean of the positive ranks has only six scores so that we can easily show how it is computed:

$$\text{Mean of Positive Ranks} = \frac{15+15+6.5+6.5+6.5+24}{6} = 12.25$$

Table 70

Data for Job Pay and Job Security for 30 Employees—Sign and Wilcoxon Test

			Security-Pay		Rank of absolute value of Security-Pay and sign of difference score	
ID	Security	Pay	Positive difference	Negative difference	Positive ranks	Negative ranks
1	3	4		-1		-6.5
2	1	9		-8		-26.0
3	6	8		-2		-15.0
4	7	5	+2		15.0	
5	6	4	+2		15.0	
6	5	6		-1		-6.5
7	3	6		-3		-20.0
8	4	4				
9	8	7	+1			6.5
10	3	5		-2		-15.0
11	4	5		-1		-6.5
12	6	8		-2		-15.0
13	6	7		-1		-6.5
14	3	6		-3		-20.0
15	7	7				
16	5	8		-3		-20.0
17	4	5		-1		-6.5
18	4	3	+1		6.5	
19	6	5	+1		6.5	
20	6	7		-1		-6.5
21	1	5		-4		-24.0
22	7	3	+4		24.0	
23	4	5		-1		-6.5
24	5	6		-1		-6.5
25	4	4				
26	2	5		-3		-20.0
27	6	6				
28	4	5		-1		-6.5
29	3	6		-3		-20.0
30	2	6		-4		-24.0

Assumptions Underlying the McNemar, Sign, and Wilcoxon Tests

The first assumption, independence, underlies all three tests. Assumption 2 is associated with all three tests when they use z approximation. As previously described, the McNemar and sign tests are disguised binomial tests. An exact p-value is computed based on the binomial distribution if there are fewer than 25 nontied paired scores, and a z-approximation test is calculated if the number of pairs of nontied scores exceeds 25 (see Lesson 38). For the Wilcoxon test, SPSS always uses a z-approximation test to compute a p-value. The third assumption is relevant for only the Wilcoxon test.

Assumption 1: Each Pair of Observations Must Represent a Random Sample from a Population and Must Be Independent of Every Other Pair of Observations

If the data are from a repeated measures design, the paired scores for each subject must be independent of the paired scores for any other subject. If the data are from a matched-subjects design, the paired scores from any matched pair of subjects must be independent of the paired scores from any other matched pair of subjects. If the independence assumption is violated, the test is likely to yield inaccurate results. It should be noted that the analysis presumes dependency between scores within pairs.

Assumption 2: The z Tests for the Three Tests Yield Relatively Accurate Results to the Extent That the Sample Size Is Large

The results for the McNemar and sign test should be fairly accurate given that SPSS requires a sample of 26 or more pairs of nontied scores before the z test is applied. However, you should be concerned about the accuracy of the approximate p-value for the Wilcoxon test if the sample size dips below 16 pairs of nontied scores.

Assumption 3 (Wilcoxon Test Only): The Distribution of the Difference Scores Is Continuous and Symmetrical in the Population

This assumption pertains to the difference scores, not to the ranked scores. If the difference scores are continuously distributed, there should be no ties in the difference scores across pairs of scores. In the sample data shown in Table 70, there are multiple ties in the scores.

Computing an Effect Size

SPSS does not report an effect size index for these three tests. However, simple indices can be reported for each of these tests to communicate the size of the effect.

For the McNemar test, a good effect index is the proportion of individuals who fall into one of the two categories on the one occasion (or condition) in comparison with the proportion of individuals who fall into the same category on the other occasion (or other condition). For our data, the two proportions being compared are the proportion of employees who are extremely concerned about job pay, which is .50 = (7 + 8) / 30, and the proportion of employees who are extremely concerned about job security, which is .37 = (4 + 7) / 30.

For the sign test, the proportion of individuals who had a positive (or negative) difference score in comparison with negative (or positive) differences can be reported. For example, the proportion of employees who showed greater concern for job pay in comparison with greater concern for job security of .77 = 20 / (20 + 6) could be reported. As an alternative, you could report the proportion of employees who showed greater concern for job security in comparison with greater concern for job pay of .23 = 6 / (20 + 6).

For the Wilcoxon test, the mean positive ranked difference score and the mean negative ranked difference score could be reported.

The Data Set

The data used to illustrate the three types of tests are on your disk in the file named *Lesson 43 Data File 1*. The set represents data from the example dealing with concern for job security and job pay. The description of the variables is given in Table 71. The sign and Wilcoxon tests are conducted on the pay and security variables, while the McNemar test is conducted on the payc and the securitc variables.

Table 71

Variables in Lesson 43 Exercise Data Set 1

Variables	Definition
pay	Concern for pay on a rating scale from 1, indicating no concern, to 10, indicating ultimate concern
security	Concern for job security on a rating scale from 1, indicating no concern, to 10, indicating ultimate concern
payc	Concern for job pay with 0 = not extremely concerned and 1 = extremely concerned
securitc	Concern for job security with 0 = not extremely concerned and 1 = extremely concerned

The Research Question

1. McNemar test: Are a greater proportion of employees concerned about job pay or job security?
2. Sign and the Wilcoxon tests: Does median concern for job security differ from median concern for job pay?

Conducting Tests for Two Related Samples

Now we will illustrate how to conduct analyses for the McNemar test, the sign test, and the Wilcoxon test.

Conducting the McNemar Test

To conduct a McNemar test, follow these steps:

1. Click **Analyze**, click **Nonparametric Tests**, then **2 Related Samples**. You'll see the Two Related Samples Tests dialog box as shown in Figure 263 (at the top of page 379).
2. Click **payc** and **securitc**.
3. Click ▶ to move them to the box labeled Test Pair(s) List.
4. Click **McNemar** in the Test Type area. Be sure this is the only option checked.
5. Click **OK**.

Selected SPSS Output for the McNemar Test

The results are shown in Figure 264 (on page 379). The *p*-value of .388 is greater than .05, and therefore the proportions of .50 and .37 do not differ significantly from each other.

Figure 263. The Two-Related-Samples Tests dialog box.

PAYC & SECURITC

PAYC	SECURITC	
	0	1
0	11	4
1	8	7

Test Statistics[b]

	PAYC & SECURIT C
N	30
Exact Sig. (2-tailed)	.388[a]

a. Binomial distribution used.

b. McNemar Test

Figure 264. The results of the McNemar test.

Conducting the Sign Test

1. Click **Analyze**, click **Nonparametric Tests**, then **2 Related Samples Test**.
2. Click **Reset** to clear the dialog box.
3. Click **pay** and **security**.
4. Click ▶ to move them to the box labeled Test Pair(s) List.
5. Click **Sign** in the Test Type area. Be sure this is the only option checked.
6. Click **OK**.

Selected SPSS Output for the Sign Test

The results are shown in Figure 265 (at the top of page 380). The sign test indicated significant differential concern for pay versus security, $p = .011$.

Conducting a Wilcoxon Test

1. Click **Analyze**, click **Nonparametric Tests**, then **2 Related Samples Test**.
2. The variables **pay** and **security** should already be selected.
3. Click **Wilcoxon** in the Test Type area. Be sure this is the only option checked.
4. Click **OK**.

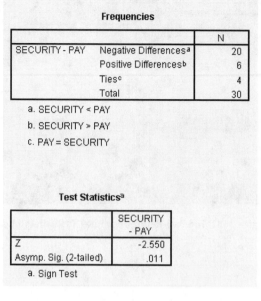

Frequencies

		N
SECURITY - PAY	Negative Differences[a]	20
	Positive Differences[b]	6
	Ties[c]	4
	Total	30

a. SECURITY < PAY

b. SECURITY > PAY

c. PAY = SECURITY

Test Statistics[a]

	SECURITY - PAY
Z	-2.550
Asymp. Sig. (2-tailed)	.011

a. Sign Test

Figure 265. The results of the sign test.

Selected SPSS Output for the Wilcoxon Test

The results are shown in Figure 266. The results for the Wilcoxon test indicated significant differential concern for pay versus security, $p = .009$.

Ranks

		N	Mean Rank	Sum of Ranks
SECURITY - PAY	Negative Ranks	20[a]	13.88	277.50
	Positive Ranks	6[b]	12.25	73.50
	Ties	4[c]		
	Total	30		

a. SECURITY < PAY

b. SECURITY > PAY

c. PAY = SECURITY

Test Statistics[b]

	SECURITY - PAY
Z	-2.626[a]
Asymp. Sig. (2-tailed)	.009

a. Based on positive ranks.

b. Wilcoxon Signed Ranks Test

Figure 266. The results of the Wilcoxon test.

Using SPSS Graphs to Display Results

Because of the simplicity of the data used in the McNemar test, it is probably unnecessary to create a graph to represent the data. However, graphs might be useful for the sign and Wilcoxon tests. The reported statistics offer no information about the shape of the distributions of the nonranked data on the original measures. Consequently, a graphical display of these data, such as a boxplot, would provide a visual representation of the distributions of the variables. See Lesson 19 for steps in creating a boxplot for separate variables. Figure 267 shows the boxplot of the nonranked pay and security scores.

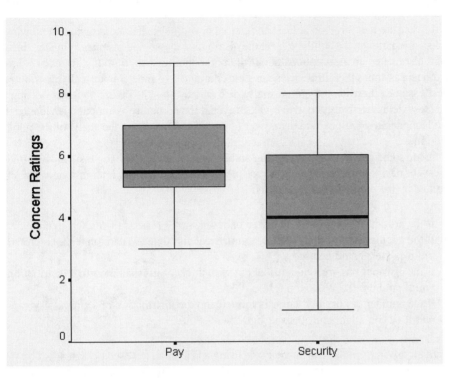

Figure 267. Distributions of pay and job security importance ratings.

Three APA Results Sections

We present sample results sections for the McNemar, sign, and Wilcoxon tests.

Results for McNemar Test

Fifty percent of the employees indicated that they were extremely concerned about job pay, while only 37% indicated that they were extremely concerned about job security. However, these percentages were not significantly different from each other based on the results of the McNemar test of dependent proportions, $p = .388$.

Results for Sign Test

Seventy-seven percent of the employees who indicated differential concern for pay versus security showed greater concern for pay. The sign test indicated significant differential concern for pay versus security, $z = 2.55$, $p = .011$. The distributions for the pay and security concern variables are shown in Figure 267.

Results for Wilcoxon Test

A Wilcoxon test was conducted to evaluate whether employees showed greater concern for pay or security. The results indicated a significant difference, $z = -2.63$, $p = .009$. The mean of the ranks in favor of pay was 13.88, while the mean of the ranks in favor of security was 12.25. The distributions for the pay and security concern variables are shown in Figure 267.

Alternative Analyses

If a study has paired scores on a quantitative dependent variable, the data from the study can be analyzed using a sign, Wilcoxon, or paired-samples t test. However, if the dependent variable is ordinal, it is preferable to conduct a sign or Wilcoxon test because medians are a more meaningful measure of central tendency.

If the data are measured on at least an interval or ordinal scale, the decision about which test to use depends partly on the ability to meet the distributional assumptions underlying the three tests. The sign test makes no assumptions about the population distribution of difference scores; the Wilcoxon test assumes the difference scores are continuously and symmetrically distributed; and the t test assumes these scores are normally distributed. The choice among tests is complex in that the t test yields relatively accurate p-values even if the normality assumption is violated if sample size is moderate or larger, and the power of the t test depends on the shape of the population distribution.

Here are some guidelines for choosing among a sign test, a Wilcoxon test, and a paired-samples t test for designs with a dependent variable that have at least an interval scale. The choices are dictated by the power of the three tests.

- If the normality assumption is met, a paired-samples t test is the preferred test.
- If the population distributions are symmetrical and flat, a Wilcoxon test or a paired-samples t test could be used.
- If the distributions are symmetrical but with thicker tails than a normal distribution, you should use the Wilcoxon test.
- If the number of possible scores is limited and the distribution of scores is asymmetrical, you might consider the sign test.

Data for a Wilcoxon test can be analyzed using a Friedman test (see Lesson 44). The Wilcoxon and Friedman tests yield identical results in that the p-values associated with the two tests are always the same for data obtained from two related samples.

Exercises

The data for Exercises 1 through 4 are in the data set named *Lesson 43 Exercise File 1* on the Student Data Disk. The data are from the following research problem.

Terri is interested in investigating if husbands and wives who are having infertility problems feel equally anxious. She obtains the cooperation of 24 infertile couples. She then interviews both the husbands and the wives and has an independent observer listen to the 48 tapes randomly ordered. After listening to each tape, the observer evaluates the anxiety level of the taped individual. Terri's SPSS data file contains 24 cases, one for each husband-wife pair, and two variables, the anxiety judgments for the husband and for the wife. For the McNemar test, the scores on the variables assessing infertility anxiety (husbandc and wifec) are 0 for not anxious and 1 for anxious. For the sign or Wilcoxon test, the scores on variables assessing infertility anxiety (husband and wife) are quantitative scores from the infertility anxiety measure (IAM). The variables are described in Table 72 (at the top of page 383).

1. Conduct a McNemar test on the husbandc and wifec variables and write a results section based on the output.
2. Conduct a sign test on the husband and wife variables and write a results section based on the output.
3. Conduct a Wilcoxon test on the husband and wife variables and write a results section based on the output.
4. Conduct a paired-samples t test on the husband and wife variables. How do your results compare to the sign and Wilcoxon results?

Table 72
Variables in Lesson 43 Exercise Data Set 1

Variables	Definition
husband	Scores on the IAM scale (mean of 50 and standard deviation of 10 in the normative sample) for husbands. Higher scores mean greater anxiety.
wife	Scores on the IAM scale (mean of 50 and standard deviation of 10 in the normative sample) for wives. Higher scores mean greater anxiety.
husbandc	Anxiety judgment about husband made by observer with 0 = nonanxious and 1 = anxious
wifec	Anxiety judgment about wife made by observer with 0 = nonanxious and 1 = anxious

K Related-Samples Tests:
The Friedman and the Cochran Tests

The Cochran and the Friedman tests are extensions of the McNemar and Wilcoxon tests, respectively. The McNemar and Wilcoxon tests can be applied to repeated-measures data if participants are assessed on two occasions or matched-subjects data if participants are matched in pairs. In contrast, the Cochran and the Friedman tests allow for the analysis of repeated-measures data if participants are assessed on two or more occasions or to matched-subjects data if participants are matched in pairs, triplets, or in some greater number. We recommend that you reread Lesson 43 about two-related-samples procedures before reading Lesson 44. The same analysis issues that apply to the NcNemar and Wilcoxon tests also apply to the Cochran and Friedman tests, and we will not present these issues in as much detail in the current lesson.

The Cochran and the Friedman tests are applicable to problems with repeated-measure designs or matched-subjects designs. With repeated-measures designs, each participant is a case in the SPSS data file and has scores on K variables, the score obtained on each of the K occasions or conditions. A researcher is interested in determining if subjects changed significantly across occasions (or conditions). For a matched-subjects design, participants are matched in sets of K participants, and each participant in a set is assessed once on a measure. Each set of participants is a case in the SPSS data file and has scores on K variables, the scores obtained on the measure by the participants within a set. The research question tested is whether the scores under the K conditions differ significantly from each other.

Applying the Cochran and Friedman Tests

Here we present two examples that are very similar to ones we introduced in Lesson 43. The major difference is that the factors for our examples in this lesson have more than two levels. For each example, we define different dependent variables to illustrate the use of the Cochran test as well as the Friedman test.

Repeated-Measures Designs

Allen, an industrial psychologist, is interested in determining if workers are more concerned with job security, job pay, or job climate. He is able to gain the cooperation of 30 individuals who work in a variety of work settings and asks each employee to indicate concern for job salary, job security, and job climate. Allen's SPSS data file contains 30 cases, one for each employee, and three variables: judgments about concern for salary level, for job security, and for job climate. The dependent variable for the Cochran test is dichotomous judgments made by employees who indicate whether they are or are not extremely concerned about salary level, job security, and job climate. The scores on these variables can be either a 0, indicating not extremely concerned, or a 1, indicating extremely concerned. The values of 0 and 1 are arbitrary. The dependent variable for the Friedman test is ratings made by employees about their concern for job salary, security, and climate. The ratings are on a 10-point scale, with 1 indicating no concern and 10 indicating ultimate concern.

Matched-Subjects Designs

Danny is interested in determining if an individual's mood state is affected by the mood of other individuals. He obtains scores on the mood measure of sadness (MMS) scale for 60 students and rank-orders their scores. He then triples up adjacent students with similar MMS scores. Accordingly, the students within a matched triplet have more similar MMS scores than they do with students from other triplets. Danny randomly assigns students within each matched triplet to one of three conditions. One student is exposed to an individual who acts depressed, a second student is exposed to an individual who acts neither depressed nor happy, and the third student is exposed to an individual who acts jubilant. After each student is exposed to one of these individuals, the student's mood state is evaluated by an independent observer. The observer is blind to the treatment condition to which the student has been exposed. Danny's SPSS data file contains 20 cases, one for each matched triplet of students, and three variables, the mood of a student exposed to a depressed individual, the mood of a student exposed to the individual who was neither depressed nor nondepressed, and the mood of a student who was jubilant. For the Cochran test, the scores on the mood measures are 0 for not depressed and 1 for depressed. For the Friedman test, the scores on the mood measures are the post-MMS scores based on the observer's judgments.

Understanding the Cochran and Friedman Tests

For both the Cochran and Friedman tests, the observations come in sets of K observations. Within a set the observations are dependent, but between sets the observations are independent. The major difference between the two tests is the scale of the dependent variable. For the Cochran test, the dependent variable has two categories, and the null hypothesis states that the population proportions are equal for the K levels of a factor. For the Friedman test, the dependent variable must be measured on at least an ordinal scale, and the null hypothesis states that the population medians are equal for the K levels of a factor.

The parametric alternative to the Cochran and the Friedman tests is the one-way repeated-measures analysis of variance (ANOVA). For all three tests, analyses involve a factor with K levels, and we are interested in evaluating whether scores differ significantly across the levels of the factor. The tests take into account the dependency among scores introduced by the repeated-measures or matched-subject characteristics of the design.

As with a one-way repeated-measures design, follow-up tests need to be conducted for the Cochran and Friedman tests if there are more than two levels of the factor of interest. These follow-up tests most frequently involve pairwise comparisons. Users can conduct these follow-up tests with the help of SPSS, but they cannot be conducted simply by choosing an option within the K-related-samples procedure.

Assumptions Underlying the Cochran and Friedman Tests

The first two assumptions are associated with both the Cochran test and Friedman test, and the third assumption is associated with only the Friedman test.

Assumption 1: Each Set of K Observations Must Represent a Random Sample from a Population and Must Be Independent of Every Other Set of K Observations

If the data are from a repeated-measures design, the scores for each participant must be independent of the scores for any other participant. If the data are from a matched-subjects design, the sets of scores from any matched set of participants must be independent of the scores from any other matched set of participants. If the independence assumption is violated, the test is likely to yield inaccurate results. It should be noted that the analyses permit dependency among scores within a set.

Assumption 2: The Chi-Square Values for the Cochran and Friedman Tests Yield Relatively Accurate Results to the Extent That the Sample Size Is Large

The results for the tests should be fairly accurate if the sample size is greater than 30.

Assumption 3 (Friedman Test Only): The Distribution of the Differences Scores between any Pair of Levels Is Continuous and Symmetrical in the Population

This assumption is required to avoid ties and to ensure that the test evaluates differences in medians rather than other characteristics of the distributions.

Computing an Effect Size

SPSS computes Kendall's coefficient of concordance (Kendall's W), a strength-of-relationship index. The coefficient of concordance ranges in value from 0 to 1, with higher values indicating a stronger relationship. The coefficient can be used as a strength-of-relationship index for both the Cochran and the Friedman tests. See Marascuilo and Serlin (1988) for further discussion about the relationship between the coefficient of concordance and these tests.

The Data Set

The data to illustrate the Friedman and Cochran tests are from our example dealing with concern for job security, pay, and climate. The data are on your disk under the name *Lesson 44 Data File 1*. A description of the variables is given in Table 73. The variables pay, security, and climate are for the Friedman test, while the variables payc, securitc, and climc are for the Cochran test.

Table 73

Variables in Lesson 44 Data File 1

Variables	Definition
pay	Concern for job pay on a rating scale from 1, indicating no concern, to 10, indicating ultimate concern
climate	Concern for job climate on a rating scale from 1, indicating no concern, to 10, indicating ultimate concern
security	Concern for job security on a rating scale from 1, indicating no concern, to 10, indicating ultimate concern
payc	Concern for job pay with 0 = not extremely concerned and 1 = extremely concerned
climc	Concern for job climate with 0 = not extremely concerned and 1 = extremely concerned
securitc	Concern for job security with 0 = not extremely concerned and 1 = extremely concerned

The Research Question

1. Cochran test: Are a greater proportion of employees concerned about job pay, job security, or job climate?
2. Friedman test: Does employees' median concern differ for job pay, job security, and job climate ratings?

Conducting K-Related-Samples Tests

We'll illustrate how to conduct the Cochran test and subsequent follow-up tests to a significant Cochran test. We also will show how to do the Friedman test and subsequent follow-up tests to a significant Friedman test. For both the Cochran test and the Friedman test, we also compute Kendall's *W*, an effect size index.

Conducting a Cochran Test

To conduct the Cochran test, follow these steps:

1. Click **Analyze**, click **Nonparametric Tests**, and click **K Related Samples**. You will see the Tests for Several Related Samples dialog box in Figure 268.

Figure 268. Tests for Several Related Samples dialog box.

2. Click **payc**, and hold down the Ctrl key and click **climc** and **securitc**.
3. Click ► to move them to the box labeled Test Variables.
4. Click **Cochran's Q** and **Kendall's W** in the Test Type area. Be sure these are the only options checked.
5. Click **OK**.

Selected SPSS Output for the Cochran Test and Kendall's W

The output is in Figure 269 (at the top of page 388). The Cochran test, which evaluated differences in proportions among the three job concerns, is significant. The effect size, Kendall's *W*, is .17. Next, we will conduct follow-up tests to evaluate comparisons between pairs of proportions. With SPSS, it is easiest to conduct these tests using McNemar's test. (See Lesson 43.)

Conducting Follow-Up Tests Using the McNemar Test

To conduct a McNemar test for the follow-up analyses, follow these steps:

1. Click **Analyze**, click **Nonparametric Tests**, and click **2 Related Samples**.
2. Hold down the Ctrl key and click **payc** and **climc**.
3. Click ► to move them to the box labeled Test Pair(s) List.
4. Hold down the Ctrl key and click **payc** and **securitc**.
5. Click ► to move them to the box labeled Test Pair(s) List.
6. Hold down the Ctrl key and click **climc** and **securitc**.
7. Click ► to move them to the box labeled Test Pair(s) List.
8. Click **McNemar** in the Test Type area. Be sure this is the only option checked.
9. Click **OK**.

Frequencies

	Value	
	0	1
PAYC	15	15
CLIMC	26	4
SECURITC	19	11

Test Statistics

N	30
Cochran's Q	10.333[a]
df	2
Asymp. Sig.	.006

a. 0 is treated as a success.

Test Statistics

N	30
Kendall's W[a]	.172
Chi-Square	10.333
df	2
Asymp. Sig.	.006

a. Kendall's Coefficient of Concordance

Figure 269. Results of the Cochran test and Kendall's W.

Selected SPSS Output for the McNemar Follow-up Tests

The results for the three pairwise comparisons are shown in Figure 270.

Test Statistics[b]

	PAYC & CLIMC	PAYC & SECURITC	CLIMC & SECURITC
N	30	30	30
Exact Sig. (2-tailed)	.007[a]	.388[a]	.039[a]

a. Binomial distribution used.

b. McNemar Test

Figure 270. The results of the McNemar follow-up tests.

As discussed in Appendix B, the LSD procedure controls adequately for Type I error across pairwise comparisons if there are three levels and the overall test is significant. If the number of levels exceeds three, then the Holm's sequential Bonferroni method or some other method will be required to control adequately for Type I error. The results of the pairwise comparisons indicated that concern for climate was significantly less than either concern for pay or security, $p = .007$ and $p = .039$, respectively. There was no significant difference between concern for pay and security, $p = .388$.

Conducting the Friedman Test and Kendall's W

To conduct the Friedman test, follow these steps:

1. Click **Analyze**, click **Nonparametric Tests**, and click **K Related Samples**.
2. Click **Reset** to clear the dialog box.

3. Hold down the Ctrl key and click **pay**, **climate**, and **security**.
4. Click ▶ to move them to the box labeled Test Variables(s) List.
5. Click **Friedman** and **Kendall's W** in the Test Type area.
6. Click **OK**.

Selected SPSS Output for the Friedman Test

The output is in Figure 271.

Friedman Test

Ranks

	Mean Rank
PAY	2.50
CLIMATE	1.68
SECURITY	1.82

Test Statistics[a]

N	30
Chi-Square	13.960
df	2
Asymp. Sig.	.001

a. Friedman Test

Kendall's W Test

Test Statistics

N	30
Kendall's W[a]	.233
Chi-Square	13.960
df	2
Asymp. Sig.	.001

a. Kendall's Coefficient of Concordance

Figure 271. Results of the Friedman test and Kendall's W.

The Friedman test, which evaluated differences in medians among the three job concerns, is significant. Kendall's *W* is .23. Next, follow-up tests are conducted to evaluate comparisons between pairs of medians. With SPSS, it is easiest to conduct these tests using the Wilcoxon test. (See Lesson 43.)

Conducting Follow-Up Tests Using the Wilcoxon Test

To conduct a Wilcoxon test for the follow-up analyses, follow these steps:

1. Click **Analyze**, click **Nonparametric Tests**, and click **2 Related Samples**.
2. Click **Reset** to clear the dialog box.
3. Hold down the Ctrl key and click **pay** and **climate**.
4. Click ▶ to move them to the box labeled Test Pair(s) List.
5. Hold down the Ctrl key and click **pay** and **security**.
6. Click ▶ to move them to the box labeled Test Pair(s) List.
7. Hold down the Ctrl key and click **climate** and **security**.
8. Click ▶ to move them to the box labeled Test Pair(s) List.
9. Click **Wilcoxon** in the Test Type area. Be sure this is the only option checked.
10. Click **OK**.

Selected SPSS Output for the Wilcoxon Follow-Up Tests

The results for the three pairwise comparisons are shown in Figure 272.

Wilcoxon Signed Ranks Test

Ranks

		N	Mean Rank	Sum of Ranks
CLIMATE - PAY	Negative Ranks	19[a]	11.21	213.00
	Positive Ranks	3[b]	13.33	40.00
	Ties	8[c]		
	Total	30		
SECURITY - PAY	Negative Ranks	20[d]	13.88	277.50
	Positive Ranks	6[e]	12.25	73.50
	Ties	4[f]		
	Total	30		
SECURITY - CLIMATE	Negative Ranks	10[g]	10.85	108.50
	Positive Ranks	13[h]	12.88	167.50
	Ties	7[i]		
	Total	30		

a. CLIMATE < PAY

b. CLIMATE > PAY

c. PAY = CLIMATE

d. SECURITY < PAY

e. SECURITY > PAY

f. PAY = SECURITY

g. SECURITY < CLIMATE

h. SECURITY > CLIMATE

i. CLIMATE = SECURITY

Test Statistics[c]

	CLIMATE - PAY	SECURITY - PAY	SECURITY - CLIMATE
Z	-2.822[a]	-2.626[a]	-.923[b]
Asymp. Sig. (2-tailed)	.005	.009	.356

a. Based on positive ranks.

b. Based on negative ranks.

c. Wilcoxon Signed Ranks Test

Figure 272. The results of the Wilcoxon follow-up tests.

The LSD procedure controls adequately for Type I error across pairwise comparisons if there are three levels and the overall test is significant. In our example, two of the three comparisons were significant.

Using SPSS Graphs to Display Results

Because of the simplicity of the data used in the Cochran test, it is probably unnecessary to create a graph to represent the data. However, graphs might be useful for the Friedman test. The reported statistics offer no information about the shape of the distributions of the nonranked data on the original measures. Consequently, a graphical display of these data, such as a boxplot, would provide a visual representation of the distributions of the variables. See Lesson 19 for steps in creating a boxplot for separate variables. Figure 273 (at the top of page 391) shows the boxplot of the nonranked climate, pay, and security scores.

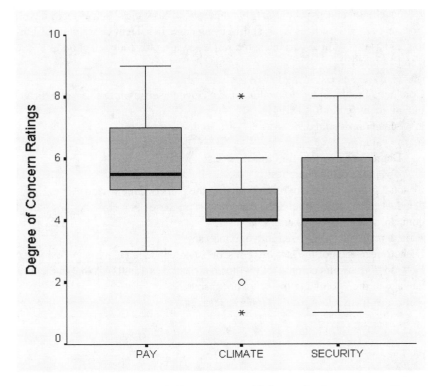

Figure 273. Distributions of climate, pay, and job security importance ratings.

Two APA Results Sections

Results for Cochran Test

Proportions of employees showing extreme concern for pay, security, and climate were .50, .37, and .13, respectively. A Cochran test, which evaluates differences among related proportions, was significant, χ^2 (2, $\underline{N}$ = 30) = 10.33, $\underline{p}$ = .006. The Kendall coefficient of concordance was .17. Follow-up pairwise comparisons were conducted using a McNemar's test and controlling for familywise error rate at the .05 level using the LSD procedure. The proportions differed significantly between concern for pay and concern for climate, $\underline{p}$ = .007, and between concern for security and concern for climate, $\underline{p}$ = .039, but not between concern for pay and concern for security, $\underline{p}$ = .388.

Results for Friedman Test

A Friedman test was conducted to evaluate differences in medians among the job concerns for pay (median = 5.50), for climate (median = 4.00) and for security (median = 4.00). The test was significant, χ^2 (2, $\underline{N}$ = 30) = 13.96, $\underline{p}$ = .001, and the Kendall coefficient of concordance of .23 indicated fairly strong differences among the three concerns. Follow-up pairwise comparisons were conducted using a Wilcoxon test and controlling for the Type I errors across these comparisons at the .05 level using the LSD procedure. The median concern for pay was significantly greater than median concern for climate, $\underline{p}$ = .005 and the median concern for security, $\underline{p}$ = .009, but the median concern for climate did not differ significantly from the median concern for security, $\underline{p}$ = .356.

Exercises

Exercises 1 through 6 are based on the following research problem. The data for these examples are in the data file named *Lesson 44 Exercise File 1* on the Student Disk.

Mary, a developmental psychologist, is interested in how girls' self-esteem develops over time. She measures 25 girls at ages 9, 11, and 14 using the Self-Esteem Descriptor (SED). The data file contains 25 cases and three variables, the self-esteem scores for each child at ages 9 (sed1), 11 (sed2), and 14 (sed3).

1. Conduct a Friedman test to evaluate the change in self-esteem over time. From the output, identify the following:
   a. Mean rank for age 9
   b. χ^2 value
   c. Degrees of freedom for chi square test
   d. p-value for chi square test
2. Conduct follow-up Wilcoxon tests among the pairs of time periods.
3. Conduct a one-way within-subjects ANOVA on these data. How do these results compare with those in Exercise 1?
4. Write a results section based on your analyses.
5. Dichotomize each of the self-esteem scores and conduct a Cochran test on them. How do your results compare with those in Exercises 1 and 3? What is the disadvantage of dichotomizing the self-esteem scores?
6. Write a results section for the Cochran test.

ID_PROF	SEX_PROF	AGE	RANK	SCHOOL	CRAB1	CRAB2	CRAB3	CRAB4	CRAB5	CRAB6
1.00	1.00	33.00	1.00	1.00	2.00	3.00	3.00	3.00	2.00	3.00
2.00	1.00	58.00	3.00	1.00	5.00	3.00	4.00	3.00	5.00	3.00
3.00	1.00	45.00	3.00	1.00	4.00	5.00	3.00	5.00	2.00	5.00
4.00	2.00	36.00	1.00	1.00	3.00	2.00	3.00	1.00	3.00	1.00
5.00	2.00	42.00	2.00	1.00	5.00	3.00	3.00	3.00	3.00	3.00
6.00	1.00	59.00	3.00	2.00	2.00	3.00	2.00	1.00	1.00	1.00
7.00	2.00	29.00	1.00	2.00	1.00	3.00	1.00	1.00	1.00	2.00
8.00	1.00	64.00	2.00	2.00	1.00	3.00	2.00	3.00	1.00	3.00
9.00	1.00	37.00	2.00	2.00	2.00	2.00	2.00	2.00	1.00	3.00
10.00	1.00	42.00	3.00	2.00	1.00	3.00	1.00	3.00	1.00	3.00

ID_STUD	ID_PROF	SEX_STUD	TEACHER1	TEACHER2	TEACHER3	TEACHER4	TEACHER5
82104	1	2.00	4.00	5.00	2.00	1.00	2.00
22466	1	2.00	5.00	3.00	1.00	2.00	4.00
75812	1	2.00	3.00	5.00	2.00	1.00	3.00
80761	1	1.00	4.00	4.00	2.00	1.00	3.00
22920	1	1.00	5.00	4.00	2.00	1.00	3.00
87172	2	2.00	3.00	4.00	1.00	2.00	3.00
98221	2	2.00	3.00	3.00	2.00	3.00	2.00
84768	2	1.00	4.00	3.00	3.00	2.00	3.00
89225	2	1.00	3.00	3.00	3.00	1.00	4.00
80623	2	2.00	3.00	5.00	2.00	2.00	3.00
94354	3	1.00	3.00	5.00	1.00	2.00	3.00
81334	3	2.00	4.00	5.00	5.00	2.00	3.00
52955	3	2.00	4.00	4.00	5.00	4.00	4.00
33191	3	2.00	4.00	2.00	5.00	4.00	2.00
55291	3	2.00	4.00	4.00	2.00	3.00	3.00
60608	4	2.00	3.00	4.00	5.00	3.00	4.00
67041	4	2.00	2.00	2.00	2.00	2.00	2.00
65719	4	2.00	3.00	3.00	5.00	3.00	4.00
40351	4	1.00	2.00	4.00	2.00	2.00	2.00
62034	4	1.00	2.00	4.00	2.00	2.00	4.00
94882	5	2.00	4.00	5.00	3.00	2.00	2.00
26841	5	1.00	2.00	4.00	2.00	1.00	3.00

ID_STUD	ID_PROF	SEX_STUD	TEACHER1	TEACHER2	TEACHER3	TEACHER4	TEACHER5
13691	5	1.00	2.00	3.00	1.00	3.00	2.00
83651	5	2.00	1.00	3.00	4.00	4.00	2.00
70778	5	2.00	1.00	3.00	4.00	4.00	3.00
70386	6	1.00	3.00	4.00	2.00	3.00	5.00
45176	6	1.00	5.00	4.00	1.00	1.00	4.00
86213	6	2.00	3.00	5.00	1.00	1.00	3.00
29627	6	1.00	2.00	4.00	2.00	1.00	4.00
24824	6	1.00	1.00	5.00	2.00	2.00	4.00
39986	7	1.00	5.00	5.00	2.00	1.00	5.00
77974	7	1.00	5.00	4.00	2.00	1.00	4.00
38396	7	1.00	5.00	5.00	2.00	1.00	5.00
78665	7	1.00	4.00	3.00	2.00	1.00	3.00
20227	7	1.00	4.00	5.00	1.00	1.00	5.00
66298	8	1.00	5.00	5.00	1.00	1.00	3.00
27423	8	1.00	5.00	5.00	1.00	1.00	4.00
79359	8	1.00	5.00	5.00	1.00	1.00	5.00
99056	8	2.00	5.00	5.00	1.00	1.00	4.00
66513	8	1.00	5.00	5.00	1.00	1.00	5.00
28796	9	1.00	2.00	4.00	4.00	3.00	1.00
67564	9	1.00	3.00	3.00	4.00	4.00	1.00
95471	9	2.00	2.00	3.00	3.00	4.00	2.00
35598	9	1.00	3.00	3.00	2.00	1.00	2.00
91744	9	2.00	3.00	4.00	3.00	2.00	3.00
77823	10	1.00	5.00	5.00	2.00	1.00	5.00
34850	10	1.00	5.00	5.00	1.00	2.00	5.00
94277	10	2.00	4.00	4.00	1.00	1.00	4.00
54217	10	1.00	3.00	5.00	1.00	1.00	4.00
99513	10	2.00	2.00	5.00	1.00	3.00	2.00

Methods for Controlling Type I Error across Multiple Hypothesis Tests

A Type I error is the probability of rejecting a null hypothesis when it is true. Alpha (α) is the probability of committing a Type I error. When we conduct a hypothesis test, we want to minimize our chances of committing a Type I error for that test and, therefore, we designate alpha to be some small value, most frequently .05.

If multiple hypothesis tests are conducted, then we may be concerned about committing one or more Type I errors across these tests. The multiple hypotheses are referred to as a family, and the probability of committing one or more Type I errors for a family is the familywise alpha (α_{family}). For any family, we want to keep α_{family} small, most frequently .05. To keep α_{family} at the .05 level, in most cases we reduce the alpha level for any one test to be a value less than .05. (An exception is for the LSD method for pairwise comparisons among three groups, as we will describe presently.)

For example, in many applications, a family of multiple hypotheses may involve pairwise comparisons among three or more groups. These hypotheses evaluate whether pairs of groups differ on a dependent variable. We'll briefly describe three methods to control for α_{family} when the family consists of pairwise comparisons. Initially, we will consider the LSD procedure, which should be used only if there are three groups. For this special application, the probability of a Type I error for a pairwise comparison, α_{pc}, is equal to α_{family}. Next, we will discuss the Bonferroni method, which requires the α_{pc} to be equal to α_{family} divided by the number of paired comparisons. Finally, we will introduce the Holm's sequential Bonferroni method that evaluates each paired comparison at a different alpha level.

Although we will look at these methods for evaluating multiple pairwise comparison tests, the last two methods (the Bonferroni and the Holm's sequential Bonferroni methods) can be used for any application involving multiple hypothesis testing. The Holm's sequential Bonferroni method is preferable to the Bonferroni method for evaluating hypotheses because it is less conservative and has greater power.

LSD Method for Control of Type I Error for Pairwise Comparisons among Three Groups

1. Set α_{family}. With the LSD procedure, $\alpha_{\bullet pc} = \alpha_{family}$.
2. Conduct omnibus F test to evaluate the difference among the three groups.
   - If $p_{ANOVA} \leq \alpha_{family}$, reject null hypothesis. Continue to Step 3.
   - If $p_{ANOVA} > \alpha_{family}$, do not reject null hypothesis. Do not proceed to next step. Declare all comparisons nonsignificant.
3. Conduct pairwise comparisons. If $p_{pc} \leq \alpha_{pc}$, then reject null hypothesis for each pairwise comparison.

Bonferroni Method for Control of Type I Error for All Pairwise Comparisons

1. Set α_{family}.
2. Define number of pairwise comparisons. N_G is the number of groups and N_{pc} is the number of pairwise comparisons.

$$N_{PC} = \frac{N_G \, (N_G - 1)}{2}$$

3. Compute alpha for any pairwise comparison.

$$\alpha_{PC} = \frac{\alpha_{family}}{N_{PC}}$$

4. Conduct pairwise comparisons. If $p_{pc} \leq \alpha_{pc}$, then reject null hypothesis for each pairwise comparison.

Holm's Sequential Bonferroni Method for Control of Type I Error for All Pairwise Comparisons

1. Set α_{family}.
2. Define number of pairwise comparisons.

$$N_{PC} = \frac{N_G \, (N_G - 1)}{2}$$

3. Rank order comparisons based on p_{pc} values from smallest to largest.
4. Evaluate comparison with smallest p_{pc} (i.e., p_1.)
   a. Compute the alpha for the first comparison, α_1.

$$\alpha_1 = \frac{\alpha_{family}}{N_{PC}}$$

   b. Conduct pairwise comparison.
      ▪ If $p_1 \leq \alpha_1$, reject null hypothesis. Continue to Step 5.
      ▪ If $p_1 > \alpha_1$, do not reject null hypothesis. Do not proceed to next step. Declare all remaining comparisons nonsignificant.
5. Evaluate comparison with next smallest p_{pc} (i.e., p_2).
   a. Compute the alpha for the second comparison, α_2.

$$\alpha_2 = \frac{\alpha_{family}}{N_{PC} - 1}$$

   b. Conduct pairwise comparison.
      ▪ If $p_2 \leq \alpha_2$, reject null hypothesis. Continue to Step 6.
      ▪ If $p_2 > \alpha_2$, do not reject null hypothesis. Do not proceed to next step. Declare all remaining comparisons nonsignificant.

6. Evaluate comparison with next smallest p_{pc} (i.e., p_3).
   a. Compute α_3.

$$\alpha_3 = \frac{\alpha_{family}}{N_{PC} - 2}$$

   b. Conduct pairwise comparison.
      - If $p_3 \leq \alpha_3$ reject null hypothesis. Continue to Step 7.
      - If $p_3 > \alpha_3$ do not reject null hypothesis. Do not proceed to next step. Declare all remaining comparisons nonsignificant.
7. And so on …

Selected Answers to Lesson Exercises

Answers for Lesson 18

1. To reverse scale the scores, use the Transform … Recode Into Same Variables option or the Transform … Recode Into Different Variables option. Alternatively, use the Transform … Compute option, type a name of a variable like item3r in the Target Variable box and type **6 - item3** in the Numeric Expression box.

3. To create a categorical age variable, use the Transform … Recode into Different Variables option. The old and new values should be as follows:

Old values	New values
Range: 20 through 29	1
Range: 30 through 39	2
All other values	3

5. Conduct the following steps to create the variable group:

   a. Compute a total coffee-drinking score using the Transform … Compute option. Type a name of a variable like **totcof** in the Target Variable box and type **sum(day1,day2,day3,day4)** in the Numeric Expression box.

   b. Create a categorical variable (e.g., cofcat) based on the coffee-drinking scores using the Transform … Recode Into Different Variables option. The old and new values should be as follows:

Old values	New values
Range: 0 through 4	1
All other values	2

   Use the Transform … Compute option and the If option to create four categories. Conduct the following steps:

   1. Type **group** in the Target Variable box. Type **1** in the Numeric Expression box. Click **If**. Click **Include if case satisfies**. Type **jobcat = 1 & cofcat = 1** in the text box. Click **Continue**. Click **OK**.
   2. Type **group** in the Target Variable box. Type **2** in the Numeric Expression box. Click **If**. Click **Include if case satisfies**. Type **jobcat = 1 & cofcat = 2** in the text box. Click **Continue**. Click **OK**.
   3. Type **group** in the Target Variable box. Type **3** in the Numeric Expression box. Click **If**. Click **Include if case satisfies**. Type **jobcat = 2 & cofcat = 1** in the text box. Click **Continue**. Click **OK**.
   4. Type **group** in the Target Variable box. Type **4** in the Numeric Expression box. Click **If**. Click **Include if case satisfies**. Type **jobcat = 2 & cofcat = 2** in the text box. Click **Continue**. Click **OK**.

7. In Exercise 6, you created a *z*-scored prosocial variable, zrating, using Analyze ... Descriptive Statistics ... Descriptives. Now use the Transform ... Compute option. Type a name of a variable like **zratingr** in the Target Variable box and type **-1*zrating** in the Numeric Expression box.

Answers for Lesson 19

1. a. Percentage men = 52%
    b. Mode is divorced (= 2).
    c. Frequency of divorced people = 11
3. The bar chart for the different sized communities is shown in Figure 274. Community sizes were ordered from smallest to largest along the horizontal axis using the Series...Displayed option. In the Bar/Line/Area Displayed Data dialog box, reorder categories in the Display box.

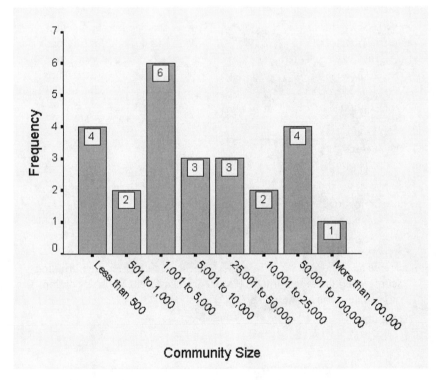

Figure 274. Number of people in different sized communities.

5. Table 74 (at the top of page 400) shows the frequencies of the types of books read.
7. The sample consisted of 50 men and 50 women. Table 74 shows the frequencies of the types of books these individuals report reading. The most popular type of book was dramatic novels ($\underline{N}$ = 16), while the least popular type was historical nonfiction ($\underline{N}$ = 6). Figure 275 (on page 400) summarizes how much the individuals in the sample read. The respondents were approximately evenly split among the four reading types.

Table 74

Type of Books Read by 50 Men and 50 Women

Type of Book	Frequency
Drama	16
Mysteries	7
Romance	10
Historical nonfiction	6
Travel books	13
Children's literature	10
Poetry	9
Autobiographies	9
Political science	8
Local interest	12

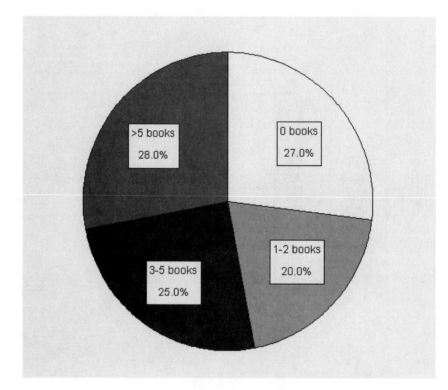

**Figure 275. Percentage of individuals who read
0, 1 to 2, 3 to 5, and greater than 5 books per month.**

Answers for Lesson 20

1. a. Skewness = .42
   b. Mean = 32.27
   c. *SD* = 23.48
   d. Kurtosis = -1.12
2. The percentile ranks for the 15 scores are 12, 24, 73, 13, 27, 77, 83, 38, 16, 17, 72, 88, 97, 73, and 19. The scores associated with the ranks of 12, 27, 38, 73, and 88 are 5, 18, 25, 47, and 60, respectively.
3. The percentile ranks are 7, 47, 53, 70, and 93, respectively.

4. The histogram is shown in Figure 276.

Figure 276. Distribution of anxiety scores.

5. Based on the graph, it does not appear that the scores are even approximately normally distributed. Accordingly, it is preferable to compute the percentile ranks not assuming that the scores are normally distributed.

7. The mean for the total attitude score for Republicans is 15.19, and the mean for the total attitude score for Democrats is 11.47. (We reverse scaled the first item, computed total scores, and then obtained means on the total scores for the two political parties using Analyze … Descriptive Statistics … Explore.)

Answers for Lesson 21

1. You can compute a total score by summing across all eight items using the Transform … Compute command. The total scores are 8, 6, 5, 7, 4, and 6.
2. The test value is 2.
3. a. Mean = 6.0
   b. t value = 6.93
   c. p-value = .001
5. A one-sample t test indicated that the mean on the emotional response scale (ranging from 2 = very sad for both segments to 20 = very happy for both segments) differed significantly different from 11, the midpoint on the summed emotional response scale, t (19) = -2.13, p = .047. The sample mean and standard deviation on the emotional response scores were 8.75 and 4.73, respectively. A d of -.48 indicated a medium effect size. The results supported the conclusion that classical music tends to make college students sad rather than happy.
6. The distribution of emotional response scores are shown in Figure 277 (at the top of page 402).

Figure 277. Distribution of positive emotional response scores.

Answers for Lesson 22

1. To obtain an overall score of life stress, sum the interpersonal and occupational stress measures at each age using the Transform … Compute option. You should have two new variables, one for overall life stress at age 40 and one for overall life stress at age 60.

3. The histogram is shown in Figure 278.

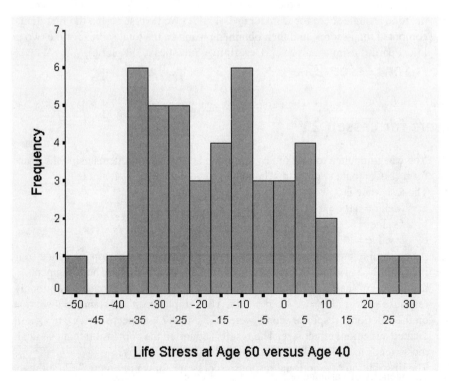

Figure 278. Distribution of change in overall life stress from age 40 to age 60.

5. Results of the analysis: A paired-samples t test was conducted to evaluate whether women's life stress declined from age 40 to age 60. The results indicated that the mean overall life stress index at age 60 ($\underline{M}$ = 136.87, $\underline{SD}$ = 9.95) was significantly less than mean overall life stress index at age 40 ($\underline{M}$ = 151.84, $\underline{SD}$ = 14.48), $\underline{t}$ (44) = -5.82, $\underline{p}$ < .001. The effect size was moderately large, $\underline{d}$ = -.87. From Figure 278, it appears that for most women, overall life stress scores declined over the 20-year period.

Two separate paired-samples $\underline{t}$ tests were conducted to evaluate whether women's occupational and interpersonal stress increased or decreased as they aged. Table 75 presents the means and standard deviations of the occupational and interpersonal life stress scores at ages 40 and 60. The results indicated that inter-personal stress levels did not differ significantly from age 40 to age 60, $\underline{t}$ (44) = -1.54, $\underline{p}$ = .131, but that women's occupational stress decreased significantly during the same time period, $\underline{t}$ (44) = -6.22, $\underline{p}$ < .001.

Table 75

Means and Standard Deviations for Occupational and Interpersonal:
Life Stress Scores at Age 40 and Age 60

	Age 40		Age 60	
Life stress scale	M	SD	M	SD
Interpersonal	78.20	11.66	75.00	7.71
Occupational	73.64	9.55	61.87	6.63

7. Results of the analysis: A paired-samples $\underline{t}$ test was conducted to evaluate whether husbands and wives differed on their levels of infertility anxiety. The results indicated that wives were significantly more anxious about fertility issues than their husbands, $\underline{t}$ (23) = -3.26, $\underline{p}$ = .003. The sample means and standard deviations on the infertility anxiety measure were 62.54 and 12.44 for wives and 57.46 and 7.34 for husbands. The $\underline{d}$ of -.66 indicated a medium effect size.

Answers for Lesson 23

1. t (38) = -3.98, p < .001 when assuming equal variances and t (30.83) = -5.40, p < .001 when not assuming equal variances.
2. a. 589 seconds
   b. 82.95 seconds
   c. F (1, 38) = 2.74, p = .106
5. Figure 279 (at the top of page 404) shows the boxplots of the time distributions for overweight and normal weight individuals.
9. The results of Levene's test, F (1, 38) = 4.10, p = .050, indicate that the homogeneity of variance assumption is violated. The variability is much greater for the regular education students who are in integrated classrooms (SD = 16.54) than those who are not in the integrated classrooms (SD = 7.41). These results suggest that the standard t test is likely to produce inaccurate p values. Consequently, the t test that does not assume homogeneity of variances should be used: t (35.85) = -2.11, p = .042.
10. Results of the analysis: The analyses addressed the question of whether students are helped or hindered academically by the inclusion of special education children in regular education classrooms. Levene's test indicated that we could not assume homogeneity of variance of the difference scores (post-achievement minus pre-achievement test scores), $\underline{F}$ (1, 38) = 4.10, $\underline{p}$ = .050. The variance of the difference

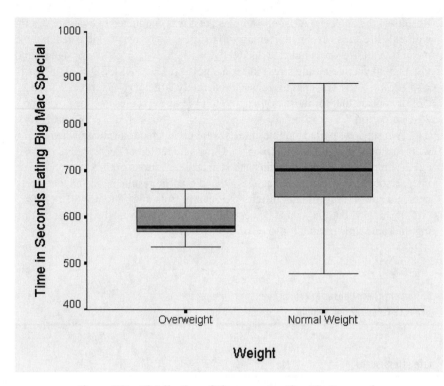

Figure 279. Distribution of time spent eating Big Mac meals for overweight and normal weight individuals.

scores for the regular education students in integrated classrooms (273.57) was much greater than the variance of the difference scores for the regular education students in non-integrated classrooms (54.91). Consequently, a $\underline{t}$ test was conducted that did not require homogeneity of variance. The results indicated that on the average standardized achievement test scores improved significantly more for students in integrated classrooms ($\underline{M}$ = 9.60) than those in nonintegrated classrooms ($\underline{M}$ = 1.53), $\underline{t}$ (35.85) = -2.11, $\underline{p}$ < .042. The $\underline{d}$ index of -.69 indicated that there was a moderate relationship between classroom integration and improvement in standardized achievement scores. Figure 280 (at the top of page 405) shows the distributions for both types of classrooms. There is considerable overlap in the distributions for the two groups. The results support the integration of regular and special education students into the same classroom.

Answers for Lesson 24

1. a. $F(2,15) = 3.51$
   b. $SS_{\text{hair color}} = 24.11$
   c. Mean for redheads = 2.33
   d. $p = .056$
2. eta squared = .32
3. Figure 281 (on page 405) shows the distributions for the three hair color groups.
5. Because the Levene's test indicates that the population variances for the three types of teachers are not equal, F (2, 37) = 14.40, p < .001, the Dunnett's C or a comparable procedure that does not require the assumption of homogeneity of variance should be used.
6. Results of the analysis: A one-way ANOVA was conducted to evaluate the effect of different behavior management strategies on classroom behavior. The independent variable was behavior management strategies with three levels—firm humanist, strict disciplinarian, and laissez-faire—while the dependent variable was the total

Figure 280. Boxplots of difference scores for regular education students in integrated and nonintegrated classrooms.

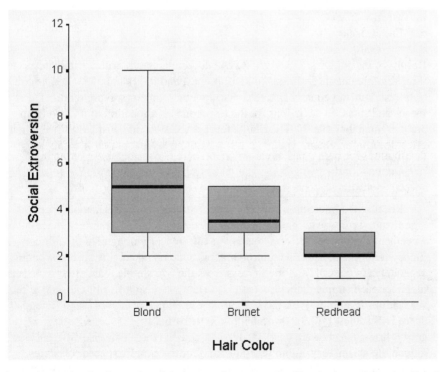

Figure 281. Distributions of social extroversion scores for blonds, brunets, and redheads.

number of times students in classrooms were sent to the office for disciplinary action. The results of the ANOVA indicated a significant relationship between behavior management strategies and the number of times teachers sent students to the office, $\underline{F}(2,37) = 5.58$, $\underline{p} = .008$. The η^2 was relatively large, .23, and indicated that 23% of the variance in the number of office trips by students could be explained by differences in behavior management strategies. Table 76 shows the means and standard deviations for each of the three types of management strategies.

To assess further the differences among groups, we conducted pairwise comparisons among the three means using Dunnett's $\underline{C}$, a multiple comparison procedure that does not require equal population variances. Levene's test had indicated that the variances among the groups differed significantly, $\underline{F}$ (2, 37) = 14.40, $\underline{p} <$ .001. Based on the results of Dunnett's $\underline{C}$, teachers who used a humanistic approach to classroom management sent students to the office significantly fewer times than did teachers who were strict disciplinarians. Laissez-faire teachers did not differ significantly from either of the other two groups in the number of students they sent to the office for disciplinary action.

Table 76

Means and Standard Deviations of Three Behavior Management Styles

Treatment groups	*M*	*SD*
Humanist (*N* = 9)	5.56	1.33
Strict, rigid control (*N* = 21)	7.29	1.68
Laissez faire (*N* = 10)	9.70	4.79

Answers for Lesson 25

1. a. F (1, 60) = 25.04
   b. Mean = 28.27
   c. Effect size = .14
   d. p = .000
3. Results of the analysis: A 3 x 2 ANOVA was conducted to evaluate the effects of three reinforcement conditions (tokens, money, and food) and two schedule conditions (random and equally spaced) on arithmetic problem-solving scores. The means and standard deviations for the test scores as a function of the two factors are presented in Table 77. The results for the ANOVA indicated a significant main effect for reinforcement type, $\underline{F}$ (2, 60) = 31.86, $\underline{p}$ < .001, partial η^2 = .52, a significant effect for schedule type, $\underline{F}$ (1, 60) = 25.04, $\underline{p}$ < .001, partial η^2 = .29, and a significant interaction between reinforcement type and schedule type, $\underline{F}$ (2, 60) = 4.78, $\underline{p}$ = .012, partial η^2 = .14.

Because the interaction between reinforcement type and schedule type was significant, we chose to ignore the main effects and instead examined the reinforcement simple main effects, that is, the differences among token reinforcers, money reinforcers, and food reinforcers for random and equally spaced schedules separately. To control for Type I error across the two simple main effects, we set alpha for each simple main effect at .025. There were significant reinforcer effects for random schedules, $\underline{F}$ (2, 60) = 20.98, $\underline{p}$ < .001, partial η^2 = .41, and for equally spaced schedules, $\underline{F}$ (2, 60) = 15.65, $\underline{p}$ < .001, partial η^2 = .34.

Follow-up tests were conducted to evaluate the three pairwise differences among the means for random schedules and for the equally spaced schedules. Alpha was set at .008 (.025 / 3 = .008) to control for Type I error over the three pairwise comparisons within each simple main effect. For the random schedules, money and food reinforcers produced significantly higher test scores than token reinforcers; the means for money and food reinforcers were not significantly different from each other. Similarly, for the equally spaced schedules, money and food reinforcers produced significantly higher test scores than token reinforcers; the means for money and food reinforcers were not significantly different from each other.

Table 77

Means and Standard Deviations for Test Scores

	Tokens		Money		Food	
Schedule	M	SD	M	SD	M	SD
Random schedule	19.64	5.03	28.27	4.76	31.45	5.28
Equally spaced schedule	26.45	4.01	37.00	4.31	32.27	2.69

6. You should conduct three pairwise comparisons among the marginal means for the three disability because (1) there is a significant disability main effect and a nonsignificant interaction and (2) the disability main effect has three levels. You should consider appropriate methods to control for Type I error across the three groups. Because there are only three groups, you could use the LSD approach.

8. The boxplot is shown in Figure 282.

Figure 282. Distributions of play time across gender and disability status of the child.

Answers for Lesson 26

1. To compute an overall scale score, *z*-score all four mechanical ability variables using the Analyze—Descriptive Statistics … Descriptives option and then sum the four *z*-scored variables using the Transform … Compute option.

3. a. $p = .013$
   b. $\eta^2 = .55$
   c. $F(1, 11) = 24.22$

5. Results of the analysis: A one-way analysis of covariance (ANCOVA) was conducted to evaluate differences in mechanical performance efficiency among three different types of professors (mechanical engineering, psychology, and philosophy), holding constant mechanical aptitude. We conducted a preliminary test to evaluate the homogeneity-of-slopes assumption for ANCOVA and found

a nonsignificant interaction between type of professor and mechanical aptitude. The ANCOVA was significant, $\underline{F}$ (2, 11) = 6.63, $\underline{MSE}$ = 1.49, $\underline{p}$ = .013. The strength of relationship between professor type and mechanical performance efficiency was very strong, as assessed by a partial eta square of .55. Type of professor accounted for 55% of the variance in mechanical performance efficiency, holding constant the level of mechanical aptitude.

The means on automobile maintenance performance adjusted for initial differences in mechanical aptitude were ordered as expected across the three types of professors. Mechanical engineering professors performed the best on the automobile maintenance as reflected by their adjusted mean of -1.88, psychology professors had the next smallest adjusted mean ($\underline{M}$ = .92), and philosophy professors performed the worst on the maintenance task ($\underline{M}$ = .96).

Follow-up tests were conducted to evaluate pairwise differences among these adjusted means. Holm's sequential Bonferroni procedure was used to control for Type I error across the three pairwise comparisons. The mechanical engineering professors performed better on the automobile maintenance tasks than either psychology or philosophy professors. The psychology and philosophy professors did not differ significantly from each other.

7. The *F* test associated with the group source is not significant, F (2,56) = 1.31, p = .279. In addition the effect size is relatively small, η^2 = .045. Based on these results, there are no significant group mean differences on depression scores among the three therapy conditions.

Answers for Lesson 27

1. a. Wilks' Λ = .176
   b. F (6, 50) = 11.52
   c. η^2 = .58.
   d. F (2, 27) = 24.31, $p < .001$
   e. Mean = 15.30

3. Results of the analysis: A one-way multivariate analysis of variance (MANOVA) was conducted to determine the effect of conflict resolution training (cognitive, behavioral, and no training) on three social skills variables. The three social skills variables were social problem-solving and teacher and parent ratings of social skills. Significant differences were found among the three conflict resolution training groups on the dependent measures, Wilks' Λ = .18, $\underline{F}$ (6, 50) = 11.52, $\underline{p} <$ .001. The multivariate η^2 of .58, indicated a strong relationship between training and the dependent variables. Table 78 contains the means and the standard deviations on the dependent variables for the three groups.

Analyses of variance (ANOVA) on each of dependent variables were conducted as follow-up tests to the MANOVA. The familywise error rate for the three tests was set at .05/3 or .017 for each ANOVA using the Bonferroni method to control for Type I error across the three tests. All three ANOVAs were significant, the parent rating of the child's social skills, $\underline{F}$ (2, 27) = 36.82, $\underline{p} < .001$, η^2 = .73, the teacher rating of the child's social skills, $\underline{F}$ (2,27) = 24.31, $\underline{p} < .001$, η^2 = .64, and the social problem-solving scale, $\underline{F}$ (2,27) = 22.52, $\underline{p} < .001$, η^2 = .63.

Pairwise comparisons were conducted to find out which conflict resolution treatment affected the social skills outcomes most strongly. Each pairwise comparison was tested at the alpha level of .017/3 or .005 using the Bonferroni procedure to control for Type I error across the multiple comparisons. For the parent rating of social skills, significant differences were found among all three groups. As shown in Table 78, the highest mean score was for the children who received cognitive conflict resolution training. The next highest mean was for children who participated in behavioral conflict resolution training. Children who received no conflict resolution training had the lowest social skills ratings. The pattern of means for the teacher ratings and the social problem-solving scale was the same as those for the parent ratings. However, there was no significant difference between the behavior and no-training groups for these two measures, but there were significant differences for the other two comparisons.

Table 78

Means and Standard Deviations for the Three Types of Conflict Resolution Training Groups

Conflict resolution training	Parent rating		Teacher rating		Social problem-solving scale	
	M	SD	M	SD	M	SD
No training	10.10	2.42	7.80	4.49	1.20	1.14
Behavioral training	15.30	4.22	10.90	4.77	2.10	.99
Cognitive training	22.00	2.31	20.50	3.34	4.00	.67

5. Wilks' $\Lambda = .274$, $F(6, 110) = 16.70$, $p < .001$.

Answers for Lesson 28

1. a. Wilks' $\Lambda = .506$, $F(2,13) = 6.34$
   b. $p = .012$
   c. Mean student stress = 49.60
3. Results of the analysis: A one-way within-subjects ANOVA was conducted to evaluate whether teachers feel more stress when coping with students, parents, or administrators. The within-subjects factor was the type of stressful situation, and the dependent variable was level of stress associated with each situation. The means and standard deviations for stress scores are presented in Table 79. The results for the ANOVA indicated a significant stress effect, Wilks' $\Lambda = .51$, $\underline{F}(2, 13) = 6.34$, $\underline{p} = .012$, multivariate $\eta^2 = .49$. These results support the hypothesis that teachers have different degrees of stress associated with different sources (students, parents, and administrators).

   Paired-samples $\underline{t}$ tests were conducted to evaluate the differences among the individual stress means, using the Holm's sequential Bonferroni method to control for Type I error across the three tests. The results indicated that teachers report a significantly higher level of stress associated with administrators than with either students or parents. Stress levels associated with students and parents were not significantly different from each other.

Table 79

Means and standard deviations for stress scores

Type of stressful situation	M	SD
Administrator	62.53	18.04
Student	49.60	15.69
Parent	52.27	14.84

5. There is a significant time effect, $F(4, 21) = 6.55$, $p = .001$, multivariate $\eta^2 = .56$
6. You could control for Type I error across the 10 paired-samples t tests using the Holm's sequential Bonferroni procedure. Alternatively, you could conduct polynomial contrasts as follow-up tests instead of paired-samples t tests to evaluate trends over time. Because the polynomial contrasts are independent of each other, some researchers may not control for Type I error across the linear, quadratic, and cubic contrasts.

Answers for Lesson 29

1. a. $p = .000$
   b. $F(3,57) = 64.86$
   c. $\eta^2 = .75$
   d. 1.48 seconds
3. Two types of follow-up tests can be conducted subsequent to the significant interaction effect, interaction comparisons and simple main effects. Interaction comparisons evaluate whether the differences between time periods are the same for novel and familiar stimuli. Although simple main effects could be conducted to evaluate the differences between stimuli for each time period, the more meaningful simple main effects would evaluate the differences in visual attention across time for each of the stimuli. This latter analysis evaluates the question of whether visual attention increases or decreases over time for novel and familiar stimuli.
5. The profile plot showing the interaction between time and stimulus type is shown in Figure 283.

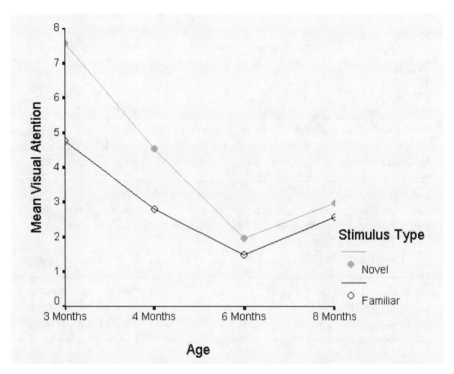

Figure 283. Mean visual attention as a function of age and type of stimulus.

6. Peter should conclude that there is no significant interaction effect, $F(1, 24) = 1.29$, $p = .267$.
8. Results of the analysis: A two-way within-subjects ANOVA was conducted to evaluate whether children rated other children more positively or negatively based on the gender and dress style (well dressed or poorly dressed). Table 80 shows the means and standard deviations associated with these data. The main effect associated with gender and the interaction effect were not significant, $\underline{F}(1,24) = 2.94$, $\underline{p} = .099$, $\eta^2 = .11$, and $\underline{F}(1,24) = 1.29$, $\underline{p} = .267$, $\eta^2 = .05$, respectively. However, the main effect associated with the dress style factor was significant, $\underline{F}(1,24) = 207.49$, $\underline{p} < .001$, $\eta^2 = .90$. These results support the hypothesis that children tend to evaluate other children more negatively when they are poorly dressed ($\underline{M} = 8.96$, $\underline{SD} = 2.08$) than when they are well dressed ($\underline{M} = 17.42$, $\underline{SD} = 1.98$).

Table 80

Means and Standard Deviations of Child Rating Scores

Gender	Well dressed		Poorly dressed	
	M	*SD*	*M*	*SD*
Boy	17.52	3.10	9.76	2.42
Girl	17.32	2.70	8.16	3.17

Answers for Lesson 30

1. a. $p = .000$
   b. $r = .828$
   c. $r = .312$
3. Results of the analysis: Correlation coefficients were computed among the four evaluation variables for the college professors. Four of the six correlations shown in Table 81 were greater than or equal to .35 and statistically significant using Holm's sequential Bonferroni approach to control for Type I error across the six correlations. The correlations between the two teaching evaluation variables (overall quality of instructor and of the course) and between the two research evaluation variables (number of publications and number of citations) were higher than the correlations between the teaching and the research variables. In general, however, the results suggest that professors who are productive in research also tend to be rated as better teachers.
5. Table 82 shows the correlations of the math and science grade point averages with the social sciences and humanities grade point averages.
7. $r = .33$

Table 81

Correlations among the Four Professor Evaluation Measures (N = 50)

Evaluation variables	Number of citations	Number of publications	Overall quality of instructor
Number of publications	.83*		
Overall quality of instructor	.31	.23	
Overall quality of course	.37*	.35*	.64*

*Significant using the Holm's sequential Bonferroni procedure.

Table 82

Correlations between Math/Science and Humanities Grade Point Averages

Subject	English	History	Social science
Math	.57*	.33*	.35*
Science	.02	-.36*	.10

Answers for Lesson 31

1. a. $r = .83$
   b. $p = .105$
   c. $r_p = .13$

3. Results of the analysis: Correlation coefficients were computed among the evaluation variables for the teaching quality and research productivity. As shown in the top section of Table 83, four of the six correlations were greater than .35 and statistically significant using Holm's sequential Bonferroni approach. To assess whether these variables were correlated due to work ethic, partial correlation coefficients were computed among the evaluation variables holding constant work ethic. As shown in the bottom section of Table 83, only two of the six correlations were statistically significant using Holm's sequential Bonferroni approach. One of the significant partial correlations assessed the correlation between the two research productivity variables, number of publications and number of citations. The other evaluated the correlation between the two teaching quality measures. The partial correlations between the two sets of variables were very small and not significant. These results are consistent with the hypothesis that the relationships between the research productivity and teaching quality variables are a function of work ethic.

5. $r = .498$.

6. The partial correlation is .382.

7. Although the correlation between the number of crimes committed and the amount of beer purchased dropped from .50 to .38 when controlling for temperature, the partial correlation was still of moderate size and was significant. These results do not suggest that temperature fully explains the relationship between number of crimes committed and amount of beer purchased.

Table 83

Correlations among the Two Sets of Evaluation Measures (N = 50)

Evaluation variables	Number of citations	Number of publications	Overall quality of instructor
	Zero-Order correlations		
Number of publications	.83*		
Overall quality of instructor	.31	.23	
Overall quality of course	.37*	.35*	.64*
	Correlations controlling for work ethic		
Number of publications	.75*		
Overall quality of instructor	.06	-.04	
Overall quality of course	.13	.10	.53*

*Significant using the Holm's sequential Bonferroni procedure.

Answers for Lesson 32

1. a. 2.32
   b. .22
   c. 11.60
   d. .93
   e. 7.83
5. a. $F(1, 48) = 21.03, p < .001$
   b. predicted number of publications = .45 Work Ethic - 2.96
   c. .55
6. The scatterplot showing the linear relationship between the number of publications and a professor's work ethic is shown in Figure 284 (at the top of page 413). Overall number of publications is predicted fairly well from work ethic. However, the prediction is not as good for high work ethic scores.

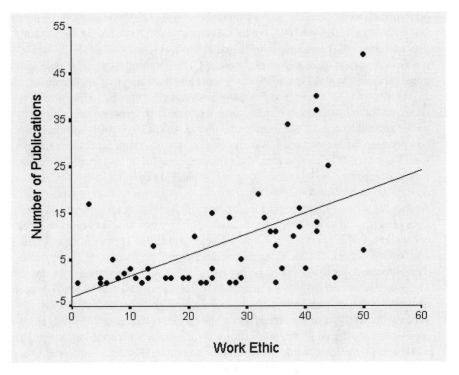

Figure 284. Relationship between the number of publications and a professor's work ethic.

7. Results of the analysis: A linear regression analysis was conducted to evaluate the prediction of the number of publications from professors' work ethic. The regression equation was

$$\hat{Y} = .45X_{work\,ethic} - 2.96$$

These results suggest that professors who have higher work ethic scores tend to have more publications. Work ethic was relatively accurate in predicting the number of publications. The correlation between professors' work ethic and number of publications was .55, $\underline{t}$ (48) = 4.59, $\underline{p} < .001$. Approximately 31% of the variance in the number of professor publications was accounted for by its linear relationship with the professor work ethic. However, as shown in Figure 284, the number of publications is predicted better for individuals who have low work ethic scores than high work ethic scores.

Answers for Lesson 33

1. The variables should be entered in two sets: (1) the high school GPA predictors and (2) the test scores. The sets would be unordered to evaluate the contribution of each set and each set over and above the other set. R^2 can be computed for each set. Also, R^2 changes can be obtained to determine the unique contribution of each set of predictors.
3. R^2 Change = .21, F (2, 94) = 13.73, $p < .001$
5. Results of the analysis: Multiple regression analyses were conducted to predict students' performance on a statistics exam from two sets of predictors: (a) high school GPAs in English, math, and all other subjects and (b) test scores in math and English. The linear combination of all five predictors was significantly related to students' performance on the statistics exam, $\underline{F}$ (5, 94) = 6.92, $\underline{p} < .001$, $\underline{R}^2 = .27$, adjusted $\underline{R}^2 = .23$. The test score predictors significantly predicted

performance on the statistics exam over and above the GPA predictors, R^2 change = .21, F (2, 94) = 13.73, $p < .001$, but the GPA measures did not predict significantly over and above the test scores in math and English, R^2 change = .01, F (3, 94) = .59, $p = .624$. Based on these results, high school GPA scores appear to offer little additional predictive power beyond that contributed by math and English test scores.

Of the two test scores, scores on the math test were most strongly related to scores on the statistics exam. The zero-order correlation between the math test scores and students' statistic exam performance was .48, $p < .001$, and the correlation between these two variables partialling out the effects of all other predictors was .44, $p < .001$. In comparison, the comparable bivariate and partial correlations for the English test scores were .20 ($p = .044$) and .18 ($p = .073$), respectively.

7. $R^2 = .38$, F (2, 117) = 36.02, $p < .001$

9. Among the social support predictors, both the amount of social support and the level of perceived social support appear to be good predictors; however the level of perceived social support was a somewhat better predictor. The zero-order correlation between amount of social support and number of relapses was .38, while the correlation between these two variables partialling out all other predictors was .29. The comparable correlations for perceived social support were .57 and .49, respectively. All zero-order and partial correlations were significant at the .05 level. Among the psychological state variables, the picture is less clear. The zero-order correlations for daily life stress ($r = .36$) and for propensity for substance abuse ($r = .31$) were significant, while the zero-order correlation for depression ($r = .08$) was nonsignificant. The partial correlations for daily life stress, for propensity for substance abuse, and depression were .12, .30, and .22, respectively. Only the partial correlations for depression and propensity for substance abuse were significant.

Answers for Lesson 34

1. a. mean = 2.92
    b. F (1, 48) = .05, $p = .826$
    c. χ^2 (4, $N = 50$) = 22.85
3. Eighty percent of the research scientists were classified correctly, and 84% of the total group of professors were classified accurately. Using leave-one-out classification, 72% of the research scientists were classified correctly, and 78% of the total group of professors were classified accurately. These results were obtained based on prior probabilities computed from group sizes.
5. Results of the analysis: A discriminant analysis was conducted to determine whether several academic factors-number of publications, amount of grant funding, teaching evaluation scores, and number of student committees-predict whether professors are research scientists or teaching moguls. The Wilks' lambda was significant, $\Lambda = .61$, χ^2 (4, $\underline{N} = 50$) = 22.85, $p < .001$, indicating differences on the four academic factors between the two professor groups.

    In Table 84, we present the within-group correlations and the standardized weights between the academic factors and the discriminant function. For both the correlations and the standardized weights, the teaching evaluation scores and the number of publications have the strongest relationship with the discriminant function. On the basis of these results, the discriminant function appears to represent an ability to acquire and impart knowledge. Individuals in the teaching group have on the average higher scores on this function.

    Professors were classified on the basis of the four academic factors. We assumed equality of the covariance matrices and determined prior probabilities from the sample group sizes. Eighty-four percent of the professors were correctly classified as teaching moguls and research scientists. To estimate how well the classification method would predict in future samples, we conducted a leave-one-out analysis. The results indicated that 78% of professors would be classified accurately.

Table 84

Correlations between Academic Performance Measures with Discriminant Function and Standardized Coefficients of Discriminant Function

Variable	Correlations with discriminant function	Standardized coefficients of discriminant function
Teaching evaluations	.78	.89
Number of publications	.44	.57
Amount of grant funding	.04	-.12
Number of student committees	.23	.28

7. The first discriminant function differentiates successful coaches as character builders from the other two groups. This function is related to all the predictors to some extent (structure coefficients ranging from .33 to .58), but is most strongly related to the average number of points per game, persistence, number of ranked high school players over the last five years, and social support. The second function differentiates the winning coaches from the winning coaches who are character builders. This discriminant function is positively related to authoritative discipline, persistence, and problem-focused coping and negatively related to the average number of points per game and number of ranked high school players over the last five years. These functions are difficult to name.

Answers for Lesson 35

1. Terrill should extract a single factor based on the results of the screen plot in Figure 285.

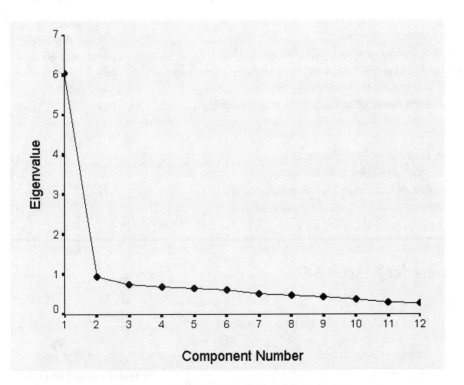

Figure 285. Screen plot for Career Values Scale

5. The correlation matrix should be read in as follows:
MATRIX DATA VARIABLES = ROWTYPE_ ITEM01 ITEM02 ITEM03 ITEM04 ITEM05 ITEM06 ITEM07 ITEM08 ITEM09 ITEM10.
BEGIN DATA
N 100 100 100 100 100 100 100 100 100 100

CORR	1.00									
CORR	-.22	1.00								
CORR	.27	-.10	1.00							
CORR	-.12	.58	.12	1.00						
CORR	.22	-.02	.59	.16	1.00					
CORR	-.09	.29	.17	.26	.07	1.00				
CORR	.23	-.16	.42	-.06	.30	.06	1.00			
CORR	-.02	.24	.04	.43	.04	.38	-.15	1.00		
CORR	.07	-.13	.34	-.01	.34	.06	.27	-.07	1.00	
CORR	-.14	.28	-.06	.18	-.04	.55	-.01	.37	.10	1.00

END DATA.

7. Results of the analysis: Factor analyses were conducted on the 10-item humor measure using the maximum likelihood extraction method. Although the eigenvalue-greater-than-1 criterion suggested that there were three factors underlying the measure, the screen plot indicated two factors. The two-factor solution was rotated using a varimax rotation to yield interpretable factors. One of the factors appears to measure self-deprecating humor, while the other factor appears to assess humor demeaning to others. The self-deprecating humor factor accounted for 18.42% of the item variance, while the humor demeaning to others factor accounted for 17.98% of the item variance. Table 85 shows the factor loadings for the items on both factors.

Table 85

Correlations of Each Humor Item with Factors

	Factors	
Item	Demeaning to others	Self-deprecating
Demeaning to others		
1. I like to make fun of others.	**.34**	-.19
3. People find me funny when I make jokes about others.	**.85**	.10
5. I frequently make others the target of my jokes.	**.68**	.12
7. I love to get people to laugh by using sarcasm.	**.51**	-.10
9. I make people laugh by exposing other peoples' stupidities.	**.43**	-.02
Self-Deprecating		
2. I make people laugh by making fun of myself.	-.19	**.67**
4. I talk about my problems to make people laugh.	.05	**.71**
6. People find me funny when I tell them about my failings.	.11	**.54**
8. I am funniest when I talk about my own weaknesses.	-.02	**.55**
10. I am funny when I tell others about the dumb things I have done.	-.08	**.47**

Answers for Lesson 36

2. a. $\alpha = .91$.
   b. Correlation between Item 3 and Item 4 = .51
   c. Mean for Item 12 = 1.55
3. Results of the analysis: Coefficient alpha was computed to evaluate the internal consistency of the total scale SCVS. The coefficient alpha was .91. These results support the conclusion that the SCVS is reliable.

6. The coefficient alpha is relatively low, .66. Inspection of the correlations among the items indicate that the Woody Allen items are not very correlated with the Don Rickles items. Because the Woody Allen items are not highly correlated with the other items, the items may not be equivalent, a violation of an assumption underlying coefficient alpha. The split-half coefficient is likely to yield a somewhat better estimate of reliability. The split is somewhat arbitrary. We split the items so that items 1, 3, 4, 6, 9 were on one half and items 2, 5, 7, 8, 10 were on the other half. The split-half coefficient of .81 is substantially larger than the coefficient alpha of .66.

7. Results of the analysis: Two internal consistency estimates of reliability were computed for the demeaning-of-others versus self-deprecating humor scale: coefficient alpha and a split-half coefficient expressed as a Spearman-Brown corrected correlation. Coefficient alpha was relatively low, .66. Because the items assessing self-deprecating humor were not highly correlated with the items assessing humor demeaning of others (based on the zero-order correlations among the items), the items may not be equivalent, a violation of an assumption underlying coefficient alpha. For the split-half coefficient, the scale was split into two halves such that the two halves would be as equivalent as possible. In splitting the items we took into account as best as possible the sequencing of the items, as well as whether the items assessed humor that demeaned others or humor that was self-deprecating. One half included items 1, 3, 4, 6, 9, while the other half included items 2, 5, 7, 8 and 10. The split-half coefficient was .81, indicating adequate reliability.

Answers for Lesson 37

2. a. Item-total correlation for q06 = .628
    b. Correlation between q05 and q09 = .259
    c. Mean for q10 = 1.50

4. Results of the analysis: Item analyses were conducted on the 12 items hypothesized to assess career valuing, after reverse scoring appropriate items. Each of the 12 items was correlated with the total score for career valuing (with the item removed). The item-total correlations ranged from .57 to .70. Based on these results, no revisions were made to the scale. Coefficient alpha for the Saxon Career Valuing scale was .91. The results of the item analysis indicate that the Saxon Career Valuing Scale does not need to be revised and that it yields reliable scores.

8. Your results section should contain a table such as Table 86.

Table 86

Correlations of Each Humor Item with Its Own Scale after Removing Focal Item and with the Other Scale

	Scales	
Item	Don Rickles	Woody Allen
Don Rickles items		
1. I like to make fun of others.	.28	-.17
3. People find me funny when I make jokes about others.	.62	.05
5. I frequently make others the target of my jokes.	.54	.06
7. I love to get people to laugh by using sarcasm.	.44	-.09
9. I make people laugh by exposing other peoples' stupidities.	.37	-.01
Woody Allen items		
2. I make people laugh by making fun of myself.	-.19	.47
4. I talk about my problems to make people laugh.	.03	.49
6. People find me funny when I tell them about my failings.	.08	.53
8. I am funniest when I talk about my own weaknesses.	-.05	.49
10. I am funny when I tell others about the dumb things I have done.	-.04	.49

Answers for Lesson 38

3. Results of the analysis: The purpose of the research was to evaluate whether one-year old girls prefer to play with other girls or prefer to play with boys. A z-approximation test based on the binomial distribution was conducted to assess whether the population proportion for girls' preference for playing with another female child was .50. The observed proportion of .57 did not differ significantly from the hypothesized value of .50, $p = .366$. The results do not support a preference by one-year old girls to play with other girls rather than boys.

4. The test value would be .50 because Emma is interested in assessing whether the cell frequencies are equal for both groups.

5. a. 33
   b. two-tailed $p = .519$
   c. .55

Answers for Lesson 39

2. a. 33
   b. $p = .000$
   c. $\chi^2(2, N = 48) = 27.12$

3. The expected frequency for each potato chip category is 16.

4. Results of the analysis: A one-sample chi-square test was conducted to assess whether potato chips taste better when fried in canola oil as opposed to fried in animal fat or baked. The results of the test were significant, $\chi^2 (2, N = 48) = 27.12$, $p < .001$. The test was significant because the observed frequency of chips fried in canola oil of 33 was much greater than the expected frequency of 16, while the observed frequencies of chips fried in animal fat or baked ($N = 7$ and $N = 8$, respectively) were less than the expected frequency of 16. A follow-up analysis was conducted to evaluate whether the proportion of individuals who prefer chips fried in canola oil and the proportion of individuals who prefer chips fried in animal fat or baked differ significantly from chance values of .33 and .67, respectively. The results of the test were significant, $\chi^2 (1, N = 48) = 27.09$, $p < .001$, indicating that individuals prefer potato chips if they are fried in canola oil rather than in animal fat or baked.

Answers for Lesson 40

1. a. 13.1%
   b. 70.0%
   c. 23.1%
   d. Pearson $\chi^2 (1, N = 130) = 9.83$
   e. phi = .27

3. Results of the analysis: A 2 x 2 contingency table analysis was conducted to assess the relationship between child-care responsibility (father only versus father and mother) and enrollment in advanced math courses (none versus one or more). These variables were significantly related, Pearson $\chi^2 (1, N = 130) = 9.83$, $p = .002$, $\Phi = .27$. The percentage of female high school students who took advanced math courses was significantly greater when they were raised primarily by their father (30%) rather than by both their mother and their father (8%).

6. Results of the analysis: A 3 x 3 contingency table analysis was conducted to assess the relationship between type of presentation (film, video, or lecture) and interest in presented information (Really Like to Know More About That; Excuse Me—You Call that a Presentation?; and Boring—Please, No More of That). The two variables were significantly related, Pearson $\chi^2 (4, N = 90) = 9.96$, $p = .041$, Cramèr's $V = .24$.

Follow-up, pairwise comparisons were conducted to evaluate the differences among the three types of presentations. The LSD method for three groups was used to control for Type I error at the .05 level across all three comparisons. The proportions differed significantly between the film and the video conditions, Pearson χ^2 (2, N = 60) = 6.67, p = .036, Cramèr's V = .33, and between the film and lecture conditions, Pearson χ^2 (2, N = 60) = 6.85, p = .033, Cramèr's V = .34, but not between the video and lecture conditions, Pearson χ^2 (2, N = 60) = 1.52, p = .468, Cramèr's V = .16. As shown in Table 87, the students found the information presented by film much more interesting than when it was presented in video or by lecture.

Table 87

Percent of Individuals Who Showed Different Levels of Interest for Each Type of Presentation

| | Interest in presentation | | |
Presentation type	Like to know more	Excuse me—You call that a presentation	Boring—Please, no more
Film	40	33	27
Video	13	33	53
Lecture	20	20	60

Answers for Lesson 41

1. a. p = .000
    b. z = -3.81
    c. Mean Rank = 24.57
2. The p-value for an independent-samples t test is the same as the p-value obtained for the Mann-Whitney U test.
3. Results of the analysis: A Mann-Whitney U test was conducted to evaluate the hypothesis that overweight individuals would eat Big Mac meals more quickly than normal weight individuals. The results of the test were significant, z = -3.81, p < .001, with the overweight individuals having a mean rank eating time of 8.30 and normal weight individuals having an mean rank of 24.57. Figure 279 shows the distributions of the time spent eating a Big Mac meal for overweight and normal weight individuals.

Answers for Lesson 42

1. Follow-up tests should not be conducted because the overall test is not significant, χ^2 (2, N = 18) = 5.96, p = .051.
3. The boxplot is shown in Figure 281.
5. Results of the analysis: A Kruskal-Wallis test was conducted to evaluate differences in extroversion among men with three different hair colors: blonds, brunets, and redheads. The test, which was corrected for tied ranks, was not significant, χ^2 (2, N = 18) = 5.96, p = .051. The proportion of variability in the ranked extroversion scores accounted for by hair color variable was .35, indicating a fairly strong relationship between hair color and extroversion in the sample, but the strong relationship may have been due to sampling error. The study needs to be replicated with a larger sample size so that the test has sufficient power.
6. The results of the median test were significant, χ^2 (2, N = 40) = 7.82, p = .020. However, the p-value may be inaccurate because two of the six expected frequencies are less than 5. See the assumptions section for additional discussion.

Answers for Lesson 43

1. Results for McNemar Test: 54% of the husbands indicated that they were anxious about infertility, while 46% of the wives indicated that they were anxious. These percentages were not significantly different from each other based on the results of the McNemar test of dependent proportions, $p = .688$.
2. Results for Sign Test: A sign test was conducted to evaluate whether husbands or wives report more anxiety about infertility. The sign test indicated that wives were significantly more anxious than their husbands about infertility, $p = .003$. The wife was more anxious for 19 couples; the husband was more anxious for 4 couples; and the husband and the wife were equally anxious for 1 couple.
3. Results for Wilcoxon Test: A Wilcoxon test was conducted to evaluate whether husbands or wives showed greater anxiety associated with infertility issues. The results indicated a significant difference between husbands and wives with respect to their anxiety levels, $z = -2.77$, $p = .006$. The mean rank for couples with husbands having higher anxiety scores was 11.75, while the mean rank for couples with wives having higher anxiety scores was 12.05.

Answers for Lesson 44

1. a. 2.62
   b. $\chi^2(2, N = 25) = 25.30$
   c. $df = 2$
   d. $p = .000$
3. The results of the one-way within-subjects ANOVA were significant, Wilks' $\Lambda = .24$, $F(2,23) = 36.07$ $p < .001$, and the results of the Friedman test were also significant, $\chi^2(2, N = 25) = 25.30$, $p < .001$. Both results indicate that there are significant differences across time in the level of self-esteem reported by girls.
4. Results of the analysis: A Friedman test was conducted to evaluate differences in medians for girls' self-esteem scores across ages 9, 11, and 14. The test was significant, $\chi^2(4, N = 25) = 25.30$, $p < .001$, and the coefficient of concordance of .51 indicated strong differences across the three time periods. Follow-up pairwise comparisons were conducted using a Wilcoxon test and controlling for familywise error rate at the .05 level using the LSD procedure for three groups. The median level of self-esteem was significantly lower at age 11 (median = 8) than at either age 9 (median = 14) or age 14 (median = 13), and self-esteem was significantly higher at age 9 than at age 14. These results suggest a curvilinear developmental trend in self-esteem where self-esteem decreases between ages 9 and 11 and increases from ages 11 to 14, although not to its original level.

References

American Psychological Association (1994). *Publication manual of the American Psychological association* (4th ed.). Washington, D.C.: Author.

Cohen, J., & Cohen, P. (1983). *Applied multiple regression/correlation analysis for the behavioral sciences* (2nd ed.). Hillsdale, NJ: Lawrence Erlbaum.

Darlington, R. B. (1990). *Regression and linear models.* New York: McGraw-Hill.

Green, S. B., Marquis, J. G., Hershberger, S. L., Thompson, M., & MacCallum, K. (1999). The overparameterized analysis-of-variance model. *Psychological Methods, 4,* 214–233.

Green, S. B., & Hershberger, S. L. (In press). Correlated errors in true score models and their effect on coefficient alpha. *Structural Equation Modeling.*

Green, S. B., Lissitz, R. W., & Mulaik, S. (1977). Limitations of coefficient alpha as an index of text unidimensionality. *Educational and Psychological Measurement, 37,* 827–839.

Hochberg, Y., & Tamhane, A. C. (1987). *Multiple comparison procedures.* New York: John Wiley.

Huitema, B. E. (1980). *The analysis of covariance and alternatives.* New York: John Wiley.

Levin, J. R., Serlin, R. C., Seaman, M. A. (1994). A controlled, powerful multiple comparison strategy for several situations. *Psychological Bulletin, 115,* 153–159.

Marascuilo, L. A., & Serlin, R. C. (1988). *Statistical methods for the social and behavioral sciences.* New York: Freeman and Company.

Maxwell, S. E., & Delaney, H. D. (1990). *Designing experiments and analyzing data: A model comparison perspective.* Belmont, CA: Wadsworth Publishing Company, 1990.

Pedhazur, E. J. (1997). *Multiple regression in behavioral research* (3rd ed.). Fort Worth, TX: Harcourt Brace College Publishers.

Wickens, T. D. (1989). *Multiway contingency tables analysis for the social sciences.* Hillsdale, NJ: Lawrence Erlbaum.

Index

LICENSE AGREEMENT AND LIMITED WARRANTY

READ THE FOLLOWING TERMS AND CONDITIONS CAREFULLY BEFORE OPENING THIS DISK PACKAGE. THIS LEGAL DOCUMENT IS AN AGREEMENT BETWEEN YOU AND PRENTICE-HALL, INC. (THE "COMPANY"). BY OPENING THIS SEALED DISK PACKAGE, YOU ARE AGREEING TO BE BOUND BY THESE TERMS AND CONDITIONS. IF YOU DO NOT AGREE WITH THESE TERMS AND CONDITIONS, DO NOT OPEN THE DISK PACKAGE. PROMPTLY RETURN THE UNOPENED DISK PACKAGE AND ALL ACCOMPANYING ITEMS TO THE PLACE YOU OBTAINED THEM FOR A FULL REFUND OF ANY SUMS YOU HAVE PAID.

1. GRANT OF LICENSE: In consideration of your payment of the license fee, which is part of the price for this product, and your agreement to abide by the terms and conditions of this Agreement, the Company grants to you a nonexclusive right to use and display the copy of the enclosed software program (hereafter the "SOFTWARE") on a single computer (i.e., with a single CPU) at a single location so long as you comply with the terms of this agreement. The Company reserves all rights not expressly granted to you under this Agreement.

2. OWNERSHIP OF SOFTWARE: You own only the magnetic or physical media (the enclosed disks) on which the SOFTWARE is recorded or fixed, but the Company retains all the rights, title, and ownership to the SOFTWARE recorded on the original disk copy(ies) and all subsequent copies of the SOFTWARE, regardless of the form or media on which the original or other copies may exist. This license is not a sale of the original SOFTWARE or any copy to you.

3. COPY RESTRICTIONS: This SOFTWARE and the accompanying printed materials and user manual (the "Documentation") are the subject of copyright. You may not copy the Documentation or the SOFTWARE, except that you may make a single copy of the SOFTWARE for backup or archival purposes only. You may be held legally responsible for any copying or copyright infringement which is caused or encouraged by your failure to abide by the terms of this restriction.

4. USE RESTRICTIONS: You may not network the SOFTWARE or otherwise use it on more than one computer or computer terminal at the same time. You may physically transfer the SOFTWARE from one computer to another provided that the SOFTWARE is used on only one computer at a time. You may not distribute copies of the SOFTWARE or Documentation to others. You may not reverse engineer, disassemble, decompile, modify, adapt, translate, or create derivative works based on the SOFTWARE or the Documentation without prior written consent of the Company.

5. TRANSFER RESTRICTIONS: The enclosed SOFTWARE is licensed only to you and may not be transferred to any one else without prior written consent of the Company. Any unauthorized transfer of the SOFTWARE shall result in the immediate termination of this Agreement.

6. TERMINATION: This license is effective until terminated. This license will terminate automatically without notice from the Company and become null and void if you fail to comply with any provisions or limitations of this license. Upon termination, you shall destroy the Documentation and all copies of the SOFTWARE. All provisions of this Agreement as to warranties, limitation of liability, remedies or damages, and our ownership rights shall survive termination.

7. MISCELLANEOUS: This Agreement shall be construed in accordance with the laws of the United States of America and the State of New York and shall benefit the Company, its affiliates, and assignees.

8. LIMITED WARRANTY AND DISCLAIMER OF WARRANTY: The Company warrants that the SOFTWARE, when properly used in accordance with the Documentation, will operate in substantial conformity with the description of the SOFTWARE set forth in the Documentation. The Company does not warrant that the SOFTWARE will meet your requirements or that the operation of the SOFTWARE will be uninterrupted or error-free. The Company warrants that the media on which the SOFTWARE is delivered shall be free from defects in materials and workmanship under normal use for a period of thirty (30) days from the date of your purchase. Your only remedy and the Company's only obligation under these limited warranties is, at the Company's option, return of the warranted item for a refund of any amounts paid by you or replacement of the item. Any replacement of SOFTWARE, or media under the warranties shall not extend the original warranty period. The limited warranty set forth above shall not apply to any SOFTWARE which the Company determines in good faith has been subject to misuse, neglect, improper installation, repair, alteration, or damage by you. EXCEPT FOR THE EXPRESSED WARRANTIES, EXPRESS OR IMPLIED, INCLUDING WITHOUT LIMITATION, THE IMPLIED WARRANTIES OF MERCHANTABILITY AND FITNESS FOR A PARTICULAR PURPOSE, EXCEPT FOR THE EXPRESS WARRANTY SET FORTH ABOVE. THE COMPANY DOES NOT WARRANT, GUARANTEE, OR MAKE ANY REPRESENTATION REGARDING THE USE OR THE RESULTS OF THE USE OF THE SOFTWARE IN TERMS OF ITS CORRECTNESS, ACCURACY, RELIABILITY, CURRENTNESS, OR OTHERWISE.

IN NO EVENT, SHALL THE COMPANY OR ITS EMPLOYEES, AGENTS, SUPPLIERS, OR CONTRACTORS BE LIABLE FOR ANY INCIDENTAL, INDIRECT, SPECIAL, OR CONSEQUENTIAL DAMAGES ARISING OUT OF OR IN CONNECTION WITH THE LICENSE GRANTED UNDER THE AGREEMENT, OR FOR LOSS OF USE, LOSS OF DATA, LOSS OF INCOME OR PROFIT, OR OTHER LOSSES SUSTAINED AS A RESULT OF INJURY TO ANY PERSON, OR LOSS OF OR DAMAGE TO PROPERTY, OR CLAIMS OF THIRD PARTIES, EVEN IF THE COMPANY OR AN AUTHORIZED REPRESENTATIVE OF THE COMPANY HAS BEEN ADVISED OF THE POSSIBILITY OF SUCH DAMAGES. IN NO EVENT SHALL LIABILITY OF THE COMPANY FOR DAMAGES WITH RESPECT TO THE SOFTWARE EXCEED THE AMOUNTS ACTUALLY PAID BY YOU, IF ANY, FOR THE SOFTWARE.

SOME JURISDICTIONS DO NOT ALLOW THE LIMITATION OF THE IMPLIED WARRANTIES OR LIABILITY FOR INCIDENTAL, INDIRECT, SPECIAL, OR CONSEQUENTIAL DAMAGES, SO THE ABOVE LIMITATIONS MAY NOT ALWAYS APPLY. THE WARRANTIES IN THIS AGREEMENT GIVE YOU SPECIFIC LEGAL RIGHTS AND YOU MAY ALSO HAVE OTHER RIGHTS WHICH VARY IN ACCORDANCE WITH LOCAL LAW.

ACKNOWLEDGEMENT

YOU ACKNOWLEDGE THAT YOU HAVE READ THIS AGREEMENT, UNDERSTAND IT, AND AGREE TO BE BOUND BY ITS TERMS AND CONDITIONS. YOU ALSO AGREE THAT THIS AGREEMENT IS THE COMPLETE AND EXCLUSIVE STATEMENT OF THE AGREEMENT BETWEEN YOU AND THE COMPANY AND SUPERSEDES ALL PROPOSALS OR PRIOR AGREEMENTS, ORAL, OR WRITTEN, AND ANY OTHER COMMUNICATIONS BETWEEN YOU AND THE COMPANY OR ANY REPRESENTATIVE OF THE COMPANY RELATING TO THE SUBJECT MATTERS OF THIS AGREEMENT.